TAKING THE FIELD

Many Wests

SERIES EDITORS:

Thomas G. Andrews, University of Colorado
Ari Kelman, University of California, Davis
Amy Lonetree, University of California, Santa Cruz
Mary E. Mendoza, Pennsylvania State University
Christina Snyder, Pennsylvania State University

Published in Cooperation with the
William P. Clements Center for Southwest Studies,
Southern Methodist University

TAKING THE FIELD

SOLDIERS, NATURE, AND EMPIRE ON AMERICAN FRONTIERS

AMY KOHOUT

University of Nebraska Press
LINCOLN

Portions of chapter 4 previously appeared in "More Than Birds: Loss and Reconnection at the National Museum of Natural History," *Museum History Journal* 10, no. 1 (2017): 83–96. Reprinted by permission of Taylor & Francis Ltd., http://www.tandfonline.com.

The University of Nebraska Press is part of a land-grant institution with campuses and programs on the past, present, and future homelands of the Pawnee, Ponca, Otoe-Missouria, Omaha, Dakota, Lakota, Kaw, Cheyenne, and Arapaho Peoples, as well as those of the relocated Ho-Chunk, Sac and Fox, and Iowa Peoples.

Publication of this volume was assisted by the McCabe Greer Book Manuscript Workshop, the George and Ann Richards Civil War Era Center, and the Pennsylvania State University Department of History.

Library of Congress Cataloging-in-Publication Data
Names: Kohout, Amy, author.
Title: Taking the field: soldiers, nature, and empire on American frontiers / Amy Kohout.
Description: Lincoln: University of Nebraska Press, [2023] | Series: Many wests | Includes bibliographical references and index.
Identifiers: LCCN 2022012100
ISBN 9781496215215 (hardback)
ISBN 9781496233769 (paperback)
ISBN 9781496234308 (epub)
ISBN 9781496234315 (pdf)
Subjects: LCSH: United States—Territorial expansion—History—19th century. | Soldiers—West (U.S.)—Attitudes. | Soldiers—Philippines—Attitudes. | Philosophy of nature—United States—History—19th century. | Natural history museums—Social aspects—United States. | Imperialism—Social aspects—United States—History—19th century. | United States. Army—Foreign service—Philippines. | United States. Army—Military life—History—19th century. | West (U.S.)—Discovery and exploration. | BISAC: HISTORY / United States / State & Local / West (AK, CA, CO, HI, ID, MT, NV, UT, WY) | NATURE / Ecology
Classification: LCC E179.5 .K68 2023 |
DDC 973.5—dc23/eng/20220518
LC record available at https://lccn.loc.gov/2022012100

Set in Questa by Mikala R. Kolander.

For Cory

CONTENTS

ILLUSTRATIONS

TAKING THE FIELD

Introduction

Preparation

A SCALPEL IS NOT A TYPICAL HISTORIAN'S TOOL. WE MIGHT hope to wield our pens like scalpels, but our tools are different. Our instruments—however sharp—are for writing, not slicing, and especially not for cutting into once-alive flesh.

Nevertheless, several years ago I found myself wearing a white coat and holding a blade. I was in a lab at the National Museum of Natural History in Washington DC with a dead Brewer's blackbird on the table in front of me. It had been collected—killed—the previous summer in North Dakota on a Smithsonian-sponsored expedition. It was put on ice for transport, and then placed in a freezer to await preparation. Blackbirds, I was told, are good birds to learn on. They are big enough to allow you to see what you are doing and small enough that a beginner might be able to complete a preparation, from start to finish, in a single day.

Christina Gebhard, my teacher and one of the museum's bird specialists, sat across from me with her own bird. We arranged our tools: the scalpel, along with a ruler, forceps, cotton, a dowel, needle and thread. She would start and I would follow, mimicking her movements. We were making scientific study skins, a process that involves removing the animal's insides, filling the skull and body cavity with stuffing, and suturing the belly shut.

Study skins are not taxidermy. They aren't mounted or posed in lifelike stances, perched on branches, grasping unlucky prey in their talons. They are soft. Their internal organs and musculature, and most of their skeletons, have been removed from their bodies and replaced with cotton. Most of these specimens are stored on their backs in shallow drawers, wings relaxed and tucked in, claws crossed. Once prepared and labeled, our birds would join others of their species in the cabinets of the Smithsonian to await future study.

We made the first incision—she on her bird, I on mine—and looked inside. Christina helped me identify and measure the tiny parts and talked me through the process of removing them. Blood and guts don't bother me; they never have. But when it was time to pick up the forceps and break my blackbird's bones below the knees, I was suddenly queasy. The sensation surprised me. Something about my size and strength, the ease with which the bones snapped, the fragility of that once-live bird—I felt it.[1]

I HAD COME TO THE MUSEUM TO SEE THE PAPERS OF Lt. Col. Edgar Alexander Mearns, a soldier who had served in both the U.S. West and the Philippines in the late nineteenth and early twentieth centuries, as part of my research into the intersection of American ideas about nature and empire. Mearns worked as a surgeon in the U.S. Army from 1883 to 1909. He completed assignments in the Southwest borderlands during the Apache wars and multiple tours of duty in the Philippines. But because Mearns was also an ornithologist, most of his materials were housed at the museum rather than at the Smithsonian Institution Archives, where I had expected to find his papers. So I made an appointment at the Division of Birds.

The Division of Birds is unlike any other archive I have ever visited. Instead of a reading room separated from the manuscripts and materials, lab tables are tucked between rows of cabinets containing the division's central resource: the birds themselves. On my first visit I sat in a small reference library off the main collection and began to look through boxes of Mearns's field notes and correspondence. Reading Mearns's papers meant reading about birds observed, birds collected, birds prepared, as well as birds missed and birds spoiled. It didn't take long for me to ask if I might be able to see one of the more than nine thousand specimens Mearns had contributed to the Smithsonian's collection. I wasn't sure what to ask for. Something important to ornithology? Something colorful? Something pretty? I also wasn't sure how to begin looking for it.

In archives of manuscripts and papers, I refer to finding aids or card catalogs to identify what I'd like to see, and then an archivist locates those items in the collection and brings them to a centralized reading room. In the Division of Birds, however, locating a specific bird begins with a database, searchable by fields including species, date, collector, expedition, and place of collection. You can also search by sex, stage of development, or kind of preparation, since a study skin is one of several ways to prepare and preserve a bird. The database reveals what is in the collection but not where to find it—at least, not exactly.

To locate a bird in the collection, you need to know something about taxonomy. Birds aren't organized by collector or by chronology but rather by species classification, which means that Mearns's birds are spread throughout the rows of drawer-filled cabinets, each in the appropriate spot for its species and perhaps sorted into more specific locations according to sex, maturity, and month of collection. Thus birds from vastly different times and climes might be found next to each other, and birds from the same time and clime are rarely nearby unless they are taxonomically quite similar. This, of course, makes perfect sense for scientific study. Like near like enables the study of categories such as species and subspecies, as well as questions related to migration and range.[2] But for a historian interested in the work of a particular collector—a historian who, at the time, was not yet even a novice birder—this organizational structure presented some challenges.

Christina and I decided to look for a few of the birds Mearns collected while serving in the Philippines. We settled on *Bolbopsittacus lunulatus*, the guaiabero, a small green bird in the parrot family, and *Ardea purpurea*, the purple heron. When Christina was looking at our database search results, she was paying attention to the taxonomic order and family for these birds, which corresponded to particular aisles and cabinets

1. Drawer of *Bolbopsittacus lunulatus*. National Museum of Natural History, 2011. Author photo.

within the Division of Birds. We walked through the collection to the parrots. After Christina pulled out a full drawer of guaia-beros (fig. 1), we went to look for the heron. We located the *Ardea* (the genus for herons) drawers and began reading each tag to find a bird labeled with Mearns's name. Familiar with his field books, I'd already begun to recognize his handwriting. When we found the correct heron, Christina gently lifted it from the drawer and carried it to a table for closer examination (fig. 2).

The conversation we had about that first bird changed the direction of this book. Up until that point I'd been thinking of the birds as interesting but still peripheral to my questions about soldiers' contributions to U.S. notions of nature and empire. Then Christina and I began to discuss what we could see, what we could know, and what we could wonder from examining the bird on the table between us. She explained the techniques Mearns likely used and the continuities between his approach and the current preparation practices of the museum.[3] She pointed out how to tell that Mearns had done a good job: the carefully arranged feather tracks, the neat incision, the her-on's full but not overstuffed body cavity.

2. *Ardea purpurea* specimen collected by Mearns. USNM 201664. National Museum of Natural History, 2011. Author photo.

All at once Mearns's birds made material the questions that I had been considering only in the realm of ideas. They added dimension to Mearns's lifetime of military service. Suddenly I could see how his medical training had made him expertly suited for his work as both an army surgeon and an ornithologist. Our conversation turned to the challenges of preparation outside a museum lab. What did it mean to do this work in the field, especially when that field might also be a battlefield? What could the birds reveal about the intersection of military and scientific work for Mearns, as well as for others who documented and collected nature in spaces they understood to be American frontiers?

The birds offered encouragement, too, to keep following soldiers and their ideas about the natural world across the geographic boundaries that often guide historical study.[4] Mearns was a man in constant motion, much like the birds he devoted himself to observing and collecting. Mearns's movements, however, were mostly dictated by the U.S. Army. This might be one of the reasons he can be hard to place and also hard to find in existing historical narratives. He doesn't quite fit into any single story; instead, his life and work cross—and sometimes connect—stories that are usually studied separately.

In this way Mearns is like many other soldiers who served in the frontier army. Their work took them to and through Indigenous homelands in service of an imperial vision. It also took them across the Pacific to the Philippines, where they fought first Spanish and then Filipino forces in a war that solidified U.S. empire in the Pacific before they returned home again. These men moved through landscapes—and histories—often considered in isolation. But soldiers' lives tie them together. Many soldiers moved back and forth across the boundaries that often divide our contemporary fields of historical inquiry, and their complex stories encourage scholars to pursue the connections between fields such as imperial history, environmental history, cultural history, military history, and the history of science.

In this book I follow Mearns and other U.S. soldiers across a range of material and cultural terrain—over land on the Great Plains and in the Southwest, across the Pacific Ocean to the Philippines, and even back to St. Louis, Missouri, where a particular set of ideas about nature and empire were displayed at the 1904 World's Fair. I also follow what soldiers sent across the landscapes of their service: details and descriptions of new-to-them people and places; articulations of love, excitement, fear, and sometimes deep ambivalence; and, in the case of Mearns, birds.

Following soldiers, it turns out, expands our understanding of how American ideas about nature and empire have been entangled. In fact, the bodies of Mearns's birds—and the experience of preparing my own bird body—showed me something that I now see unfolding almost everywhere in the period I study: that preservation, long thought of in relation to parks and protected places, as a set of processes that keep species and systems thriving, can also involve creatures long dead, unnaturally resting in drawers far from where they roamed in life. For many Americans in the late nineteenth and early twentieth centuries, preservation was a much more capacious—and more violent—concept than our popular narratives capture.

When Americans think about preservation in the context of the nation's history, we tend to center on land—on national parks, on the West, on the grand vistas both created and reinforced by generations of landscape painters, photographers, and tourists. This is especially true for the late nineteenth century, when the first national parks were created, the first environmental advocacy groups were established, and conversations about resource scarcity and the so-called end of the frontier rose to national prominence.[5]

But these decades also mark the expansion and acceleration of U.S. empire. Precisely at the time in U.S. history when industrialization and urbanization led to many Americans becoming increasingly alienated from the natural world, soldiers were uniquely positioned to understand and construct nature's ongoing significance for the work they were doing and for the nation as a whole. During the same period often framed as foundational for contemporary environmentalism, U.S. soldiers offered the nation an expansive picture of the nature of the North American West. Their private letters and official reports reveal ideas about nature laden with assumptions about U.S. imperial power over Indigenous peoples and their land. Preservation—of Indigenous cultures thought by many Americans to be vanishing (without attention paid to the ways federal Indian policy actively displaced Native nations and disrupted their cultural practices), of new plant and animal species encountered in the West, and of land for American uses, whether under settler ownership or federal management—was inseparable from conquest. Only recently have we seen more mainstream attention given to Indigenous history and U.S. settler colonialism. That the violent dispossession of Native nations from their homelands preceded the creation of parks in these same landscapes is often left out of our national narratives.[6] Soldiers did this work at the behest of the U.S. government. They then were tasked with managing both the land they had taken and the people they had displaced.

As U.S. military actions shifted from the West to the Pacific, the role of empire in soldiers' ideas about nature became even more pronounced: the unfamiliar tropical context heightened links between new environments and imperial work, and words used to describe American environments and opportunities to enjoy them were redeployed in the Pacific. As they had done in the U.S. West, soldiers described the possibilities they saw in Philippine landscapes even as they also devoted paragraph upon paragraph to the difficulties of tropical military service. They bound together the strenuous work of climbing Philippine mountains with the violent work of warfare against a hard-to-find enemy under the heading "hiking."[7] They marveled at the beauty of this unfamiliar place even as they carried out acts of destruction. And throughout, Mearns continued his collecting, in contexts where the boundaries of scientific inquiry and military duty became increasingly blurred, all of it contained within the growing work of U.S. empire.

CALLS TO CONNECT U.S. COLONIALISM IN NORTH AMERICA and across the Pacific in the Philippines are not new. In a landmark 1980 article Walter L. Williams linked federal Indian policy in the U.S. West to the nation's imperial designs in the Philippines by emphasizing the way politicians in 1898 drew on their almost universal belief in the righteousness of U.S. actions toward Indigenous nations in the previous century. "To admit doubt," he wrote, "would have undercut the whole history of the nation."[8] Indeed, reframing what many white nineteenth-century Americans would have named westward expansion as an imperial and settler-colonial project requires sustained attention to the violence at the heart of U.S. history—violence that has often been imperial in nature. Ned Blackhawk has argued that "despite an outpouring of work over the past decades, those investigating American Indian history and U.S. history more generally have failed to reckon with the violence upon which the continent was built."[9] Studying U.S. soldiers—and their words, their ideas—is one way to reckon with their violent work. It is also an approach that illuminates the shape and reach of U.S. empire.

The observations Williams made in 1980 about the continuities of U.S. colonialism on multiple frontiers are in dialogue with recent charges to more critically examine U.S. history—and U.S. imperialism—everywhere it leads. While Williams focused on how imperialist politicians linked conquest in the U.S. West and the Philippines, studies of U.S. imperialism have moved beyond statesmen to consider the experiences of those who lived within, labored in the service of, or actively resisted U.S. empire. Following the lead of several scholars interested in thinking about the imperial history of the United States, I suggest that returning to U.S. soldiers can show us more about how U.S. empire operated on both sides of the Pacific.[10] Paul Kramer has argued for the imperial as an analytical category—an approach that can help historians think "about power, connection, and comparison."[11] Daniel Bender and Jana Lipman, in the introduction to their edited volume, *Making the Empire Work*, push scholars "to consider the labor that formed, worked, and rendered the U.S. empire visible."[12] Though there is "a persistent case of empire denial" in many accounts of U.S. history, Kristin Hoganson and Jay Sexton advocate for moving beyond naming empire where it exists to "ask what empire does."[13] Attending to empire's actions directs our gaze away from high politics, and toward on-the-ground, in-the-field experience.

I take up this challenge by examining how soldiers, whose labor was crucial to the material work of U.S. empire on both sides of the Pacific, made sense of the landscapes of their service, and then described and narrated these landscapes for both intimate and more public audiences. The work of empire, soldiers reveal, was not just physical. Imperial work was not limited to military tasks, as soldiers who were also writers and collectors make clear. Agents of empire followed well-traveled pathways, imperial circuits that carried people and ideas. In the sites this project links, local people participated in the work of empire: Indigenous North Americans served as scouts, translators, and guides for the U.S. Army during its campaigns against Native nations, and similarly, Filipinos participated in constabulary units and worked as porters and guides during the Philippine-

American War and later U.S. occupation of the archipelago. While some of these figures appear in these pages, they are not the focus of this study. Instead, this book looks at how the labor of U.S. soldiers made the empire work and how imperial visions both shaped and relied on a set of nineteenth-century ideas about the natural world.[14]

Linda Nash suggests that "by and large, American environmental histories are still written as if the nation's imperial engagements mattered little to domestic stories, and conversely, as if environments mattered little to the culture and politics of American imperialism."[15] Soldiers offer the opportunity to write a different story, one that centers voices we usually hear only within military history. Mary Renda writes that "imperialism can never be an unmediated expression of armed might. Culture, consciousness, and identity both direct and are affected by, among other things, the taking up of arms and the harming of human bodies."[16] I suggest here that soldiers—officers and enlisted men—expand the resources we rely on to make sense of American ideas about nature, and that they demonstrate how their experiences in the service of empire shaped and were shaped by these ideas.

Soldiers' words and their work make visible some of U.S. empire's most persistent features: the kind of labor it required, often in new and challenging environments; the violence those working in its service meted out; and the way its narratives were told and retold in different places and contexts. Ann Stoler emphasizes the importance of "the familiar, strange, and unarticulated ways in which empire has appeared and disappeared from the intimate and public spaces of United States history," including "how relations of empire . . . indelibly permeate—or sometimes graze with only a scarred trace—institutions and the landscapes of people's lives."[17] Soldiers, through their writing about and work in the landscapes of their service, reveal a much broader set of ideas and attitudes about nature than a purely continental story of U.S. environmental thinking provides.[18] Their on-the-ground perspectives (sometimes also about the ground they moved through) show us how soldiers' notions of nature intermingled with their understandings of their work and with how they saw their roles within a growing U.S. empire on both sides of the Pacific.[19]

As empire's direct agents, U.S. soldiers exercised power over other peoples, their homelands, and their resources. Soldiers in the frontier army employed what Patrick Wolfe has called a "logic of elimination": they dispossessed Native nations of their homelands, furthered genocidal policies, and actively protected Anglo settlements on stolen land.[20] They also carried out "eliminatory" work through less material means: official reports, articles, and prose meant for a variety of publics. Later some of these men remembered their frontier service with nostalgia—for an older West, for the ways their experiences affirmed a particular kind of manhood—even as they lamented changes that they had enabled.[21]

Taking the Field begins on the plains in the 1870s, with soldiers serving in campaigns of genocidal violence and dispossession against Lakotas and Cheyennes. Soldiers' perspectives remain mostly white and mostly male, but in contrast to the artists and travelers who have shaped our understanding of how nineteenth-century Americans thought about nature, soldiers were working in—not just looking at—new environments.[22] And their work regularly brought them into direct confrontation with the people who lived in these landscapes. Soldiers sometimes concluded that places they were expected to think were "splendid" should be left to the Indigenous peoples who already lived there.[23] At other times soldiers used official reports to figuratively empty Native homelands in anticipation of white settlement and resource exploitation, effectively reproducing popular narratives of what the West was "supposed" to be. The material transformation of the landscapes of their service, landscapes that were anything but empty, was often accompanied by a figurative reworking of these places in prose.

Soldiers' private letters, official correspondence, and published reports reveal the many modes through which western landscapes were remade. Their words make clear that soldiers, not often the sources we rely on to understand cultural production, made critical contributions to American ideas about the landscapes of the West by shoring up and sometimes critiquing the ideologies underpinning their work, even as they continued to do it.[24]

Imperial violence took many forms. Edgar Mearns was assigned to serve as a medical officer in what the United States called Arizona Territory. As he traveled on official army business with Gen. George Crook through Apache and Yavapai homelands, he documented and preserved birds, generating an archive of specimens that later found a home in the Smithsonian. This natural history work was dependent on and shaped by U.S. military power. Across Native homelands the U.S. Army established territorial control and enabled colonial science, a set of practices that emerged from the strategies global empires regularly used to describe and categorize the world's resources and cultures. The natural history techniques Mearns employed—collecting, categorizing, describing, and labeling—resemble the tactics Crook used to regulate and contain Apache and Yavapai people. Indigenous people resisted these new tactics, just as they had fought against other strategies of removal and control. These resonances between the techniques used by nineteenth-century naturalists and the U.S. Army signal the pervasive, violent, and multidimensional nature of American empire in the U.S. West.

Soldiers continued the work of empire across the Pacific, bringing their ideas and assumptions with them to the Philippines and sending home letters, artifacts, and in Mearns's case, specimens to museum curators and collaborators. These materials helped shape American ideas about Philippine nature—and Filipino people. Many of these soldiers, career army men and volunteers brand new to soldiering, made rhetorical moves linking their service in the Philippines with earlier campaigns against Indigenous nations in the U.S. West. Some signaled the destructive nature of their work with words more commonly associated with the natural world. In an imperial context "wilderness" took on other, unsettling meanings: it could be something soldiers made with force.

Though U.S. empire took different forms on opposite sides

of the Pacific Ocean—and had separate goals—key similarities connect landscapes and imperial projects too often considered in isolation.[25] These similarities stretch from the extractive designs the United States brought to both frontiers to the strategies employed and struggles experienced by soldiers, many of whom had served in both places.[26] They extend to the rhetorical choices and cultural framing these men used to make sense of their work, including the violence they carried out in the service of U.S. empire. These continuities all suggest that connecting histories of empire, nature, and labor in the U.S. West and in the Philippines can help us understand how and through whom empire worked, as well as how ideas about the natural world figured into U.S. imperial visions in the late nineteenth and early twentieth centuries.

In fact, nature and empire are impossible to separate; even in death they remain intertwined. Mearns's work as soldier, surgeon, and collector animates these connections. By the time he was deployed to the Philippines in 1903, he had strong relationships with Smithsonian curators, who had high hopes for what his new assignment could do for their collections. But in these Pacific landscapes, military and scientific work became even more tangled: Mearns fought Moro people with his collecting gun, skinned specimens while bullets flew around him, and looted ethnographic materials from villages made accessible by force. Once collected, his Philippine specimens still needed to survive a long journey to be of use to the museum. But Mearns didn't just preserve natural history specimens—he took skulls from Filipino graves and preserved the bodies of U.S. soldiers killed in action. The bodies of birds, of Filipinos, and of U.S. soldiers all traveled the same route: back across the Pacific in boxes.

Imperial pathways connect multiple "fields" with intersecting meanings. Specialists develop expertise in different fields of study. Scientists conduct fieldwork away from homes and labs. Soldiers serving away from posts or bases are deployed to the field, and the violent work of war takes place on the battlefield—though not only there. To take the field is to occupy a space. In this book what constitutes a "field" is blurred; ideas, actions, orders, and assumptions layer it with meaning. And sometimes the spaces between fields—whether battlefields or fields of study—momentarily collapse, creating unexpected narrative opportunities.

Taking the Field concludes by returning to the U.S. West, to St. Louis and the 1904 Louisiana Purchase Exposition. There the book's two frontiers and their many fields were no longer separated by the vast Pacific but only by temporary walls of staff and plaster. Fairgoers could cross over a replica of the Bridge of Spain to enter the fair's version of the old walled city of Manila, and then cross back again to exhibits on western landscapes so recently transformed by soldiers' labor. People and materials were transported across the Pacific so that traditional homes could be constructed, displayed, and inhabited by Filipinos in living exhibits. North American Indigenous people were exhibited, too, positioned within a story that drew a straight line from continental to Pacific empire. This narrative, one that seamlessly linked the Louisiana Purchase, campaigns to dispossess and eliminate Indigenous peoples, and the U.S. colonial project in the Philippines, was the fair's central display. And soldiers, laboring across many fields and on both sides of the Pacific, played their parts and sometimes even helped tell this story. As workers and writers, as collectors of specimens and souvenirs, and as agents of empire moving within patterns and structures not of their own making, soldiers in the late nineteenth and early twentieth centuries show us their roles in the production of American notions of nature and demand that we more fully acknowledge the centrality of empire to those ideas.

SOLDIERS TOOK—AND TOOK FROM—MULTIPLE FIELDS IN the service of the U.S. Army and, more broadly, the U.S. imperial regime. Their taking, and their documentation of it, forms the backbone of this book, which opens up critical questions about sources, where they come from, and how we interpret them. Jean O'Brien talks about reading and interpreting sources produced by colonizers: "We cannot and should not simply toss out this colonial archive. Instead, we need to find ways to use it judiciously."[27] In *Taking the Field*, I argue that historians have overlooked what U.S. soldiers have said about their work as imperial agents, about the landscapes of their service, and about the nature of empire itself. These perspectives illuminate continuities between U.S. empire on both sides of the Pacific, but beyond that, they reveal the shape, reach, and texture of U.S. empire and especially how ideas about nature became further entangled with understandings of imperial work, even in sites far from fields and battlefields.

These sites include museums. Following soldiers whose service carried them across the North American continent to the Philippines and back again has carried me to many different places too. But at the start of this project I hadn't imagined that it would take me to natural history collections. Museums are key sites for reckoning with colonial violence; these institutions hold art, ancestors, historical artifacts, cultural belongings, scientific specimens, and so many people and objects gathered, purchased, prepared, and taken. As I write this there are ongoing efforts to hold these institutions to account—to rework the narratives they display but also to return, to repatriate, to make restitution—not just for the initial violence that built these collections but for the ongoing display and interpretation of these materials.[28] Bird collections, though often housed within institutions that need to grapple with these critiques, open up different, if related, questions.

When I first visited the National Museum of Natural History's Division of Birds, I could not believe the scale of the collection: more than 640,000 specimens, reflecting roughly 85 percent of the world's birds known to scientists.[29] They are here primarily for scientific study, available by appointment or loan request for use by staff researchers, visiting scholars, and a historian who arrived to see field books and then asked to see birds.

To view these drawers full of birds from across time and space is to be overwhelmed, at least at first. There are so many. But it is through comparison that species and subspecies are differentiated, that migratory patterns become visible, and that home ranges are defined. Their movements make them harder to understand; their frequent motion—governed by forces larger than a single bird on the wing or an individual surgeon in the U.S. Army—interferes with our attempts to know them until their circuits and pathways become clear.

Scientists study birds in museum collections to understand their lifeways; I have come to realize that as a historian, my focus is on how they came to be in the museum itself: on their death, their preparation as specimens, their journeys to the museum, and their service to science as parts of these collections, constructed and preserved through centuries of care and carefulness. The unending care work that ensures the birds' continued preservation—work that makes them timeless or perhaps pulls them out of time—may have an unintended effect: it separates them from the specific contexts of their collection, from the large-scale processes and individual choices that brought these birds to the museum.

Examining the interplay of military service and imperial science has shown me that empire is everywhere. It may be harder to see in drawers of birds than in the histories of wars fought to create empire and then extend it. But there it is, shaping what was seen and collected, and shaping possibilities for future study. These birds are an extraordinary record. They embody a tangle of nature and empire and labor that has become so naturalized that it can be difficult to recognize. Spend some time with a drawer of ornithological study skins, though, and you will see it all: the beauty of centuries-old feathers, the institutions named on multiple labels, the handwriting on each tag, notes and measurements on tag backs hinting at additional contextual clues, the careful work it took to empty and then suture the bellies of all these birds. These clues reveal where the birds have been—and also where agents of empire traveled to collect them. These links between birds and their collectors, between institutions and their agents, and between empires and the fields they took from are all visible in a drawer full of birds, if you know to look for them.

My blackbird, though a twenty-first-century specimen, is also part of this tangle. His presence—his unnatural permanence—encourages us to think about the practices and the ideologies that allow him to remain. My complicated and incomplete relationship with my blackbird is encoded in his body, in the labor of transforming him from dead thing to preserved specimen.[30] My specific moves are written there—each incision, each stitch sewn—but so much of what I know to be there is hard to see. Skinning and stuffing a blackbird forced me to pay attention to my own embodied experience, to the intimacy and violence bound up in this particular form of preservation work. Breaking a bird's bones in order to preserve its body might be a metaphor for the story of this book. Writ large, it demonstrates how agents of empire carried out the work of conquest over and over, in the U.S. West, in the Philippines, and then again in miniature at the 1904 St. Louis World's Fair. Conquest and preservation are two sides of the same story; thinking with them together affirms the driving thread of this book: to understand American ideas about nature we must grapple with U.S. empire. And to do this we need to be willing to follow soldiers, their stories, and their specimens wherever they lead: west and farther west, across the Pacific and back again, into an archive of birds.

1

The Nature of Frontier Army Work

"YOU HAVE NEVER BEEN STATIONED IN A COUNTRY AS MEAN as that at Powder River," wrote Capt. Samuel Ovenshine in an August 1876 letter to his wife, Sallie, who was back at Fort Leavenworth. Ovenshine was camped with the Fifth Infantry where the Powder River flows into the Yellowstone, near what is now Terry, Montana. As the Fifth made its way west to the site of a future army post where the Tongue and Yellowstone Rivers meet, Samuel had much to say to Sallie about the landscapes of his military service: "You may count on the miserable Yellowstone, out of God's world, as your future home."[1] Lt. Frank Dwight Baldwin, stationed elsewhere in Dakota Territory, characterized the landscape similarly. To his wife, Alice, he wrote in July 1876, "The country up here is not as fine as I had expected to see." A few weeks later, from a camp at the mouth of Rosebud Creek, he told Alice that what she'd heard "about this country by parties who have been up here telling how beautiful + etc, well it has all been exagerated." In the two hundred miles he'd traveled from the Missouri River, he'd seen "a most dreary + desolate country." Baldwin continued, "They all say that a little farther up the country improves. But I have seen enough."[2]

These letters from Samuel Ovenshine and Frank Baldwin to their wives, like those of so many other soldiers in the field to their loved ones back home, are a window into the social world of the U.S. Army. Soldiers' letters reflect the often-challenging working conditions soldiers navigate, as well as a range of social and cultural histories and norms. And the letters sol-

19

diers received from loved ones reflect their contexts, too—the daily rhythms of life at a frontier army post. These letter writers had news to share and also relationships to preserve, to strengthen despite periods of long separation.

We do not have equal access to both sides of these conversations; in fact, the conditions of frontier army service have materially shaped contemporary archives.[3] Think about it: a letter from home reaches a soldier like Ovenshine, stationed in a place he calls "one of the most desolate and forlorn looking places you ever saw."[4] He reads it and tucks it away somewhere—a chest pocket, a saddlebag, or maybe even the driest corner of his makeshift home on the banks of a remote river at the site of a soon-to-be-built army post. Samuel's letters, by contrast, travel across the Yellowstone River and down the Missouri on a steamboat, arriving at a fixed address at Fort Leavenworth, where they are safe from weather, if not wear. Given these different pathways and circumstances, it is a wonder that both sides of any personal correspondence between soldiers and their families survived for historians to examine. The letters between Samuel and Sallie that remain—a flurry of correspondence back and forth for a short period in time—offer a brief glimpse of the life of a military family between the U.S. Civil War and the Philippine-American War. To read these letters from summer and early fall 1876 is to wish for all the pages not in the archives.

Still, what exists is evocative. Captain Ovenshine's description of the confluence of the Yellowstone and the Tongue—"mean," "miserable," "out of God's world"—got so stuck in my head that I drove to see the country for myself, to have one of what William Wyckoff, in his field guide to reading the U.S. West, calls "tactile, terrestrial encounters."[5] With Ovenshine's words in my mind, I marveled at Montana's big sky, at the green of the cottonwoods near the confluence, at the flow of both rivers. Where Ovenshine saw "as miserable [a] part of the U.S. as we could get into," I saw beauty.[6] And I took pictures (figs. 3 and 4).

Of course, we were not looking at the same place; the natural world is not constant, even without the human-driven changes

3. Confluence of the Tongue and Yellowstone Rivers, June 2017. Author photo.

that transformed an 1876 winter army camp into part of the contemporary riverfront of Miles City, Montana. And even if Ovenshine and I had, by some magic, been there at the same time, our perspectives as viewers would likely have generated different perceptions of the same space. Landscapes, as scholars of environmental history, geography, and aesthetics have

4. Probable former site of the Tongue River Cantonment, the 1876 camp that later became Fort Keogh, on the south side of the confluence (though the site for the construction of the fort was shifted a bit farther away from the river), June 2017. Author photo.

shown us, are constructed through the act of looking. "A landscape, unlike an environment, with its strong scientific connotation of the objectively material and scientific, is always a profoundly human creation made out of profoundly nonhuman stuff," writes Daegan Miller.[7] This distinction helps separate what I saw when I looked at the confluence of the Tongue and Yellowstone in 2017, on a trip to celebrate the seventieth wedding anniversary of my now-husband's grandparents, from what Samuel Ovenshine saw and chose to describe almost a century and a half earlier. Simon Schama writes, "It is our shaping perception that makes the difference between raw matter and landscape."[8] I can reflect on what I brought to that beautiful bend joining two rivers. But Captain Ovenshine and the Fifth Infantry were doing far more than looking: they were working, and that work remade the West—as both material environment and cultural landscape.

The nineteenth-century U.S. West was a place filled with the work of reshaping terrain. While the most persistent imagery of this period might be of agrarian families farming and homemaking, others toiled for low wages in mines, along railroads, and in industries providing services to those who came west in search of new opportunities. But soldiers in the frontier army were also workers whose labor was deeply tied to the material transformation and cultural construction of the landscapes of what became the American West.[9]

Conceptualizing soldiers as workers opens up new ways of understanding the complexity of their labor. First, they were carrying out the violent work of war, what nineteenth-century Americans routinely called "Indian fighting." Soldiers were also tasked with literal state building: army post construction, route making and roadbuilding, and management of both newly created national parks and reservations where Indigenous people were incarcerated. Elsewhere, U.S. soldiers were also tasked with other kinds of labor: the work of enforcing Reconstruction in the South and strikebreaking and enforcement during the large labor conflicts of the Progressive Era.[10]

Cultural terrain was being remade too. In the late nineteenth century ideas about both identity and whiteness in the United States became far more rigid; many Americans united around imperial expansion and settler colonialism in Native homelands, and the political and cultural transformations of the post–Civil War nation foregrounded clashes over labor, citizenship, empire, and modernity.[11] U.S. soldiers lived these changes, bringing ideas encountered earlier in their lives west with them to the sites of their military service.

Soldiers assigned to frontier outposts occupied a hybrid position in the western landscapes where they served: temporary, though not tourists; stationed in these landscapes, though not stationary. They moved west, sometimes with their families, and made homes and lives at army posts. But they weren't settled there; new orders could arrive anytime. In some ways they were placeless, grounded instead in routines and protocols, in communities defined by rank and regiment. Despite this, many soldiers developed deep attachments to the West—certainly as a place but as an idea too, a kind of imaginary that took hold in their minds as well as in the mythology of the nation.[12] Whether more recent immigrants or Civil War veterans who had already fought to preserve or advance their vision of the nation, soldiers in the U.S. Army had been steeped in ideas about what America was and could be—and about the role of the West in those visions. Though these men were not separate from notions of progress and ideas about the future circulating in American culture in the late nineteenth century, they didn't universally embrace them.[13]

As representatives of the United States, soldiers legitimated settlers' claims to the West, first with their presence and then with their actions. But some had concerns. And while these concerns did not lead to a full-scale critique of American empire and the worldview sustaining it, they do demonstrate that anxieties about the particular shape of American progress in the late nineteenth century extended beyond the sectors of society where we tend to look for and locate alternative perspectives. Some soldiers were unsure of this work. Still, they continued it.

Soldiers were often the first to describe western landscapes for American audiences, whether privately, as in Captain Ovenshine's letters to Sallie, or publicly, as in official reports and published accounts of expeditions through Yellowstone and the Black Hills. In both private and public writing U.S. soldiers represented landscapes transformed by their physical labor as well as by their work with the pen to a variety of readers. Here I bring together the writing of soldiers who worked in different plains landscapes: Ovenshine at the confluence of the Yellowstone and Tongue Rivers, Lt. Gustavus Doane at the future site of Yellowstone National Park, and Col. Richard Irving Dodge in the Black Hills. I pull from the writings of other officers and enlisted men to flesh out what frontier army service was like and how soldiers remembered it, how they interacted with the natural world, and what they, as a group, offer both environmental and imperial history. The things they wrote, the stories they told, reveal not simply agents of empire, carrying out the work of conquest and colonization—though they certainly show us this—but also soldiers expressing curiosity, frustration, and sometimes ambivalence about both their assigned tasks and the landscapes of their service. Centering soldiers' stories makes visible the deep roots of a more capacious and complex constellation of ideas about preservation. These ideas were at the heart of U.S. imperial expansion.

Wonderland?

"It is spoken of as a splendid country but Leavenworth will suit me. I have seen enough of these splendid countries. They rarely ever turn out to be what they are said to."[14] Capt. Samuel Ovenshine wrote these words to his wife, Sallie, in late July 1876. When Ovenshine spoke of the Yellowstone, he meant the Yellowstone River, an almost seven-hundred-mile-long tributary of the Missouri River that flows north out of the Rockies, through Yellowstone National Park and then north and east across present-day Montana and into North Dakota. There it reaches the Missouri. Though north and east of Yellowstone National Park, the site Ovenshine was heading toward, a future post at the confluence of the Tongue and Yellowstone, might easily have been linked with ideas and images of the park in both the popular and military imagination.

While many marveled at the landscapes they encountered as part of their military service, some, like Ovenshine, reacted differently. Douglas McChristian suggests it was unfamiliarity that prompted some soldiers to express ambivalence or even displeasure about these landscapes.[15] In contrast to voices expressing wonder—"It is as beautiful and rich a country as I ever saw," wrote Cpl. Maurice H. Wolfe in 1867—others offered different impressions. "Dakota I do not like at all," wrote Pvt. Henry Hubman in 1881. And Pvt. Herman S. Searl wrote to his parents in 1868, "It seems as though this country was made for the Indians, what us[e] is it to the United States I have not seen any yet."[16] In McChristian's project, these examples help prepare the reader to imagine leaving an army post and entering the field. In that context they work quite well to suggest the newness of western landscapes. But they also suggest that when U.S. soldiers critiqued the aesthetic qualities of these landscapes, they were also commenting on the ways the West had been represented to them in popular culture.

Myriad texts and images about the West were in wide circulation by the time men like Wolfe, Hubman, Searl, and Ovenshine wrote from their posts on the plains. Martha Sandweiss describes how the West "was for many nineteenth-century Americans a fabled place of fantastic topography, exotic peoples, the place where the nation's future would unfold."[17] Soldiers in the U.S. Army were, in fact, tasked with enabling a particular version of that future.

While we cannot know what exactly soldiers had read or seen before the army sent them to experience the West for themselves, nineteenth-century American landscape painting, which linked nationalism and nature, provides one set of sources for the ideas that pervaded the white American culture that produced these men. From Hudson River School artist Thomas Cole's work, which could be quite ambivalent about the balance of the country and the city, as in *The Oxbow* (1836), to the work of later landscape painters who focused on particularly imperial representations of the West, such as Albert Bierstadt, especially his paintings of the Rocky Mountains and the Sierras, visual representations of American landscapes were deeply connected to American culture, even as the artists had different ideas about the relationships between nature and the state. They reflected these ideas in their paintings. So whereas Cole explored the tensions between American nature and the American nation, for the next generation of painters the American landscape, especially the western landscape—as they chose to represent it—contained none of these contradictions.[18] Instead, they depicted western places as naturalized landscapes where imperial expansion and Native dispossession had already occurred. Even as U.S. soldiers were tasked with emptying the West and readying it for settlement, artists were painting the West as if these soldiers had already finished this work.[19] Enabled by prose, paintings, and photographs, tourists were primed to look for—and to see—certain qualities in the landscapes of the U.S. West.[20] Soldiers were too.

When army men like Ovenshine articulated a critique of "splendid countries," they were revealing the gaps between the artistic representations they had consumed and the landscapes they encountered in their work as soldiers. And when they suggested in private letters that the territory where they served should be left to Indigenous people, they were speaking against pervasive narratives that presented the West as destined to be American, rather than already Native. These glimpses of unease, these personal articulations in opposition to nationalistic framings of the West, remind us that alongside the artistic and literary renderings of the West as wonderland were other impressions and observations about what western landscapes were like and whom they were for. I highlight these gentle critiques, these moments of ambiguity, to make visible the work of constructing and crystallizing the West as wonderland. Glimpses of doubt about the on-the-ground reality of American cultural understandings animate the active work of constructing these assumptions about land and landscapes.

Yellowstone National Park was created by Congress and signed into existence by President Grant in 1872. Yellowstone was to be "set apart as a public park or pleasuring ground for the benefit and enjoyment of the people."[21] This designation set a significant preservation precedent, though the decision was less about a commitment to wilderness than it was about limiting certain kinds of private development in the region.[22] Support for the protection of Yellowstone grew out of a series of expeditions undertaken to survey the region in 1869, 1870, and 1871, each one contributing to the energy spurring on the next. In the summer of 1869 Charles Cook, David Folsom, and William Peterson explored the area, and the following year Henry Washburn led a larger expedition accompanied by an army escort under Lt. Gustavus Doane. The published work this expedition produced affirmed existing expectations about the Yellowstone landscape as a kind of wonderland and reinforced ideas about whom this wonderland should be for.

Nathaniel Langford participated in the Washburn Expedition and published a two-part piece in *Scribner's Monthly* the following year titled "The Wonders of the Yellowstone."[23] In Langford's telling, the group encountered marvel after marvel, each one surpassing the next. "A grander scene than the lower cataract of the Yellowstone was never witnessed by mortal eyes," he wrote, and then the group reached the upper falls: "The sun shone brightly, and the laughing waters of the upper fall were filled with the glitter of rainbows and diamonds." They had never seen anything like it. "Nature, in the excess of her prodigality, had seemingly determined that this last look should be the brightest, for there was everything in the landscape illuminated by the rising sun, to invite a longer stay."[24]

The trip wasn't all "rainbows and diamonds," though. Langford detailed the challenges of traveling ("but another name for scrambling") through the terrain, grizzly bear and mountain lion encounters, and the fear of attacks by Native people. What Langford described as a journey "through a country until then untraveled" discounted Indigenous presence in the region, except as a source of fear, and reproduced the work of erasure necessary to make this sort of claim.[25]

As the Washburn Expedition's military leader, Doane submitted a report to the secretary of war, who then shared it with the Senate Committee on Territories. Doane's report corroborated Langford's assessment of the Yellowstone region as splendid. He described a geyser in Firehole Basin as "the most lovely inanimate object in existence." Of waterfalls he wrote, "Every great cascade has a language and an idea peculiarly its own, embodied, a[s] it were, in the flow of its waters." Doane's report, intended for his military superiors (and perhaps Congress), is filled with measurements, distances, and details. He paid attention to the region's use value, noting areas suitable to settlement and irrigation, and even pointing out cedars "yielding most beautiful material for small cabinet work, and of a nature susceptible of an exquisite finish."[26]

These observations are more common at the start of Doane's report; once deep into geysers, sulfur springs, and mountainous territory, he no longer made these recommendations. Instead, he focused on describing what he saw. Even though this report was Doane's work product—an official military document— the language slips easily into more lyrical imagery: "Standing on the brink of the chasm the heavy roaring of the imprisoned river comes to the ear only in a sort of hollow, hungry growl, scarcely audible from the depths, and strongly suggestive of demons in torment below." Doane drew on notions of the sublime to convey the scene: "It is grand, gloomy, and terrible: a solitude peopled with fantastic ideas; an empire of shadows and turmoil."[27]

These descriptions painted quite the picture of the Yellowstone region for a range of readers and lecture circuit attendees. In addition to his *Scribner's Monthly* feature, Langford gave public talks in which he described the region as containing the "greatest wonders on the continent." F. V. Hayden, director of the Geological and Geographical Survey of the Territories, attended a Langford lecture and added Yellowstone to the itinerary for his 1871 civilian expedition.[28]

These materials were deployed for political goals too. Copies of Langford's "Wonders of the Yellowstone" and Doane's military report were distributed to members of both houses of Congress to aid them in their decisions regarding S. 392 and H.R. 764, identical bills that would create Yellowstone National Park. Park supporters worked to aid the bill's passing. Hayden brought specimens from his 1871 survey trip to display in the

Capitol rotunda, along with sketches by Thomas Moran and photographs by William Henry Jackson, who had both participated in his expedition.[29]

The bill passed, though not because of deeply held beliefs in the value of Yellowstone as wilderness. Rather, the bill sought to protect Yellowstone's "natural curiosities" from private ownership. Many of Yellowstone's early visitors forecast its value as a site for tourism and scientific study, not agriculture and settlement.[30] Even Doane, in the conclusion to his military report, called it an unparalleled "country for sightseers" and also "probably the greatest laboratory that nature furnishes on the surface of the globe."[31] And Gen. William Tecumseh Sherman, in a note accompanying the report, reminded readers who might be swept up in the fantastical experiences of Doane and his men of the value of these words for those "studying the resources of our new Territories."[32] Sherman visited Yellowstone in 1877, and the report he wrote about his encounter with "the National Park or 'Wonderland' as it is called here" regularly slipped into the language of the sublime and the picturesque. For example, Sherman called the Yellowstone "the best trout-fishing stream on earth" and wrote, "The falls and cañon of the Yellowstone will remain, to the end of time, objects of natural beauty and grandeur, to attract the attention of the living."[33] Surely he recalled the reports of earlier Yellowstone expeditions as he experienced this "Wonderland" for himself.

The note Sherman wrote to accompany Doane's report of the 1870 Washburn Expedition described terrain already subdued and ready for exploration and development—an idea that was clearly conveyed in Doane's report. Of Yellowstone's Indigenous inhabitants Doane wrote, "Appearances indicated that the basin had been almost entirely abandoned by the sons of the forest." Doane reported "no recent traces of them" and even offered this popular (if untrue) explanation: "The larger tribes never enter the basin, restrained by superstitious ideas in connection with the thermal springs."[34] Karl Jacoby explains that these erasures were grounded in American ideas about land and property, not in actual use: "Drawing upon a familiar vocabulary of discovery and exploration, the authors of the early accounts of the Yellowstone region literally wrote Indians out of the landscape, erasing Indian claims by reclassifying inhabited territory as empty wilderness."[35] Similar arguments were made by soldiers tasked with surveying the Black Hills a few years later.

In spite of its supposed emptiness, the newly established park required policing, and in 1886 the U.S. Army was deployed to Yellowstone. Though framed as temporary, the military management of Yellowstone that began that year stretched on for more than three decades.[36] The soldiers deployed to Yellowstone, in particular, found themselves at the intersection of competing Wests: a West of frontier labor—the work of American state building through Native dispossession and genocide, the work of policing the users of these preserved-for-some, protected-from-others spaces—and a West that was supposedly a timeless, pristine wonderland.

Some of these soldiers enjoyed their unexpected detour into national park protection and service. Others detested the tasks accompanying a Yellowstone deployment—work that to them didn't seem much like the soldiering they had expected.[37] Still, when viewed against the backdrop of what frontier service entailed, perhaps a park deployment wasn't so different. While frontier regiments serving in campaigns against Lakotas and Cheyennes dispossessed Native people of their land, constructing empty spaces that could then be occupied by U.S. settlers, Yellowstone soldiers fought poachers. They surveilled and preserved western landscapes to be experienced and enjoyed by tourists who increasingly came to see the wonders they had heard the park contained—wonders depicted in paintings, photographs, and prose. And whether inside the boundaries of a national park or out in the field, U.S. soldiers contributed to a growing body of written impressions of the U.S. West.

Writing the West, Narrating the Frontier Army

On August 1, 1876, a decade before soldiers were deployed to protect Yellowstone National Park, Samuel Ovenshine described the Tongue River Cantonment, the site chosen for the new army post on the Yellowstone, to his wife, Sallie, back at Leavenworth with their children, this way: "It is a fair-looking locality taking into consideration all things. . . . There is no nice place in the whole country, but as I said before, we will be lucky to get any place."[38] The persistence of these descriptions of the terrain along the Yellowstone River might prompt a reader to wonder whether these landscapes were new to Ovenshine. But the distance, though difficult, wasn't a fresh challenge. Neither was the work of soldiering in the West; he'd fought against the Apaches, Arapahos, and Cheyennes who lived there. Samuel Ovenshine had already been a soldier for fifteen years, and for twelve of them he was married to Sallie. Perhaps the distance had always been hard, or perhaps something not in these letters made it harder. "No news from home, and no hopes of any," his letter continued. "It seems as if it were useless for you to write to me but if you do now and then write enough to say how you are. I might get one of the letters sometime, though no doubt many of them I will never see."[39]

In his letters to Sallie, Samuel offered candid comments about his professional obligations. Perhaps Ovenshine had once held optimistic views about the work of the army, about what the West could offer him.[40] But his letters to Sallie contain evidence of many kinds of hardship. He described the evening of August 8, 1876, as "a miserable night," writing, "After being tired out I could not sleep for the mosquitos and heat together." A few days later, Ovenshine described a more layered struggle, with bad weather to match his sadness: "It is a wet dismal morning which will add to the already dismal appearance of the place I am to be put off at. I know we are both on this day thinking of the little one we have lost. I feel homesick anyway and all together things are very depressing." A few lines later: "If the Sioux have slipped through I suppose Terry and Crook will still follow them but no one knows anything about it. I wish we were well out of this business." In the same letter, Ovenshine wrote, "It is also thought likely that our Regt. will get stuck at some of the Sioux Agencies on the Mo. River—all fearful places—as these agencies are on or will be turned over to the Military. I am disgusted with this whole business and were it not for bread and butter would get out of the Army."[41] "This whole business" was the everyday work of the frontier army, what Manu Karuka calls "countersovereignty" work: finding, fighting, and forcing Native nations and peoples into more contained spaces under more regulatory control.[42]

Ovenshine was part of an army in transition, an institution with "dual missions": both enabling imperial expansion across the continent, which primarily meant fighting a series of military campaigns against Indigenous peoples across North America, often grouped together under the label of the "Indian Wars," and enforcing Reconstruction policies in the postbellum South.[43] Despite responsibilities stretching in all cardinal directions, the army suffered steady congressional cutbacks in size and funding. The "frontier army" in which Samuel Ovenshine served on the plains included no more than twenty-five thousand enlisted men and an officer corps of just over two thousand as a result of an appropriations bill passed in 1874.[44] While half of the frontier army was American-born, including six African American regiments, its ranks were filled with recruits from more than forty countries, with significant numbers of both German and Irish immigrants. Later in the nineteenth century the makeup of the frontier army shifted toward a more fully American-born force.[45] What compelled these men to take up work for low pay and in extremely rough conditions? In a period marked by financial panics and labor strikes, the steady employment the frontier army offered drew men from different walks of life. Many were laborers, though some were farmers and tradesmen. Others had been soldiers before. And for some the excitement and opportunity frontier army service might provide was appealing too—thanks in part to ideas about the West and Indigenous people circulating nationwide.[46]

The officer corps included Civil War veterans who had been volunteers, West Point graduates, and enlisted men who had been promoted to commissioned officers. Sherry Smith explains that army officers "were among the most educated, articulate, and informed people in the West."[47] Ovenshine, though not a product of the military education system, fit this description. He'd been on his way to a career in law, but the Civil War changed his plans. Commissioned as a second lieutenant, he served in the Civil War's western theater in Kansas and New Mexico.[48] As an officer he was able to settle his family at a western army post before following orders into the field; enlisted men needed permission to marry. This, along with different pay scales for officers and enlisted men, was a key difference in soldiers' experiences at frontier posts.[49]

Baldwin and Ovenshine, along with the Fifth Infantry, were in pursuit of Lakotas as part of the U.S. military response to Lt. Col. George Armstrong Custer's decisive defeat at the Battle of Greasy Grass (known to soldiers and in American popular memory as the Battle of the Little Bighorn).[50] Nick Estes writes that "Cheyennes, Lakotas, and Arapahos made Custer and his Seventh Cavalry famous."[51]

On July 12, 1876, less than three weeks after Custer and the Seventh Cavalry fought Indigenous forces and lost, and only one week after the news of Custer's death reached the media via the telegraph at Bismarck, Dakota Territory, Ovenshine's company and several others from the Fifth Infantry left Fort Leavenworth for the Yellowstone River. Not long after reaching the plains Ovenshine noted in his diary, "Reports . . . say that Indians at Standing Rock have clothing of Custer's men."[52] As a plan was formulated, Samuel wrote to Sallie daily, speculating about what might be ahead without saying too much: "I can't, of course, tell you much about what we will do, but at present all I can pick up indicates we will start in about a week or maybe sooner and go up the Rosebud." And in the next day's letter he said this: "I don't dread an action at all. I feel that your arms protect me but if anything should happen you know my faith and love always have and will be yours my precious one."[53] Uncertainty is everywhere in Ovenshine's letters, and it was a feature of many soldiers' service on the plains. To Alice, Frank Baldwin wrote, "When I shall have an opportunity to send you another letter no one can tell. . . . I shall expect so many of your good letters when I return to my lonely tent on the banks of the Yellowstone."[54]

Military service in the U.S. West was different from what many soldiers had experienced in the East.[55] The army established a series of small, often understaffed forts across the western landscape, positioned not just to facilitate military strategy but also to accommodate settler concerns.[56] Though the substantial number of soldiers ordered to the Yellowstone after Greasy Grass/Little Bighorn was the exception rather than the rule (more often small groups of soldiers scouted their assigned patrol areas, using frontier army posts as jumping-off points), the work of Ovenshine's company was certainly representative of the frontier army experience: *hard.* His letters to Sallie describe grueling days of roadbuilding in extreme weather conditions, one day so hot that he couldn't touch the metal of his belt, the next day gray, damp, and rainy. From his regiment's camp at Rosebud Creek he wrote, "Our company marched with the train to assist it to day. The assistance consisted in pushing the wagons up hill, letting them down by ropes, digging roads, fixing crossings and all that nature of work. As we have over 200 wagons, you may know it was no easy task. . . . We left camp at 5 A.M. and got into camp about 5 P.M. taking 12 hours to make ten miles. All this is owing to the train as roads for it have to be made."[57] Some soldiers were assigned the work of "pioneering," preparing the path for the rest of the group to advance—labor that included grading streams and removing rocks and other debris.[58] Though the physical environment was different, this work wasn't entirely new for army veterans. Road and bridge construction had been central to the movement of troops and supplies during the Civil War.[59]

The marching Ovenshine described was part of a U.S. response to the decisive victory of the Lakotas over Custer and the Seventh Cavalry. Congress approved the construction of two posts on the Yellowstone River, and additional troops were ordered to the region in pursuit of Lakotas. Soldiers divided among the commands of Gen. George Crook, Gen. Alfred Terry, Col. Nelson Miles, Col. Wesley Merritt, and Lt. Col. Elwell Otis all headed for the Rosebud and Yellowstone Valleys. The Fifth Infantry under Miles, of which Ovenshine was part, marched in a column of 1,700 soldiers on August 8 and 9, 1876. On August 10 forces under Terry and Crook unexpectedly converged in the Rosebud Valley. Coordinating their efforts, Terry ordered Miles and his men (Ovenshine among them) to the Yellowstone River to prevent Lakotas from fleeing to Canada. Rain and mud further slowed Crook and Terry's forces, and plans to continue their fruitless search fizzled. Miles and his men were detailed to the Yellowstone Valley for the winter months, and the challenge of transporting wagons and supplies added to the hardship of these orders.[60] Samuel Ovenshine had anticipated much of this in his letters to Sallie. On August 2 he had written, "Things have such a forlorn look that it is enough to discourage me. . . . My darling, I would give worlds if I had them to be with you."[61]

Writing about the West was everywhere: personal experiences of overland travelers, letters to family members, how-to manuals for others hoping to make the trip, short and long fiction pieces about this new, exciting, dangerous place.[62] And though settler accounts seem to have earned more attention, soldiers' writings are a voluminous part of the written record of the West. Officers like Ovenshine, who had brought their families west, sent letters back to the fort while in the field. But some accounts from enlisted men remain. Fred H. Tobey, a member of the "L" Troop of the Seventh Cavalry, kept a diary that seems to have been one layer removed from his immediate experiences—not letters, written in the moment and sent off to loved ones, but entries that may have instead been recopied for safekeeping. Tobey mentioned skirmishes with Native people; an encounter with a Native woman he described as "fair and dusky and for a wonder rather clean," to whom he showed some pictures; and the small improvements he made to the tent he occupied in "this baren unsivilized country": "a carbine rack, a rustic shand-alier," and decorations of leaves, flowers, and sage. Sometimes Tobey described the wildlife he saw along the Yellowstone, and in other places he documented "hard fatigue during the day."[63]

Though accounts like Tobey's exist, much of what has been written about the frontier army draws from the accounts and experiences of officers—many of them individuals with far more power than Ovenshine.[64] This might be in part because officers assigned key leadership roles were also assigned professional writing tasks. They drafted official prose: telegrams, orders, reports. Everything in the frontier army required documentation, and the remaining paper trail is extensive. But some soldiers displayed this attention to detail in their writing beyond their military service, keeping diaries or publishing books about the places they had seen.

Col. Richard Irving Dodge generated one such written record. Tasked with leading the 1875 Black Hills Expedition, Dodge knew he would have an official report to write. But after a lifetime as an officer in the infantry (Dodge graduated from West Point in 1848 and had been in the army for twenty-seven years when he helmed the Black Hills Expedition), he also seems to have been imagining a broader audience for his prose. His immediate observations, in diaries, military reports, and the books he published for public consumption, demonstrate his contributions to an American discourse about the nature of the frontier.

The Black Hills

Dodge was not the first to lead a military expedition to the Black Hills; Lieutenant Colonel Custer had done so in 1874 to scout a location for a new fort and to explore the possibilities— especially the geological prospects—of this territory, despite a treaty that affirmed Lakota ownership of the land.[65] Looking back on these days from 1891 Capt. John Gregory Bourke, an aide to General Crook, described the "smouldering discontent among the Sioux [Lakotas] and the Cheyennes, based upon our failure to observe the stipulations of the treaty made in 1867 [1868], which guaranteed to them an immense strip of country, extending, either as a reservation or a hunting ground, clear to the Big Horn Mountains. . . . Reports of the fabulous richness of the gold mines in the Black Hills had excited the cupidity of the whites and the distrust of the red men." Indeed, Custer helped create this hype by reporting, according to Bourke, that the Black Hills contained gold "from the grass roots down."[66]

In 1875 the federal government, through the Office of Indian Affairs, authorized a scientific expedition to the Black Hills to assess its mineral wealth at the same time that Oglala and Brulé delegations made their way to Washington for meetings about their lands and treaty rights. The scientific expedition was assigned a military escort. While this pairing was not uncommon—western scientific expeditions were still ventures into contested territory—it illuminates the blurriness of the borders between scientific and military aims. And given the terms of the 1868 Treaty of Fort Laramie, it is hard not to see this as another imperial scoping trip "camouflaged as a scientific endeavor."[67]

Colonel Dodge, the officer assigned to command the military escort of this expedition, crossed paths with Red Cloud (Oglala Lakota) and Spotted Tail (Brulé Lakota), who were on their way to Washington; Dodge was en route to Fort Laramie to begin his highly publicized assignment. "They say I will have trouble, possibly a fight with northern Sioux who are now in Black Hills," Dodge wrote in his journal on May 9.[68] At Fort Laramie the expedition was assembled: John Gregory Bourke was assigned as engineer officer, and Wayne Jenney, a civilian geologist, headed the scientific mission. Dodge's sixteen-year-old son, Fred, joined the expedition, and once it was underway, even Jane Dalton (better known as Calamity Jane) was discovered among the group, disguised as a cavalry officer.[69]

The 1875 Black Hills Expedition was an extensive undertaking: five months of route finding, road making, and gold seeking. The military escort included 452 men (and Jane), 376 horses, and 71 supply wagons, and these "with a proportionate number of civilian employees—not to mention the scientists with their gear—were to be moved together over yawning divides, across treacherous streams carrying unhealthy alkaline water, through thickets, and by some means over a more than 2000-foot rise in elevation into the central hills." From the perspective of Dodge and his superiors, the expedition was an unqualified success: peaceful confirmation of the possibilities waiting beneath the surface of the Black Hills. This expedition "opened up more than 1,500 miles of wagon road, and the scientists and surveying parties had established more than 6,000 miles of horse trail."[70] Though there had been no trouble of the sort Dodge had been warned about, the expedition—its very presence a violation of the 1868 treaty—made marks on a sacred landscape.[71] He Sapa (the Black Hills), or "the heart of everything that is," holds great meaning for Lakota people: it is "the beating heart of the Lakota cosmos," central to the Lakota origin story. But the Black Hills are meaningful to many other Native people; Nick Estes writes that "more than fifty Indigenous nations" have relationships with He Sapa.[72] The U.S. Army caravan disregarded these relationships as well as the terms of the 1868 Treaty of Fort Laramie.

Black Elk remembered the caravan. John Neihardt writes that during their conversations in 1930–31 Black Elk told him, "In the spring when I was twelve years old (1875), more soldiers with many wagons came up from the Soldiers' Town at the mouth of the Laramie River and went into the hills." Black Elk remembered Custer's expedition from the previous year and also the way that "yellow metal" made soldiers and settlers "crazy." "Our people knew there was yellow metal in little chunks up there," he said; "but they did not bother with it, because it was not good for anything."[73] But it was exactly what Dodge, Jenney, and Bourke were looking for.

Colonel Dodge filled several diaries with his thoughts about the experience and the terrain. These journals look something like reporters' notebooks: small, with stiff cardboard backing and pages that flip up to allow the author to write on the reverse side. Army officers were expected to document their observations when traveling in new-to-them country; this was especially true for Dodge in 1875, as the whole purpose of this trip was to get the lay of the land, both above and below the ground. And the journals he kept cover this ground and more, including a recounting of each day's route and events, important milestones in his son Fred's riding and shooting and hunting experiences, reflections on Custer's earlier trip through much of the same territory, and more personal details: his frustration with the reporters accompanying the expedition, the quality of his sleep, the fact that the gypsum in the water made him ill, the view from his tent. May 30: "Had to build a corduroy & bridge over 200 feet long. It took three solid hours of work." June 11: "Wagons had a hard day." June 12: "Bog, bog, all the time—16 mules on a team, & as many men as could get hold prying & lifting the bed out of the mud."[74] And later that afternoon: "Today we struck for the first time—*Gold*—undeniable unmistakeable. It is only a little 'show'—but it is *gold*."[75]

Wayne Kime has painstakingly edited Dodge's journals, making them far more accessible—and legible—to researchers, but I looked at this section in Dodge's journals in the archives at the Newberry Library. Something about that phrase "undeniable unmistakeable" made me want to see the words in Dodge's hand, with "gold" underlined both times. Dodge carefully documented the determination and muscle each mile demanded, so when I arrived at this entry about gold, "undeniable unmistakeable," Dodge's underlining of the element—*Gold, gold*—felt exuberant, even more than a century after those lines were drawn. But of course, this is what entries like this can do: bring along the readers, catch them up in the energy of discovery, in the glimmer of gold. And then prompt them to pause, to see how the lines beneath the gold in Dodge's journal lead directly, in his own narration, to Native dispossession. Dodge continued, offering a confident prediction: "In ten years the Black Hills will be the home of a numerous & thriving population, & all the Administrations & Interior Departments cant stop it. It is not an Indian Country."[76]

Dodge's forecast for the region revealed an expectation that the work of the expedition, the mapping, route-finding, and path-breaking they were doing, would ease the way for this "thriving population." Dodge and his men encountered miners who had been drawn there by reports and rumors of gold. Their presence was not sanctioned by the federal government, and the military was under orders to remove miners found in the

Black Hills. Though aware of these instructions, Dodge chose to interpret his responsibilities as the expedition's escort as absolving him from rounding up miners in violation of federal policy. He didn't have the resources or manpower to enforce these instructions, and he didn't want to. On June 16 Dodge sent a letter to his commanding officer, Gen. George Crook, in which he offered his vision for the future: "All the power of the Administration cannot keep this country in possession of the Indians, and I confess my sympathies are all with the miner and settler."[77] This sense of inevitability, the push of a particular kind of progress, runs through all of Dodge's writing. He chose to write it this way, as a foregone conclusion, a determining kind of description waiting for fulfillment.

The following week Dodge wrote in his journal, "The mail brings us information that the Indian Chiefs have returned from Washington badly snubbed, & in an ill humor, which means war, & the death of many good men. From the newspaper reports of the conferences, there is no doubt that this end is intended."[78] Here Dodge hinted at his opinions about the federal treatment of Native people in the West, a topic he later wrote about quite forcefully. Despite his critiques, Dodge's articulations grew out of assumptions about Native people as primitive wards of the state, not as autonomous and capable peoples, tribes, and nations.[79] He advocated assimilation into a preordained American destiny rather than unconditional sovereignty; like many of his contemporaries, Dodge did not think Indigenous people could—or should—make their own futures.

Dodge had already decided what kind of narrative he would write, what story he was part of: a linear tale of expansion that moved westward across the map, a steadily upward story of American progress. "I am very sure that no part of the wilderness is as well known as the Black Hills are now," he wrote to General Crook on September 4, 1875. After all, he was leading the military escort of the team that would make it "known." He was most of the way through the five-month expedition and beginning to turn his attention to report writing and mapmaking. In the same letter Dodge asked Crook for permission to supervise the map himself rather than hand it off to the engineers.[80] The map ultimately accompanied his military report, which Dodge mined for a small volume he published under his own name in 1876. Dodge explained the book project this way: "It is not my purpose to attempt to follow the expedition in all its windings, its explorations, its labors, its troubles, and its pleasures; but so to sum up the information gained as to give an idea, as perfect as possible, of the nature of the country, its climate, soil, resources, and value." This "idea" was refracted through Dodge's vision of the terrain the expedition covered. Its potential is repeatedly stressed, alongside what "the nature of the country" could offer the nation.[81]

For John Bourke, the expedition's engineer officer, the Black Hills initially provoked "a feeling akin to loneliness." Bourke compared the "undulation of these immense fields" to the "gentle roll of the sea in a time of calm."[82] Dodge focused on the possibility of this new landscape: "The scenery is very grand and beautiful. The valley, owing to the number of streams, is a rich green. On each side rise ranges from one to two thousand feet, their tops covered with the dark, thick growth of pine which gives the name 'Black' to the 'Hills.'"[83] Gone is the focus on the work of moving through this terrain. The difficulty of route finding and road making, constant concerns throughout the group's five-month journey, figure into Dodge's published treatment of this newly reconnoitered territory only when the details add to the expedition's accomplishments. The labor slips under the text; Dodge's words instead highlight the beauty the expedition encountered. "Each portion of the Hills has its own especial peculiarities of scenery," he wrote. "The tops of the grand mésas are lovely with long grass and flower-covered slopes, set as it were in frames of the dark green forests of pine. Lower down, the slopes become ravines, then cañons."[84]

Dodge portrayed a landscape that alternates between gentle and grand: hills robed in flowers "become ravines"; ranges rise to shelter a verdant valley. Though he emphasized the view, the value he saw extended beyond the visual pleasure of this landscape. For Dodge the scenery held deep development potential for those pioneers willing to labor in this paradise. This wilderness, thanks to the Black Hills Expedition, was now "known"—and ready to be put to use. And this knowledge—"an idea, as perfect as possible"—had been constructed both with words and with roads. Dodge wrote and built a picture "of the nature of the country," and his published account, *The Black Hills: A Minute Description of the Routes, Scenery, Soil, Climate, Timber, Gold, Geology, Zoölogy, Etc.*, conveyed that vision to his readers.[85]

Others had previously described these hills—most recently Custer, but before that Francis Parkman had called the Black Hills both "wild" and "thickly peopled," noting that on his 1846 excursion, "in the deep stillness of those lonely mountains the stroke of hatchets and the sound of voices might be heard."[86] Likewise, in *Roughing It*, Mark Twain characterized Laramie Peak as "looming vast and solitary," an "old colossus frown under his beetling brows of storm cloud." Beyond adding to the growing body of writing about this "hostile Indian country" (Twain's words), Dodge's expedition, with its expert scientists, could offer a definitive picture of the possibilities in the Black Hills and could address the rumors of what might lie beneath them.[87]

Dodge's vision revised contemporary realities about the Black Hills and their use by the Indigenous people who, by their presence and through formal treaty negotiations, held the rights to this land. In *The Black Hills*, Dodge focused on the future: opportunities for settlement, development, and tourism in an area he framed as fully ready for American expansion. While he expressed some sympathy for the treatment of Native people, especially by corrupt officials, Dodge made it quite clear that any value the Black Hills held for Lakota people mattered less than their potential use value for the United States.

Dodge failed to understand the shape and structure of Lakota communities; he had decided that Indigenous people did not have historical relationships with the Black Hills, and that they should not have ongoing connections to this land and its resources. He wrote this as a confident declaration: "It is not an Indian Country."[88] But as Dodge and the members of his expedition were beginning to traverse Lakota territory, Spotted Tail was speaking in Washington about this same land: "I know my country is a good country, because I put things in the ground and they grow up. . . . You speak of another country . . . but, if it is such a good country, you ought to send the white men now in our country there and let us alone."[89]

One way to make the case that the Black Hills were "not an Indian Country" was to argue that Lakotas were not actually using the land. This idea that claims could be validated through a particular kind of improvement, consistent with much of the legal framework used to justify U.S. colonization of the West, erased Lakota uses—and thus the legitimacy of Lakota claims in the eyes of the state.[90] Jeffrey Ostler calls this the "thesis of Lakota nonoccupancy": Lakota people did not live in the Black Hills and visited only occasionally and thus might agree (or be forced) to sell or cede them. Ostler demonstrates that key members of the Black Hills Expedition made this argument in their private and public writings, though these same sources also offer plenty of evidence to contradict the notion that the Black Hills were devoid of sustained Lakota use.[91]

Bourke's personal papers reflect an understanding that openness did not necessarily mean emptiness. He saw and described evidence of Lakota life in the Black Hills, and he wondered at what appeared to him to be their unusual absence. Early in the Black Hills Expedition he wrote in his diary, "The absence of Indians means something, in my opinion; none have come near us thus far, altho' it is evident we are now in a part of their country often visited if not permanently occupied by them." Bourke's entry continues: "Great trails have been seen, broad and well travelled, and the indications of a great camp having been here not many months ago can be found in all directions."[92]

Dodge's writings suggest the effort required to construct a version of the Black Hills as an insignificant place for Lakota people. Early in *The Black Hills* Dodge offered up an anecdote about one of the scientists needing another blanket because his horse was developing saddle sores. This man used a green blanket the group had found wrapped around "dry bones" in a Native grave. Dodge went on to describe the scientist's discomfort each time the group encountered Lakotas as they traveled—meetings that "occurred so frequently" that the scientist's reaction, which was to "immediately [find] something specially important in another direction," seemed, for Dodge, worth retelling in his book. Dodge introduced the story with an observation about Lakota burial practices and the significance of the color green: "In almost all of the graves examined by our party, the blankets in which the remains were wrapped were green."[93] Dodge and the expedition regularly encountered Native people and, it seems, routinely dismantled (and dismembered) the contents of Indigenous graves. This was not a new practice; settlers had been disturbing Native graves since at least 1620.[94]

On June 1 Dodge confessed that he felt sorry, though he did nothing, when a grave in a cottonwood tree "was rifled by the Doctors of the Expedition (there are two (2) military and several civil Doctors) & the head & all curious articles carried off." If some of this collecting was for science, not all of it was. Dodge noted that Dr. McGillycuddy "got the lower jaw, which he proposes to take home as a present for a dear friend to be used as a pen holder."[95] Respect for the dead, then, did not extend to Native people. McGillycuddy's actions suggest that looting Indigenous graves and desecrating the ancestors within—as specimens for study or as souvenirs to be displayed—was considered acceptable to many soldiers and scientists.[96]

After Dodge's anecdote about the horse's saddle sores early in *The Black Hills*, he shifted his focus to narrating the geology, topography, and scenery of the area. Dodge described resources in terms of how he might envision using them: "These trees are just the right size for railroad ties, and this forest will furnish enough for all the roads which are likely to be constructed within a reasonable distance in the next hundred years." Dodge continued, in case his meaning was not clear: "These poles are also admirably suitable for building small log houses, barns, cribs, etc.; and scattered through the smaller growth are larger trees sufficient to furnish the boards necessary for floors, doors, etc."[97] This is what use—and occupancy—looked like to Dodge.

He dismissed the possibility that the Black Hills were home to Crow people before the Lakota, writing, "If this country had been used as a residence, even thirty years ago, some marks of its occupation would still be visible." Dodge didn't see—or chose not to see—these marks; he saw only movement, peripheral use for the occasional lodgepole, the occasional hunting party. In a word: nonessential. He overlooked graves, camps, trails, and treaties and stated clearly his position on the subject of homeland: "My opinion is, that the Black Hills have never been a permanent home for any Indians."[98] This emphasis on permanence—permanence made visible through "marks"—reveals how differently Dodge and the U.S. military understood their own relationships to land. Dodge framed the Black Hills in terms of settlement, prospecting, and profit; for Lakotas the Black Hills carried—and continue to carry—meanings in many registers.

Graves and evidence of large camps, big trails, and regular encounters with Lakota people did nothing to change Dodge's representation of the Black Hills as underutilized territory, ready for the taking. And this move was made again and again by soldiers and settlers. Despite evidence to the contrary—well-worn paths in Yellowstone, evidence of large camps in the Black Hills—agents of U.S. empire actively misread these landscapes as devoid of prior use by Native people and full of potential for Anglo development.

Even Bourke seemed to adopt this thesis in later diary entries. He wrote, "Look where we might, turn where we would, new beauties obtruded their claims upon our bewildered attention, each demanding, each in turn receiving the palm of superiority." The Black Hills became beautiful scenery in Bourke's account, picturesque parks that required a photographer to capture their full loveliness so that "the sun-portraits [may] speak for themselves." Gone is the sense of the Black Hills as Bourke initially described them, "an immense area of country with scarcely a tree to give shelter against the cutting edge of the wintry 'Norther', or the fervid rays of the noonday sun."[99]

The expedition covered a lot of ground, and it is possible that Bourke found some parts of the landscape more compelling, more beautiful. But allowing for changes in the scenery doesn't explain the erasure of Native people in his account of these landscapes. Bourke articulated his view of the land's underutilization and its potential in the form of a question. "Why," he asked, "have these Black Hills, greater in area than several of the New England states, and which have never been of any value to the nomads who claim them as their own, and are never visited even save at rare intervals to obtain lodge-poles for the Sioux and Cheyenne camps—why have these lovely vales and hills been sequestered from the national domain?"[100] The Black Hills, in Bourke's telling, had become pristine again. No longer "their country," these landscapes were remade as sites waiting for both appreciation and U.S. settlement.

Some Americans were already staking their claims. Dodge encountered miners in the Black Hills who had been removed and returned multiple times. Meanwhile, the federal government set a January 1876 deadline for Lakota people to gather at agencies inside designated reservation lands under threat of force. Additional troops moved into the plains as spring approached, and many Lakotas and their allies prepared to fight. At a Sun Dance held on the Rosebud River in early June, Sitting Bull had a vision of American defeat. In the Battle of the Rosebud, Sitting Bull, Crazy Horse, and their men forced back General Crook and his men. The following week Custer's Seventh Cavalry found their way to the Greasy Grass. Few left alive.[101]

Though a clear victory on the battlefield, this win ultimately solidified the loss of the Black Hills for Lakota people. At the next negotiation the United States demanded that the Lakotas surrender claims to the Black Hills; if they did not, the federal government would cease all monetary and in-kind support—support that had been promised in the 1868 Fort Laramie Treaty.[102] In *All Our Relations* Winona LaDuke talks to Gail Smalls, a Northern Cheyenne activist who recounted learning the story of Custer's defeat. "'I remember hearing the old people tell this story often when I was growing up in Lame Deer,' Gail continues the story. 'And it always ended with the moral that war does not bring peace.'"[103] President Grant sent the Manypenny Commission to the Black Hills to formalize Lakota compliance with the government's demands. Though illegal—the terms of an earlier treaty required the signatures of three-fourths of adult men for land to be ceded, but the commission gathered only 10 percent—the commission did as it was asked.[104] This agreement created the Black Hills that soldiers like Custer, Dodge, and Bourke had already described: empty, unused, and ready for American settlement and development. In many ways their reports and published accounts did as much of the work of remaking the West as their expeditions, of enacting the visions painted on those pages of a new West, an empty West—an American West.

In the varied descriptions they offered of western landscapes, soldiers' words helped construct the West as an idea. Brutal landscapes became beautiful. Through prose, homelands were emptied. This process of erasure—a key part of the construction of the American notion of wilderness in the nineteenth century, an idea that persists in policy and cultural attitudes today—is visible in soldiers' writing.[105] Bourke's "feeling akin to loneliness" recedes. In his public writing Dodge emphasizes opportunity and wonder over work. Soldiers, like other western writers, both reflected and produced contemporary cultural ideas about the American West. Their experiences and writings were part of the construction of the pervasive myth of the West as a garden ready to be occupied—a garden they helped prepare.[106]

"A Special Record"

Colonel Dodge had experienced far more of the West than the Black Hills landscape he described as "the finest country I have ever seen."[107] In fact, he spent many evenings, even while leading the Black Hills Expedition, working on his first book manuscript, a project based on his years of military experience on the plains.

When I was a schoolboy my map of the United States showed between the Missouri River and the Rocky Mountains a long and broad white blotch, upon which was printed in small capitals, "The Great American Desert—Unexplored." What was then "unexplored" is now almost thoroughly known. What then was regarded as a desert supports, in some portions, thriving populations. The blotch of thirty years ago is now known as "The Plains." Like an ocean in its vast extent, in its monotony, and in its danger, it is like the ocean in its romance, in its opportunities for heroism, and in the fascination it exerts on all those who come fairly within its influence.[108]

These words open *The Hunting Grounds of the Great West: A Description of the Plains, Game, and Indians of the Great North American Desert*. Part natural history, part hunting how-to guide, the book was Dodge's definitive treatment of the West. Born of a friendship and collaboration with William Blackmore, an English lawyer and venture capitalist interested in the American West (and especially in American Indians), the volume was published in both London (1876) and the United States (1877).[109] The American edition carried an alternate title, *The Plains of the Great West and Their Inhabitants, Being a Description of the Plains, Game, Indians, &c., of the Great North American Desert*.

Dodge's book begins with the impact the plains apparently had on a man: "The first experience of the plains, like the first sail, with a 'cap' full of wind, is apt to be sickening." Or at the very least, unsettling. But once that feeling passes, the plains offer unique opportunities: "At no time and under no circumstances can a man feel so acutely the responsibility of his life, the true grandeur of his manhood, the elation of which his nature is capable, as when his and other lives depend on the quickness of his eye, the firmness of his hand, and the accuracy of his judgment." Dodge pitches the Great West as a place to be a real man, to be one's best self: "There is no lack of such occasions on the plains."[110] Dodge's nostalgic vision reflects a particular kind of Victorian masculinity and would have fit right in among the guides, manuals, and narratives produced by both American and British elites. Hunting became framed "as a scientific hobby, one that advanced the hunter's understanding of natural history"; in fact, according to Monica Rico, "each stage of the hunt demonstrated the hunter's scientific knowledge of his quarry and his ability to read the landscape for its presence."[111]

In writing *The Hunting Grounds of the Great West* Dodge was establishing his own credentials as a true frontiersman—even if the opportunity to encounter the West Dodge knew as an army officer had, in his mind, disappeared.[112] Now all that Dodge had left was his "special record of a particular time and place." To traverse the plains used to be "the work of a whole summer," he wrote, and groups attempting the route were "lost to the world." Dodge's nostalgia remade the world he remembered. Though filled with uncertainty and struggle, most of Dodge's adventures occurred within the framework of the army and its web of printed orders, letters, and telegrams—hardly a world of "no mails, no news, no communication of any kind with civilisation."[113]

"Now," Dodge wrote in the nation's centennial year, "all is changed. There is no longer an unknown." He compared civilization to a cuttlefish with incredibly destructive powers. It "has passed its arms of settlements up almost every stream, grasping the land, killing the game, driving out the Indian, crushing the romance, the poetry, the very life and soul out of the 'plains,' and leaving only the bare and monotonous carcass." Civilization did these things, Dodge wrote, but in developing this metaphor, he failed to make explicit his own position in this process. As an officer in the U.S. Army Dodge participated in "crushing the romance" of the plains.[114] The nostalgia Dodge expressed for a West he had helped reshape through his service, his hunting, even his writing, is a particular kind. Anthropologist Renato Rosaldo calls it "imperialist nostalgia," a kind of lament "where people mourn the passing of what they themselves have transformed."[115] For Rosaldo it isn't that actors like Dodge were unable to acknowledge their place in these changes, but rather that they lived with the tension, with complicated feelings about their role in change, in the "civilizing" process.[116]

Other soldiers, reflecting on military careers spent in the West, articulated similar emotions as they relived memories of their service, especially long after the fact. William H. C. Bowen, of the same Fifth Infantry that Samuel Ovenshine served in, wrote about his military experiences both in an unpublished autobiography of his army career and in shorter pieces detailing specific battles and campaigns. His papers contain longhand manuscript drafts describing an 1880 expedition in pursuit of Native people who had just raided the pony herds of ranchers on the Porcupine River. Bowen was stationed at Fort Keogh that spring, on the Yellowstone River. News of the raid came late in the afternoon, and Bowen's company was ordered to attempt to "overtake the spoilers and recover the stock." Bowen's account is undated, but the appreciation for the bitter cold that creeps into his words suggests that he was home, safe and warm, as he wrote, "A march through the snow on a cold Winter night is not the most cheerful and enjoyable amusement imaginable but after all there is something in it which stirs the blood of the young and keeps it tingling." Still in pursuit the following day, the company encountered a herd of deer, and that evening the men cooked bacon and venison, "the odors from which were enough to make the ghosts of the dead and gone frontiersmen arise from their graves and join us at the feast."[117]

Bowen narrated his company into a thick and glorious past: the spirits of those already departed approved and were summoned by the spoils of the hunt. He gloried in a lineage he saw himself as part of—the ghosts of those who had gone before, though not the ghosts of those on the other side of these campaigns. In later writings Bowen recognized his place in the West's transformation but also the challenges faced by his opponents.

Many soldiers remembered their frontier experiences with nostalgia, and some returned decades later to the landscapes of their service. Others took to writing memoirs, and some collected clippings and other artifacts that reflected elements of their own roles in transforming the West.[118] But some soldiers took to collecting the frontier even as their work remade it.

Colonel Dodge did so in words. *The Plains of the Great West* is filled with detailed descriptions of the game and Native people of the West. Even the structure of his book suggests the fluidity of late nineteenth-century notions of natural history and anthropology—notes on animal traits and behavior are followed by a discussion of "Indian" characteristics and practices.[119] Next Dodge began working on *Our Wild Indians: Thirty-Three Years' Personal Experience among the Red Men of the Great West*, more than fifty chapters of detailed observations and anecdotes about his interactions with Native people, as well as commentary on army life—both general "plainscraft" and specific conflicts.

Amid chapters on religion, death, art, weaponry, and governance, Dodge articulated his position on the treatment of Native people by the U.S. government and its agents. He offered critiques of the rampant corruption among Indian agents and government officials, as well as of federal Indian policy. He described what happened when treaties were made and not kept, when the food that was promised was not delivered, when corrupt bureaucrats and white men who married into Native families gamed the system, and he wholly condemned these practices. William Tecumseh Sherman wrote the book's introduction and found much to praise in what Dodge called a "minute and careful study of the social or inner life of the wild Indian of the present day."[120] But Sherman wasn't shy about stating his disagreement with Dodge's conclusions about the treaty system, the behavior of the federal government, or the character of Indian agents and traders in the West. His introduction affirmed the government's work in the West and invited Dodge's audience "to read this book carefully, to the end that public opinion may aid the national authorities to deal justly and liberally with the remnants of that race which preceded us on this continent."[121]

While Dodge and Sherman disagreed over what federal Indian policy should look like, they were united in their narrative framing of Indigenous peoples and cultures as "remnants" of some deeper past.[122] But Dodge's convictions about both the transformation of the frontier and the shape of federal Indian policy—though not the structures of settler colonialism and empire driving it—led him to document three decades of army service and to participate in the process of preserving and producing a particularly freighted "knowledge" of the "remnants" Sherman wrote of.

And it seems he had an audience. Dodge's work prompted letters from politicians like Henry Dawes, a strong advocate for the creation of Yellowstone National Park and architect of the Dawes Act (1887), which pushed Native assimilation through individual allotments of reservation land, undermining existing treaties between Indigenous nations and the United States. Conservationist William Hornaday wrote to ask Dodge about buffalo herds. Dodge also received offers to write about his encounters with Native people for a children's magazine, though it seems that the drafts he submitted were deemed unsuitable for its audience. The editor wanted lively stories, but Dodge was offering detailed observations.[123] This mismatch illuminates the different ways in which Dodge was contributing to a body of colonial knowledge about the American West: while *The Black Hills* described the landscape and offered encouragement to potential pioneers, both *The Plains of the Great West* and *Our Wild Indians* described animal behavior and human cultural practices. This emphasis on description of people and animals in decline echoes the nostalgic laments offered by Dodge and others concerning the transformations they'd not only witnessed but also helped bring about.

Anthropologist Jacob Gruber coined the term "salvage ethnography" to describe the impulse of nineteenth-century anthropologists to collect as much information as they could about people and communities they perceived to be in the process of vanishing: "Throughout the century and within whatever theoretical framework, the refrain was the same: the savage is disappearing; preserve what you can; posterity will hold you accountable."[124] The notion that Native people were destined to vanish was a particularly pernicious part of the progress narrative that shaped the ideas and practices of many nineteenth-century people and institutions. In *Firsting and Lasting: Writing Indians out of Existence in New England*, Jean O'Brien explains how narratives of disappearance crafted by local and regional writers were then "customized for their locality and replicated across the landscape of the nation."[125] Despite persistent Indigenous presence throughout North America, even before the Civil War most white Americans believed in the inevitability of Native disappearance; furthermore, Steven Conn suggests that these extinction stories repositioned Indigenous people "as part of natural, rather than human, history."[126] Late nineteenth-century science, especially the collecting and studying led by the Smithsonian's Bureau of Ethnology, affirmed these false narratives about Indigenous disappearance.

This sense of Native people as part of the nation's past but not its future motivated people like Dodge to participate in a particular kind of preservation work. Dodge wrote multiple volumes based on his experience and observations in the West, but he also supported the efforts of the Smithsonian Institution and the Bureau of Ethnology to gather information and artifacts from Native people. Dodge corresponded with Garrick Mallery at the bureau about Indigenous languages and communication. Mallery was working on a glossary of Indigenous signs and sent diagrams and word lists for contributors to fill in with drawings and prose. Clearly sensitive about his position in Washington (not in the field or on the frontier), in one letter Mallery boasted that he'd had plenty of opportunities to communicate with Native delegations who had made trips to the U.S. capital: "The Sec. of the Interior gives an order—and the Indians and interpreters are *mine*—for days or weeks."[127] Dodge assisted in this project—one with clear military and political aims, as well as the ethnographic goal of preserving linguistic practices—but he also helped increase the Smithsonian's collection of specimens and artifacts. His correspondence with Spencer Baird, then secretary of the Smithsonian, reveals that Dodge sent "plants and flowers" in addition to ethnographic artifacts. Acknowledging the receipt of these materials, Baird asked for more, especially bird eggs, smaller mammals, and "well-preserved aboriginal relics in the form of pottery, pipes, scrapers, hammer stones + the like."[128]

Understanding Native cultures as inevitably declining and encountering them, through military work, as either enemies or wards of the state meant that acquiring ethnographic and archaeological material—from the living and the dead—did not appear problematic to many of these collectors. But of course it was—and is. Beyond the explicit violence of grave robbing, the removal of ancestors and cultural belongings added another layer of disruption. And the collection of ordinary or supposedly representative belongings enabled particular representations of Indigenous peoples in the arguments made by ethnologists and museum curators—in prose but also in exhibits designed for others to view.[129]

While part of a deep history of imperial knowledge production, Dodge's collecting work, much like his written work, also helped make a particular vision of the West: removing Native ancestors and cultural belongings emptied western landscapes. Tribal governments and museum curators are now working to reverse this and return these ancestors and cultural belongings to their homelands.[130]

Collecting and Countercollecting

Lt. John Gregory Bourke aided this emptying of the West with his prose and with collecting of his own. Like Dodge, Bourke kept a detailed diary. And like Dodge, Bourke was interested in Indigenous cultural practices and belongings.[131] Though Bourke did not publish accounts of his military experiences until the 1880s and 1890s, his position as General Crook's aide-de-camp provided him with access to a wider audience. In his work as a press agent for Crook, he articulated the thesis of nonoccupancy in ghostwritten newspaper articles and advocated for American expansion into the Black Hills and war with the Lakotas. But soon after his service on the plains, something within him changed. His biographer points to the end of what Americans called the Great Sioux War as a turning point for Bourke's ideas about Native people: "After 1876 he came as a student of their cultures, not as an enemy soldier."[132] Perhaps it is more accurate to suggest that he was attempting to be both; we must also recognize that as both student and soldier Bourke represented the interests of a settler-colonial nation. Soldiering and ethnography were both weapons wielded by the United States against Indigenous people.

The year 1876 had been a hard one for Bourke: lots of campaigning in brutal landscapes and bitter weather. He'd nearly lost his foot to frostbite at Powder River. Bourke fought in the Battle of the Rosebud alongside Crow and Shoshone allies, and he fought in the press amid controversy over the performance and character of officers involved in the battle. Then Custer died and Crook and Terry set off in pursuit of the Lakotas, Northern Cheyennes, and Arapahos who had defeated their comrades at Greasy Grass/Little Bighorn. Bourke's diary, according to Joseph Porter, "became a litany of the miseries that followed the column" in the same country that Samuel Ovenshine had called "mean" and "miserable" in his letters to Sallie.[133] But 1876 had been harder still for Native people on the plains.

Bourke's plains combat days ended with a surprise attack against the camp of Morning Star (a Northern Cheyenne chief also known as Dull Knife to Lakotas and to U.S. soldiers). Colonel Dodge was there, too, as was Lt. Henry Lawton, a soldier who was later venerated for his service in Apache homelands and in the Philippines. On November 25, 1876, Northern Cheyenne warriors in Morning Star's camp along the Red Fork of the Powder River were startled by the arrival of U.S. cavalry forces and Native scouts. They quickly worked to get their families up and out of the canyon.[134] Iron Teeth, a Northern Cheyenne woman, described what happened: "They killed our men, women and children, whichever ones might be hit by their bullets. We who could do so ran away."[135] The fight lasted until the afternoon, when the army took control of the village—burning winter supplies, confiscating ponies, and recovering materials "bearing Seventh Cavalry markings" collected by Native warriors from Greasy Grass.[136]

In addition to burning supplies, U.S. soldiers destroyed belongings with great value to Cheyenne history and culture—corn, sacred objects, painted tipis, and artifacts that "would have been gems in the cabinets of museums," according to Bourke.[137] Not everything was burned, however; some Cheyenne cultural belongings were taken, including war bonnets, robes, pipes, shields, and tobacco bags. In his memoir one soldier wrote, "In my collection of Indian curios I had several items which came out of this Cheyenne village."[138] Bourke's collections included a necklace belonging to High Wolf, a Cheyenne medicine man, which had been "found" in Dull Knife's camp and "given" to Bourke.[139] It was a necklace of great value, made from carefully preserved human fingers—and, according to Bourke, "among the bitterest losses of valuable property suffered by the Cheyenne on this occasion." Two necklaces had been taken from Dull Knife's village, Bourke wrote, but "Gen. Crook did not wish to have kept more than one specimen, and that only for scientific purposes," so the other necklace was buried.[140]

The destruction of Dull Knife's village ended the war for the Cheyennes.[141] Iron Teeth remembered watching as the "lodges and everything in them burned."[142] This attack, along with the looting and burning that accompanied it, is one example among many of the work frontier soldiers did in the service of U.S. empire. What Iron Teeth witnessed was settler colonialism in action: burning to destroy, to remove, to erase.

Snow fell after the fight, exacerbating the challenges facing the Cheyennes who had survived the attack. Still, they kept moving, in smaller groups to avoid the soldiers they expected to pursue them. Temperatures were well below freezing. Many people were injured, and more, including several children, died from exposure in the nights following the attack on their camp. It was not until the following April that Morning Star surrendered at Red Cloud Agency. These Cheyennes had endured months of harsh weather and hunger since the November attack on Morning Star's camp.[143]

After 1876 Bourke moved to Omaha. He traveled often to fulfill his military duties—purchasing supplies, conducting inspections, participating in court-martial cases, or accompanying General Crook's hunting trips, including an 1880 expedition to Yellowstone National Park. In his diary for the trip he wrote, "I am making no attempt at a description of this Wonderland:— such a task would be beyond my feeble powers."[144] Despite this, his entries for each day of this trip reflect the beauty he perceived all around him. In his efforts to orient himself in the landscape, he made regular mention of the sites of his plains service. From Yellowstone Lake, "the heart of our great country," Bourke described the waters of the Bighorn River "passing the spot where Custer and his men went down to bloody graves."[145] Bourke had visited Greasy Grass/Little Bighorn in 1877, along with General Crook, as part of an escort to General Sheridan, lieutenant general of the army. Some of the soldiers' bodies, buried where they'd fallen, had been washed out by a recent storm. Members of the expedition reburied them.[146] Much attention was given to how and where U.S. soldiers who died at Greasy Grass/Little Bighorn should be buried; members of the Seventh Cavalry were sent to exhume and retrieve officers' bodies in 1877, not long after Bourke's visit.[147] A body presumed to be Custer's was reburied in the West Point Cemetery that October.

Multiple U.S. soldiers wrote that objects belonging to members of the Seventh Cavalry were found in Native camps and villages across the region. That soldiers emphasized these objects is curious; given their widespread looting, confiscation, and destruction of cultural belongings found in Indigenous camps and villages, why would Native possession of objects found on the battlefield at Greasy Grass warrant soldiers' attention?[148] Perhaps most obviously, the presence of objects from the Seventh Cavalry affirmed for U.S. soldiers that they were trailing the "right" people—a large part of the army's initial response after Custer's defeat was to mobilize more troops and set off in search of the victors.

But reflecting on Lakota and Cheyenne collectors, and the "countercollecting" practices they employed, reveals another dimension of the work of U.S. empire on the plains. When

U.S. soldiers collected Indigenous cultural belongings—and ancestors—they did so, it seems, without remorse. They took military trophies for personal collections and ethnographic materials destined for museum study and display. But when Lakota and Cheyenne collectors took items from the Greasy Grass battlefield—including guns and cartridges, horses, metal and paper money, saddles, boots, bugles, a pocket watch, and a compass—these items were considered stolen property, rather than spoils rightfully taken after victory.[149]

Thomas Marquis learned of some of these objects while working as a doctor in Lame Deer; he later established a museum in Hardin, Montana, in 1931, where he displayed items collected by Cheyennes from Greasy Grass. Much of what was there is now in the permanent collection at the Little Bighorn Battlefield National Monument, where in 2010, as part of an exhibit focused on Cheyenne memories of the battle, objects collected by Cheyenne warriors—including a cartridge belt, saddlebags, and a bag made from a U.S. soldier's boot— were displayed alongside photographs of the collectors with the artifacts.[150] These items, originally taken by victors, were recollected by agents of the battle's losing side and are now displayed in a museum at the site of the battle, which continues to occupy an outsize place in national frontier lore. These particular artifacts have not traveled very far in the generations since the battle at Greasy Grass, but their movement back and forth across the lines that determine how they are used and for what purposes they have been collected and displayed suggests their power.

IN 1881 CAPTAIN BOURKE MET MAJ. JOHN WESLEY POWELL, the director of the Bureau of Ethnology. Powell saw value in Bourke's work, and encouraged him to continue his study of Indigenous cultures. Rather than work for the Bureau of Ethnology, Bourke asked military leadership for approval to study American Indian tribes under the auspices of the army. With military approval and Crook's support, Bourke embarked on eight months of ethnographic observation among the Bannock,

Shoshone, Lakota, Oglala, Navajo, Hopi, and Zuni peoples.[151] These travels generated more collecting and more than a thousand pages of notes, and Bourke returned to Omaha to review them—and to rest. This would have to wait, though; Bourke's first obligation was still to the army, and in the summer of 1882 General Crook and Captain Bourke received orders to return to Arizona Territory.[152]

Bourke and Crook had been stationed in Apachería a decade earlier.[153] It was where they began working together and where Bourke's interest in Native cultures and practices had originated. And now he was returning, bringing with him all that he'd seen and learned in the intervening years. He'd changed some of his opinions about Native people and the federal government's policies toward them, and his biographer generously describes Bourke after 1880 as a man with more worry, more doubt than he'd displayed before. But he, and many others, continued to work in the service of the state and its settler-colonial mission. Bourke eventually returned to his notes and his collections; in 1891 cultural belongings from the landscapes of his service were accessioned by the Smithsonian Bureau of Ethnology—more than one hundred items, many likely taken from, rather than given by, Indigenous peoples across the West. High Wolf's necklace, which Bourke called "a ghastly relic of savagery," isn't listed in the public-facing register, though Bourke wrote that it had been sent first to the United States Military Academy and then on to the Smithsonian, where it remains.[154]

Responsible for much of the material transformation of the West, U.S. soldiers remain a critical source for understanding nineteenth-century American empire. But soldiers were also key contributors to the construction of broader ideas about the nature of this newly American West. They helped create a persistent cultural imaginary at the same time that they fought campaigns against Indigenous nations and built infrastructure that extended the reach of the state. That these tasks occurred simultaneously is not coincidental; the material and cultural work soldiers did blurred together. Supposedly pristine landscapes were made that way through soldiers' labor—on the ground and on the page. Indigenous communities did not fit into this vision and were removed—written out of it. But anxiety about the limits of wonderland, about the realities of not-so-splendid spaces, emerged around the edges—in private letters, in efforts to collect and preserve, and in carefully framed nostalgia for a misremembered past.

2

Collecting the West

IN MARCH 1884 EDGAR ALEXANDER MEARNS BEGAN THE
journey west with his wife, Ella, and their daughter, Lillian,
not yet two years old, to take up their post in what the United
States called Arizona Territory. "The Collecting List of Edgar
A. Mearns," an oversize leather-bound book with catalog and
narrative entries describing birds seen, walks taken, and specimens prepared, also contains an account of the trip. Mearns
was observing through the windows of the train, making notes
about species he recognized and those he'd never seen or heard
before. For example, Mearns described seeing a pileated woodpecker "on the top of one of many huge dead trees, standing
beside the Railroad": "As the train passed it flew into the forest, its red crest gleaming in the sunlight."[1] He also described
the trees, shrubs, and flowers they observed along the way:
yucca, cottonwood trees, cacti—all new, all hints of the landscape where the Mearns family would soon make their home.

At Ash Fork, while waiting for a military ambulance to take
them the rest of the way to Fort Verde, Mearns "went out to see
the country." On this day trip Mearns brought along his gun, and
together with his observations, the entry for March 17 includes
descriptions of two specimens, his first in the West: "Near the
Cañon I saw a number of ravens, one of which I made a good
wing shot at and 'collected.'"[2] Mearns didn't mince words; he
regularly acknowledged the killing that was—and is—part
of the work of ornithological collection. Here, though, he put

"collected" in quotes, pointing, perhaps, to the ways that this particular word obscures the violence that collecting requires.

An avid naturalist, Dr. Mearns understood the opportunities that military service might offer him to explore the natural world beyond his home in Highland Falls, New York. Though not yet thirty years old at the time of his first military assignment, Mearns had been cultivating his interest in birds and mammals for years. His father, who died when Edgar was a teenager, had taught him to hunt and trap. According to Charles Richmond, assistant birds curator at the Smithsonian, who became one of Mearns's closest friends, "Every natural object interested and attracted him," both as a boy and as a young man.[3] Natural objects—botanical specimens, especially—also attracted Ella Wittich and were perhaps part of the attraction between Ella and Edgar. They married in 1881 after Edgar finished medical school. He sat for the army medical examination in 1882 and then, while awaiting his commission, devoted the winter to curating a cabinet of vertebrate zoology at the American Museum of Natural History in New York.[4]

In September 1883 Mearns attended the first meeting of the American Ornithologists' Union (AOU), founded by three leading naturalists: J. A. Allen, William Brewster, and Dr. Elliott Coues. Coues was an army surgeon who collected, studied, and published prolifically while serving at posts all over the U.S. West (including in Arizona Territory), until he was named the secretary and naturalist of the Geological and Geographical Survey of the Territories.[5] Mearns had already begun corresponding with Allen, an ornithologist and zoologist at Harvard's Museum of Comparative Zoology. Other giants of American ornithology attended that first meeting of the AOU, including Capt. Charles Bendire. As an enlisted man in the dragoons and the cavalry, Bendire, who was later commissioned as an infantry officer, had begun paying attention to birds.[6] He developed an interest in oology, the study of birds' eggs, and while on leave from the military in 1883 he became the honorary curator of the National Museum's Department of Oology.[7]

The following spring the Mearns family made their way west.

While waiting in Prescott, Arizona Territory, for their luggage to arrive, the family went for a "short ramble in the woods amongst the tall pines which," Mearns said, "we used to read about with envy in the writings of Dr. Elliott Coues."[8] Coues had resigned his military commission at the age of thirty-nine to pursue natural history work full-time.[9] Mearns may have hoped to follow in his footsteps—literally: "Now we were free to tread where his illustrious feet preceded us, and much we enjoyed doing so."[10]

That Coues and Bendire pursued scientific and specifically ornithological work alongside their military service was likely quite encouraging to the newly commissioned Mearns and perhaps to other soldiers who would become Mearns's peers and colleagues throughout his twenty-five years in the army's employ. Robert Ridgway, the curator of birds at the Smithsonian, had begun his formal career in ornithology at sixteen when he joined Clarence King's 1867–69 survey of the fortieth parallel as the expedition's zoologist.[11] Large surveys under the leadership of Clarence King, George Wheeler, Ferdinand Hayden, and John Wesley Powell were a central feature of U.S. exploration of western North America in the middle of the nineteenth century. Though the surveys had military escorts, these were civilian operations.[12] Nevertheless, much of the information generated from these civilian expeditions would be put to military use: the availability of mineral resources certainly influenced paths of expansion and extraction, and the maps and reports pointed the way.

General Crook, Captain Bourke, and Dr. Mearns were not in the Southwest to make maps and locate mineral wealth; their assigned tasks were even more explicitly imperial than the surveys that had crossed the West in earlier decades. As officers of the U.S. Army, they were its representatives in what they called Arizona Territory, charged primarily with containing Yavapai and Apache people on designated reservations and ensuring "peace" and the protection of pioneer property in steadily growing Anglo settlements.

Removing Indigenous people from their land was a violent

process; even when actual fighting was avoided, forced relocation ruptured connections between people and their land. While
for the United States land was often abstracted or reduced to the
ways it could produce profit, whether through mining, farming,
or settlement, for Native people land carried—and continues
to carry—more layers of meaning. Michi Saagiig Nishnaabeg
writer Leanne Betasamosake Simpson explains how Nishnaabeg
knowledge is deeply situated in place: "Indigenous education
comes through the land." In discussing what she calls "expansive dispossession," Simpson shares that she grew up "physically disconnected from" her territory. She writes, "A great deal
of the colonizer's energy has gone into breaking the intimate
connection of Nishnaabeg bodies (and minds and spirits) to each
other and to the practices and associated knowledges that connect us to land, because this is the base of our power." Though
Simpson is describing what she calls the "meta-relationship
my Ancestors and I have with Canada," her reflections on the
centrality of land to Indigenous identity are critical for understanding the impact of the settler-colonial work the U.S. military carried out across the Southwest borderlands.[13]

Not only were Apache and Yavapai people removed from
their land by the U.S. Army, but these acts strained and severed intergenerational connections to Indigenous homelands.
The U.S. Army further destabilized Native groups by incarcer-
ating people from different tribes, groups, and bands together;
the San Carlos Apache Reservation is one such example.[14] Contemporary nations, boundaries, and tribal governments reflect
the violent dispossession and dislocation of Native people in
the late nineteenth century, and attempts by anthropologists
to describe Western Apache people often reproduce categories
constructed through U.S. settler colonialism.[15]

The Tonto Basin

Mearns might have heard that Gen. George Crook, recently
reappointed to lead the Department of Arizona after service
on the plains, was sympathetic to his interest in natural history. Crook's skills as a hunter and an outdoorsman were well

known—skills he had deployed successfully, from the U.S. perspective, at the helm of the Department of Arizona from 1871 to 1875. Crook had taken significant ground from Yavapai and Apache groups and had developed strategies that became hallmarks of frontier campaigning. He relied on Native scouts and embraced the art of mule packing. To defeat those Yavapai and Apache people the U.S. military labeled "renegades"—those who refused to stay on bounded reservations—Crook divided his troops into mixed groups of soldiers and scouts and sent them into the Tonto Basin in pursuit. The basin was, in Crook's words, "some of the roughest country in the United States and known only to the Indians."[16]

The Tonto Basin is part of a vast stretch of Yavapai and Apache homelands. Where soldiers and settlers saw land—and landscapes shaped through a set of dominant cultural ideas about the possibilities of the newly American West—Native people saw homelands that held, and continue to hold, complex histories and cultural identities.[17] Anthropologist Keith Basso explains how Western Apache history is oriented around specific geographies. Placemaking is historical narration; where something happened is central to accessing what happened there.[18] What Basso writes about Western Apaches is similar to the "memoryscapes" Christine DeLucia examines across the Native Northeast. She describes them as "geographies bearing layers upon thick layers of meanings, accessible to and transmitted by Indigenous past-keepers who learned to navigate particular terrain and routes as well as relations stretching across time and into other-than-human domains."[19] The Tonto Basin and Verde Valley were—and are—spaces holding deep meaning for Yavapai and Apache people; Daniel Herman writes that they were part of "a world infused with history and magic," sacred landscapes that Yavapais and Apaches honor in many different ways.[20]

Maps created by and for U.S. military, mining, and settler interests depicting the land in and around the Tonto Basin amplify a colonial sense of territorial control. To look at colonial maps is to see Native people contained within what Nick Estes calls the "carceral reservation world" created by the United

States, drawn within boundaries imposed by the U.S. government.[21] But in the 1870s and 1880s this was contested ground. Colonial maps might project U.S. power, but the letters and reports that remain from the U.S. conquest of the Southwest demonstrate the tenuousness of this control, the refusal of Native people to accept or comply with U.S. directives, and the challenges presented by the desert terrain. These texts show us the material and figurative work soldiers did to extend U.S. power in the Tonto Basin and across the Southwest borderlands.

The U.S. Army used brutal violence to push Indigenous people out of the Tonto Basin and onto reservations—massacres litter the record of General Crook's first tour of duty in Arizona. But army officials also employed tactics of imperial control that resembled the natural history techniques some officers used to describe, collect, and study southwestern environments. Looking beyond official military actions to the ways individual soldiers interacted with southwestern landscapes reveals the shape and reach of U.S. empire throughout Indigenous homelands in the late nineteenth century.

As on the plains, one of the U.S. Army's tasks in the Southwest was to protect white settlers and their property. The ruggedness of the Tonto Basin likely insulated it from settler interest, at least at first. Trappers and surveyors passed through these Indigenous homelands earlier in the nineteenth century, but even those heading west to California in the 1850s via Yuma stayed away from central Arizona Territory and the Tonto Basin's difficult terrain. Then news of gold in the early 1860s drew outsiders—first in La Paz, then near Prescott, then in Kingman. This rapid growth—thousands of placer mines and a rush of miners and settlers—set the stage for conflict. Those in search of good farmland found the Verde Valley, "a Shangri-la by Arizona standards, fed by no fewer than six perennial streams."[22] This valley, just northwest of the Tonto Basin, was already home to many Yavapai and Dilzhe'e (Tonto Apache) people. But settlers moved in anyway, taking rocks from nearby ancestral Puebloan ruins to mark sites for future homes.[23] Targeted acts of violence—a Native family murdered, an army man killed—prompted the construction of a string of U.S. military posts: Whipple Barracks, Camp Verde, Camp McDowell, and Camp Date Creek.[24]

In 1871 General Crook received his first set of Arizona orders, just after the Camp Grant Massacre, an early-morning slaughter of Apache people, mostly women and children, by a group including Anglo Americans, Mexican Americans, and Tohono O'odham people in Aravaipa Canyon.[25] Some survivors made their way to the San Carlos Apache Reservation, which was under Crook's control.[26]

Crook sought to force an Apache surrender, and he accomplished this goal through a mixture of unending harassment—"until they could no longer grow crops, hunt, or even rest"—and violence, most significantly the massacres at Skeleton Cave (1872) and Turret Butte (1873).[27] Skeleton Cave earned its name after Crook's men fired into a cave sheltering over one hundred Dilzhe'e and Yavapai people, the bullets bouncing off the stone in all directions. A boy named Hoomothya, captured by U.S. soldiers a few days before while out looking for a horse, lost the rest of his family that day. After the massacre soldiers brought him into Skeleton Cave, where he saw the body of his grandfather. Writing decades later as Mike Burns, he described that day, concluding, "In all history no civilized race has murdered another as the American soldiers did my people in the year 1872. They slaughtered men, women, and children without mercy, as if they were not human."[28] A few months later scouts tracked a group of Yavapai and Dilzhe'e people to the Agua Fria River. Soldiers scaled Turret Butte in the middle of the night and attacked the group at dawn. Most of the Native people at Turret Butte died, some from enemy bullets and others when they jumped off the butte where they had been cornered.[29] The killing continued after the Turret Butte Massacre, as Crook's scouts and soldiers crisscrossed the Tonto Basin looking for any Indigenous people who remained.[30]

Crook had stressed its ruggedness, but the Tonto Basin's beauty was not lost on army men and their families. Even as Crook's men were working to find every last Native person, every last hiding place, Martha Summerhayes, the wife of an officer assigned to Arizona Territory, was marveling at the scenery. In *Vanished Arizona: Recollections of My Army Life*, Summerhayes reflected on her experience of the basin: "The scenery was wild and grand; in fact, beyond all that I had ever dreamed of; more than that, it seemed so untrod, so fresh, somehow, and I do not suppose that even now, in the day of railroads and tourists, many people have had the view of the Tonto Basin which we had one day from the top of the Mogollon Range."[31] Summerhayes pointed out the pristineness of the vision before her, the expansiveness of the scene she encountered. Though not a tourist, as her account of "joining the army" with her husband, Jack, well attests, when she reflected on the experience of looking into Tonto Basin, she employed the rhetoric used by many visitors to describe the wonders of the U.S. West: "wild," "grand," "untrod," "fresh."[32] Her words echo descriptions of Yellowstone and the possibilities soldiers like Dodge and Bourke saw in the Black Hills. Nowhere did she mention the ongoing work of soldiers, her husband among them, to make the Tonto Basin "untrod" and "fresh" again by removing the basin's Indigenous residents.

To U.S. soldiers a decade later much of Arizona Territory likely still appeared to be the way Martha Summerhayes had described it. The trail Summerhayes and her husband's regiment had traveled along in 1874 had since become an established route for traversing the hard country. But much of the territory remained difficult to move through. Capt. John Bourke described the southwestern landscape this way: "To look upon the country was a grand sensation; to travel in it, infernal."[33]

Like the labor required of U.S. soldiers on the plains, the varied work of the frontier army in the Department of Arizona was demanding, involving not just fighting but also cutting paths, moving supplies, and constructing posts.[34] This work continued to shape how army men thought about the landscapes of their service. But army men engaged with more than landscapes, as they observed, hunted, and collected what they found in and on land that was not theirs. And these outside interests—interests literally outside, in the cultures and ecology of the Southwest—were deeply intertwined with their military assignments. Sometimes army work shaped, limited, or enabled scientific work; sometimes scientific work influenced military—and imperial—practice.

A Surgeon and a Naturalist in the Field

The Mearns family made it to Fort Verde on March 25, 1884. Edgar's entry for this day describes several bird species encountered on the descent into the Verde Valley. The party was warmly received by the fort's officers and their wives. And Dick ah Moon, a Chinese man the Mearnses hired in Prescott to accompany them, was apparently "tendered courtesies from his countrymen." Mearns described his new home this way: "Verde is built on a little plain in the open Valley, about 100 feet above the River, which, upon the Post side has low sandy banks, but on the farther side the bank rises through several irregular terraces crowned by grassy mesas to high steep and rocky walls of limestone rock, which were occupied by Aztec inhabitants, whose cave dwellings may be seen from the Post."[35] These ruins, evidence of the deep human history of the Verde Valley, would occupy much of Mearns's free time. But already there was work to do.

The next day Mearns traveled six miles through snow and hail to see a patient. The day after that he went shooting with one of the lieutenants, and his entries detailed the Verde Valley wildlife. And then, not long after Mearns and his family arrived at Fort Verde, his entries in "The Collecting List" stop. Pressed between blank pages near the end of the volume, though, are three botanical samples. Two are reddish and one is brown, but all seem to be from the same plant. They aren't described, documented, and cataloged like the rest, perhaps kept only as souvenirs from the Mearnses' westward journey or from their first days in their new desert home.

The surgeon's quarters at Fort Verde still stand; retracing some of Mearns's steps is easier than following the flow of Montana rivers. Fort Verde State Historic Park is open to visitors, and you can even walk inside the building where Mearns lived

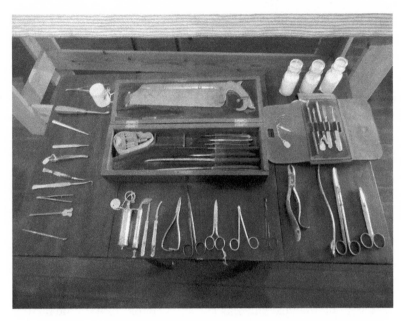

5. Surgeon's quarters, home "office." Fort Verde State Historic Park, August 2012. Author photo.

and worked. The adobe walls are whitewashed now, just as they are in photographs from when Mearns lived there. There is a generous wraparound porch. I know it isn't new because someone took a picture of Dr. Mearns here. He is sitting in a rocking chair. His legs are crossed, and he appears to have been reading moments before the picture was taken. Rocks, and maybe fossils, are arranged on a stand near the door. Metates, stone surfaces that ancestral Puebloans ground grains against, are lined up under the window, revealing the doctor's interests outside the realm of medicine.

I imagine these artifacts piling up inside as well, though not exactly in the way they are arranged today. Contemporary visitors to the fort walk in through the front door of the surgeon's quarters. The living space is to the left; to the right is a doctor's workspace. An examining table occupies the center of the room. A desk and a side table display carefully laid-out surgical tools: scissors, scalpels, pliers, and what looks to be a bone saw in a case (fig. 5). One of the bookshelves holds labeled bottles, while a lower shelf houses cotton stuffing, tongue depressors, more liquids, and powders. Every other surface in the room supports specimens and artifacts: arrowheads, animal skulls, pottery, taxidermy.

Of course, this isn't how Mearns left it. He wasn't the last surgeon to serve here; this doctor's office turned curiosity cabinet reveals more about the fort's history and its trajectory from private parcel to public park and museum than it does about Mearns's time at Fort Verde.[36] It is unclear where all these objects come from and who collected them, but this assemblage of materials crossing time, space, and cultures reflects a particular kind of Victorian collecting impulse. Cabinets of curiosities are often framed as precursors to the kinds of ordered and categorized displays that appeared in nineteenth-century museums. Sometimes they reflected a person's travels or their capacity to acquire objects and artifacts from much farther afield. They signaled what a collector might care about or what they might want to reflect to those in their social circles.[37] The objects in this present-day rearticulation of Mearns's workspace can't tell us much about his own collecting desires; still, I'm certain that the view from the back porch of the surgeon's quarters hasn't changed too much (fig. 6).

I took a similar picture when I visited Fort Verde State Historic Park in August 2012. I stood on the back porch and looked out across the Verde Valley, over the river and toward the buttes and mesas in the distance (fig. 7).

Mearns wrote of getting used to life at Verde and to the unfamiliar chorus of song from the Brewer's blackbirds that covered the parade grounds each morning.[38] Despite being assigned to a post, rather than to a company and regiment, Mearns had plenty of opportunities to travel.[39] Because reservations were under military supervision, General Crook crisscrossed Arizona Territory, meeting with federal Indian agents and Apache leaders. In letters Mearns boasted of Crook being "particularly interested in my pursuits, and has chosen me to accompany him on two long expeditions through the wildest and least known portions of Arizona."[40] The first of these, in October 1884, took

6. View of Verde Valley and Beaver Creek from surgeon's quarters, Fort Verde, Arizona. Photographic print by Edgar Mearns, ca. 1884–87, no. 204. Edgar A. Mearns Collection, Prints and Photographs Division, Library of Congress.

Mearns from Whipple Barracks near Prescott to Fort Apache and the San Carlos Apache Reservation and then back to Whipple by way of Globe (see fig. 8).

The purpose of the expedition was to meet with Western Apache and Chiricahua leaders. In the spring of 1883 (before Mearns's arrival) Crook, his men, and a substantial number of Native scouts headed south into the Mexican Sierra Madre to locate Geronimo and the Chiricahuas traveling with him and return them to reservation lands north of the U.S.-Mexico border. By the spring of 1884 they were back at San Carlos, and a few months later the Chiricahuas negotiated a move to Turkey Creek, near Fort Apache.[41] Most accounts of this period in U.S.-Apache relations gloss over late 1884; Crook's October expedition was routine.

This was the context for the expedition Mearns accompanied, but his account offers little information about the military objectives of the journey. On one afternoon Mearns described "a grand pow-wow with the Apache Indians" at Fort Apache organized by General Crook—but it is observations of birds, mammals, and terrain that occupy the pages of Mearns's report.

7. View from surgeon's quarters. Fort Verde State Historic Park,
August 2012. Author photo.

Occasionally there were medical tasks for Mearns to do, but his
expedition narrative privileges the land and its creatures over
all other details. In fact, this mention of the meeting at Fort
Apache is deployed to set up Mearns's true focus: "I spent half
of the day listening. In the afternoon I followed the south Fork
of White River up into the cañon and climbed up a high hill to
get a few of the country, and a magnificent panorama I saw—a
view to be remembered."[42]

Mearns used his already well-practiced skills as a field naturalist to keep three kinds of lists in his notes for this expedition accompanying General Crook across Arizona Territory:
birds seen, mammals seen, and specimens collected. Mearns
listed scientific names, always underlined, often accompanied
by common names. Some entries include a bit of description,
such as the October 3 notes for Maximilian's jay: "Large flocks
were flying about before daylight, uttering their loud, plain-
tive cry. . . . Occasionally a few would drop out of the ranks as
they skimmed over the pine tops; but they were too shy to be

8. Map of Arizona Territory, 1883. David Rumsey Map Collection, David Rumsey Map Center, Stanford Libraries.

easily shot."[43] Some entries noted the presence of a particular bird or its call; others indicated that Mearns had managed to collect—kill—a creature. While early mornings seem to have yielded more regular success in this realm, Mearns also managed to observe and collect specimens while on the move as a member of Crook's expedition.

Reading Mearns's field books prompted me to take a beginner birding course—a humbling experience that expanded my appreciation for Mearns's scientific work. I struggled to match birds and their songs from the excellent vantage point my old porch offered, and now, even in the most ideal circumstances, it requires all my attention—and my binoculars and bird book.[44] Mearns was in a new-to-him place, encountering species he'd never seen before, and he managed to document what he saw in impressive detail.

Specimen collecting and marching were not an ideal pairing, as Mearns well understood: "The objection to rapid marching in field collecting and observation is that nearly everything that is small, inconspicuous or shy is almost certain to be overlooked." Mearns praised his horse Daisey, "a lean cadaverous beast," because he stood still enough that Mearns was "even able to kill birds on the wing from his back."[45] Or at least those birds not scared away by the movement of a marching column of soldiers.

That Mearns managed to pursue his scientific interests while following military orders, rather than only in his spare time, suggests that it would be too simple to frame Mearns as an army surgeon first and a naturalist second. Profession or occupation can serve as a kind of shorthand for making sense of people in the past and the present. But for someone like Mearns, work was a many-layered thing. Examining the nature of Mearns's work—how Mearns the medical officer and Mearns the naturalist coexisted, shared time, needed each other—reveals some of the ways the spheres of nature and empire intertwined.[46]

During the October 1884 expedition Mearns wandered off from the group repeatedly. Sometimes this was intentional: Mearns left a meeting at Fort Apache to hunt specimens, or he chose to get up early to do some birdwatching near the previous night's camp. But sometimes he just got lost, or let himself get lost, and then took advantage of the opportunity. This practice wasn't available to everyone; Mearns's position as an officer and a surgeon afforded him far more flexibility than most.

Getting lost had the obvious benefit of distancing Mearns from the group of marching soldiers—and more specifically, from the noise and commotion that their daily marches produced.[47] When the sun appeared, he located the trail, hiked back for Daisey, and then continued onward to camp: "I trotted swiftly over a trail where I would have delighted to linger for days. At length I came to an open space to the right of the trail and, riding out into it I beheld one of the grandest, most exquisite scenes that could be imagined. I found myself upon the very verge of the high rim-rock of Tonto Basin, and looking down from the top of the gigantic wall of rock, a hundred times hig[h]er than the great wall of China, which shuts in this beautiful basin." Continuing, Mearns broke from scientific observation and specimen collection to reflect on the scene before him: "A miniature and beautiful world seemed spread before me, making a panorama so exquisite in its loveliness, so naturally beautiful, and so delightfully solitary and lonely, that I stood entranced until aroused by the sight of a Peregrine Falcon (*Falco peregrinus naevius*) which settled upon a dead pine-top."[48]

Mearns wasn't the first to be "entranced" by the Tonto Basin and write about it; recall Martha Summerhayes's narrative of arriving at the basin a decade earlier and finding it "beyond all that [she] had ever dreamed of."[49] Indeed, the descriptions of the Tonto Basin offered by Summerhayes, Mearns, and others evoke many features common to environments Americans considered lovely: rolling hills, green forests, an expansive view. It must have been a sight, especially when contrasted with the less-watered portions of Arizona's desert landscapes.

What strikes me about Mearns's description here isn't just how taken he is with the beauty of the Tonto Basin; it's his attention to how alone he is as he stares at the scene before him. That Mearns describes the basin as "delightfully solitary and lonely" certainly captures the expansiveness of the view, the sheer spread of this "miniature and beautiful world," but it also highlights a key condition of Mearns's ability to wander into the basin in the first place: its emptiness. A decade earlier the Tonto Basin had been Yavapai and Apache territory; it remains a Yavapai and Apache homeland. But the army's work—finding and fighting Native people and containing them on reservations—had been largely successful, enabling Mearns

9. Nineteenth-century wagon ruts still visible along the state route named General Crook Trail Road, August 2012. Author photo.

to wander through the basin on his own, away from the officers and enlisted men of the expedition. Though not part of this description of the scenery, Mearns knew this history, knew of the violence that preceded his journey to the Southwest and his participation on this expedition.

Even the trail Mearns was following that day was the product of the army's work in this landscape. It had been built to move men and supplies between Prescott and San Carlos; today much of it is part of a state route named General Crook Trail Road. In some spots along the roadside you can still see the wagon ruts, the cuts into the hillside made by Crook's men in the 1870s and then traveled steadily afterward (fig. 9).[50]

A few days later, though the command began marching at dawn, Mearns and the expedition's steward stayed behind to hunt and collect specimens. Mearns described this day as "the pleasantest one of the trip. The trail was excellent, birds were abundant, and the part of Tonto Basin through which we rode was the most beautiful place that I ever saw." Then Mearns connected this vision of the basin to the work assigned to Crook's command, writing, "It seems little wonder that the Apaches were so brave and fierce in defending their beautiful home from the whites."[51] Mearns's use of the past tense here wasn't exactly wrong; most Apaches were elsewhere, confined by the U.S. Army, and even well-known Apache warriors like Geronimo and Chatto were farming at Turkey Creek in the fall of 1884. And his specific language signaled an awareness of an increasingly racialized frame for American expansion; despite a multiracial U.S. Army and diverse non-Native settlement in the Southwest, Mearns named "whites" as the aggressors in the Tonto Basin.

Mearns's acknowledgment of the violent history of the recent past articulates an important piece of the construction of "naturally beautiful" and "delightfully solitary" landscapes like the Tonto Basin, the Black Hills, and countless other panoramas: Indian removal made them empty, and army occupation kept them that way. Except not quite; while Mearns repeatedly emphasized the emptiness of the Tonto Basin, he also described encounters with Apache people: men on "tough, wiry horses" interested in tobacco, a couple he met with turkeys to sell.[52] So even within accounts describing U.S. military victory and subsequent Native removal, we see the incompleteness of these processes and the continued presence of Apaches in supposedly empty landscapes. Despite narrating the violent work done by Crook's command, Mearns's field book also offers evidence of Indigenous refusal to comply with the broader imperial project of the U.S. Army. Apache people were still in the basin, even after repeated campaigns to remove them.[53]

Deployed to Arizona Territory after Crook's ruthless Tonto Basin campaign, Mearns emptied this southwestern landscape in a different way. When looking out over the basin, he took a shot at that peregrine falcon he spotted. He knocked a few feathers off the bird but didn't severely injure it—a fact that pleased him once he realized that if he'd killed it, "the bird would have fallen down perhaps a thousand feet before striking the sidewall and would of course have been lost."[54] So perhaps "empty" is too strong a verb for the specimen collecting Mearns did; U.S. colonial control over the people, land, and resources of the Southwest could only stretch so far. Mearns's failed attempt to collect the birds of the basin reflects, in miniature, the limits of his—and by extension, his government's—reach.

Mearns's approach to observing, documenting, shooting, and collecting birds in the service of ornithological study wasn't the only way to see, know, or value these birds. Mearns—and practitioners of Western science—were interested in studying, describing, and naming these birds; building collections enabled this form of knowledge production. Apache people used birds in other ways. Many of the Apache cultural belongings that are currently part of collections at the Arizona State Museum—collections born of imperial and settler-colonial pathways—draw from or incorporate references to southwestern birds: dolls dressed in 1880s clothing, a cane used in young women's puberty ceremonies, *gaan* masks, buckskin caps, a war charm necklace. These items include flicker, eagle, owl, and turkey feathers. A late nineteenth-century shield depicting a hummingbird is ringed with eagle feathers.[55] So Apache people were collecting and preparing birds, too—but for different reasons. The methods and practices Mearns had learned were only one approach to knowing and using these species.

Ornithologists and natural history museums still prepare birds in much the same way that Mearns would have; some of the materials have changed, but nineteenth-century methods have persisted because they work and also because field conditions in remote locations today present many of the same challenges that naturalists encountered in the past.[56] When Edgar Mearns collected a bird, he began by shooting it. He used appropriate ammunition—the small stuff. There's a reason we call it "birdshot."[57] Birds shot while marching or wandering would likely go into his saddlebags, or sometimes the ambulance wagon, until Mearns could find time to prepare them. Preliminary notes made in the moment could be expanded and refined later. Many specimens were lost at this stage of the process to rot and ruin.[58] While my blackbird could be saved for several months in a Smithsonian freezer, awaiting preparation, Mearns was operating within a much smaller window.

In the time he could find amid his military obligations, Mearns was preparing birds. My first bird preparation took a full day; Mearns, well practiced, could probably transform a bird into a specimen in fifteen minutes.[59] He would have performed the same steps I learned more than a century later: document and carefully remove the insides, insert a stick for structure and surround with stuffing, suture the belly, arrange wings and feather tracks, label and complete the corresponding field book entry, and pin the bird in place to dry. Our names are on the tags of specimens in the Smithsonian's collection now; we are both participants in these imperial circuits of removal, collection, and preparation.

The specimens that bear Mearns's name at the Smithsonian suggest that he consistently did an excellent job: Christina Gebhard, my bird preparation mentor at the Division of Birds, compared even the work he did as a young man favorably with specimens of naturalists with far more experience. Though it might seem obvious that men trained as surgeons would be skilled at specimen preparation, Mearns's early birds, specimens prepared before he began medical school, suggest that perhaps it was his naturalist work that prepared him for his military medical responsibilities. The quality of this work becomes even more impressive when considered in context.

It is easy to imagine Mearns's work as solitary, but his letters reveal community interest and sometimes expertise. In a letter to Ella from a camp outside Deming, New Mexico, he wrote, "My dearest wife . . . We have pleasant times in camp—all the officers come around to my tent and tell stories, cuss the K.O. and make merry; but I skin birds all the same." Mearns often took day trips from the post with Lt. Charles Vogdes, and in the evenings he routinely walked up the Verde River. Sometimes Ella and Lillian walked with him, and every so often Ella contributed to the specimen pile.[60] (Mearns was careful to indicate which birds were shot by others in his notebooks.) Mearns described an afternoon spent learning a different skinning technique from Crook while accompanying the general and Captain Bourke to a Havasupai village: "I found a good place under a large cedar and skinned up my birds, while Captain Bourke, within earshot, was pumping Cowarrow the Hualpai dry on the subject of the religion of his tribe, using Charley Spencer for interpreter." Mearns continued, "The General then showed me how he liked to skin birds by opening them under the wing as most of my Danish specimens are skinned. I tried the operation on my first Arizona specimen of *Junco* [*hyemalis*] and made a success of it."[61]

Though more of a hunter than a scientist, Crook valued what even Mearns's superiors in the army medical command structure understood to be his "favorite studies" and supported his efforts by providing him with specimens from the field.[62] Not satisfied with birds alone, Mearns also encouraged Crook to complete data sheets for the birds he shot. Crook wrote to Mearns, "The difficulty in filling up the blank you sent me is that I don't know the technical names of the birds + in many instances would be unable to make myself understood."[63] As Crook was both an interested colleague and Mearns's commanding general, his support seems to have been crucial to the collecting Mearns and others did while on assignment in Arizona Territory. But Mearns also received support for his collecting activities from farther afield. After all, his access to the Southwest, and later the Philippines, offered significant opportunities for museum-bound medical and scientific personnel to expand their collections and subsequently their expertise in their respective fields.

Working with Museums

In March 1885 Mearns received a letter from Spencer Baird, the secretary of the Smithsonian Institution, in response to a letter he'd written a few weeks before requesting Smithsonian publications. Baird's letter explained that Smithsonian materials were limited, only for "formal correspondents," and that he could not "give them out simply on call, even though the applicant be known as a student of science." Baird acknowledged Mearns's "zeal as a student of natural history, especially for ornithology," and invited him to become a contributor. "There are a great many ways in which you can assist us in our work," he wrote, "especially in making collections of reptiles, of fishes, and of Indian remains. Of course, anything in the way of birds or their eggs would be gladly received."[64] Baird connected natural history collecting work with the looting of Indigenous graves and was never shy in asking for what he wanted for the museum. This request hints at widespread awareness of the Smithsonian's interests and suggests how easily grave robbing was bundled into the work of "making collections."

Baird's correspondence network was substantial: while assistant secretary of the Smithsonian, Baird and his team had been writing more than five thousand letters a year. Baird became the second secretary of the Smithsonian Institution in 1878 and continued this correspondence, though not at the same rate. In writing to Baird, Mearns was participating in a broad, decentralized network of collectors and nature enthusiasts.[65] Army men were certainly a feature of this network; museums relied on officers (especially doctors) collecting specimens alongside their military responsibilities. The network of amateur naturalists that Baird had cultivated had peaked earlier in the century; scholars who study the professionalization of science often argue that late nineteenth-century shifts toward specialization left little room for laypeople in these fields.[66] But these broad trends obscure figures like Mearns, who maintained complex identities and occupational expertise in both medicine and natural history. Though he did not follow prescribed professional pathways to scientific expertise, Mearns's skills and his access to harder-to-reach fields combined to make him a particularly desirable correspondent and collaborator.

At the time of his deployment to Fort Verde, though, Mearns was still mostly unknown to those at the Smithsonian. Though he had corresponded with department-level curators like Robert Ridgway, he hadn't yet begun collecting for the United States National Museum. Many of Mearns's southwestern specimens eventually found permanent homes at the Smithsonian, but neither Mearns nor his specimens are listed in the annual reports for the museum's divisions in the 1880s, where museum staff named key collectors and outlined their most significant acquisitions each year.[67] Rather than pointing solely to the Smithsonian, the correspondence from Mearns's Fort Verde assignment suggests a range of possible destinations for the products of his scientific fieldwork.

For instance, Mearns received inquiries about specimens from the Army Medical Museum. Established in 1862 amid increased attention to documenting, managing, and sometimes stealing the dead, the museum solicited specimens from army surgeons across the continent.[68] These requests could sometimes be quite specific. In 1885 new curator Dr. John Billings wrote to Mearns "to request that if a specimen was preserved in the case of Private Wm. H. Taylor, Troop M 10th Cavalry, who died in the post hospital at Fort Verde from the effects of a shot wound of chest, it be forwarded to the Army Medical Museum."[69] It is unclear whether Billings was after the bullet or the tissue where the bullet was lodged, but his attention to individual casualties and their possibilities hint at the museum's role in military practice, especially during the U.S. Army's campaigns against Native people in the West.

Though the outgoing curator wrote to Mearns that the Army Medical Museum did not intend to "enter into any rivalry with the National Museum," the museum did extend its interests to include not only specimens useful for the study of military medicine but also ethnological and biological specimens. Billings wrote to Mearns, "It is hoped that medical officers of the army in making collections will give this Museum the first choice of specimens which they may collect." Billings had heard that Mearns had committed a set of specimens to the American Museum of Natural History, where he'd worked before taking up his commission in Arizona Territory, and Billings wanted to remind him that the army would be happy to have those materials—or anything Mearns might want to send. Even if the museum wasn't going to use the specimens directly, they could still be useful in trade to obtain what was necessary "to make in this Museum a complete collection of specimens in comparative Anatomy to illustrate the development and morphology of man."[70] The desire to order human societies along a linear spectrum of supposed advancement runs through much of nineteenth-century natural history and ethnography; displaying physical specimens was one strategy for representing racial theories about progress and civilization, ideas now dismissed as pseudoscience and scientific racism.[71]

An 1880 listing of all the anatomical specimens at the Army Medical Museum demonstrates that one of the museum's key trading partners was the Smithsonian Institution. The specimens on the list are arranged by purpose, anatomical or ethnological, and then by type and place.[72] The "Aztec Indians" section has eight listings, several of which come from the area surrounding Fort Verde, revealing settler ideas about the origins of ancestral Puebloan sites nearby.[73] And several skulls and incomplete skeletons are listed as coming from Civil War battlefields.[74] Only a few have names, and while most of the listings don't contain any information about how these people might have died, other than those describing soldiers' skulls gathered directly from battlefields, there are some clues. Maybe the bones sent by hospital stewards came from people who died at post hospitals? Perhaps. But the anatomical list overwhelmingly indicates looting: Native ancestors were exhumed, burial sites were disrupted, and mounds and shell heaps were turned over in search of specimens for the museum—for study but also for show. Many of the museum's ethnographic specimens were taken by medical officers stationed at posts in the U.S. West.[75] Ann Fabian characterizes the Army Medical Museum as a combination of a "war museum, an anatomical cabinet, and an ethnographic laboratory" that brought forty thousand visitors through its doors annually in the 1880s.[76]

Edgar Mearns participated in what Fabian calls "imperial body collecting"—though for him, and for others, the category covered more than human bodies.[77] Bird specimens, bone fragments, mammal skins, metates—Mearns collected all of these from the area surrounding Fort Verde. But in addition to demonstrating Mearns's varied pursuits, this range reflects the interests of nineteenth-century institutions. Ethnography, especially when conducted under the aegis of the federal government, shared much with mid-nineteenth-century natural science—including its practitioners.

John Wesley Powell drew on his background in geology in his role as the first head of the Bureau of American Ethnology. Powell applied natural science methods to the work of mapping and measuring Indigenous communities; he systematized the bureau's approach and attempted to conduct surveys of Native nations in the same manner as the geology surveys he'd supervised previously. While Powell's leadership standardized the fieldwork of the bureau, it also helped solidify Western science's racist placement of Native people in a hierarchy alongside natural resources—a hierarchy that withheld from Native people the dynamism and individual agency afforded to white people, who were positioned such that there were myriad possibilities for how their choices, ideas, and politics might play out. Which isn't to say that Powell himself understood Indigenous people solely as static elements of newly American landscapes; his interactions with Native communities were complicated, part of a wide-reaching career that enabled U.S. imperial expansion while signaling some ambivalence about its outcomes. Still, the systematic surveying of Native communities and cultures he implemented was a precursor for their removal; mapping often precedes extraction, and this kind of knowledge in the hands of a settler state did great harm.[78]

Natural science and ethnography, especially as organized under Powell, shared more than methods; these practices also shared products. The material outcomes of the large surveys of the West—in the form of stuffed animal skins, pressed plants, rocks and geodes—trumpeted both the wealth and the strangeness of the frontier. The surveys collected these specimens for study and for display at the United States National Museum and at international expositions. Public and private institutions were deeply interested in what expeditions across the West produced, and museum interests helped shape collecting practices. Anthropological artifacts, both historical and contemporary, followed these same pathways from the field to museums for study and display.

Most of the scholarly attention to these pathways has focused on the history of ventures like the U.S. Exploring Expedition (1838–42), which included a mixture of military and scientific members and whose collections were foundational to the Smithsonian, and the later Wheeler, King, Hayden, and Powell surveys of the U.S. West.[79] But Edgar Mearns and his military colleagues remind us that these large-scale efforts aren't the only way that museums acquired material.[80] Military collectors like Mearns had access to sites and specimens not easily reached or acquired by larger expeditions, both in the U.S. West and farther afield. Crook's encouragement had expanded that access, as had other military naturalists.

In May 1886 Capt. Charles Bendire wrote to Mearns from the Smithsonian. Retired from military service the previous year, Bendire had relocated to Washington DC to spend time working in the zoological collections of the museum.[81] "My dear Doctor," Bendire wrote, "I presume . . . that you are as hard at work as ever and judging from your former letter you must by this time have a grand collection of about everything that is to be found in that portion of Arizona." Bendire told Mearns that he understood the particular challenges of pairing naturalist work with military service—and then turned toward his own fascination, nests and eggs: "Have you taken anything new + especially interesting in the Nest + egg line about Verde. I have not seen anything published from you anywhere that I remember."[82] This single question reveals much about Mearns's participation in ornithological networks.

Like Bendire, Mearns was more than simply a source of hard-to-get specimens for museum specialists; he was not only a collector but also a scientist. Mearns had an excellent model in Bendire for combining scientific and military work. But he had work to do to get there. In the mid-1880s he was barely on Spencer Baird's radar, but that would change. He collected steadily and studied extensively. And he began to publish, perhaps using Bendire and Coues as inspiration.

Though reviewers highlighted Coues's rhetorical style (one labeled Coues's bird entries "rugged narratives"), Bendire also wrote about birds and their habits in an engaging way.[83] Describing the blue jay, Bendire wrote, "Even his best friends cannot say much in his favor, and though I have never caught one actually in mischief, so many close observers have done so that one cannot very well, even if so inclined, disprove the principal charge brought against this handsome freebooter." Coues was interested in "mak[ing] natural history entertaining and attractive as well as instructive, with no loss in scientific precision." He took the writing of natural history quite seriously: "Nor is it a matter of little moment so to shape the knowledge which results from the naturalist's labors that its increase may be susceptible of the widest possible diffusion."[84] It does not seem a stretch to see the influence of both Bendire and Coues in Mearns's writing.

In the January and July 1886 issues of the *Auk* Mearns published pieces on "Some Birds of Arizona." Mearns did not limit himself to the birds' behavior, but instead narrated his first view of the Verde Valley and the fort that would become his home: "It was a dismal and desolate outlook truly, but possessed of the beauty of wild loneliness. A few days' residence at the Post more than reconciled us to our surroundings, and we soon discovered that Nature had here scattered her treasures with lavish prodigality, though veiling them from the vulgar gaze never so cleverly."[85] Mearns goes on to describe the hawks he encountered while out observing the work of beavers, as well as a trip with a fellow officer and an escort of two enlisted men. The army context functions as a backdrop for Mearns's storytelling, and he says nothing about the particular military work occurring all around him. It simply sets the scene.

Mearns introduced the Verde Valley similarly in an 1890 article he wrote for *Popular Science Monthly* about the excavations he had conducted in the area surrounding Fort Verde. When writing for a general audience, Mearns used his military service to strengthen his credibility; though he was not an archaeologist or anthropologist, his familiarity with the region and his army

10. "'Montezuma's Castle,' Beaver Creek, Arizona, 3 miles from Fort Verde, A.T., showing the creek in the foreground, instantaneous / E.A.M." The site is now Montezuma Castle National Monument, part of the National Park Service. Photographic print by Edgar Mearns, 1887, no. 12. Edgar A. Mearns Collection, Prints and Photographs Division, Library of Congress.

medical work helped Mearns distance himself from those he called "unscientific relic-seekers." He cited "numerous tours of field-service and authorized hunting expeditions" as providing him with the opportunity to explore ruins like those along Beaver Creek, including a Sinagua cliff dwelling that still carries the name Montezuma's Castle (fig. 10), thanks to settlers who imagined an Aztec presence in this part of Arizona.[86] Montezuma's Well is not far from the site Mearns described for *Popular Science Monthly*, and it continues to hold great meaning for Yavapai and Dilzhe'e people as their "emergence place."[87]

Mearns did not frame these sites or the people who inhabited them as Aztec, and his article marvels at the tools and artifacts he took from a handful of sites along the Verde River. He detailed the exhumations of several skeletons, including the bones of children, taken from carefully constructed vaults "covered with large, flat stones, some of which were painted red." Mearns noted that the skeletons would be sent to the Army Medical Museum and the tools and artifacts he had collected would go to the American Museum of Natural History. Mearns used his platform in *Popular Science Monthly* to advocate for a more "systematic exploration" of these ruins, and soon, so that the site's "treasures" would not be "scattered." Collecting artifacts and ancestors for museum collections, "in order that our knowledge of them may become as comprehensive as the material procurable for study will permit," made Mearns, at least by his own determination, different from the "unscientific relic-seekers" he critiqued.[88] Carefully buried ancestors became "material" for study, and their exhumed bones became specimens alongside everything else Mearns sent to join museum collections.

In 1888, after four years at Fort Verde, Mearns requested six months' leave time, ostensibly to pursue his scientific work. This kind of leave was not unheard of; the military records of Coues and Bendire certainly suggest that assignments to Washington or leave for naturalist's work had occurred before. But Mearns's request, though approved, was never granted. A letter he received from the Surgeon General's Office in the War Department acknowledged Mearns's service but cited the "great dearth of medical officers" as the reason that it was "impossible to grant indulgencies to those who have won the right to them by hard work on the Frontier." A few weeks later Mearns was notified that he was to be transferred to Fort Snelling, an arrangement that the author hoped might enable Mearns to get some leave time sooner than if he were to remain in Arizona. Apparently the medical director there was "a warm supporter" of natural history.[89] The larger politics of the frontier army's hierarchy and needs shaped the contours of Mearns's service, but it seems that the most significant factor enabling his naturalist work was his immediate command structure.

Bendire acknowledged this indirectly in his May 1886 letter to Mearns. After asking Mearns about his collecting and publishing, Bendire turned toward army politics: "How do you like the new change of administration, I hope that Genrl Miles will give you as many facilities as Genrl Crook did."[90] The "change of administration," as Bendire called it, was no small switch. General Crook and General Sheridan fundamentally disagreed about how the ongoing military campaign should be handled, especially about Crook's use of Apache scouts. This clash had occurred against a backdrop of disputes over civilian versus military supervision of reservations and as part of a deeper rift in ideas about military strategy. The broader foundations of American policy—the state's dismissal of Indigenous sovereignty and embrace of a settler-colonial strategy—were not questioned.

The relative peace of Mearns's first two years at Verde was fragile, built on the assumption of Apache capitulation to American demands. Amid the increasing greed of white settlers, corrupt behavior by Indian agents, and disagreements about the terms of reservation life, new forms of Apache resistance emerged. In May 1885 a large group of Chiricahuas left reservation land and headed for Mexico. This group, labeled "renegades" by the United States—forty-two men and ninety-two women and children in all—included leaders Geronimo, Naiche, Mangus, Chihuahua, and Nana.[91] Thus began the final military campaign of the Apache wars.

"Tagging" as Colonial Violence

Not since Custer's death had so much American attention been focused on the frontier. Geronimo's name was known everywhere, and the campaign to find him received almost continuous national press coverage.[92] Even now the pile of popular and scholarly accounts of the Apache wars (almost all of them from army or settler perspectives) could occupy an interested reader for a lifetime. I do not intend to add to that pile here. Rather, I am interested in what the Apache wars can reveal about the intersection of ideas about nature and empire.

In particular, the regulatory tactics employed by Crook to manage Apache people bear strong resemblance to natural history practice. Apache men were described, labeled, and made to wear tags, a system that sounds much like the procedures Mearns and other natural history enthusiasts followed when collecting—whether for themselves or for institutions like the Smithsonian and the Army Medical Museum. Though not parallel—animal specimens were killed, while Apache men were labeled and contained—these processes echo each other in ways that require scholars to reckon with the relationships between them. The categorization, codification, collection, and later display of Native people were interrelated acts of violence that grew out of the close proximity of scientific and military work, both of which functioned within a worldview that affirmed both settler colonialism and white supremacy.

Already I have been drawing attention to the language U.S. soldiers used to describe the landscapes of their service; these details help illuminate the relationships between soldiers' work and their ideas about nature. But what words did soldiers use to describe Apache people? Frontier soldiers regularly likened Native people—Apache people in particular—to animals. Sometimes this language expressed awe or even a kind of admiration. Bourke described the challenging terrain but also how the scouts handled it: "Up and down these ridges our Apache scouts, when the idea seized them, ran like deer."[93] And Crook described Apaches as "very independent and as fierce as so many tigers" in a telegram to General Sheridan, his superior in Washington.[94] Animal comparisons went both ways; Odie Faulk wrote that Crook's nickname among the Apaches was "Grey Fox" because of his graying beard. But Mike Burns (Hoo-mothya, in Yavapai) noted that Yavapais and Mojave Apaches called Crook names that meant "Old Woman's Face" and "old woman's eyes," emphasizing a different dimension of Crook's physical appearance.[95]

Other observers deployed animal comparisons to denigrate Apache people. For example, Assistant Surgeon L. Y. Loring acknowledged the courage of Apache people and then attributed that courage to "ignorance and an animal nature," rather than to their humanity, thus grounding his assessment in hierarchical notions of progress and human development widely believed by white America in the late nineteenth century.[96] The pursuit of race science, a set of now debunked ideas about racial differences and racial hierarchies, affirmed a persistent belief in white superiority and produced typologies of races and cultures, with white, European societies at the top. Those who embraced these approaches to ordering the "natural" world regularly made connections between human and animal communities, especially when discussing their possible or even impending extinction.[97]

In examining the language used by soldiers to describe Native people, we should also consider the language that historians of these campaigns have relied on in their own descriptive and analytical work. Janne Lahti highlights the uncritical adoption of late nineteenth-century language by many historians of the Apache wars—especially words like "hostiles" and "renegades." Deploying these words reproduces the perspectives of army men and reflects what Lahti calls "the often subtle influence of colonial knowledge."[98] We must recognize the perspectives embedded in the sources we rely on—and also the resonances between the official and unofficial work of army men, especially when those resonances have consequences.

During his first tour of duty in Arizona Territory Crook had implemented a "tagging" policy on reservation lands, both "for the better protection of the Indians" and "to enable the commanding officers to tell at a moment's notice just where each and every one of the males capable of bearing arms was to be found."[99] Newcomers to San Carlos, such as those from the Rio Verde Reservation, were issued metal tags with identifying information on them. Henry Irving, a Dilzhe'e man who had been forced to relocate to San Carlos with others from Rio Verde, was issued a tag with the designation "S.E. 8."—S for San Carlos, E for "E band," and 8 to identify Henry as an individual.[100] Bourke described the tags as being "of various shapes, but all small and convenient in size." Different shapes signaled different tribal affiliations. Bourke wrote that there were "crosses, crescents, circles, diamonds, squares, triangles."[101] The tags were to be worn at all times. While this practice echoes tactics of control deployed in other contexts—passes written by enslavers, tokens issued to wage laborers in mines—the components of Crook's tagging policy strongly resemble the procedures used by nineteenth-century naturalists.[102]

Army men articulated tagging's effectiveness for controlling and ordering Apache men and their families. The callousness of their descriptions is striking. For example, an officer in the Fourth Cavalry wrote, "Any American who would attempt to burden himself or his memory with a number of Indian names would soon be hopelessly lost, but tag numbers and the records made it very simple to locate a special individual." Civilian actors sometimes used this system to their advantage. For example, Charles Elliott remembered a complaint from the Silver King Mine: the clerk at the company store had noticed the tags some Apache men were wearing and had written down the letters and numbers he saw. Those tag band IDs were then used to identify—and punish—those who had left the reservation without army permission.[103]

Some Apache men refused this practice. They hid in the mountains to avoid being tagged by the army—to avoid being marked as belonging to an agency or as under the power of the U.S. government. Others fled, and troops and scouts were dispatched over and over to find them. Gen. Wesley Merritt wrote that Apache men received the tagging order with "sullen dissatisfaction because, if carried out, it checkmated their roving."[104] Others, such as General Raguero of Mexico, did not think the practice was effective; apparently Crook had "told him of the tag system, and it had rather amused him, as there was not the slightest way of preventing an Indian from leaving or punishing him properly when he came back."[105]

While Bourke's earlier account identified the tags as passes to track movement, Merritt described what he called "the daily verification of the Indians." The "counting officer" walked among the tagged men, arranged in concentric circles, and "checked off the numbers on the tags."[106] Crook and his men continued to use the practice of tagging Apache men to monitor their travel and compliance when he returned to lead the Department of Arizona.[107]

In fact, this tagging policy, used throughout the Apache campaigns, sounds eerily similar to the natural history practices of specimen collection deployed by officers like Mearns.[108] Murat

11. Tagging of Apache men. The tag hangs from the necklace seen on "Nal-te, the San Carlos Dude, White Mountain Apache." Studio portrait by Ben Wittick in the 1880s. Photographic print, ca. 1880–90(?), no. 015907. Palace of the Governors Photo Archives, New Mexico History Museum, Santa Fe.

Masterson of the *Prescott Arizona Democrat* interviewed Crook about how it worked: "The Indians in each band were all numbered and each given a brass tag or check, the different bands having different-shaped tags, so that the tag shows not only the band its owner belongs to but his number in the band. A record of these together with a full and complete description of the owner is kept in a book. They were then instructed that anyone found outside the reservation or without his tag would be considered as hostile and treated accordingly."[109] The practice of tagging didn't just organize; it standardized and surveilled. The shapes, numbers, and letters on the tags corresponded not just to tribe and band but also to a descriptive entry of the tag wearer, "kept in a book" by army officers. Bourke called this description of each man "a full recital of all his physical particularities," and to me it sounds not unlike an entry in a naturalist's field book, with measurements and distinguishing characteristics documented for each collected specimen.[110]

Despite regular mentions of this practice in military sources from the Apache campaigns, physical evidence is hard to find. The tags, if worn, are hard to see in the pictures we have from this period. But I've located one image, a studio portrait of a San Carlos Apache man named Nal-te wearing a tag, taken in the 1880s (fig. 11). Archaeological surveys of battle and massacre sites from the Apache wars have turned up some of these tags, and histories and ethnographies of Apache communities sometimes mention an individual's tag-band ID in parentheses.[111] And the Department of Anthropology at the Smithsonian's National Museum of Natural History contains a brass tag collected by Captain Bourke, though the notecard accompanying its accession records does not include any information about the person to whom it had been issued.[112]

I went looking for more evidence of Crook's tagging practice in military records, in search of the volumes containing the written physical descriptions of Native men that sounded so much like the natural history descriptions entered by Mearns into his field books. I didn't find them, though I carefully unfolded and refolded hundreds of items in the records of the military's

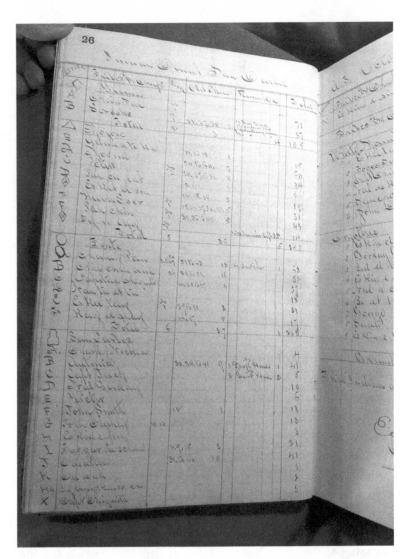

12. Inside page, detailing shapes assigned to each band, from "San Carlos Census of Reservation Indians," October–November 1882, in Record Group 393: Records of the United States Army Continental Commands, 1821–1920, part 5, entry 406-27, National Archives and Records Administration. Author photo.

Department of Arizona at the National Archives. I encountered department reports, muster rolls, letters, telegrams, blank forms, details about rations, official orders, even small scraps of paper likely once tucked in breast pockets for safe passage across unfamiliar ground—now preserved alongside others, waiting to be reviewed again by whoever opens the boxes next.

Though the registers U.S. soldiers described eluded me, I did find evidence affirming that tagging was used by the army to identify, describe, and track Native men. For example, the Department of Arizona's records for 1886 contain a list of the Native scouts in Companies A, B, C, and D of the Second Infantry, with columns for rank, name, and tag-band ID number.[113] In documents that list prisoners sent to post jails for various infractions, enlisted men were entered by name and rank, while Native men were instead listed by nation, tribe, and the assigned letter of their band. And the October–November 1882 "San Carlos Census of Reservation Indians" was structured according to Crook's tagging practice: the almost daily census taking was organized around tribes and band chiefs (fig. 12).[114] Each tribe had been assigned a shape, which presumably corresponded to the material form of the brass tag issued to each man. A letter was assigned to each band, identified by the name of that band's "chief." The census has rows for each band and columns for indicating those present, those working as scouts for the U.S. Army, those who were sick, those who were old men, out on passes, or otherwise absent. Sometimes the census lists how many people met each column's criteria, and sometimes the census-taker instead wrote down the individually assigned numbers for those who fit into a particular category, such as all the numbers for those labeled "old men." Across the army records I have examined, these tag-band ID numbers were often used instead of individual names.[115]

The residue of tagging persisted long after the Apache campaigns. Though often framed as an Apache reservation, San Carlos contained people representing multiple nations, tribes, and languages—as evidenced by the San Carlos census, which included categories for Yuma and Mojave people (both categories used by the military to describe Yavapais), as well as categories for four different Apache bands: Tonto, San Carlos, White Mountain, and Coyotero. These lists demonstrate how colonial categories reshaped Native communities; contemporary Indigenous nations, such as the Yavapai-Apache nation, have navigated this forced construction of a single political presence while honoring their "dual heritage."[116] Anthropologist Grenville Goodwin, who conducted fieldwork focused on Western Apache culture, described the imposition of the tag-band system as "an alien patrilineal system of inheritance," an example of "government usurping of chiefs' power and function."[117]

In her memoir, titled *Don't Let the Sun Step over You: A White Mountain Apache Family Life, 1860–1975*, Eva Tulene Watt reveals the persistence of tag-band IDs as she shares the interconnected personal histories of members of her family and community. She explains how tag-band IDs sometimes accompanied individual names, especially those of relatives and community members who survived the Apache wars: "My grandmother Rose had two brothers and one sister. William Lupe, F-1, was the oldest. He was the leader of the people living at Oak Creek and Chediskai." Later, when describing her mother's uncle, William Goshoney, she refers to him as "A-2." And John Lupe was Z-3; Watt writes, "That was his brand."[118] That some Apache families repurposed this tactic as a strategy for cattle management hints at the persistence required to navigate the long and ongoing history of violence toward Apache people by the United States.[119]

On its own, the practice of tagging sounds like the work of empire: an imposition of colonial power and increased surveillance and management of colonial subjects.[120] It is ugly and dehumanizing, and it is also a legible (if awful) part of a military operation—and occupation. It has many echoes across time and space. Examined in the context of natural history practice, though, the similarities between specimen labels and field notes and the tags and descriptions documented in army ledgers seem too great to be a coincidence. Specimens were shot, skinned, stuffed, described, and labeled. Native people were collected too—incarcerated on reservations, and tagged with labels keyed to physical descriptions. Some historians have suggested to me that tagging might have its origins in the army's existing record-keeping practices; I certainly found muster rolls containing physical descriptions of U.S. soldiers in the

Department of Arizona papers I was searching through. But the act of tagging Apache men pushes me to look beyond military practices and into the describing, ordering, and labeling central to nineteenth-century science.

The focus on men, too, resonates with natural history practice. The individual specimen used as the basis for identifying a new species is called the "type" specimen for that species. A specific description of the type specimen is published, and it becomes the representative example of that species. Most often (especially historically) the type specimen for birds is male.[121] Women and children were not listed individually in the San Carlos census, nor were they tagged by the U.S. Army. Instead, they seem to have been included in the total numbers for each band, though nowhere is this clearly stated.

But of course, specimen collection and tagging are not the same—in one case birds and other creatures are killed in the service of science, and in the other living people are labeled, their movements controlled and curtailed, as part of strategies devised to accomplish military goals. Recognizing their differences, though, does not diminish the correlation between these practices. Instead, it suggests the reach of U.S. imperial practice, as well as the stakes of refusal. Indigenous people, in the face of resources weaponized and wielded against their right to even exist, evaded capture and categorization whenever possible. The work of U.S. empire in Apache and Yavapai homelands had expanded to incorporate strategies more commonly used to practice Western science. This resonance demonstrates what becomes visible when we consider environmental and imperial history together—that seemingly separate ideas and practices might carry unsettling connections, might implicate natural history more fully in the work of settler colonialism.

The act of transforming a living being into a specimen is an exercise in stopping time. No longer breathing, no longer flying, the birds shot by Mearns, Crook, and others became prepared scientific specimens, preserved seemingly for all time—forever futureless. These words—futureless, preserved for all time—might also describe, in different ways, the visions Anglo-America had for Apache people. Arizona settlers actively campaigned for Apache removal; the residents of Cochise County went so far as to pass a resolution demanding that Apaches be removed from what the residents described as "the middle of our territory."[122]

While U.S. settlers made their desires known, the U.S. Army continued implementing the state's strategy to make Native lifeways futureless—either by ending them or by forcibly changing them. The tags the army required Indigenous men to wear fixed them in place. Tagging was a form of emptying, a tactic of elimination, in that it restricted the movement of Indigenous people, removed them from large sections of their homelands, and reduced them to letters, numbers, and shapes.[123] Daily counts, as reflected in Capt. Emmett Crawford's San Carlos census book, demanded that Yavapai and Apache people present themselves according to the categories engraved on their tags. Native families were expected to farm specific pieces of land, and Crook, in his 1884 annual report, described what he framed as his great success: "The change already effected within the last year is remarkable, and I am in hopes of being able to accomplish a more complete and radical transformation with time."[124] Crook advocated assimilation and, in so doing, affirmed his vision of Native cultures as fixed in the past. To move forward, in his mind, was to move away from Indigenous beliefs, practices, and political sovereignty. As evidenced by the departure of several families from Fort Apache in 1885, Native people did not agree.

General Crook's tagging practice, part of the carceral world of reservations established by the United States, was a key feature of how settler colonialism operated in Yavapai and Apache homelands.[125] Kelly Lytle Hernández labels incarceration "human caging." Reading her work on the long history of incarceration alongside descriptions of tagging suggests how this practice contributed to U.S. goals: tagging was a strategy designed to control, contain, cage, and functionally eliminate Yavapai and Apache people from their homelands—from land that settlers wanted.[126]

U.S. settler and army ideas and practices increasingly lim-

13. *Geronimo* by A. Frank Randall, 1884. National Portrait Gallery, Smithsonian Institution.

ited Indigenous sovereignty in the Southwest—and in 1885 led Geronimo and a group of Chiricahua Apache people to leave Fort Apache. The American public had long been fascinated by Geronimo (fig. 13); when what would become the final military campaign of the Apache wars began, one did not need to look far for Anglo characterizations of the Apache warrior. And of course, he'd been issued a tag; in a table constructed by Edwin Sweeney based on the tagging of Chiricahua and Warm Springs Apache men, Geronimo is listed as the chief of Chiricahua Band B.[127]

Describing Geronimo and his band in 1883 Bourke wrote, "In muscular development, lung and heart power, they were, without exception, the finest body of human beings I had ever looked upon."[128] Soldiers who knew Geronimo had mixed opinions.[129] Lt. James Parker remembered him as "friendly and good natured" while at Fort Apache.[130] Another officer wrote that Geronimo had "the most arresting" countenance and "a look of unspeakable savagery, or fierceness," continuing, "When he was mad he simply looked like the devil, and an intelligent devil at that."[131]

Other sources described his kindness. Marietta Wetherill remembered encountering Geronimo near Willow Springs in 1885, probably while he was on the way to Mexico. Marietta's father was out looting Puebloan ruins, and she'd been left at her family's camp because she hadn't finished her daily lessons. A group of Apaches rode up and asked for water; they seemed impressed that eight-year-old Marietta responded in Navajo. Geronimo called her an "Apache girl" and said he'd take her with him and give her a pony. In response she said that her mother would cry; besides, she already had a pony. The men watered their horses and gave Marietta a quarter of beef from their supply. She didn't realize she was talking to Geronimo, and her father didn't believe her when she told him that Apaches had visited their camp while he was away. And then the army arrived, asking questions. Geronimo had been kind to her, she recalled in a 1953 oral history interview, so she didn't quite tell the soldiers the whole truth about which direction the Apache men had gone.[132]

A few years earlier Crook had been interviewed about Indian affairs by the *New York Herald*. He said the Apaches were "the shrewdest and best fighters in the world," so in May 1885, when Geronimo, Naiche, Chihuahua, Mangus, and Nana left

14. *Council between General Crook and Geronimo.* Cañon de los Embudos, Sonora, Mexico, March 1886. Photograph by C. S. Fly. Prints and Photographs Division, Library of Congress.

Fort Apache with members of their families, Crook sprang into action.[133] He moved his base of operations south to Fort Huachaca and organized expeditions comprising cavalrymen and Apache scouts to sweep the area on both sides of the U.S. border with Mexico. Boundary lines—lines used to break up Apache homelands, to separate reservations, to divide nations— crisscrossed the southwestern borderlands. And so did the U.S. Army; a March 1886 conference between Crook and Geronimo took place in Sonora, Mexico. C. S. Fly, a photographer from Tombstone, Arizona, captured the meeting's participants on film (fig. 14).

Crook and the Chiricahuas discussed possible terms for surrender. By meeting's end it seemed that a tentative agreement—one that included the right of Apaches to return to their homelands after two years in the East—had been reached. (These terms were not approved by General Sheridan or President Cleveland.) But afterward a small party including Geronimo and Naiche hurried into the mountains, prompting Sheridan to question Crook's tactics and his trust of the Native scouts in the army's employ: "It seems strange that Geronimo's party could have escaped without the knowledge of the Scouts."[134] A flurry of telegrams revealed an impasse. "I have spent nearly eight years of the hardest work of my life in this department," wrote Crook as part of a formal request to be relieved of his post.[135]

Gen. Nelson A. Miles was dispatched to take over Crook's assignment: this was the leadership change Captain Bendire referenced in his letters to Mearns. Miles sent Capt. Henry Lawton into Mexico after Geronimo, into what Lawton called in letters to his wife, Mary, a "godforsaken country."[136] He wrote letters to her almost daily during the summer of 1886, and they are filled with accounts of the challenges of the field. "It's hard for you to realize the hard work we have to do," he told her; no sign of "the hostiles," as he called them, and on some days no sign of their or any other trail. The bugs were bad, and either water was hard to find or the rivers were too high and rough to ford. And on top of that they were short on supplies, and Lawton blamed the government for not fully supporting "soldiers who are laboring their very best, very hard and patiently in these wild and awfully rugged mountains." "This is an *awful* country," Lawton complained, though he later acknowledged his dour tone: "Well, I have given you another growl today." But there are moments when Lawton's letters lift: "I forgot to tell you we are in the land of parrots—not the small ones, but the great big green and red fellows . . . it seems funny to have parrots flying about wild." The parrots provided a small distraction from the task Lawton worried over. He articulated the stakes this way: "I shall try very hard to catch Geronimo because I know I cannot get home until I do."[137]

At the end of August Apache scouts found Geronimo's camp. The Chiricahuas outlined a plan for surrendering to Miles. In her biography of Geronimo Angie Debo highlights "the strength and stability of Apache institutions," their "democratic manner of reaching decisions," even (or perhaps especially) in the context of war.[138] To Mary, Lawton wrote, "This morning Geronimo with 12 or 13 of his men came in to my camp and I have been talking with him all the morning. . . . He says he and all his people are anxious to make peace but he wants to see and make peace with General Miles."[139] Miles eventually agreed to meet the Chiricahuas at Skeleton Canyon. There he used stones to explain that the Chiricahuas would be reunited with Chihuahua and his band, who had already been sent east to Florida.[140]

The details of this meeting remain unclear; Geronimo never learned that the terms of his earlier agreement with Crook were not acceptable to the U.S. government. And certainly Miles had made promises he could not keep—promises of a reservation for all Chiricahuas, promises of good land, water, and resources.[141] Geronimo later said to Stephen Barrett, while recounting his life story through a translator, "I do not believe that I have ever violated that treaty; but General Miles never fulfilled his promises."[142] Geronimo and the remaining Chiricahuas, including Apache scouts who had served in the U.S. Army, were collected and ordered onto trains headed east, yet another example of the kind of emptying of the West that was central to the imperial work of the frontier army. The Chiricahuas were now prisoners of war, and their journey reflected this: the windows and doors were closed shut, even in the desert heat, as the train hurtled eastward, first to San Antonio, Texas, and then onward to Florida (fig. 15).[143]

A white soldier said that Apaches made the country "uninhabitable"; their departure from Apache homelands to a Florida prison seemed to many white Americans to herald the beginning of a new age on the western frontier: its end.[144] But that did not stop Americans from flocking to Wild West shows, world's fairs, and even to the site of Geronimo's imprisonment to affirm that the West had indeed been "won." Visitors bought crafts and autographs and paid money to watch Apache dances.[145] Perhaps going to see Geronimo allowed these Americans to indulge in a kind of frontier nostalgia. Or maybe they understood him as the ultimate curiosity, a living, breathing part of the natural and human history of the "wild" West.

15. *Geronimo and Fellow Apache Indian Prisoners on Their Way to Florida by Train.* September 10, 1886, no. RC02773. State Archives of Florida, Florida Memory.

THOUGH HE REMAINED STATIONED IN ARIZONA TERRITORY throughout the campaign against Geronimo and the Apaches, Mearns wrote nothing about him; Mearns's field books for 1885 and 1886 are filled with detailed descriptions of bird and mammal specimens.[146] In 1888 Mearns received orders to report to Fort Snelling in Minnesota, also occupied Native land. At Bdote, the Dakota name for the confluence of the Minnesota and Mississippi Rivers, life for Mearns was quieter. His field books describe walks around the post and specimens collected from the yard—no General Crook to invite him on expeditions, no ruins to excavate and loot. But perhaps because of the quiet, an opportunity that overlapped with Mearns's scientific skills and interests presented itself: an invitation to serve as the medical officer for the United States–Mexico International Boundary Survey. It wasn't the leave he'd requested a few years before, but it was a chance to combine his medical and scientific work in a more official capacity—and to return to the Southwest borderlands. Between January 1892 and September 1894 the survey team traversed the border, located and rebuilt the monuments marking it, and collected specimens: thirty thousand bugs, birds, plants, and mammals.[147]

Meanwhile tourists, including many newspaper editors who described their experiences in print, visited Pensacola to see the nation's most famous prisoners of war.[148] During the fall of 1887 and the spring of 1888 Geronimo's band was transferred to Mount Vernon Barracks in Alabama. Apache people still in the Southwest tracked these movements; Paul Conrad describes an Apache woman named O-Neelth, who drew a picture of her son's "reservation brass tag, 'San Carlos D,' though she could not remember the number anymore," in trying to locate him among the Apaches at Mount Vernon Barracks.[149] About the move Robert Utley writes, "Pensacolans were dismayed by the loss of their prime tourist attraction."[150] Florida had not been kind to the Chiricahuas imprisoned there. They had difficulty adjusting to the damp and humid climate, and many of the Chiricahuas battled "consumption"—tuberculosis—during their seven-year stay in the East.[151]

Finally, as a result of War Department reports and advocacy by philanthropic associations and U.S. officers, including General Crook and Captain Bourke, Congress authorized a move for the Chiricahua prisoners to Fort Sill, Oklahoma.[152] William H. C. Bowen, a member of the Fifth Infantry who had served under General Miles on the plains, described watching the Chiricahuas board the train for Fort Sill on October 1, 1894. There, with the opportunity to farm, Bowen wrote, "it is expected that they will become self-sustaining and partly, if not wholly civilized."[153] The move to Oklahoma meant fewer visitors. But in the years that followed, Geronimo became a much-desired display at world's fairs and expositions, as well as at Theodore Roosevelt's inaugural parade.

In separating Geronimo and many Chiricahuas from their land, the United States furthered its settler-colonial mission: to empty Native land and make it available for U.S. settlement.

But separation did not sever the link between Apache people and their homelands. Geronimo petitioned repeatedly to return to the Southwest borderlands, including directly to President Theodore Roosevelt. His requests were always denied.[154]

Collection practices—the preservation and removal of birds, artifacts, and even living people—advanced Western natural history and extended American imperial power over Indigenous people and their homelands. Whether soldiers understood these processes as connected, they were deeply tangled together: Mearns's natural history work was directly shaped by his military tasks and travel, and the U.S. Army employed techniques resembling scientific specimen collection to describe, tag, and contain Native people on reservations. These connections make visible the particular shape and reach of U.S. empire and amplify the tangled way that military action, scientific knowledge production, and imperial desire combined to restrict and incarcerate Native people. They reveal the range of imperial practices Native people resisted. More broadly, these resonances demonstrate the layered, violent, and interconnected histories of collection and dispossession.

Interlude 1

Revising and Remembering

DR. PAUL FLETCHER OF ST. LOUIS, MISSOURI, WORKED AS a contract surgeon during the Philippine-American War. His wife, Hughine Coyle Fletcher, copied large sections of his letters to her into a bound notebook. Its pages are more fragile now, but the volume, and with it the record of Paul's service that Hughine preserved, remains intact. I'm grateful for Hughine's careful transcription; her husband's handwriting is more angular than her round script. But I have questions about the passages she chose to transfer—for safekeeping? for comfort?—and which sentences she might have left behind.

Two photographs are pasted inside the book's front cover: one of Paul holding their infant son, Robert, who seems to be wearing a christening dress, and one of Hughine with Robert, perhaps on the same day (fig. 16). Except Hughine has been removed, her figure torn from the image. I don't know why, but this removal seems important somehow, given that it opens a volume dedicated to preserving Paul's words.

Fletcher's letters pivot quickly. A typical message might move from a porpoise sighting to a wish to give Robert a whale ride to the number of vaccinations he administered on the ship to the sublime nature of the Pacific Ocean—the trip, Fletcher wrote, "exhausts all expression."[1] A later letter covers a whirlwind tour of Nagasaki and describes the workers coaling Fletcher's ship, closing with a kiss for Robert. There's an immediacy to these letters—and an intimacy too. I've lost afternoons reading them.

It is easy to forget Hughine's editorial presence, that her

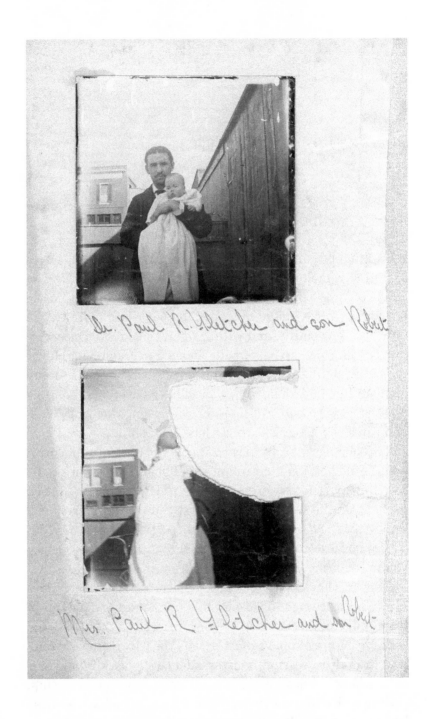

16. Inside cover of Hughine Fletcher's letterbook.
Missouri Historical Society, St. Louis.

pen touched each page, that she decided which of Paul's letters would be preserved to read. Although this set feels more complete than many other collections of correspondence from this war, it, too, is a fragmentary record. I haven't found any of the letters Hughine wrote to Paul. Maybe he didn't keep them. Maybe they didn't survive his service in the Philippines, though he did. Maybe she didn't want her letters, that version of herself, to be saved. I'm left to wonder.

Other figures rewrote, revised, and returned to earlier words on the page. Sometimes, as in the case of Dr. Edgar Mearns, earlier entries served as a kind of to-do list. His field books, housed near his specimens in the Smithsonian's National Museum of Natural History, are filled with little checkmarks next to the names of individual birds (fig. 17). I read these checkmarks, the occasional underline or question mark, as evidence of Mearns's process, of his regular return to his bird lists, notes, and narrative entries. Marks in pen and pencil suggest that he checked and double-checked words against birds and birds against the words in his field books. His papers contain examples of notes distilled into itineraries, reports, and specimen lists. Neater versions replace older, messier drafts. This means I've read some of Mearns's accounts over and over again.

Col. Frank Baldwin's papers reflect a similar pattern, though his papers are not at all concerned with birds. As the leader of a military expedition in the Lake Lanao region in 1902 intended to locate Moros suspected of murdering American soldiers (an expedition that led to the Battle of Bayan), Baldwin was responsible for creating an official record.[2] His papers contain draft after draft of his official expedition report, each one more marked up than the last. Some versions model the kind of revision practice encouraged by my middle school English teacher: literal cutting and pasting, with whole paragraphs reattached on top of the sentences they were meant to replace (fig. 18). Baldwin's practice of snipping out full paragraphs, replacing them and rearranging them in the larger document, highlights the work he put into narrating the war and its component parts. The attention soldiers gave to revising, reframing, and renar-

17. Notes and itineraries from travels on the island of Sulu, Zamboanga, Borneo, Mati, Mindanao, Rio Grande, Parang, Manay, and Malabang, November 11, 1903–March 19, 1904. Edgar Alexander Mearns Papers, Smithsonian Institution Archives, Record Unit 7083, image no. MODS13675.

rating their actions in the Philippines signals the importance they placed on their written work, whether officially required or personally significant.

In some ways these writing practices reflect American conquest in miniature. This was an iterative process—each version looks slightly different, but the connections are there, in the repetition of particular tactics and techniques, both on the ground and on the page. In the U.S. West soldiers regularly removed Native people from the landscapes they constructed in their writing on the page, while also participating in the large-scale processes of violent dispossession and incarceration on the ground. Techniques fundamental to natural history practice were applied to effect imperial control. And in the Philippines rhetorical links between the work of conquering

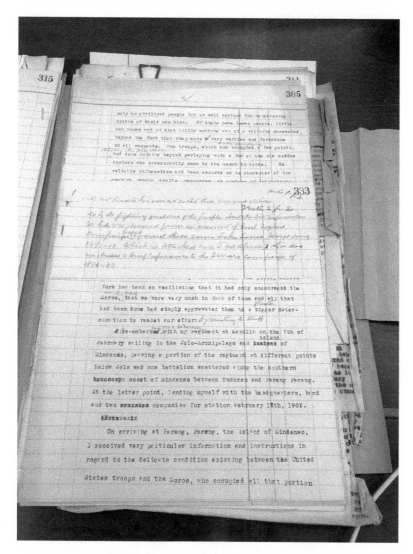

18. Frank Baldwin's revision practices. Huntington Library, San Marino CA.

the Philippines—and Filipinos—and the campaigns against Indigenous people in North America were abundant, made by soldiers, their superiors, and even their opponents. These connections are particularly visible in the letters soldiers wrote home, in the ways they worked to narrate themselves into a story of conquest or to express some concerns about the places they occupied in this narrative.

Through their writing soldiers constructed and collected particular versions of the war, the past, and the natural world. Soldiers serving in the U.S. West employed these practices to make sense of their service, to explain it to their families and, more broadly, to the American public. Soldiers serving in the Philippines employed them too. Miguel Martínez, writing about soldiers and their words across the early modern Hispanic world, explains, "Soldiers were usually the first to reach the edge of empire and the last to leave, so they had a particularly intense and concrete experience of imperial space."[3] The soldiers I study wrote of these experiences on pages they sent home to loved ones, expressions of euphoria and despair scattered between descriptions of daily routines. The letters, traveling along circuits formed by empire, were often fragile, prone to ruin. That words once sent up and down rivers on steamships in the U.S. West, or overland before crossing the Pacific to and from the Philippines, might still be readable today has much to do with what happened to them after they reached their destination.

Some soldiers' words were reprinted in local newspapers. Others were kept safe at home but given to an archive or museum generations later. And Hughine—one layer removed from the work Paul Fletcher was doing as a contract surgeon in the Philippines—preserved his letters by transcribing some portion of them. By crafting a record of her husband's service, she chose which letters might survive into the future, which materials might help shape historians' narratives—also drafted and reworked over and over again.

3

The Nature of the Philippine Frontier

FROM THE BLUFFS AT MARIQUINA IN MARCH 1899, NEAR some waterworks his regiment had been tasked with defending, Pvt. Edwin Segerstrom of the First Colorado Regiment of Volunteers wrote to his mother and sister, "I wish I could describe the view as I can see it from my bed in this end of the tent. Spread at our feet away below is the beautiful valley which is 6 or 7 miles wide as far as I can judge." Cpl. Selman Watson, stationed nearby, echoed Segerstrom's observations in a letter to his family: "This place is by far the prettiest we ever were in camp. . . . On the other side of the valley rises the first chain of a Range of Mountains tall, blue, and grand, dotted to the tops with tropical verdure." The next month Segerstrom wrote that the volunteers were being replaced by members of the regular army, meaning he might not be in the Philippines much longer. Though the work was "getting a little tiresome," Segerstrom did not tire of the landscape. Still camped near Mariquina in May, he wrote home that "the sight of the valley and hills bordering it is a beautiful one now and if I were a poet, I think I could create some great verses about the scenery here."[1]

Those verses, as yet unwritten, together with Segerstrom's descriptive letters, were part of a flood of words sent home by soldiers who framed the Philippines as a tropical paradise.[2] Paradise, writes Vernadette Vicuña Gonzales, "is by no means natural—it is conjured through imaginative labor." Gonzales writes about the intersection of tourism and militarism in the twentieth-century Pacific world, but her analyses of "sites of fantastical imaginings and military occupations" point to deeper histories—to earlier wars and the soldiers who fought in them, and to the continental empire that came before soldiers like Segerstrom found themselves waxing poetic about the Philippine landscape.[3]

Like soldiers who served in the U.S. West during the late nineteenth century, U.S. soldiers deployed to the Philippines wrote extensively about the landscapes of their service. They described the challenges presented by new and difficult terrain, and they played a part in shaping American ideas about the nature of the Philippines, half a world away. But U.S. soldiers in the Philippines were not starting from scratch; they were drawing from a rich tradition of writing about American frontiers. Whether they had experienced the "Indian Wars" firsthand, many soldiers made explicit links between the U.S. West and the Philippines—as landscapes and as sites of U.S. imperialism. That many soldiers traveled across the North American West as part of their journey to the Philippines only amplified these connections.

Capt. Matthew Steele was one of the regulars Segerstrom described. He had already performed fifteen years of service all over the western frontier. He'd been stationed in other landscapes often considered hard, sparse, and desolate, in Texas, Montana, and Dakota Territory, where he had participated in the arrest of Sitting Bull.[4] He fought in Cuba in the Spanish-American War. Now, as part of this war with Spain, Steele was leading a new group of volunteers (men who enlisted when the war began, rather than men already part of the regular army) to the Philippines. But before they began the trip across the Pacific, they first had to cross the mountain West by train.

From "On top of the Rocky Mts.," Steele wrote to his wife, Stella, "Whew! but it's cold up here 8000 feet in the sky." He described how "a large black board stood there with the words 'The Summit of the Rockies' painted upon it." He was "gliding along a thinly grassed plateau as flat as a dinner table," traveling by rail to San Francisco, where he and his men would board a navy transport vessel to cross the Pacific Ocean. Though no stranger to the rhythms—and hardships—of military service in the West, Steele reserved a special epithet for the Great Basin desert expanse between the Rockies and the Sierra Nevada: "the Godforsakenest country I ever saw."[5] Maybe it was the apparent emptiness of this terrain or the aridity of the Great Basin. Or perhaps he'd learned to expect this "Godforsakenness" from the accounts of white travelers who had made similar journeys earlier in the nineteenth century.

Crossing the Pacific

A few months earlier Beverly Daly had crossed the West to San Francisco, where he boarded a navy transport vessel bound for the Philippines. In a letter to his mother he described "a practically desert country—although we passed some very interesting groups of rocks—like those in Kirk Munroe's story—'The Painted Desert.'" Munroe characterized the desert Daly moved through as "a place to be avoided by all men" and also "terribly beautiful and changeless." In Munroe's tale a Baltimore boy visiting his geologist brother gets "lost in that fearful wilderness of sand and towering rocks" in the novel's first few pages and must rely on wits, luck, and the friendship of a Native boy named Nanahe to survive.[6] Perhaps Daly replayed this story in his mind as he peered through the windows of the train. Though he wasn't the only soldier seeing the mythic West he'd read about, as his train cut through the desert, Daly did have a particularly personal connection to the Apache campaigns: his father, a miner, had been killed by Apaches in 1881.[7] Daly and his mother had moved east after that. Even for those without a personal link to the U.S. West, these journeys across the continent reinforced soldiers' understandings of the continuity of empire.

Like Steele, Daly, and a host of other soldiers ordered to the Philippines, Acting Assistant Surgeon Paul Fletcher also commented on the scenery he traveled through on his way to San Francisco.[8] Fletcher left St. Louis on August 20, 1900. His letter of August 23, written from Ogden, Utah, describes riding the Denver and Rio Grande Railroad through Colorado's Royal

Gorge: "It is in the heart of the Rocky Mts. and is a magnificent structure of Nature reaching towards the clouds."[9] These experiences of the West—brand-new visions for volunteers and contract surgeons like Fletcher, familiar sights to career army men like Steele and westerners like Daly—were journeys filled with anticipation of the places, people, and work ahead of them.

Lieutenant George Telfer wrote to his wife, Lottie, "If there is to be a fight I want to see it."[10] As an officer with the Oregon Volunteers Telfer was among the first to be deployed. His journey across the ocean began in May 1898, and it was rough: cramped quarters, seasickness, filth, lice, hunger. But stopping in Honolulu raised his spirits—there he had access to food, drink, more kinds of fruit than he could keep track of. And then it was back to the ship and onward across the Pacific. In the open stretches of ocean Telfer seemed almost forlorn: "We see no ships. We are out of the world and we all wonder what you will think when we are not reported from any place."[11]

When Paul Fletcher looked at the sea, he thought it sublime. He reserved his most vivid language for the Pacific itself. To his wife, Hughine, he wrote, "I never fully realized the expansiveness of the great Pacific Ocean before. Morning after morning as I cast my eyes out of the narrow window of my state-room and see the vast and seemingly endless waste of rolling water, I feel how utterly insignificant we mortals really are and how great the universe is."[12] Though framed differently from Telfer's sense of being "out of the world," Fletcher's "seemingly endless waste" also evoked the desert and even recalls John Gregory Bourke's initial impressions of the Black Hills, whose "immense fields" were like the "gentle roll of the sea in a time of calm."[13] During the crossings these men seemed to be at the limits of their facility with language—they were not equipped to explain the sea. The huge, open spaces before them could be oceans or deserts; what seemed to matter was their emptiness.

The space provided by the journey, and perhaps the expanse of the sea, offered plenty of opportunity for reflection on what the future might bring. Beverly Daly's letters reveal a young man eager for adventure: "My life has been so hum drum, and thought less, that now I am up against the stern realities, I have to pinch myself once in a while, to convince myself that I am not dreaming." But it wasn't just that Daly was going to get to do something important, something exciting. There was also a sense of destiny: "One thing is sure Mamma—this experience will make a man of me unless it is ordained that I am to die, as my father died. However, I don't fear the future, and haven't been losing any sleep by wondering whether a Filipino bullet will find in me, its billet—or not." Underneath this bravado Daly was worrying and wondering about what might happen—he was, after all, going off to war: "Oh Mamma—if I am taken, please don't think of my foolish and wasted boyhood, but remember that in the end, I tried to be my father's son—I have broken down completely and must close."[14] By invoking his father, Daly linked the danger of the western frontier with the challenges he would face as a soldier in the Philippines. This new war activated older fears about gruesome violence and the supposed savagery of unfamiliar enemies.

Paul Fletcher hinted at his own worries. He told Hughine of a "fearfully scarred" doctor he had met in San Francisco. The man had been "boloed" in the Philippines—"slashed . . . with lightening-like rapidity over neck and shoulders and left . . . for dead."[15] The things that might happen to Fletcher once he reached his assigned post were left unsaid. As the Philippines— and thus the war—grew nearer Fletcher's letters home turned to politics. He was traveling in the autumn of 1900. A presidential election approached, and Fletcher repeated an idea that had taken hold for many soldiers: if William Jennings Bryan, rather than William McKinley, won the election, the whole army would be home very soon. After talking to other soldiers in port at Nagasaki, Fletcher told Hughine that the consensus seemed to be that the United States should either leave the Philippines or send in a larger force of "two or three hundred thousand men and wipe them off the earth."[16] This casual description of genocidal action, though perhaps common rhetoric in a time of war, demonstrates the pervasiveness of settler colonial logic; if

American occupation of the Philippines was the goal, removal and erasure of its people appeared to many to be the next step.

Others shared these concerns about what would be required to take control of the Philippines and what that would mean. Similar questions were being asked by soldiers' families at home and debated vigorously by newspaper editors and politicians. This is well-trodden terrain for historians who have long analyzed McKinley's decision-making.[17] Military historians, too, have detailed the state of the U.S. Army and Navy at the end of the nineteenth century, the transport system, and the process of calling up volunteers to supplement the nation's too-small supply of experienced officers.[18] The Philippine-American War has received a smaller share of scholarly attention in the history of modern warfare; renewed interest can be traced back to the 1960s and U.S. military intervention in Vietnam.[19] And questions about insurgency and torture—issues that were central to the Philippine-American War—concern us still.

Despite this it is a war that seems to have been mostly forgotten, excluded from textbooks or glossed over quickly with a mention of the U.S. naval victory over the Spanish fleet at Manila Bay. This erasure fits easily with interpretations of U.S. history that cast 1898 and its aftermath as an aberration, a blip, a brief experiment with empire, rather than one example among many in a long history of U.S. imperialism, both across the North American continent and across the Pacific. But recent moves to reframe U.S. history as a history of empire, and to examine exceptionalist narratives that obscure the foundational nature of imperial expansion to the history of the nation, have also brought renewed attention to the Philippine-American War and U.S. colonialism in the Pacific.[20] And increased emphasis on settler colonialism and the persistence of white supremacy at home and around the world has drawn scholars from a range of fields and disciplines to examine U.S. colonialism in the Philippines.[21] But with few exceptions, this work does not follow soldiers or center their ideas or their labor.[22]

As both consumers and producers of U.S. culture, soldiers drew from a broad range of experiences and texts to describe the tropical landscapes of the Philippines and weigh in on the work of empire they had been assigned. In doing so they made connections between Indigenous people in the U.S. West and the Filipinos they fought, and they pulled from familiar framings of the nature of the U.S. West to explain Philippine environments. Natural beauty, challenging terrain, resource abundance, the rhetoric of outdoor recreation, and even the shifting meanings of wilderness all found their way into U.S. soldiers' service— and the records they made of their service—in the Philippine-American War.

"Some Relic of the War"

After weeks of travel the coastline of the Philippines was a welcome sight. "June 19th. Woke up this morning in Manila Bay!" wrote Daly. "As we came in at night, we were unable to see any of the sunken Spanish ships. This morning, however, the 'Baltimore,' the war ship that silenced the Cavite batteries and completed Dewey's victory, is off our starboard bow."[23] Adm. George Dewey's decisive victory had expanded the theater of the Spanish-American War halfway around the world; his decimation of the Spanish fleet also expanded visions of U.S. empire in the Pacific.

John McCutcheon, a reporter for the *Chicago Record*, had been at the right place at the right time to cover the story. He had been on a round-the-world voyage in 1898 when the U.S. Treasury Department vessel he was on was reassigned to the U.S. Navy. McCutcheon stayed with the ship as it traveled to Hong Kong. On April 17, 1898, the *McCulloch* joined Commodore Dewey's fleet. Ten days later all the ships under Dewey's command sailed for the Philippines, and McCutcheon remained with the *McCulloch* as a war correspondent. He made detailed drawings and descriptions of the Battle of Manila Bay in small reporter's notebooks, some of them no larger than my palm.

While positioned off the coast of Luzon McCutcheon wrote down his first glimpses of the shore: "The land . . . looks very pretty in the bright sunlight this morning. It suggests the outline of Cuba approaching Havana from the north. There are

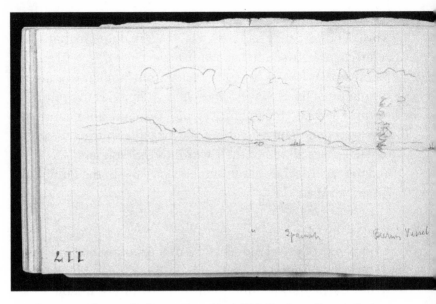

19. "Burning of Spanish ships, 11 AM, May 1." McCutcheon Papers Series 3: Works: Diaries and Notebooks, January–May 1898, vol. 14, pp. 84–85, McCutcheon Special Collections, Newberry Library, Chicago.

faint blue lines of hills and mountains with little patches of dark colored features on the coast." These words show anyone who can read his handwriting (some of it tiny enough to warrant a magnifying glass) the horizon: "A bluish haze hangs over the land and the hills and mountains grade off in tints until the far-thermost range is a mere flat line."[24] It sounds lovely, though in that hanging haze there is a hint of the battle to come. The reference to the coastline of Cuba is imagined—McCutcheon had not been to Cuba—perhaps meant to call up the connections between Havana and Manila or even to suggest that the land-scapes of U.S. imperialism were interchangeable. As McCutcheon sketched, the *McCulloch* moved steadily onward, at the end of a line of ships led by the *Boston* and the *Concord*, "now so far ahead of the fleet that only the smoke from their furnaces mark[s] where they are."[25]

On May 1, 1898, very early in the morning, Dewey led American ships past Corregidor and toward the Spanish fleet near Cavite. The night before the battle the U.S. ships turned off all

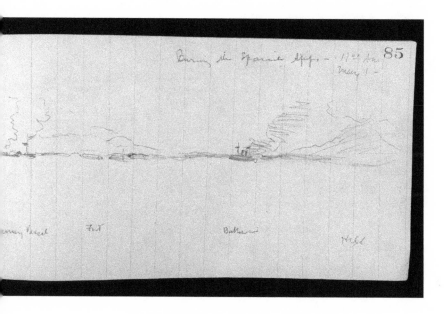

their lights, invisible but for the lightning. McCutcheon wrote, "It is only when one of these flashes illuminates the sky that the black bodies of the ships are seen."[26] When the battle began McCutcheon could see it all from the deck of the *McCulloch*: the shells hitting their targets, the Spanish ships burning. He sketched the scene, the destruction clear even though the ships and seascape are only outlines drawn in pencil on tiny pages (fig. 19).

The Battle of Manila Bay was a definitive American victory.[27] The following day McCutcheon rowed out to the remains of the Spanish fleet and "went around among the wrecks, making photographs and collecting souvenirs of the fight." He reported that the *Castilla*'s "insides are burned completely out, only the blackened iron work being visible." McCutcheon did not say what he recovered from the wreckage, but he noted that he was not the only one after a memento: "Boatloads of officers and seamen have been to her [the *Castilla*] all afternoon, pillaging her of souvenirs of the battle. Scraps of signal and boat

20. *Battle of Manila Bay, 1 May 1898.* U.S. Naval Historical Center photograph no. 902937, courtesy of the Naval History and Heritage Command. Donation of Lt. C. J. Dutreaux, USNR (Ret.), 1947.

flags, charts, books, small anchors and dozens of little relics have been eagerly seized. Sailors have been diving down and bringing forth all sorts of trophies, from clocks and compasses to chains and pieces of Spanish guitars."[28] Edward C. Veberhagen wrote to a friend serving in the Philippines, "Wish you would gather some valuable relics and send to me pieces of some destroyed ships if only a screw or a splinter or a piece of metal." Everyone, it seemed, wanted "some relic of the war."[29]

This souvenir collecting was not a new practice. Civil War soldiers had done it too, gathering bits and pieces from bloody battlefields, items to save or enclose with a letter home. Megan Kate Nelson argues that these sometimes macabre mementos "seemed to conflate time: they embodied both present and past, allowing veterans and their relatives to narrate their autobiographies by recalling where they were and what they were doing on a certain day." Civil War soldiers collected bullets, picked flowers and cotton, and took items from the dead and the wounded. In doing so, "soldiers anticipated their futures,"

futures that involved making it home, where they might look at these relics and remember.[30] Some army men who had served in the nineteenth-century campaigns they called the Indian Wars in the U.S. West had done the same—collected pieces of the West even as their labor transformed it. And at Manila Bay, soldiers and spectators like John McCutcheon rummaged for relics amid the still-smoking wreckage of the Spanish fleet (fig. 20). "In a day or two," McCutcheon wrote, "the bodies will be coming to the surface."[31]

The souvenir hunters no doubt recognized the significance of the battle; the little that remained of the Spanish ships was a testament to the strength of the U.S. Asiatic Squadron. The things they collected reflected not only a great victory but also, for many soldiers, an approaching opportunity. U.S. forces had not yet landed in the Philippines. Despite soundly defeating the Spanish Navy, to the Americans the islands remained a collection of faint blue lines to the east.

U.S. soldiers knew very little about the land or the people who lived in the vast Philippine archipelago of more than seven thousand islands. And just as it is problematic to flatten diverse Indigenous peoples in North America, with different histories, cultures, and languages, into a single category, it is important to recognize the variety of peoples and cultures in the Philippines. While many Americans thought of the archipelago's residents simply as Filipinos, the Philippines was and is home to several different ethnic groups, among them large communities of Tagalogs, Kapampangans, Ilocanos, Bicolanos, Cebuanos, and Visayans. Muslims in Mindanao were grouped together by the Spanish as Moros, a category including three main tribes: Taosugs, Maranoans, and Maguindanoans. Smaller groups living more remotely interacted infrequently, if at all, with Spanish colonizers. The Igorot peoples, clustered because they lived in the highlands of Luzon, the archipelago's largest island, drew much American attention, especially when representatives were later displayed as part of the U.S. government's Philippine Exposition at the 1904 St. Louis World's Fair.[32] Given the archipelago's diversity, a sense of political identity as Filipinos was forged for many through resistance—first to Spanish and then to American colonialism.

Dewey had cut the telegraph wires between Manila and Hong Kong, so it took several days for news of his victory at Manila Bay to reach the United States. With the news came confusion—what next? The Spanish fleet had been defeated, but technically it still held Manila. Dewey thought that five thousand men was all he would need to take the city.[33]

In the aftermath of the destruction of USS *Maine* in Havana Harbor on February 15, 1898, President McKinley had set in motion plans to send troops to Cuba and to the Philippines—regiments from both the regular army, composed of career military men, some of whom had served in the Civil War and in campaigns against Native people in the U.S. West, and from the newly formed volunteer army. In the week before Dewey sailed for Manila Bay, Congress declared war with Spain and McKinley called for 125,000 men to join the army as volunteers.[34] But what were they to do? Historians continue to debate what, exactly, McKinley wanted General Merritt, assigned to helm U.S. operations in the Philippines, and General Miles, now the commanding general of the U.S. Army, to accomplish. (This was the same Miles who had replaced Crook during the Apache campaigns.) Brian Linn points to the words Miles used in the days following the Battle of Manila Bay: everything from "occupy" and "possess" to more limited goals focused on holding the harbor—and on not starting "a war to conquer." Linn argues, "even as the United States stood on the threshold of a great leap toward Pacific empire, no one knew what the agents of empire were supposed to be doing."[35]

As these agents, both regulars and volunteers, made their way to San Francisco to board transport vessels for Manila, Emilio Aguinaldo, the leader of the Philippine effort against the Spanish, returned to Cavite, overlooking Manila Bay, where the remains of the Spanish ships were slowly sinking. Cavite had been the site of another important Spanish defeat—but at the hands of Filipino forces led by Aguinaldo a few years earlier. Now that the Spanish had suffered a devastating loss, Aguinaldo sought to capitalize on the opportunity to renew the revolution. In June 1898 Aguinaldo declared the independence of the Philippines from Spanish rule and set plans for self-government in motion. Filipino revolutionaries fought against the Spanish. Meanwhile, U.S. troops continued to assemble.

On arrival at Cavite Harbor Lt. George Telfer of the Second Oregon Volunteers wrote to his wife, "A campsite will be selected in the morning and it will be then decided how we are to be killed." The letter lightened, though, when he described what he and the other Oregon Volunteers saw from their ship: "Of course we have not been on shore—but we are all entranced with what we see from shore. We all talk of locating here—if the U.S. holds it."[36] Even before his feet touched the ground Telfer was imagining the aftermath of U.S. conquest: U.S. settlement. That Telfer and his fellow soldiers saw themselves as possible pioneers reveals how naturalized this process of expansion, conquest, and settlement was for them.[37]

In his letters Telfer also anticipated how his family would get news of him: "My daily life is the same as that of the balance of the 3,000," he wrote in early July, "and the only satisfaction we have in having the newspaper correspondents around is that they do our letter writing to a certain extent."[38] One of those, John Bass, a correspondent for *Harper's Weekly*, described what those early days were like: "Delay, delay, delay; no one knew why. The days dragged."[39] One Nebraska private, Henry O. Thompson, described soldiering during this period as "a good and lazy job."[40] Everyone was waiting for the Americans to advance on Manila.

Brig. Gen. Francis Vinton Greene described what was at stake in a rousing Fourth of July speech delivered on the deck of the *China*, a navy transport vessel carrying Greene and a ship full of U.S. volunteers across the Pacific. The Declaration of Independence was read aloud, and Greene began: "Comrades, when Thomas Jefferson wrote the immortal words which you have just heard read, he little dreamed that one hundred and twenty-two years later they would be read in the middle of the Pacific Ocean to an expedition of American soldiers bound to the conquest of a group of islands off the coast of China." (In fact, Greene's typed copy of the speech provides specific coordinates: "Pacific Ocean, Longitude 166° East, Latitude 19° North.") And then Greene imagined how Jefferson might have understood the possibilities the Philippines presented for the United States. To the troops before him Greene said, "The vigor with which Jefferson acted in acquiring Louisiana proves that were he alive to-day he would be the first to seize the opportunity which Admiral Dewey's glorious victory in Manila Bay has placed within our grasp." For Jefferson, Greene declared, "there would be no hesitation as to our duty"; the Philippines was American "destiny."[41]

Greene's speech was meant to encourage and inspire the mostly inexperienced men who had by that point spent several weeks in cramped quarters on the *China*, but his words also reveal how he—and many others—understood their actions within the larger narrative of U.S. history.[42] Greene linked their (still unclear) mission in the Philippines to the vision of Thomas Jefferson, the 1803 Louisiana Purchase (which doubled, or more, the size of U.S. territory), and the apparent inevitability of the task before them. Greene situated the "opportunity" the Philippines offered as a natural extension of Jefferson's vision and service to the nation. For many in Greene's time, as well as for readers today, his words laid bare the continuities between U.S. imperial expansion across the North American continent and across the Pacific. But for others the era of Jefferson and the U.S. Declaration of Independence suggested a different path— not to U.S. occupation of the Philippines, but to independence *for* the Philippines from their Spanish colonizers.

The first American Anti-Imperialist League formed on June 15, 1898, and by the following year it had grown into a mixture of local chapters that engaged in a coordinated critique of U.S. actions in the Philippines. Comprising reformers, scholars, writers, labor leaders, and politicians, the Anti-Imperialist League struggled to articulate a coherent message.[43] Matthew Frye Jacobson explains that many anti-imperialists were concerned about the implications of imperialism not only because of the difficulty of reconciling it with U.S. democratic ideals but also because of what annexation might mean: an influx of Filipino people, who might one day want to become citizens. Thus anti-Asian racism shored up arguments both for and against U.S. imperialism in the Pacific.[44]

The league used soldiers' words to make its points in the pamphlets it printed and circulated. For example, an 1899 publication quoted Sgt. Arthur H. Vickers of the First Nebraska Regiment, who wrote, "I am not afraid, and am always ready to do my duty, but I would like someone to tell me what we are fighting for."[45] In fact, Cheryl Berudo has argued that one of the league's most critical interventions was the creation of an "anti-imperialist archive." The league recognized that collecting more information—and more varied perspectives—was a necessary precondition for influencing public opinion.[46] Newspapers and popular magazines around the country editorialized about the Philippines and how the United States should proceed. Though anti-imperialists mobilized in impressive ways to combat U.S. colonial expansion across the Pacific (and some, such as Herbert Welsh, also advocated for "Indian Rights" at home), their efforts did not sway enough U.S. decision-makers.[47] Those in favor of annexation and colonial control over the archipelago made arguments about how the United States would be different from Spain as a colonial power and the commercial opportunities available both within the Philippines and reachable from them.[48]

Theresa Ventura has reconstructed the career of Ramon Reyes Lala, a Manila-born naturalized American citizen who wrote and lectured about the Philippines at a moment when Americans were clamoring to learn more about this faraway place. Lala advocated U.S. empire alongside citizenship for Filipino subjects while critiquing Spanish rule, adding to already loud voices in favor of extending U.S. imperial expansion across the Pacific. Ventura unpacks Lala's "deft maneuvering" in a space where he could claim to provide "an insider's perspective" while highlighting his ambivalence about key dimensions of American visions for the Philippines.[49] Still, Lala's efforts contributed to the political momentum in favor of U.S. colonial control over the Philippines. Richard Welch calls turn-of-the-century anti-imperialist efforts "not a failure of will but of political strength" and shows that once McKinley articulated a policy of annexation, many who had opposed annexation got on board.[50]

Meanwhile, a few days after Greene's rallying speech on the decks of the *China*, and despite significant organized resistance from the Kanaka Maoli (Indigenous Hawaiian people), the U.S. Congress passed the Newlands Resolution, which asserted that Hawai'i was a U.S. territory.[51] The U.S. flag was raised at 'Iolani Palace in Hawai'i, with plenty of U.S. soldiers present to affirm U.S. colonial control. This move, made in the face of ongoing and coordinated Native resistance, was certainly part of a broader U.S. colonial strategy: Hawaiian ports served as coaling stations for U.S. naval vessels bound for the Philippines.[52] July victories for the United States in Cuba resulted in Spanish surrender, and American military leadership turned its attention toward Manila.[53]

In 1898 Samuel Ovenshine, more than twenty years out from his service on the Great Plains and now a colonel in the U.S. Army, received orders to ship out to the Philippines. His papers contain very little from his Pacific service, but there is a narrative—possibly part of a letter—about the events of August 13, 1898. Ovenshine commanded troops from the Twenty-Third U.S. Infantry under General MacArthur's Second Division. After the "delay, delay" mentioned by Bass, instructions arrived. At 6:30 a.m. on August 13 Ovenshine marched his men to Pasig. At midmorning they "heard the *Olympia* shelling the Spanish trenches," and after a telegram from MacArthur, they "hurried on for Manila." Ovenshine described finding Spanish trenches empty—soldiers had retreated as a result of the shelling. Merritt, Greene, and MacArthur each led brigades into the city, and U.S. forces took Manila. Ovenshine wrote that he had orders to "keep the Insurgents from going into the Walled City," which was the older city center of Manila.[54] These orders were an indication of things to come.

The United States might have held Manila, but it did not

hold much of anything else. U.S. and Filipino troops were on edge, even as Aguinaldo agreed to move his men farther outside the capital city. Despite his incomplete conquest of the islands McKinley could—and did—claim significant victories over the Spanish in both hemispheres, and as a result, representatives from both sides met to negotiate an end to the Spanish-American War. They reached an agreement in Paris in the final weeks of 1898. After much back and forth over matters of territory, the delegates decided that Spain would transfer the Philippines into the possession of the United States (along with Guam and Puerto Rico) for a sum of $20 million.[55]

Meanwhile, with the Spanish defeated, Filipino leaders held a convention to decide on a governmental system and write a constitution. While deliberations over imperial boundaries unfolded in Paris, Filipino leaders were busy drafting governing documents and articulating their autonomy. The Philippine Republic was established in early 1899, with Emilio Aguinaldo installed as the new nation's first president.[56]

Americans often overlook this part of the story; when the emphasis is on U.S. victory it is easy to lose sight of the ongoing revolution many Filipinos were fighting. But for them this moment was crucial; it was when the United States decided not to affirm Philippine independence and instead to extend U.S. imperial visions farther west. Before the Philippine-American War, before the Spanish-American War, the Philippine Army of Liberation had already been doing the work of challenging Spanish colonial rule. The revolution of 1896–97 was an uprising against the Spanish with participants from varying parts of Philippine society; a temporary end resulted in negotiations that sent Aguinaldo to Hong Kong in exile. But once U.S. aspirations were clear, revolutionary forces reorganized their efforts, and the Malolos government, or Philippine Republic, was established.[57] This history helps further explain the mounting tensions between American and Filipino troops in the weeks following both the Paris negotiations and the founding of the Philippine Republic. And it makes clear that the Philippines was already both a colonial and a postcolonial space when the

United States launched a war to occupy and control it.[58] While some Filipinos initially saw the U.S. defeat of the Spanish as a victory that would enable Philippine independence, after the Treaty of Paris they realized that the United States planned to replace Spain as the colonial power in the Philippines.

An attempt by U.S. forces to occupy Iloilo City offers additional evidence that regardless of what Spain and the United States had agreed to in Paris, the Philippines was not actually under U.S. control. After Spain lost control of Manila Gen. Diego de los Rios took over Spanish leadership of the Philippines and established himself at Iloilo City, where he asked local leaders to form militias; only later did he learn that he did not have their loyalty. Instead, local people sought independence. Lacking local support, Rios asked for approval to turn Iloilo City over to the Americans, and in late December the United States dispatched the *Baltimore* to peacefully establish a military government. But local forces had already declared their independence as the Federal State of the Visayas, ostensibly allied to the newly formed Philippine Republic. With orders to convince the Filipinos of the supposed kindness of American intentions, the *Baltimore*'s commander attempted to negotiate.

It quickly became clear that the Americans were not welcome. When presented with the opportunities the United States could offer the Philippines, Raymundo Melliza explained that the Philippines did not require American help; its residents were ready to self-govern and were doing so already. The Americans responded that the Philippines was technically U.S. territory, as decided in a treaty recognized by other nations. Besides, U.S. troops could just destroy the city. Melliza's response? Basically, to go ahead—the city was filled with foreigners' property. But if U.S. troops attacked, Melliza said, "we will withdraw to the mountains and repeat the North American Indian warfare."[59] The *Baltimore* returned to Manila.

A few weeks later the Philippine-American War officially began. On February 4, 1899, U.S. soldiers on patrol in Manila shot and killed two Filipino soldiers who supposedly failed to stop. Historians have offered a range of interpretations of this incident: was the start of the war an accident, or was the incident instigated intentionally, cleverly timed to encourage the U.S. Senate to ratify the Treaty of Paris and formally agree to U.S. ownership and occupation of the Philippine archipelago? Competing narratives persist. David Silbey writes, "The insurgents and later Filipino historians claimed that the American soldiers fired without provocation. The American soldiers and historians believed that the Americans fired after the armed and advancing Filipinos refused an order to halt."[60] Susan Harris notes what news traveled to Washington—namely, that the first bullets had come from insurgent guns, rather than from the weapons of American soldiers. Luis Francia states that after two Filipino soldiers were killed, Willy Grayson of the Nebraska Volunteers yelled racial slurs to rally his fellow soldiers. And Stuart Miller suggests that the events of February 4 did not have to turn into the full-fledged battle that followed on February 5; it was possible, Miller argues, to let the skirmishes die out.[61] But that's not what happened.

In a letter home to his parents Pvt. Henry O. Thompson described the fight: "Our guns were so hot that we burned our fingers on them." After explaining how the battle began—Thompson said Filipino soldiers didn't stop at the checkpoint—he told his mother and father, "Well, I got a chance to shoot at a Filipino, if I didn't get a shot at a Spaniard. One thing I don't know, that is how many I shot and killed."[62] Casualties are hard to determine, but the Philippine side experienced significant losses on February 5, in terms of both soldiers and supplies.[63] The U.S. Senate ratified the Treaty of Paris on February 6, 1899—the same day Thompson wrote in his diary, "You ought to have heard the bullets whistle"—and thus the United States assumed control (however abstract) of the Philippines.[64] U.S. military leaders drew up plans to subdue what they framed as an "insurrection" against their legal authority to occupy the nation's newest territorial possession.

The word *insurrection* is everywhere in the military and civilian records of the period. To call the conflict a war, as we do now, is to acknowledge the legitimacy of Filipino claims to self-government. In 1899, though, the United States did not accept this. To many Americans this was not a war, and Filipinos were not justified in fighting for their independence. Thus they were called "insurrectos" or insurgents.[65] President McKinley used this language to frame Filipino resistance to U.S. imperialism.

Just before Matthew Steele's transcontinental trip to San Francisco, McKinley campaigned in Pittsburgh. He called those fighting for Philippine independence "insurgents" and described their engagement with U.S. troops outside Manila as "a foul blow." "Our kindness was reciprocated with cruelty, our mercy with a Mauser," he said. McKinley continued: "Peace brought us the Philippines, by treaty cession from Spain. The Senate of the United States ratified the treaty. Every step taken was in obedience to the requirements of the Constitution. There was no flaw in the title, and no doubtful methods were employed to obtain it. (Great applause.) It became our territory and is ours as much as the Louisiana Purchase, or Texas, or Alaska."[66] McKinley's campaign speech narrated a seamless story. Just as the United States had purchased much of the North American West, it had negotiated a treaty and purchased the Philippines. Gone from this story are the conflicts between U.S. settlers and Indigenous communities who did not recognize the "purchase" of their land—a purchase negotiated between imperial powers without any attention to the sovereignty of Native nations. Gone are the individual treaties negotiated and broken, the brutal campaigns the army fought against Native people. Gone is any recognition that Filipinos were fighting for independence. McKinley's story was of purchase and expansion, not violence and occupation. But soldiers who had served in the West knew otherwise. They understood that imperial expansion required blood.

So did the soldiers too young to have previously served in the U.S. West. And they relished it. Mary Renda characterizes what boyhood—white boyhood—had emphasized for young men who served in the U.S. occupation of Haiti: virility, strength, "youthful savagery" that would prepare them well when they were men. She stresses the "cultural supports for white manhood"—among them frontier warfare turned spectacle, in the form of Buffalo Bill's Wild West show, the displays at the World's Columbian Exposition in Chicago in 1893, and Theodore Roosevelt's version of his Spanish-American War service in *The Rough Riders*. These elements shored up soldiers' ideas about themselves in relation to service in the Philippines too.[67] Pvt. Henry Thompson told his parents, "I don't care to come home now while there is war, as I like it all right, to hear those bullets whistle past our ears—only my shoulder is black and blue from shooting so much."[68]

After the initial battles for Manila and the surrounding area, U.S. military leaders mapped out strategies for transforming abstract ownership into territorial conquest. And many soldiers found time to write home about the work they had been doing and all that they'd seen. They described beautiful scenery, hard work, and the violence of war. Some relished the opportunity to shoot at Filipinos with abandon. A. A. Barnes of the Third U.S. Artillery wrote to his brother, "I am probably growing hard-hearted, for I am in my glory when I can sight my gun on some dark-skin and pull the trigger."[69] Telfer's letters echo this sentiment. He told his wife, Lottie, "It is great fun for the men to go on 'n—— hunts.'"[70] Many soldiers took pleasure in using their military-issued weapons to inflict pain on their newly appointed enemies; that white soldiers reproduced slurs and both racialized and dehumanized Filipinos underscores how white supremacy and U.S. colonialism often overlapped.

Whether they shared the attitudes of men like Barnes and Telfer, some soldiers regretted having volunteered to serve in the Philippines. Pvt. Frank Loucks of the First California Volunteers wrote home to his brother George, "Well you can thank your lucky stars you stayed at home. The next time Uncle Sam calls for volunteers—I will stand on the sidewalk [and] cheer them as they pass—Go it boys I was a sucker once."[71] Even Barnes told his brother, "Do not be so patriotic as to come here."[72]

Describing the Philippines to People at Home

When Matthew Steele reached Manila, he wrote to his wife, Stella. He outlined the orders he had received—to take over some trenches and, soon, to join Gen. Henry Lawton farther inland (the same Lawton who had won accolades for his role in Geronimo's capture)—and then devoted much of this letter to instructions related to Stella's planned arrival in Manila.[73] This was not unusual; many officers' wives moved to Manila for the duration of their husbands' service, even if they were stationed quite far from the capital city. In fact, Mary Lawton was already established in Manila.

In addition to corresponding with family and friends, Mary Lawton wrote letters describing her new surroundings for her hometown newspaper in Redlands, California. On August 10, 1899, from "HOME," as she typed it, in all caps above her address in Manila, Mary began, "Notwithstanding the accurate descriptions given in the many books and magazine articles on the Philippines, I do not think one realizes at all the actual facts. One must <u>see</u> it to understand the prettiness of the place, and wants to be brought in contact with these people, to appreciate their attractiveness." She continued, "I am wondering what impression my pen pictures give you, and if I can present to you, even in a small way, a correct idea of the many things that interest me so much."[74]

Mary Lawton had an eye for detail, and her position as the wife of a high-ranking officer allowed her access to areas outside Manila. "Occasionally, after an expedition, I am permitted to visit the captured country," she noted, referring to the army's work outside the city. U.S. soldiers moved steadily through the Philippines, establishing outposts, confiscating weapons and ammunition, and receiving notice of surrender from village after village. She described one such visit this way: "We had a real soldier's luncheon at Pasig, of substantial stew, and coffee in tin cups, then, went on our way, close enough to see without glasses, a beautiful country, well cultivated and thickly settled." Of course, Mary knew that the picturesque countryside contained far more than was on display for her benefit. Of her experience witnessing a ceremony of surrender, she wrote, "Who, to look at them, would suspect they had guns hidden in the thicket—who could guess an insurrecto uniform was buried, ready at a moments notice, to cover those 'flags of truce' on their little persons?!"[75] This challenge—the difficulty of identifying the enemy—runs through many accounts of marches in contested territory, and it is bundled together with frequently deployed racialized, and often racist, characterizations of Filipino people.

Newspapers and magazines at home in the United States were desperate for information about the Philippines, and in addition to correspondents like Mary Lawton, several soldiers contributed to local and national publications while they served overseas. Some soldiers also contributed to newspapers produced in the field; James Berkey highlights how these publications helped readers on both sides of the Pacific "see themselves as part of an imagined community of empire."[76] Pvt. Walter Cutter, for example, and his colleague C. L. Clark both wrote letters addressed to newspaper editors or even just to "Dear Folks at Home," with descriptions of their experiences. They took pictures too—one newspaper published a photograph of bodies lying in a field and captioned it "'Just before the Burial': Dead Filipinos Found on the Firing Line after an Engagement," under the heading "Daily Sights with Clark and Cutter at Manila."[77]

Both men were members of the Seventeenth Infantry and documented their experiences for readers in the United States. A September 30, 1899, letter written by Clark offered a description of the Philippine countryside: "More and more I am impressed with the lovliness of the place. The flowers are beautiful but are all strange to me. I do not know the name of any of them."[78] To the editor at the *Farmers' Cabinet* Cutter described the view from his new post at San Carlos, Luzon: "These mountains are grand, especially in the sunset glow. In speaking of the country the other day one of the boys said, 'They can tell of God's country, but the angels must have slept here.'"[79] Though Cutter mentioned the beauty of this faraway country in his published letters over and over again, he did not shy away from describing (or depicting, as in the burial photograph) the less lovely parts of the job. In December he wrote about a hanging but noted that the prisoner's "eyes roamed for a second over the beautiful hills and mountains and then he stepped quietly under the noose."[80]

Other reports of the war also provided photographic evidence of victory—and violence. In *Campaigning in the Philippines Illustrated*, an 1899 volume by Karl Irving Faust, several maps and photographs accompany detailed accounts of the volunteer regiments of the U.S. Army in the Philippines. Alongside descriptions of fighting there are several photographs of the bodies of Filipino soldiers in trenches or on battlefields. Captions for these images describe these bodies—these deaths—as the "work" of one regiment or another: "Work of the Kansas Boys" describes ten or so bodies laid in a line; "Trench Showing Work of Washington Regiment" labels an image of bodies crumpled in a seemingly endless trench; "At the Battle of Tondo.—Work of Minnesota Men" captions a much messier image.[81] These images undermine any arguments for the ease of establishing U.S. control—they make graphically clear what the "work" of empire looked like.

These photos aren't on every page. There are also photographs of soldiers preparing for and engaging in battle and photographs of soldiers burying their dead. Faust, the volume's author, ended the book by highlighting the danger and difficulty of taking photographs "in the open battlefield, under the fire of the enemy." He continues, "It requires as much nerve to take a photograph of a company of soldiers charging the enemy's trenches, as to be one of those engaged in the movement—possibly more, when the enemy is firing wild, or when they happen to select the camera for a target." Faust made a point of acknowledging his own bravery, but he also provided contact information for the other photographers whose pictures were included, "for the benefit of those who may be collecting war views."[82] This small aside hints at a market for these photographs beyond interest in Faust's 1899 volume, published as the war continued.

In 1901 both Cutter and Clark were reassigned. Cutter traveled south to Jolo, "the garden spot of the Philippines." "It is an island paradise," he wrote, describing parks and parrots, flowers and fruit. Cutter noted a coffee plantation, a local hemp industry, and a reservoir from a "cool, clear mountain stream."[83] The paradise he depicted was pastoral; park benches and possibilities for future development added to Jolo's charm, and pearl fisheries and forests filled with valuable timber completed the picture. In personal letters Beverly Daly offered a similar portrait of the island of Negros: "This is certainly a fine island and its resources, which are as yet almost totally undeveloped, are very great. As soon as the Americans begin to colonize, and the engineers get to work remedying the results of Spanish carelessness, Negros is bound to boom."[84] Almost seamlessly, these soldiers connected the paradise they saw with possibilities for future profit, echoing a story that had been told before about the abundance to be found in a supposedly new world.[85]

When Pvt. Needom Freeman of the Twenty-Third Infantry's Company A looked at the Philippines, he saw "a rich country," where "almost anything can be raised that is desired in the line of field and garden crops; fine timber is plentiful and saw mills are yet unknown."[86] Paul Fletcher detailed the abundance of many things, from "cocoanuts" to chocolate, and told his wife, "To be short, anything in the world can be raised here."[87] To an investor interested in the Cagayan Valley, Col. William H. C. Bowen wrote, "Americans who would go there with capital and machinery, pluck and patience, can do anything that can be done in any virgin country."[88] And Maj. Matthew Batson wrote in a field notebook, "Altogether I think the islands are well worth holding and that it would be a great mistake to let them go."[89]

The possibilities the archipelago could offer seemed endless to many Americans. These public and private accounts reflect what Julie Tuason notes in her analysis of National Geographic coverage of the Philippines: emphasis on the commercial potential of Philippine resources, especially in the early years of U.S. military and colonial intervention.[90] So the Philippines would be, could be, a commercial paradise—with the proper (read: white, American) management. In fact, as Rebecca Tinio McKenna demonstrates, though the war was just beginning, U.S. colonial agents were already planning to construct a mountain retreat in northern Luzon.[91] Baguio, a hill station embodying what McKenna calls the "imperial pastoral," was designed by Daniel Burnham (the architect of the White City at the Chicago World's Fair in 1893) and was described by a later visitor, Frank Carpenter, in 1925 as "a garden that would be the pride of any multimillionaire if he could drop it down near New York or Chicago."[92]

While Baguio was still only a vision, U.S. soldiers articulated the possibilities they saw for the islands in their letters. In addition to describing mineral riches and predicting a mining boom that would "attract more people than the Klondike ever did," Freeman used the familiar metaphor of the desert in bloom to describe the archipelago's potential: "Luzon and some other large islands are very fertile, and under proper agricultural management would yield millions and blossom as the rose, but as yet they are blighted by the uncivilized natives." Opportunities that could be developed from the archipelago's natural resources were described alongside possible dangers. Freeman wrote, "A man would be taking his life in his hands to go out in to the country and try to engage in anything. As conditions existed when I was there, bands of hostile Filipinos were scouring the whole interior." Whether he intended the comparison, Freeman's description of local people as "bands of hostile Filipinos" evoked a familiar description for Indigenous people who resisted U.S. control. In Freeman's estimation, it was these "hostile Filipinos" who were responsible for "devastation" of an otherwise "fertile" land.[93]

Walter Cutter, too, contrasted Jolo's beauty with the Moro settlements outside the city's walls. According to Cutter, "A Moro is a savage, pure and simple. Filthy, ignorant, and happy to be so." Though he mentioned no conflicts with these Moros, Cutter noted both their religion (Islam) and their weapons (the barong, a knife that "cuts a man's head from his body at one blow").[94] At the same time that Moros were framed as different and dangerous, soldiers described them with familiar language, positioning them as "savages" in need of a particular form of "civilization"—a racist rubric for progress deployed on both sides of the Pacific at the turn of the twentieth century.

Black soldiers in the U.S. Army served as correspondents for African American newspapers, especially those whose editors were not pleased with the coverage white newspapers typically gave to Black soldiers—coverage that amplified examples of their supposed misconduct and downplayed evidence of their valor and hard work.[95] Multiple soldiers wrote home to correct these representations and also to comment on both the Philippines and Filipinos. Pvt. P. C. Pogue of the Twenty-Fifth Infantry wrote home to the *Cleveland Gazette* on November 24, 1899, to tell how three companies of African American soldiers had captured a garrison and confiscated weapons, documents, ammunition, and supplies. Pogue also described a pamphlet, supposedly written by Aguinaldo, titled, "To the Colored American Soldier," which urged Black soldiers to "consider your situation and your history" in thinking about where their allegiance should lie and made reference to the 1899 lynching of Sam Hose. Pogue explained that "a few [pamphlets] were kept as souvenirs" and then responded this way: "Colored Americans are just as loyal to the old flag as white Americans and it will always be so."[96]

In a February 7, 1900, letter Capt. F. H. Crumbley described the Philippines as "a beautiful country" and declared that "Americans should, and would if they but knew the extent of the value of these islands, feel a great pride in our national acquisition." He highlighted the kindness Filipinos displayed toward African American soldiers and advocated that Black churches send missionaries "as soon as possible."[97] Cpl. C. W. Corbin wrote on November 18, 1899, "This is a fine country in the interior" and in the same letter characterized the Filipinos as "immensely 'human.'"[98] These letters reflect the challenges Black soldiers faced as they navigated a racialized colonial discourse; some expressed different forms of solidarity with Filipinos, strengthened, no doubt, by the behavior of white American soldiers, while others articulated their commitment to country and to the colonial "civilizing" mission, a commitment that offered a possible pathway toward racial uplift for Black soldiers and their families at home.[99] Black soldiers were not monolithic in their thinking about U.S. empire in the Philippines and their role in it, even as they found themselves positioned between white supremacy at home and a racialized imperial hierarchy in the Philippines. Black regiments also had widely variable experiences while serving in the Philippines—what Cynthia Marasigan calls "the unevenness of war" in her examination of Black soldiers' service across at least ten provinces. Different environments and different opportunities for interacting with local communities influenced Black soldiers' ideas about U.S. empire.[100]

An unsigned letter sent to the *Wisconsin Weekly Advocate* offered a direct critique of the American project. The author believed that the Filipinos had a "just grievance." After describing having to listen to white soldiers deploy racist slurs "with impunity" at Filipinos, noting that "at home this is the same vile epithet they hurl at us," he wrote, "I want to say right here that if it were not for the sake of the 10,000,000 black people in the United States, God alone knows on which side of the subject I would be." The letter writer closed by describing the acquisition of the Philippines this way: "Expansion is too clean a name for it."[101]

Hiking and Fighting

It was the pursuit of opposition forces that drew U.S. soldiers farther into the country. But as Mary Lawton and many soldiers noted, identifying "insurgents" was no easy task. Those fighting for independence and against the United States were not always in uniform. Paul Fletcher wrote to Hughine that "the farmer of to-day turns into a fighting man to-morrow."[102] Many Filipinos were fighting to defend their homes and fields against the tactics of total war routinely deployed by U.S. forces—and thus revolutionaries might be among the villagers who welcomed

U.S. soldiers arriving to "capture" more of the archipelago's territory, their weapons and ammunition hidden until needed.[103]

While regiments stationed near Manila adapted to unfamiliar environments, those sent beyond Manila into other parts of Luzon (or to other islands altogether) learned feetfirst how to navigate difficult terrain. Several soldiers described the work of patrolling in search of insurgent forces and supplies not as marching but as "hiking." Soldiers often placed this word in quotation marks, as if to indicate the ways in which hiking was not an adequate descriptor for all they were doing. To a modern-day reader, hiking evokes being surrounded by natural scenery and suggests a certain degree of effort or difficult terrain. Some soldiers linked the terrain of the Philippines to the mountains of the U.S. West; one quoted a commanding officer as saying that "the extreme ruggedness of the range" they traversed in the Philippines "could only be equalled by the Teton Range of Wyoming and Idaho."[104]

Hiking is a form of walking that often requires navigating uneven terrain and more varied environments. These factors can make it challenging; still, many hike for pleasure, for the experience of using our muscles to move through the woods, and sometimes for the reward—a summit, a scene, or maybe a swimming hole. In the late nineteenth century naturalist John Muir wrote in national publications about the importance of preserving California's wild places. Articles he wrote for *Century Magazine* about Yosemite reached two hundred thousand readers, and his words contributed to the swift passage of a bill creating Yosemite National Park in 1890.[105] A few years later he founded the Sierra Club, an organization for "exploring, enjoying, and rendering accessible the mountain regions of the Pacific Coast."[106] Over the following decade the Sierra Club's membership grew, and along with enjoying the California mountains, the group embraced wilderness advocacy. And in 1901, as U.S. soldiers "hiked" through rice fields and mountain ranges on the other side of the globe, Sierra Club members also embarked on a hike, the organization's first High Trip.[107]

Rebecca Solnit writes about wandering in the mountains

as a political act, linked to the preservation at the heart of the Sierra Club's mission: "Walking—or hiking and mountaineering, as the club tended to call it—became its ideal way of being in the world: out of doors, relying on one's own feet, neither producing nor destroying."[108] The word began appearing in early twentieth-century descriptions of adventure and recreation. For example, in a 1901 column called "City Fables" in the *Los Angeles Times*, Albert, a grocer, reads everything he can about camping so that he will be ready to "Hike for the Wilderness."[109] And the *Oxford English Dictionary* points to a 1904 *Chicago Evening Post* article about three girls who "had hiked up the dizzy trail along the face of Glacier to the summit."[110] Even Maud Jenks, in the Philippines alongside her anthropologist husband, Albert, used the word to describe traveling through the "treacherous beauty" of Benguet Province, though a closer look reveals that both Albert and Maud were carried by local people for most of the journey. In her entry for December 30, 1902, Maud wrote, "It has been very tiring riding in a chair."[111]

But U.S. soldiers claimed this word as their own. And from the letters they wrote, it seems that soldiers in the Philippines were hiking—or "hiking"—much of the time. They didn't just use the word in letters home; they also sang it. A stanza meant to be sung to the melody of "I've Been Working on the Railroad" began "Oh, sing a song of hikers, On Datu Ali's trail."[112] Like California Sierra Club members, American soldiers relied on their feet. But in addition to covering an impressive amount of ground, they produced plenty of destruction.

Capt. Charles D. Rhodes proudly characterized his service on patrol as "unceasing vigilance and indefatigable troop movement," to the tune of 2,200 miles covered over a period of eight months in 1901.[113] Pvt. Edwin Segerstrom, who wrote so frequently of the beauty and verdure of his camp outside Manila, used different language to explain more recent experiences: "A person ought to have an iron constitution in order to go through this kind of a life all right."[114] Pvt. Peter Lewis of the New York Volunteers described several "hikes" in letters to his brother, including this one: "We had a pretty hard time of it on that 'hike' most of the time we were up to our waists in mud you see we had to go through Rice fields . . . and we had to plow through them, as it happened we did not come across any amount of Insurgents, but I held a Filipino up and took his Bolo away from him."[115] "Hiking," it seems, included not only extended marching across difficult terrain but also any ensuing encounters with the enemies these soldiers were searching for.

Several soldiers emphasized the physical challenges they navigated while out "hiking" in their letters home. In November 1899 Maj. Matthew Batson of the Fourth Cavalry narrated a challenging route in a letter to his wife, Florence: "The farther we penetrated the jungle the worse it got and the less marked. Soon we were tramping in mud which the carabao had tramped into a slush which pervaded our boots and ground between our toes."[116] And earlier that fall Beverly Daly told his brother Arthur about a gunboat fight, an expedition to Calatrava, and a night march "over horribly muddy mountain trails, through jungles and along the beach." Nowhere near as detailed an account as Batson's, Daly's letter promised that more was to come: "You will get the full account when I send on my journal, which great work is as yet only projected."[117]

War correspondents also covered (figuratively but sometimes literally) the challenging terrain soldiers traveled. John McCutcheon reported on the marching of the Thirtieth Infantry. "Col. Cornelius Gardiner and his men of the 30th have been out walking," he wrote in a piece for the *Chicago Record*. "One day you hear of them at one end of Batangas province and the next day you learn they are in Laguna, while on the third day you're likely to hear that they crossed a mountain range or two and are fighting in Tayabas. A record of their wanderings would include nearly every place on land south of Manila." McCutcheon marveled at the speed and the duration of these marches. "Out walking," quipped McCutcheon, before relaying that the Second Battalion had covered forty miles in twenty-seven hours. While sometimes soldiers traveled along existing roads, many of the paths they followed required scrambling and wading, sometimes even sliding and crawling. McCutcheon described one path that led "through a range of mountains, winding up and down, in some places almost impassable and in all places very hard, even on troops which had been hardened by four-teen days of constant hiking."[118]

Batson described similar challenges: leeches, terrain so steep they needed ropes to avoid falling. Another mission was delayed by the darkness of the night sky. When daylight arrived, Batson wrote, "the rain had obliterated the trail of the band we were following so we retraced our steps." And then he described his exhaustion: "I went to sleep while I was undressing to take a bath in my wet clothes." He told his wife, Florence, "This is the sort of work we are doing all the time now. Not very pleasant either. I think we earn our pay though."[119]

Capt. Frank G. Russell, of the Thirty-Fourth Infantry's Company F expressed similar sentiments. He wrote several letters to recommend recognition of "meritorious service" for a group of men who conducted a rescue mission "over mountains here-tofore thought impassable for white men and through a river whose swift flowing current and rocky banks threatened the life of everyone who crossed."[120] Col. Frank Baldwin made a similar claim in the reports he wrote detailing his 1902 roadbuilding expedition to Lake Lanao: "Troops of no civilized nation had ever penetrated this country to the lake from the south."[121] In the reports they produced for their superiors both men deployed popular ideas about race, "civilization," and climate to empha-size the difficulties encountered—and defeated—by the men under their command. While Russell's Company F completed 3,211 miles of "actual hiking on Luzon" between October 1899 and March 1901, Baldwin's men met with felled trees, thorny brush, and later flooded trenches when their expedition became an all-out attack on Fort Pandapatan, resulting in hundreds of Filipino casualties.[122]

Others extended their descriptions to include the violent dimensions of the work they carried out. Paul Fletcher described endless "hiking" in his letters home to his wife, Hughine. In Feb-ruary 1901, from his post in Cebu ("like a paradise"), he wrote, "We had a terrible 'hike' through mountains, climbing incessantly. It is terrible work, and I am about exhausted." He was also sore: "My feet are covered with blisters tonight and will not need to be rocked to sleep." Fletcher's letters often mentioned Santa Lucia, the destination of a hike that was the worst he had witnessed during his Philippine service. Sometimes he pointed to the physical challenge: "My ankles and knees were dreadfully swollen—forty-four mile-march without food or sleep." Other times he alluded to the trauma: "We have not engaged the enemy since Santa Lucia. I can never forget my feelings as I saw men killed all around me."[123] And a few weeks later he noted, "Tomorrow is my birthday. . . . I will be twenty-four—just a boy. I am aging very rapidly."[124]

Fletcher's letters slipped into this kind of sadness regularly, but never for too long. Thoughts of home seemed to help. But so did the surrounding landscape. To Hughine he wrote, "Here and at it again with the sound of the incoming tide to sooth my restlessness." And the view, too, seemed to bring him comfort. Fletcher was careful to highlight that it was the sight of the mountains—"all around us they rise in grand array"— that calmed him: "I assure you, however, that looking at them appeals far more to the 'bump' of sublimity than climbing them. I know from experience in both."[125] Fletcher preferred his experiences of looking at the mountains to the work of "hiking" in them—and to the violence of fighting. He returned from the field to gaze at the mountains and be soothed by the sound of the waves. For Fletcher, it seems, the beauty of nature was separate from the site of his hard work. But sometimes violence and natural beauty were part of the same field of vision.

John McCutcheon described a battle that occurred in the shadow of Mayon, a volcano that he found particularly impressive. On the morning of January 21, 1900, from aboard the *Helena*, he sketched the volcano and, beneath it, the entrance to Sorsogon Bay (fig. 21). McCutcheon was tagging along on an expedition to open the hemp ports of the Philippines, which involved asserting U.S. control over port cities and then installing customs and revenue agents at them.[126]

Numerous sketches and journal entries demonstrate

21. Sketch of entrance to Sorsogon Bay. McCutcheon Papers Series 3: Works: Diaries and Notebooks, January 1900–March 1901, entry for January 21, 1900, McCutcheon Special Collections, Newberry Library, Chicago.

22. Sketch labeled "Mayon the Beautiful." McCutcheon Papers Series 3: Works: Diaries and Notebooks, January 1900–March 1901, entry for January 21, 1900, McCutcheon Special Collections, Newberry Library, Chicago.

McCutcheon's fascination with the volcano (fig. 22). "One feels that he could gaze at the volcano for days without tiring," he wrote.[127] For the *Record* he described his view of the volcano behind the port city of Legazpi: "The great Mayon volcano, its lofty top shrouded in a clinging bank of clouds, stood alone in its majesty behind the town and looked serenely down on the waving palm trees at the beach and the sparkling waters of the bay." McCutcheon praised Mayon's symmetry, describing how the volcano "rises from the sea in one long gentle slope and then springs up to its enormous height in lines as geometrical as if human hands had shaped it," before pivoting away, grudgingly: "Other events soon drew our thoughts from the contemplation of scenery."[128]

The Battle of Legazpi began with Mayon in view, and McCutcheon's transition from the volcano standing watch to the clash between American ships and Filipino soldiers in the port is an effective narrative device. The scene is set, and the action begins: "On all sides the noise was deafening. The sharp reports of the Krags, which sounded hollow and metallic from the iron sides of the ship, the clatter of bullets on the stone godowns and walls, and the rattling echoes coming back to us; the steady shock of the *Nashville*'s big guns, so near that we on the *Venus* could feel the blast of air; and then the occasional trip-hammer clacking of the Colt's automatic combined, creating a din that was distracting."[129] Kobbé's forces encountered eight hundred Filipino soldiers with fortifications. As the ships fired in support, a small group of American soldiers landed and worked their way around their enemies, ultimately securing the city.[130] McCutcheon described the sights and sounds of the battle, and the mountain was exchanged for the lagoon, accounts of combat on shore, and the bodies of the dead lined up and laid out afterward, "all bolo-men, armed with rough, heavy wooden knifelike clubs."[131] With the port opened, Kobbé and his men, McCutcheon with them, moved on to Catbalogan.

This juxtaposition of the volcano and the firefight reminds the reader that McCutcheon was a reporter, not a soldier. His work was in the observing, in the telling, and to do his work he paid special attention to nature in both his sketches and his written pictures of the war. Some of his sketches feel like notes: a way to document the position of ships or to capture key details about a scene, for later retelling in prose or illustration.[132] Sometimes the details came from interviews, and other times his stories came from his own experiences embedded with U.S. soldiers as they shelled ports, shot "insurgents," or "hiked" nonexistent trails in search of enemy forces and supplies. He wrote that he could "gaze at the volcano for days"; against the backdrop of the most unsettling parts of the war, Mayon seemed to offer some relief. In his notes on the Battle of Legazpi McCutcheon wrote that the "pleasure the men exhibited afterwards was rather sickening."[133] Statements like these distance McCutcheon from the soldiers; though he was right there with them in this Philippine workscape, he was not doing the same work. He could step back and sketch the volcano.

Though Paul Fletcher often separated the beauty of the sea and his view of the mountains from his experiences performing military work in Philippine landscapes, he sometimes read the brutality of war in the land itself. In one letter he linked the terrain with the question of his own survival: "In this wild and uncertain country, death may come swift and certain without one moment's warning." And one day in April three Filipinos were brought to him in his role as an acting army surgeon, their bodies "almost hacked to pieces by bolos and spears." He described these people as "the most horrible looking objects that I ever seen alive," continuing, "This is a bad part of the country."[134]

Sometimes it was U.S. soldiers who materially transformed the Philippine environment into "bad" country. After "insurrectos" cut communication wires linking U.S. forces at Balamban, Cebu Island, with other regiments in the area, Fletcher received orders to take a "hike" of destruction. "On Dec 4th at 11:30 P.M.," he wrote, "Capt. Malley, myself, and forty-two other men went on a 'hike' south of Balamban covering some seventy-five miles of country and mountain region, burning and destroying everything in our way." This was very early in

Fletcher's tour, and it stayed with him: "I can see them now, with the tears streaming down their cheeks begging—entreating the Capt. and then me to save their homes." Still, to Hughine, he attempted to justify his actions: "It was terrible but we had our orders and it was necessary to burn and destroy everything on the west coast of Cebu."[135] Here soldiers transformed the landscape, but not in the service of "improvement." This was violence on the land itself, the burning of "everything" a punitive strategy for a victory that was proving to be far more elusive than the United States had anticipated.

"Indians" and Filipinos

Fletcher's letters repeatedly signaled that while surrender was happening on other islands, it was not happening on Cebu. There local forces were digging in, continuing to fight. Their unwillingness to concede, for Fletcher, seemed at first to justify the brutality of his orders, even if the act of destroying homes and fields left him unsettled. Fletcher's experiences at Santa Lucia shook him, drove him to pray, to commit to being a better man. He critiqued the violence he was part of, but he also wrote about teaching his son to be a soldier, even teaching him to fight with a bolo. Sympathy for Filipino people seemed to exist alongside Fletcher's persistent belief in their savage nature. To Hughine he wrote, "Kiss my boy and tell him that I will make a soldier out of him but want him to fight civilized people. These fellows are worse than Indians." Fletcher made the connection between "Indian fighting" and fighting Filipinos on multiple occasions. Though he wrote, "To paraphrase the adage applied to our own American Indian: 'A dead Filipino is a good Filipino,'" Fletcher had never participated in the campaigns against Indigenous people in the U.S. West; he was both too young and a contract surgeon, not a member of the regular army.[136] Still, he heard and repeated this comparison, placing himself within a frame that connected U.S. settler-colonial violence in the North American West to war in the service of U.S. empire in the Pacific.

Fletcher wasn't the only one to make this link. Pvt. William

Oliver Trafton's memoir is riddled with descriptions of local Filipinos as "indians," their homes as "wild indian villages," their weapons as "tomahawks." In his retelling of a particular skirmish in northern Luzon, he described hearing Tagalog scouts "yelling like a bunch of Comanches." He wrote that one of his fellow soldiers "seemed to think it great fun to fight indians" and also highlighted that his commanding officer had served with Custer in 1876.[137] Another soldier, George Telfer, had served in the Minnesota National Guard before joining up with the Oregon Volunteers. He sometimes drew on his earlier experiences to make comparisons between Filipinos and Indigenous North Americans in the abstract, but more often he relied on racial slurs rooted in anti-Blackness when describing his specific encounters with Filipino forces. Sean McEnroe traces how Telfer's accounts increasingly "show no remorse" and reflect the ways many U.S. soldiers racialized their Filipino opponents as the war progressed.[138]

Describing the charge of U.S. soldiers at Manila in February 1899, Pvt. John Bowe wrote with similar callousness: "The Indians were stampeded, and this sort of hunting was too good sport for our men to stop."[139] Col. Frederick Funston, a key player in the 1901 capture of Aguinaldo, also deployed these comparisons, writing, "I, for one, hope that Uncle Sam will apply the chastening rod, good, hard, and plenty, and lay it on until they come into the reservation and promise to be good 'Injuns.'"[140] David Silbey notes the use of a slur to describe local women linked with U.S. soldiers, which he calls "another echo of the American West."[141] But some soldiers made more positive comparisons between Filipinos and Indigenous North Americans. In a November 9, 1900, letter published in the *Colored Citizen*, Black soldier Arthur Peterson offered a few paragraphs describing Igorot people as both "semi-civilized" and "the most moral people I ever saw." After complimenting their agricultural practices, Peterson wrote, "They are something like our North American Indian."[142]

It would be a mistake to interpret these connections as evidence that soldiers simply brought ideas formulated in other contexts to their service in the Philippines. U.S. soldiers were continuing to work out their ideas about nature and empire as they served, rather than simply projecting a fixed set of assumptions and expectations onto their new circumstances. In fact, some soldiers' experiences as agents of empire changed their perspectives—whether serving to further entrench a set of racist ideas about other peoples and cultures or to open up avenues for critiquing the violence employed in the service of a supposedly "civilizing" mission.[143]

Still, U.S. newspapers covering the Philippine-American War repeated these connections between Filipinos and the Indigenous peoples of North America, especially when writing about Gen. Henry Lawton. Robert Carter, a family friend of the Lawtons who tracked Henry's career meticulously, left behind a scrapbook of letters, reports, and newspaper clippings describing Lawton's successes and his legacy. The two had become friends in the early 1870s and kept in touch while stationed separately. Letters from Henry and Mary are carefully pasted into the scrapbook alongside articles from newspapers and national magazines about Lawton's role in these wars. Headlines like "Sharpshooters Did Fine Work, and Our Men Fought in Regular Indian Style" and captions of Lawton sketches such as "General Lawton, Who Fights Filipinos in Indian Fashion" suggest that Lawton and his men, some of whom fought in the U.S. West against Native people, deployed strategies used successfully by Indigenous warriors against new foes in another frontier setting.[144]

Articles profiling Lawton often mentioned his role in Geronimo's capture as a way of signaling his experience and skill. And still others made him larger than life: a Manila-based newspaper called the *American* headlined a May 1899 article "Lawton, Fighting Machine," with subheadings ranging from "Otis Has Six Feet of Animated Steel as a Lieutenant" to "He Is as Tireless as a Wolf and Can Go a Week without Food or Sleep."[145] In the space of two sentences Karl Irving Faust, author of the 1899 *Campaigning in the Philippines*, called Lawton "the Indian Exterminator" and "the grizzly fighter."[146] Here positioning Lawton in relation to both human and animal targets affirms all the ways he embodied a kind of frontier masculinity, as well as how he presented opportunities for narratively linking U.S. imperial expansion across the North American continent to occupation of the Philippines.

Several histories of the Philippine-American War highlight that many of the men leading army efforts in the Philippines had begun their careers as "Indian-fighters."[147] Some use the past experiences of these officers to illustrate the respect and admiration regulars and volunteers had for their leaders, while others use them to shore up already compelling arguments about race and empire. In still other cases this background is used to make inferences about American political and military strategy.[148] For example, in Katharine Bjork's work tracing the role of scouts and scouting in the U.S. West, Cuba, the Philippines, and Pershing's Punitive Expedition to Mexico in 1916, she shows that the equivalencies soldiers constructed—comparing Native people in the U.S. West to Moros in Mindanao—enabled officers with previous frontier experience to deploy strategies and tactics they had used against Indigenous people to control Filipinos. They created units of scouts, went on missions to remote villages in search of "insurgents" and their supplies, and implemented policies that surveilled, contained, and terrorized Filipino people. "Put another way," Bjork writes, "the Muslim south was Indian Country, a territory far from imperial centers of power where terms laid out in international compacts between colonial powers were contested on the ground by headmen with regional influence who had not been party to their creation."[149] And Stefan Aune has examined how an Indian Wars discourse became portable, constructed and expanded by soldiers and writers looking to make the war in the Philippines legible—for themselves and for their readers.[150]

In her consideration of the visual culture of the Spanish-American War, Bonnie Miller notes that while these connections between Filipinos and Indigenous North Americans were made in prose, political cartoonists mostly chose not to pursue this comparison in their illustrations, perhaps because this would draw attention to dimensions of U.S. settler colonialism that many did not want to remember. Instead, cartoonists made choices that often Africanized their Filipino subjects, amplifying the racial dimensions of colonial domination. Miller makes clear that cartoonists and others deploying these tactics didn't simply impose existing "domestic racial visions" onto new subjects; rather, "cartoonists created an amalgamated racial-imperial type that infused new and often contingent meanings into a shared imperialist vocabulary at home."[151]

As consumers of contemporary media, but also as cultural producers in their own right, soldiers contributed to the construction of cultural ideas about both the Philippines and Filipinos. They reproduced the slurs and insults born of the racist worldview underpinning arguments for colonialism made the world over—racist framings that they would have also consumed in the visual culture of the late nineteenth and early twentieth centuries. But when soldiers encountered material that conflicted with their own experiences, they offered revisions.

For some soldiers the links between Filipinos and Native North Americans circulating in U.S. newspapers had their limits; such readily available and oft deployed comparisons did not always capture their experiences in the field in the Philippines. For example, in an April 1899 letter home Pvt. Edwin Segerstrom of the First Colorado Regiment wrote, "We have been reading with combined amusement & indignation in papers from the states about some of the Insurgents being armed with bows and arrows. I have not run up against any of them so armed in a fight and don't know of any one who has."[152] Maj. Matthew Batson elaborated, writing that Americans "seem to be under the impression that we are fighting a lot of ignorant natives dressed in breech clouts without organization and armed with bows and arrows." Instead, Batson described "an army of patriots armed with Mausers and Remingtons and apparently an abundance of ammunition."[153] Note Batson's use of "patriots" rather than "insurrectos"; this choice seems to hint at his thinking about what Filipinos were fighting for. A few weeks later he told Florence, "They are not savages," even suggesting that missionaries planning to come to the Philippines should be told that "they had better put their missionaries to work in New York."[154]

Though Batson thought that people at home were underestimating the threat, he believed the fighting would be over soon. In December he wrote to Florence, "There will be no more fighting out here to amount to anything . . . so I am willing to go home. But I did enjoy the scraps I have been in, and I have been in a good many. In fact, I think I have had about my share."[155] His "share" included a foot injury that hobbled him for some time and plenty of service under Gen. Henry Lawton, a man Batson considered a friend. This letter about being "willing to go home" was written just a few days after Lawton was killed in battle at San Mateo, felled by a bullet while fighting forces commanded by a Filipino general named Licerio Geronimo. The echo from Lawton's Apache campaign days did not go unnoticed by those remembering him or by men who continued to serve in the Philippines.

Batson did not go home in 1899 as he'd expected and went on to lead the Macabebe Scouts, a regiment of Filipinos willing to serve with the Americans against the "insurrectos." The structure—Filipino scouts led by a U.S. cavalry officer— mirrored a strategy used by some of the frontier's most famous commanders.[156] Batson recounted his skirmish with Licerio Geronimo, the Filipino general, and his account made ample use of the comparative possibilities available to him. To his wife he wrote, "You have, no doubt, seen Geronimo's name mentioned a great many times. He is a man similar to the famous Indian Chief of the same name, and uses much the same tactics. He is a wiley old devil, and though I have been within an ace of getting him several times, he has always managed to elude me." Batson lost Geronimo's trail, but he did claim the soldier's saber as his own. He described it for Florence and then declared, "I will get him yet though. He will not always escape me."[157]

Henry Lawton was the highest-ranking U.S. officer to die in the Philippine-American War. His death devastated many of the men who served alongside him, and the nation mourned. After a military funeral in Manila, his body was shipped to San

Francisco and escorted to Washington DC, where he was given a state funeral and buried at Arlington.[158] Lawton's death amplified the physicality of loss: newspaper coverage tracked the movement of his body from the battlefield, across the Pacific, and then eastward across the country to his final resting place. He embodied, perhaps especially in death, in the circuits of empire his body traveled, the connections between imperial violence on multiple frontiers. And his preserved body reminded the nation of his record of service in both the West and the Philippines.

While General Lawton received a hero's funeral, U.S. forces in the Philippines found themselves fighting in what had increasingly become a guerrilla war. Some soldiers, even as they deployed turn-of-the-century ideas about race and landscape in the letters they sent home, questioned aspects of their participation in the U.S. occupation of the Philippines. In February 1901 Paul Fletcher critiqued what he perceived to be the "hypocritical platitudes" of his government. Right or wrong, the United States needed to be in or out of the Philippines: "If we own them, we own them; if we do not own them, we should get out." He continued, "Above all things, let us do what we do thoroughly; no half-way half-hearted policy, as though we were overstepping our ground."[159]

In Fletcher's mind the imperial project had potential but required fuller commitment. He wrote, "The virgin soil is good and wholesome and it remains to be seen whether we will so fertilize it that a strong, vigorous people will spring up to bless our nation and to revere our flag."[160] This reference to virgin soil— both the material conditions of the Philippines and the political potential for growing a Philippine democracy (or protectorate)— echoed older notions about an earlier American frontier and the possibilities it offered the nation. This idea is captured in the language of "improvement," which has a deep history. To improve, in this context, was to remove land from the wilderness, taking it, claiming it, taming it, and making it productive.[161]

"Improvement" often signaled a particular set of ideas about what sorts of uses—or which users—made land valuable. Soldier's descriptions of both land and resources in the Philippines as "virgin," as awaiting U.S. exploitation, rather than already in use by Filipino communities reproduced the language regularly used to describe both the prospects and the projected outcomes for settler-colonial expansion across North America over the previous century. And Fletcher's language about growing a "strong, vigorous people" reflected the widely embraced frameworks of scientific racism and eugenics, as well as the rhetoric deployed by proponents of assimilationist violence enacted in other imperial contexts, including in U.S. federal policy toward North American Indigenous peoples.

On July 4, 1901, a few days after Fletcher wrote home to Hughine about the "virgin soil" of the Philippines, formal authority over the archipelago was transferred from the U.S. Army to the newly established American civilian government under the leadership of the Philippine Commission and a newly named governor-general, William Howard Taft.[162] Perhaps Fletcher found this encouraging, a step toward formalizing the colonial project and expanding its reach into Philippine society. Or perhaps he thought it another hypocritical action, gesturing toward peace and progress when the military work was not yet done. His letters do not say.

Hughine wrote to Fletcher that their local newspaper was reporting the war's end. His response, dated July 12, 1901, disputed that news and offered as evidence a story titled "A Cebu Adventure." It isn't clear whether Fletcher lived this story, heard it told, or even made it up, but the style is different from the rest of his letters. Fletcher, writing from Cebu, used third-person narration to describe a detachment leaving on a night "hike" amid sublime natural scenery. He contrasted the experience of a new soldier with those who had already done quite a lot of hiking: "To the eye of the young recruit who had just joined, the surroundings were very beautiful, but to the men who had been months in the miasmatic climate enduring rain and sun, the scene was old the poetry all gone."[163] Fletcher doesn't claim these feelings as his own, but it is hard not to hear echoes of his own experiences in lines like "the scene was old the poetry all gone." The story ends abruptly with the capture of two men who were coerced, under threat of death, to lead the U.S. soldiers to an insurgent arsenal. Then Fletcher's first-person voice returns, asking Hughine to give their son a kiss.

Fletcher's next letter describes how, "by the order of an officer wearing the uniform of the United States army," a Filipino man who'd been repeatedly beaten was shot for not knowing where to find insurgent forces. Fletcher's growing disgust for the war and for the behavior of U.S. soldiers becomes clearer with each subsequent letter home: "Until this war, our country had been clean, our national escutcheon had had no stain; but now, I say, that in letters of blood—in dishonor and crime, we have unfurled our flag and become oppressors."[164]

"A Howling Wilderness"

The Philippine-American War is remembered, if at all, for its brutality. And while historians disagree about how widespread certain kinds of violence were, some particularly violent moments became focal points for those who critiqued the U.S. military presence in the Philippines.[165] In June 1901 Paul Fletcher framed his critique in terms of basic decency: "The degradation of a human being by his fellow man is a serious offense in the eyes of God. I do not want to hear more of our civilization + progress after witnessing 'man's inhumanity to man' as typified here."[166] Some of the most brutal events of the war occurred on the island of Samar in the fall of 1901, and they, too, violently transformed the Philippine landscape.

On the front page of the April 9, 1902, *Los Angeles Herald*, the headline rang out: "Instructions of Major Waller: Told to Make Samar a Howling Wilderness; General Smith Directed Him to Kill and Burn and Said the More He Killed and Burned the Better He (Smith) Would Like It." The *New York Journal* kept its headline short, choosing "KILL ALL" in large capital letters.[167] These headlines came from the court-martial of Maj. Littleton Waller Tazewell Waller. (That is not a typo; Stanley Karnow calls Waller "improbably named.")[168] Waller was being investigated for excessive brutality on Samar, specifically for the summary execution of eleven local guides.[169] The proceedings were highly publicized, and as several historians have detailed, they have become stand-ins for the war itself in popular memory.[170] Waller's actions were part of a program to subdue Samar, a response to what Americans called the Balangiga Massacre, when in September 1901 Philippine forces surprised Company C of the Ninth U.S. Volunteers at breakfast and killed forty American soldiers. Twenty-four of the twenty-six remaining soldiers in the company were wounded in the fight. All who could fled to safety.[171]

As a result of the attack at Balangiga, Gen. Adna Chaffee appointed Jacob Hurd Smith to lead the Sixth Separate Brigade, a special force assigned to respond to insurgents on Samar. Smith was a Civil War veteran whose background as an "Indian-fighter" was often mentioned as part of his military experience.[172] Indeed, some of Smith's comments to reporters encouraged this connection. Smith said that fighting Filipino "insurrectos" was "worse than fighting Indians."[173] Under Smith's direction, U.S. forces "tightened a vise on Samar by land and sea."[174] Using a naval blockade and strict licensing rules, Smith sank or confiscated unauthorized boats—226 of them before the end of the year. Residents of Samar endured forced relocation to "zones of concentration," a policy that recalled the treatment of Indigenous people in the U.S. West.[175] Outside these zones U.S. troops wreaked havoc, destroying homes, crops, and livestock. They also tortured suspected "insurrectos" and Filipino civilians and carried out executions without judicial proceedings.[176] Waller was called to defend his actions, and the broader Samar campaign, in the spring of 1902.[177] Waller testified that Smith had instructed him to "make the interior of Samar a 'howling wilderness.'"[178] All these actions—what Thomas Bruno points to as "the triple press of concentration, devastation, and harassment"—were part of carrying out that order.[179]

The words Smith allegedly spoke have a long legacy. There is scholarly debate about whether Smith said the words Waller quoted and, if he did say them, whether he meant them.[180] Some suggest that it may have been General Chaffee who instructed

Smith to make Samar into a "howling wilderness" and that this mission was then passed on to Waller and the Sixth Separate Brigade.[181] Everyone agrees that no matter the wording, the instructions were to employ "the harshest methods."[182] And "howling wilderness" stuck. It found its way into newspaper headlines, and Jacob Smith became known as "Howling Jake."[183] The exact wording of the instructions might not matter for our understanding of their material impact; we have a pretty good idea of what U.S. forces did on Samar.

But the "howling wilderness" is important not only for what it became on the ground but also for what it meant to soldiers and, more broadly, to the American public—to those who read accounts of Waller's and Smith's testimonies. These words offer insight into a frontier mindset that the U.S. military took to the Philippines, a mindset that was then further shaped by soldiers' experiences there. For to create a "howling wilderness" where one had not existed was essentially to destroy—to kill and burn, erasing evidence of cultivation and community.[184]

In U.S. environmental history the wilderness is a central concept; it is foundational to the field. The idea of wilderness helps us understand how Americans have made sense of the natural world and their places in it. The notion of the "howling wilderness" is biblical—outside of Eden, antithetical to paradise. "Wilderness" calls up something dark and primordial, a kind of "beforeness." It was supposedly what pioneering settlers encountered when they arrived in the New World and what generations after those initial transplants met when they moved farther inland. Pioneers struggled against the wilderness to make homes and eventually communities. Wilderness, in this framing, is not something to make; rather, it is something North American settlers consistently sought to unmake—to tame and civilize. Of course, this wilderness was itself an idea, a culturally rooted set of expectations and perceptions imposed on the North American continent by settlers. Environmental historians have devoted ample time to tracing the emergence of the idea of wilderness, at least for white Americans, as a pristine place without people.[185]

However, what looked like wilderness to some was not wilderness to all. What settlers understood to be untouched, unaltered, wild nature was—and is—something entirely different to the Indigenous communities living in these landscapes.[186] For Native people these were not and are not wildernesses; they are homelands. To speak of them as places where people are not is to embrace a worldview that assumes that this kind of separation is natural or desirable. While it may have been desirable for some, it was not for all. In fact, even in the nineteenth century, amid the ongoing settler-colonial violence of Indigenous dispossession, amid growing tensions between a system built on Black enslavement and visions of a world where all were free to work for their wages, wilderness could—and did—serve for some as a place to make a home.[187] Scholarship has recently taken a turn toward expanding our understanding of what wilderness meant in the past; of expanding where—and to whom—we look for ideas about the natural world.[188]

But many U.S. soldiers brought dominant notions of wilderness with them to the Philippines, and they would have been familiar with both versions of it—the older, darker, more terrible wilderness and the newer understanding of wilderness as sublime, pristine, and without people. The soldiers serving under Smith and Waller likely heard echoes of these ideas in their instructions to turn Samar into not just a wilderness but a "howling" one. The younger U.S. soldiers serving in the Philippines were a generation removed from the Civil War, which meant they were also only a generation, maybe two, removed from the peak of U.S. imperial expansion westward. And among the more experienced soldiers were men who had enabled those processes by dispossessing Native nations of their land and by protecting invading U.S. settlers from Indigenous peoples defending their homelands. These men had done the work of transforming western landscapes into just this kind of desirable wilderness—emptied of Indigenous people and ready to bloom—and some of them were career soldiers who had already served at posts within newly designated national parks like Yellowstone and Yosemite.[189] Whether newly enlisted or career army men, many soldiers had heard, read about, or even seen the western landscapes regularly framed as pristine and sublime. In addition to these associations with wilderness, however, soldiers serving in the Philippines might also have recognized more recent resonances.

For example, in the fall of 1901 John Muir published *Our National Parks*, a book based on a series of pieces (sketches, he called them) he had written for the *Atlantic Monthly*. It opened this way: "The tendency nowadays to wander in wildernesses is delightful to see. Thousands of tired, nerve-shaken, over-civilized people are beginning to find out that going to the mountains is going home; that wildness is a necessity."[190] Wilderness wandering was not exactly what American soldiers were doing in the Philippines, but they would have been aware of the growing popularity of the activity, as evidenced by their appropriation of "hike" to describe the long marches and accompanying violence that constituted much of their work in the field.

Muir was perhaps the best-known advocate for American wilderness; he wrote extensively about his adventures in the mountains and forests of the Pacific Coast, and he continued to escape into the Sierras or the Alaskan backcountry or the Pacific redwood forests whenever he could. He celebrated the nation's four national parks—Yellowstone, Yosemite, General Grant (now part of Kings Canyon National Park), and Sequoia—and thirty-eight reserves adding up to forty million acres, which Muir described as "unspoiled as yet," though they were endangered by those in the mining, grazing, and lumber industries. When describing the Black Hills and the million-acre reserve there "made for the sake of the farmers and miners," Muir repeated false claims about Indigenous disappearance: "The Indians are dead now. . . . Arrows, bullets, scalping-knives need no longer be feared; and all the wilderness is peacefully open."[191] But even this now "peacefully open" wilderness, in Muir's telling, needed protection from exploitation and development.

In fact, Muir pointed to national parks under the care of the U.S. cavalry as examples of forests that were "flourishing, protected from both axe and fire."[192] U.S. soldiers had been detailed to guard and manage Yellowstone, the nation's first national park, since the 1870s. And U.S. soldiers were tasked with managing both Yosemite and Sequoia, park landscapes dear to Muir, until 1913.[193] Members of the Ninth Infantry, one of the nation's Black regiments, under the leadership of Capt. Charles Young (the third Black graduate of West Point), were detailed to Sequoia and General Grant National Parks in 1903 after their Philippine service.[194] Road construction was one of their many tasks, and during their tenure in these parks Young's men extended one road to the base of Moro Rock—so named not for Muslim Filipinos but apparently for a bluish-tinged mustang belonging to a Mr. Swanson in the 1860s.[195] Still, for soldiers returning from the Philippines, the echo would have been hard not to hear.

These seemingly disparate places of rugged beauty were linked by more than the soldiers who moved through them. Rather, soldiers and their service were evidence of much deeper connections between dispossession, preservation, occupation, and empire. Stolen land undergirded it, along with a narrative of conquest that soldiers heard, performed, and retold. Different pieces of the story might stand out more in one place or another, but whether soldiers were serving in the Philippines or the U.S. West, or had been deployed specifically to protect and preserve national parks, they were participants in a broad imperial project.

U.S. soldiers still stationed in the Philippines—soldiers whose earlier service included tours of duty in the West, on the plains and in the Southwest—would have recognized the military's ongoing relationship with North American wilderness. Younger or newer soldiers, both regulars and volunteers, would likely have carried with them to the Philippines an awareness of the language of preservation, as well as some knowledge of the army's role in emptying land of Indigenous people before setting this same acreage aside for white settlement, for parks, and for forest reserves. They would also have encountered the proliferation of prose, paintings, and photographs depicting western wonderlands as spaces for the kind of wandering in the newly protected wilderness Muir and other preservationists advocated as a balm to soothe the stresses of daily life at the turn of the twentieth century.[196] Some men, Fletcher and McCutcheon among them, made regular use of Philippine nature as a kind of salve for their worries and discomfort.

This context makes Smith's instructions to Waller rather curious. Given these turn-of-the-century associations with wilderness, what did it mean to "make" one? We know that the directive to turn Samar into a "howling wilderness" was understood by U.S. soldiers: not only did earlier American meanings of wilderness (and the crucial inclusion of "howling") square with what the U.S. military did on Samar, but soldiers with experience in earlier theaters would have recognized in Smith's words the tactics of "hard war" or "total war" deployed both in the Civil War and in campaigns against Indigenous people. Lisa Brady has written about the agroecological destruction ordered by Union generals as part of a broader strategy to win the U.S. Civil War.[197] This particular directive to "make" a wilderness on the island of Samar demanded that soldiers enact older visions of wilderness—"howling," terrible, a place without civilization—even as they engaged with newer cultural understandings of wilderness as pristine and beautiful.

Though scholars continue to probe the historical meanings of wilderness for more and different communities, a dominant framing of American wilderness as pristine, as a place without people, crystallized in the late nineteenth and early twentieth centuries, as figurative erasure followed material dispossession of Indigenous people in what became the U.S. West. In the Philippines soldiers demonstrated their facility with multiple visions of wilderness in this new-to-them context: they noted the archipelago's beauty and the possibilities it presented for U.S. interests, and they understood instructions to transform Philippine landscapes in ways that unmade them, returning them to what U.S. soldiers imagined to be a "howling" state. Wilderness, then, was a culturally constructed—and at Samar, a physically created—product of U.S. colonialism.

U.S. soldiers in the Philippines also signaled their deftness with multiple visions of empire. They described a civilizing project that was benevolent on the page and brutal in practice. They imagined themselves conquerors, forecasting possibilities to cultivate or exploit local resources. And they used "nature" language to narrate imperial work, expanding the definition of hiking to include the techniques of total war. In orders given, letters written home, and accounts published in local papers, U.S. soldiers made use of previous encounters with both nature and empire to describe the landscapes of their service and to convey what the work of empire was like. And sometimes their on-the-ground experiences prompted reflection on—or revision of—their commitment to that work.

4

Collecting the Philippines

IN FEBRUARY 1901 GIFFORD PINCHOT, THE CHIEF FORESTER of the United States, received a letter in the mail from his old friend George Ahern. Captain Ahern had been assigned to lead the newly formed Philippine Bureau of Forestry, a position he hoped to retain after the formal transfer of power from the U.S. military to the U.S. colonial civilian government in the Philippines.[1] "Dear Pinchot," he wrote. "By this mail I send you a specimen of the leaf + flower of a new tree species, 'Cananga Aherneana,' as named by our botanist Regino Garcia who was with me on a recent trip to Mindanao where this species was discovered."[2] Clearly thrilled, Ahern exclaimed, "This is fame! When McKinley's statue is in dust 500 years hence my Cananga will flourish." And then for reference Ahern linked "his" *Cananga* to existing taxonomies, identifying its relation to the ylang-ylang tree (scientific name *Cananga odorata*), "from the flowers of which a celebrated perfume is extracted."[3] The local name for the tree, ylang-ylang, may be connected to the Tagalog word for "wilderness," *ilang*; other possibilities include "wild," "isolated," and "desert," all reminders that naming practices can reflect existing power structures and deeply contextualized local connections.[4]

Regino García's choice of name, *Cananga Aherneana*, situates this particular species in place and time and, more specifically, in empire. While ostensibly honoring Ahern in name, following patterns established by European botanists who themselves were following the habits of earlier colonizers, *Cananga Aher-*

neana operated as a kind of marker, making visible the connections between U.S. occupation of the Philippines and the colonial scientific knowledge production it enabled.[5]

At the time of Ahern's letter to Pinchot, moves toward a civilian colonial government in the Philippines continued apace. In the summer of 1901 William Howard Taft was appointed governor-general of the Philippines by President McKinley. In September McKinley was shot at the Pan-American Exposition in Buffalo, New York; he died from his injuries, and Theodore Roosevelt was sworn in as president of the United States. The Balangiga Massacre and "Howling Jake" Smith's violent response followed soon after. In early 1902 court-martial proceedings catapulted what had happened on the island of Samar into the headlines, but even as the testimony revealed the brutal tactics deployed by U.S. soldiers, the tide was turning. Much of the Philippines was already under U.S. colonial management, an outcome with an "astonishing cost," writes Christopher Capozzola.[6] And though significant parts of the south still resisted U.S. control—indeed, fighting there would continue into the second decade of the twentieth century—President Theodore Roosevelt declared the war over on July 4, 1902.

Later that year Pinchot traveled to the Philippines by way of Russia and the newly completed Trans-Siberian Railroad. Perhaps in part he was responding to Ahern's 1899 invitation, "Come out here as soon as the war is over + your head will swim at the variety and beauty of the woods."[7] But he was also traveling in his capacity as chief forester of the Division of Forestry under the U.S. Department of Agriculture. He toured Russian forestry efforts before reconnecting with his old friend in Manila.

Pinchot's impression of the Philippine coastline from his transport vessel was not so different from what U.S. soldiers saw as they approached the islands. As a forester Pinchot paid particular attention to the trees of the Philippines. Even from the water he observed that "forests run from the summit of the Mountains down to the edge of the water, and, as we see them from a distance of a couple of miles, they are evidently composed, at least in part, of large trees."[8] On arriving in Manila

Harbor and receiving an invitation from Governor-General "Will" Taft and his wife, Helen, to stay at their palace, Pinchot immediately marveled at "the beautiful floors—wide planks of dark narrawood, polished by rubbing with bitter oranges cut in two."[9]

Though Pinchot was pleased with his reception, he was eager to get out of the palace and into the islands' forests. Taft gave Pinchot the use of his gunboat and outfitted him for a preliminary survey of Philippine forest resources. Pinchot described the trip this way: "Nothing could be more delightful than cruising among these wonderful islands, where there are new things to be seen at every landing, and where the variety of forest and topography is so great that interest never flags."[10] To his father he described his "first real sight of a tropical forest," writing, "It was full of the keenest interest, although somewhat bewildering to be dropped into the midst of a forest not one tree of which I knew."[11] No matter. Despite the mystery of all these new kinds of trees, the more Pinchot saw of the Philippines, the more he began to develop a picture of their timber potential.

As the lead forester of the United States, Pinchot would have been balancing a range of concerns about the practice of forestry back home: the management of federal forests, the growth of a department that needed to be staffed by trained and knowledgeable foresters, and the politics of advocating for conservation of the nation's natural resources. These resources now included Philippine forests, and scholars of empire and imperial forestry have noted the ways that resource extraction and management techniques were observed, borrowed, and shared.[12] U.S. officials participated in these processes too.

While Pinchot's 1902 exploratory trip through Russian and Philippine forests could situate him as a more broadly international—and imperial—forester, his tour is scarcely more than a footnote in U.S. environmental history. Pinchot's place in that field is as the voice of conservation, the wise use of resources, the "greatest good to the greatest number"—an approach to natural resource management regularly positioned opposite John Muir's preservation, a perspective steeped in celebrating the beauty of western landscapes whose adherents pushed for the protection of large swaths of the West from development or destructive use.[13] But this framing of these two men as oppositional embodiments of competing worldviews, while a useful shorthand for turn-of-the-century U.S. environmental thinking, is a bit too neat. Conservation and preservation were overlapping approaches to managing U.S. public lands— sometimes in tension but often aligned around outcomes, if not ideas.[14] Neither approach challenged the settler-colonial foundation of protecting as U.S. federal property lands stolen from Indigenous people. And though each offered strategies for navigating the frenetic world of the late nineteenth and early twentieth centuries—Muir recommended spending time in the wilderness, while Pinchot advocated for better planning and scientifically managed natural resources—neither argued against U.S. imperialism. Empire, it seems, was capacious enough for the ways both men approached the natural world.

Both men traveled along imperial pathways that led them to the Pacific. Pinchot's Philippine journey occurred in 1902; he visited to evaluate its timber resources in his official capacity as the nation's lead forester. Muir also made time to see the Philippines in 1904 while on a round-the-world trip that had been framed as a botanical collecting expedition. Muir's trip began alongside Charles Sprague Sargent, a Union Civil War veteran who directed Harvard's Arnold Arboretum; it opened with a European circuit and then followed in Pinchot's footsteps across Russia by way of the Trans-Siberian Railroad. In China Muir and Sargent parted ways, and Muir traveled through Singapore, India, the Himalayas, Egypt, and then on to Australia and New Zealand, botanizing and pressing plants for his personal collection as he went.[15]

From on board a ship named the *Empire*, Muir sailed north to the Philippines. He noted in his diary the Sulu archipelago's "beautiful shores" and "nobly massive" trees and commented that Mindoro was a "gloriously beautiful isle." Though he made only a short visit, Muir was also received by Ahern and even escorted on "a most instructive trip" during which he "saw many villages, rice fields, battlefields."[16] Muir praised the cultivation practices he observed outside Manila. As a grower himself—Muir was by marriage the proprietor of a substantial ranch in California's Alhambra Valley—his appreciation came from a place of familiarity, even as he encountered new species and practices.

But California was never all that far away. While in Manila he met a Mr. Fitzgerald, who, Muir wrote, "showed me many fine photos of Hetch Hetchy region made while making surveys for San Francisco water supply."[17] The work of natural resource management, it seems, was critical for controlling both Californian and Philippine environments, and agents of the state on both sides of the Pacific were busy observing, surveying, naming, and ordering the nature they were tasked with governing.

Pinchot's 1902 Philippine trip covered much more ground—or sea—than Muir's; the southern leg of his Philippine forest survey encompassed about 2,300 miles, much of it on Taft's gunboat.[18] Pinchot's notes include assessments of the potential of various forests, as well as brief descriptions of even the smallest islands. His account conveys a sense of great possibility: "The forest was the most luxuriant I have yet seen"; "the untouched forest was in a superb condition"; "it is exceedingly rich"; "its value is unquestionably very great." Pinchot also found some of the islands particularly beautiful, calling one collection of limestone islands "the most picturesque I have ever seen."[19]

Pinchot also commented on the challenges of moving through the country. Of Malabang he wrote, "The vigor of the life in this forest was most striking. Much of it was literally so dense that a man without a bolo would find it impossible to make more than a few yards an hour."[20] Pinchot's descriptions of the challenging terrain were similar to the ways soldiers described the country they "hiked" in search of supposed insurgents. Navigating this ground himself, Pinchot found much to praise when it came to the U.S. Army. "The army has certainly had a much harder time out here than most people know about," he told his father, "and is doing its work in a way that should win admiration instead of attack."[21] To illustrate this point Pinchot highlighted the continuing danger posed by moving through territory only nominally under U.S. control. While camping at Mataling Falls he noted, "No one leaves the tents in this camp, even within the line of sentries, without being armed. . . . It happened not uncommonly in the early part of the trouble that sentries, and even outposts, were cut up at night."[22]

Pinchot relayed his impressions of the American army to Roosevelt in letters sent from the Philippines, alongside comments about the "enormous resources in timber" he found there. He stressed the "enormous difficulty of the country in which our troops are at work" and described the officers he encountered as "men of so high a grade that it makes me proud to be an American every time I see them."[23]

While Pinchot was touring Philippine forests, Maj. Edgar Mearns was collecting birds and mammals in and around the wonderland of Fort Yellowstone, within the boundaries of Yellowstone National Park. Fort Yellowstone was the headquarters for the park, which remained under the administration of the U.S. Army until 1918. In fact, after serving at multiple posts in the U.S. West and then suffering an injury in the Spanish-American War, Captain Ahern had hoped to become the park's military superintendent, but politics got in the way. Only after it became clear that Yellowstone wasn't an option did Ahern request an assignment in the Philippines.[24] As part of the military occupation of the Philippines, he took over the existing Spanish colonial forestry bureau in April 1900 and began reviewing existing records and making plans.[25] Ahern's interest in national parks and natural resources in the West and the Philippines is one example of the connections between soldiering and work focused on managing the natural world. From different vantage points, then, Pinchot, Muir, Ahern, and Mearns were all part of an imperial network dedicated to colonial science and natural resource management. While Captain Ahern was assigned to a military role in the colonial government, Mearns was to be in the field, part of the U.S. forces engaged in ongoing fighting to fully occupy the south.

As an agent of U.S. empire through both his military appointment and his contacts within the Smithsonian, Mearns's Philippine service illuminates the interconnected nature of military violence and natural history collecting, from the increasingly blurred boundaries between fighting and fieldwork to the overlapping networks engaged in the military occupation of Mindanao and the collection of scientific specimens, and later to the vision developed for the display of the Philippines at the 1904 St. Louis World's Fair. A kind of imperial vision made the Philippines an exciting place for men like Mearns and Ahern to practice natural history and forestry; this vision also shaped the expectations of those not with them in the field.

Encouragement from the Smithsonian

When the war with Spain began Major Mearns was stationed at Fort Clark, Texas. In letters to his museum colleagues he wondered when—and where—he might be deployed overseas. Charles Richmond, the assistant curator of birds at the United States National Museum, wrote to Mearns that in Washington "war rumors are in the wind."[26] But Mearns was not sent to Cuba. Instead, he was ordered east to Chickamauga and then Camp McKenzie in Georgia to work with the Reserve Hospital Corps. He was next assigned to Fort Adams, in Rhode Island. After several months of medical leave he was ordered to head west again, to Fort Yellowstone, and then back to Fort Snelling in Minnesota. He kept up his correspondence with museum curators and scientists even as he moved around the country— and it is the letters these colleagues wrote in response to news of Mearns's orders to report to the Philippines that hint at his feelings on the subject.

Frederick W. True, the curator of biology at the National Museum, wrote, "My Dear Dr. Mearns: I can understand exactly how you feel about going to the Philippines. Under the circumstances, it seems as if another officer might have been selected. It must be very disheartening to have one's affairs upset so ruthlessly." We can hear an echo of how Mearns shared the news in True's next line: "Of course, as you say, that has to be expected in the service, but it *does* seem to me that you have not been treated fairly in this case—I should think you might have been left at Ft. Yellowstone or Ft. Snelling for at least two years." And from there the letter turns lighter. True asked, "Why don't you retire and let the younger men do a little hustling around? Then you could finish up your reports and get some satisfaction out of life."[27]

Numerous letters mention Mearns's health, and not just because many of his contemporaries believed that white people were not well suited to tropical environments. Mearns contracted malaria early in his career, and it seemed to recur with some regularity. In fact, a few years earlier Mearns had received twelve months of sick leave, part of which he spent collecting specimens for the Smithsonian in Florida—after being fitted for a special medical corset to stabilize his stomach and spleen, which seem to have been displaced by the malarial "paroxysms" he sometimes experienced.[28] While resting and collecting in Florida Mearns wrote to his wife, Ella, "I hate the thought of an army post again. How I wish I had been retired! (But don't tell anybody so.)"[29]

Mearns seemed surprised to be sent to the other side of the world; although he didn't let his medical issues get in the way of his avid pursuit of scientific specimens, he wasn't the picture of health in 1903. But his fellow naturalists and scientists sent consoling, encouraging words—think of what he'd see in the Pacific!—and others offered advice on gathering and preparing specimens for transit around the world.[30] Some focused on what Mearns's presence in the Philippines could mean for the National Museum. For example, one colleague wrote, "The only thing that saves our material from there from being disgraceful is that we haven't any, so the prospect of getting something from you is very gratifying. After you get over there I think you will be glad you were sent particularly if you can help moving about."[31] And True, referencing contemporary concerns about whiteness and tropical environments, told Mearns, "Now, don't get the idea into your head that the climate will kill you—we won't make any provision for such a contingency. I have faith and believe you will come back all right, with a good lot of valuable material."[32]

The paper record suggests that Mearns's colleagues at the National Museum were sincere in their excitement about what Mearns might encounter—and collect. Alongside letters of encouragement are letters of introduction, fixed with the seal of the Smithsonian. And there are requests: freshwater shells but not "large and showy marine shells"; "plants of all kinds, large and small" for the herbarium. These were in addition to the birds Mearns was expected to obtain.[33] Leonard Stejneger, the museum's reptile specialist, asked Mearns to "pay special attention to the small, inconspicuous, dull-colored, nocturnal or burrowing species," while E. J. Brown, a friend from Mearns's Florida trip, asked for seeds of "desirable fruits, that so far as you know have not been introduced here." He also quipped to Mearns, "Be careful that some of the natives don't serve you up as a novelty, 'Broiled ornithologist on toast'"—which gives us an idea of the kind of "information" circulating in the United States about the Philippines.[34]

While the Smithsonian scientists seem to have stayed away from commenting on the politics of Mearns's new assignment, one zoologist, Mary Rathbun, may have hinted at some ambivalence about the larger U.S. imperial project in the Philippines when she asked Mearns for freshwater crabs.[35] "If you could get a good lot of these crabs from many localities," she wrote, "we shall not have taken possession of the Philippines in vain."[36]

The Smithsonian offered materials to aid Mearns in pursuing his work as a naturalist. Perhaps True said it most directly: "If you *are* going to the Philippines, we want you fixed to get specimens to the best advantage. That is rather a selfish way of looking at the matter, but you will understand that a museum has no modesty."[37] Mearns did understand—and the potential the Philippines presented him for growing the museum's collections may have offered him some comfort at this point in his career. Armed with literature on Philippine nature from his friends at the museum, Mearns traveled west to San Francisco, where he reported for duty.

Mearns set sail for the Philippines on July 1, 1903. "Weighed anchor after luncheon + passed through Golden Gate," he wrote. He had managed to see and hear birds at Golden Gate Park, Cliff House, and the Presidio before departing on the *Sherman*. Mearns recorded seeing albatross, flying fish, terns, and petrels on the way to Guam (also occupied by the United States as a result of the Treaty of Paris, which authorized the purchase of the Philippines from Spain), where he went ashore and "got skull of deer." On July 25 Mearns noted that they had seen land that afternoon, and he made a list of things to do on his arrival, including "Visit Capt. Ahern," "Visit Manila Museum," "Call on Chief Surg. Officer," and "Try on suit."[38] Amid lists and lists of birds appear occasional lists of tasks; daily life creeps into Mearns's records of birds seen, shot, and collected. Mearns did not stay in Manila long; by early August he was already at his assigned post on the island of Mindanao. Richard McGregor of the Manila Museum told Mearns in a letter, "You are going to a good island."[39]

Mindanao was "Moroland" to U.S. forces, home to predominantly Muslim Filipinos grouped together by the Spanish under the category "Moro." Even though President Roosevelt had declared the Philippine-American War over the previous July, the fighting had not stopped in Mindanao.[40] While Governor-General Taft continued the work of establishing a civilian colonial government—aided by passage of the Organic Act, which spelled out governing structures, citizenship status, and future plans for a colonial legislative assembly composed of Filipino members—the U.S. military was tasked with quashing ongoing resistance to the U.S. occupation in the south.[41] Civilian governors were named for other islands and provinces, but military authorities remained in control of Mindanao.[42] Pointing to the reestablishment of military control over regions beyond Mindanao in the years that followed Roosevelt's initial proclamation, Paul Kramer calls the end of the war "a beleaguered fiction that broke down in unflattering reversals."[43]

Still, for many in the Philippines the war had ended, and the Philippine Commission, along with Taft, established a colonial government that installed U.S. department heads while working to cultivate collaboration with Filipino elites. Ahern led the Bureau of Forestry, and Dean Worcester became the secretary of the interior.[44] American colonial bureaucrats drafted plans for managing the people and resources of the Philippines. The formal work of imperial administration, which Michael Adas describes as a "vast engineering project," had begun.[45]

Meanwhile, in Mindanao the U.S. military pursued its own strategies for colonial governance. When Mearns arrived Gen. Leonard Wood had just assumed the military governorship of Moro Province, which included Mindanao, Palawan, and the Sulu islands to the south. Wood took a more active approach to imposing U.S. rule in Mindanao: he organized local military-led governments, levied taxes, established American schools, and confiscated and reallocated land. He implemented rules that challenged societal norms and undermined the power of local leaders, called datus.[46] And he led a series of punitive expeditions, using violence to persuade the residents of "Moroland" to adjust to U.S. power throughout the south.[47] Flattening the people of Mindanao and the Sulu archipelago into a single category was, as Oliver Charbonneau has pointed out, "a strategy of colonial rule."[48] This move to simplify and reduce echoes practices used by the U.S. government to order and control Indigenous people in North America.

Wood had served with Gen. Henry Lawton in the Apache campaigns and most recently in Cuba as its governor-general.[49] Hermann Hagedorn opens the second volume of his Wood biography with an evocative description of Wood's new post:

In tropic waters, a vast, green crab stretches out an irritated claw after a school of minnows skipping off in the direction of Borneo. The crab is the island of Mindanao, the minnows are the Sulu Archipelago. Southward along the menacing claw the steamer bears the new governor. On the left is a jagged shore rising three thousand feet or more to a ridge

dark with forests; on the right is the purple placidity of shel-
tered waters where white-winged *lorchas*, schooner-rigged,
carry cargoes dreamily this way or that across the Sulu Sea,
or naked men in queer outrigger canoes float on the swells
like huge birds. The air is heavy in the midsummer heat.[50]

Hagedorn's pen practically oozes imperial prose. He describes
the languid life of those in the tropics, all the while demonstrating that ideas about "primitive" peoples and practices circulating in Wood's time persisted in Hagedorn's. He writes of "the
world of the white masters" in describing structures built by
the Spanish; he calls Moro homes "filthy and picturesque"; he
speaks of the "monsoon [that] blows softly" and of "Arabian
Nights."[51] Hagedorn is not wrong that Mindanao looks like a
crab, but beyond that his prose mostly demonstrates how colonial officials might have viewed Mindanao through racist and
imperialist glasses. Hagedorn portrays Wood's Mindanao as "a
wild country" with "a wilder people."[52] And in order to govern
Mindanao, Wood decided he needed to experience it.

On August 8 Wood was aboard the *Borneo* to tour this new-
to-him territory. Hagedorn calls it "a country to stir Wood's
blood."[53] Mearns was aboard the *Borneo* on the following day.
His notes are rather scattered and initially more focused on
the birds he saw than on his direct orders. But if his papers
are any indication, during his first few months of service he
rarely stayed in one place. The pages of Mearns's Philippine
field books are filled with bird lists from all over Mindanao; the
potential for collecting materials new to the Smithsonian—
and perhaps even new to western science—was already clear.

To Mearns collecting work paired easily with his military
medical assignments, but not everyone in the army shared this
view. As early as 1899 Mearns had written a letter to True at
the Smithsonian about the ways "bug doctors" were perceived
by their higher-ups in military circles. It seems that True had
floated an idea for integrating the museum's goals into existing
military operations by identifying an officer serving as part of
the immediate staff of the commanding generals everywhere

the U.S. military was stationed—Cuba, Puerto Rico, the Philippines—in order to "act as an agent and supervise the collection of ethnological and historical materials in those countries."[54] The Army Medical Museum had requested similar service of medical officers stationed across the North American West earlier in Mearns's career, emphasizing the collection of cultural belongings and Indigenous ancestors.

Now, though, Mearns told True that "outside interests are severely discouraged by the War Dept.," prompting Mearns to postpone work on some of his earlier collections because of concerns related to his prospects for promotion. Mearns conceded to True that some doctors had earned "the feeling hostile to general scientific pursuits" because they pursued science while "grossly neglect[ing] their profession and patients." Mearns did not approve of those men. "My own policy," he wrote, "is to work quietly and avoid friction, biding my time. When I reach the head of my department, scientific research will be encouraged throughout the Corps—medicine first, but all science as well. The naturalists of our corps made a strong showing during the last war—better than the 'military' doctors!"[55] When Mearns wrote this letter he did not yet know that he would soon be ordered to the Philippines, and that from there he would be able to do exactly what he and True had imagined in their letters.

Imperial Violence

Unlike the registers and reports from Mearns's earlier frontier postings, his Philippines field books are raw and unpolished— works in progress, filled with smudges and strikethroughs. Put plainly, some of them look as though they've been through a war. And according to the entries Mearns wrote inside them, they have. Nowhere in Mearns's records of his service in the U.S. West does he write of combat; even when serving during the Apache campaigns he wasn't on any kind of front line. But now Mearns was fully in the field, and that meant fieldwork of all kinds. These field books contain descriptions of combat: "Went on a hike to capture the Sultan of Bacayauan named

Macabato," Mearns wrote on August 20, 1903. "I helped to kill the sultan's brother, and took his war bag, containing, powder, bullets, balls of brass, poisoned stones in wooden tubes, Crag [Krag] shells + bullet, bolts + other missiles [?] for use in guns in lieu of bullets."⁵⁶ In a typed itinerary detailing his fieldwork, Mearns further clarified his role in the fighting: "The command was fired upon, and in the fight that followed, 14 of Macabato's men were killed. (Three of them I killed with my shotgun.)"⁵⁷ Here Mearns seems to be clarifying that he fired his collecting gun at Moro people, further blurring the boundaries between military and scientific work.

Mearns's notes on the violence against Moro people are consistent with Wood's activities on the island of Jolo—the same place Pvt. Walter Cutter had described as a paradise a few years earlier. On Jolo Wood went after Datu Panglima Hassan, who moved inland to resist U.S. occupying forces. Wood described the march to find him as "one of the hardest and roughest marches I have made for a long time."⁵⁸ Hassan escaped after Wood's men captured him, but this series of "hikes" resulted in somewhere between 1,200 and 1,500 Moro casualties (and 17 on the American side).⁵⁹ Campaign after campaign ended with massive Moro losses, but Wood's attempts to bring Mindanao under complete U.S. military control remained unsuccessful. Mearns accompanied Wood on several of these punitive expeditions, ostensibly to provide medical care to wounded soldiers. The small number of U.S. casualties seems to have allowed Mearns to participate in the fighting and collect when he could.

The notebooks from Mearns's Philippine service, especially from these early months, preserve the shifting nature of the field: sites of specimen collection became battlefields and then scientific field sites again immediately afterward. For example, the entry for November 12, 1903, begins with white cockatoos and "a few small flocks of large green parrots." The following line reads, "Brown Java Sparrows," and the next, "1 Moro killed + 2 wounded." After that is a note about where to find good shells, the name of an island with pigs, and then this: "Killed 20–30 Moros + wounded many."⁶⁰ A few days later, on November 16,

Mearns wrote, "Three columns of troops moved forward. Dr. Hicks on right, Patterson with major Bullard's central column, Lewis and Gynn with Scott's column on the left. I remained in camp at foot of Crater Lake Mt."[61] And then a list begins:

Cockatoo, Quail, Dove, Crow
Brown Java Sparrow, Gray
Martin, Chelidon, Yellow-
Bellied Wagtail, Sedge Warbler
Black Starling
125 Moros killed, 76 in
one stand.
Little Dark Bittern
White-tailed Tattler, sirge flavipes
Small flocks great green parrot,
flight + notes like duck.
Flock of 1–200 Cockatoos at
evening feeding in corn + tapioca fields.[62]

These lists are both ordered and messy. For some dates, like this one, there's a brief narrative of the day's activities—miles marched, species seen. It is not unusual to find a discussion of birds shot mixed with a record of the number of Moros killed. Sometimes the phrasing is passive, a record of what has transpired; other times Mearns indicates that he is the one doing the killing. These lists seem to suggest that Mearns was documenting birds seen and people shot in real time; in this tangled composition Filipino casualties and birds observed are entries in the same list. Even if he intended to separate them, each kind of work seems to bleed into the written record of the other: his scientific field books document the military violence Mearns participated in, while the typed itineraries that document his official duties occasionally veer into scientific territory.

Local partners, too, are obliquely visible in Mearns's field books, through notes on naming and vocabulary, as well as the occasional mention that someone—a local boy, a soldier from another detail—had a specimen for him. These glimpses of collaborators and informants serve as a key reminder that fieldwork was rarely solitary, an observation that might be doubly true for collectors working in new-to-them contexts and landscapes and for collectors actively serving in the U.S. military. In a narrative detailing a single expedition, Mearns describes enlisting Moro paddlers and a Hospital Corps soldier. With their help, Mearns "went out on Lake Liguasan and shot some birds."[63] Elsewhere Mearns mentions Filipino cargadores, or paid porters, many of whom regularly abandoned their positions. And he notes which parts of the lotus plant Moros ate, as well as local names for streams, suggesting regular interaction with Filipino people, many of them hired to support the army's work. Few of these people are named in Mearns's reports, though their work and knowledge enabled much of his travel and collecting.[64] As in the U.S. West some army men worked to gather information about the people they were tasked with subjugating. Some focused on local vocabulary lists, while others generated amateur ethnographic reports.[65] More broadly, many Americans in the Philippines, whether in military or civilian roles, participated in processes of imperial knowledge production—processes that relied on, and then often downplayed, the significance of local labor and expertise.

By the start of December 1903 both Wood and Mearns were in Zamboanga, the port city on the tip of the crab claw of Mindanao. One morning Mearns and Wood got up early to go hunting, and in just a few hours they managed to bring in snipes, plovers, sandpipers, a rail, and a tree duck. They "shot at a huge iguana, which escaped in the grass."[66] Mearns knew Wood from his service in the Southwest, but it is not clear how well. Now that Mearns was stationed under Wood in the Philippines, their shared interests in hunting and natural history made them a predictable pair. On December 7, 1903, Mearns wrote that he "tramped 9 hours"; in the description of birds that follows, it is clear that Wood accompanied him and shot two herons.[67] This entry shifts into a more organized specimen list, with numbers, collection locations, scientific names, and even some measurements. These birds weren't just seen; they were collected— shot, skinned, stuffed, numbered, and set aside to be shipped to the Smithsonian for future study, evidence of how the support of one's commanding officer could open up opportunities to serve not only the army but the museum as well.

Collecting for the Museum

Mearns, though focused primarily on natural history specimens, collected widely, just as he had when serving in Apache homelands, where, in addition to collecting and preparing birds, he had excavated local ancestral Puebloan sites, uncovering and removing ancestors from their resting places. When his military assignments allowed, Mearns collected more than birds; his notes and museum acquisition records indicate that he removed cultural artifacts and dug up Filipino graves to build Smithsonian collections.

Though Mearns was an experienced collector and preparer—his papers include records for birds shot and stuffed as early as 1874, meaning that he had been skinning birds for close to thirty years by the time he was sent to the Philippines—this assignment presented a new set of preparation challenges. Even carefully preserved materials degraded quickly in the hot, humid climate, and the distance specimens had to travel between the Philippines and the Smithsonian was vast.

Mearns's friends and colleagues at the Smithsonian had much to say about tropical preparation, and the instructions began arriving even before he boarded his ship for the Philippines. Charles Richmond sent detailed advice, saying, "Your way is clear as far as packing birds is concerned. If you follow my directions all will be well."[68] Of all of the remaining correspondence between Mearns and the museum, the letters with Richmond suggest the closest friendship. Before leaving for the Pacific Mearns wrote to him, "I wish you were to be a fellow passenger!"[69]

Richmond's instructions to Mearns began, "In the first place, take out the tendons in the legs of birds larger than an ordinary pigeon, or where the tarsus is heavy. Use a mixture of arsenic + alum on the skins. Keep a solution of bichloride on hand, and paint the feet, tarsi (when naked), bills, and any naked spots on head, with it."[70] The arsenic and alum were intended to protect against bugs; the bichloride was actually mercuric chloride, a mercury solution that museum preparators recommended be applied to certain parts of skins (as well as ethnographic materials) to prevent damage from pests.[71] These instructions continue with details about how to wrap the birds—use a paper that is porous, like newspaper, but not cotton—so that they would arrive "in beautiful shape." Next Richmond had advice about the boxes—tin-lined were preferable—and about adding a drop or two of formaldehyde before sealing them, which "would absolutely prevent the formation of mould."[72] The technical nature of these instructions makes clear the care and skill necessary to prepare Pacific specimens and then pack them for safe transport to the other side of the world.[73]

As he worked to collect widely, Mearns received advice from many museum curators on how best to prepare and preserve the specimens they valued most. For example, Leonhard Stejneger, the Smithsonian curator for reptiles and amphibians, sent advice for collecting and preparing herpetological specimens: "In labeling use only paper labels with indelible ink or pencil writing, not tin tag. Wrap specimens well in cheese cloth or Japanese paper." He advised curing these specimens in formalin and to avoid crowding them into too small a space before fully cured.[74] Frederick V. Coville of the National Herbarium described a box of plant specimens, supposedly from Mearns, that "were so badly moulded and rotten when they reached us as to be unsuitable for preservation." Coville wrote that he "presume[d] they were prepared by some inexperienced volunteer collector," differentiating, it seems, between the quality he had come to expect from Mearns and his assessment of this particular box of specimens.[75]

Still, specimens that all knew to be Mearns's sometimes arrived in poor condition. In early February Gerrit Miller sent Mearns a letter about the mammals he'd sent to the museum: "I am sorry to say that the specimens in your last shipment were badly damaged by dampness. By careful treatment, however, we were able to save the rats and the flying fox, though their fur was already slipping. . . . I think it might be a good plan to try the experiment of sending some small mammal skins in packages by mail. They would undoubtedly travel more rapidly and might be safer from harm."[76] And even when Mearns's packages arrived unscathed, museum curators worried about them. Richmond wrote in December 1903 "to call [Mearns's] attention to the fact that parcels coming from the Philippines in the mails are very liable to be *smashed*, unless forwarded in tin boxes or strongly reinforced cigar boxes." Richmond suggested stockpiling specimens until Mearns had a larger lot to send and to consider sending boxes express or using the military transport system through the quartermaster general.[77]

In early February 1904 Mearns received a letter from Richard Rathbun, the assistant secretary for the entire Smithsonian Institution and the person in charge of the United States National Museum. After praising Mearns's "unabated zeal in making a thorough investigation of the natural history of the Philippine Islands" and confirming that the museum would "gladly furnish all the collecting material required," Rathbun, too, turned to the condition of specimens received. "I am sure you will not think I am criticizing anything you have done for us by inclosing a copy of a memorandum which Dr. Richmond has sent me in regard to the condition in which some of the specimens already sent by you arrived," he began. "I fully understand the difficulties under which you are laboring, and for this reason it is natural that we should be anxious about the preparation and packing of the specimens, so that the fruit of your labors may not be wasted."[78] Richmond's memo, passed along to Mearns by Rathbun, certainly confirms the soggy, moldy ruin of much of what the box in question contained. But it also tells us what exactly was in the box: "ethnological material, mammal skins and skulls, osteological material, insects, living and dead shells, samples of nuts or fruit, coral, birds' eggs and nests, and 138 bird skins."[79] Richmond's memo isn't dated, but it was sent with Rathbun's letter of February 13, suggesting that the specimens and artifacts inside the box were gathered in the fall of 1903, when Mearns and Wood traveled throughout Mindanao.

The contents of this ruined box suggest the breadth of Mearns's collecting in the Philippines. Though his primary natural history interest was birds, Mearns collected widely, taking from the field all that might interest his contacts at the museum. Different museum divisions identified the material they wanted in notices sent to their network of contacts and collectors. For example, among Mearns's 1903 papers is a notice outlining the three "objects needed most by the Division of Physical Anthropology, U.S.N.M.": first, "brains of pure-bloods of any tribe; also those of monkeys and animals or birds of any kind"; second, "embryos, foetuses and infant bodies of pure-bloods of any tribe"; and finally, "skulls and other parts of skeletons of pure-bloods of any tribe." This list is accompanied by instructions for preparation and this clarifying note: "Male adult brains or heads are more important than others." The list is followed by detailed instructions for documenting specimen measurements, removing brains from skulls ("as early as possible after death, using freely the aid of a chisel"), and clarifying that "animal brains or heads are treated in the same way as human."[80] This brief memo is not on letterhead, nor is it signed. Its matter-of-fact tone implies that there was nothing unusual about this request. It echoed earlier requests that ethnographic material and human remains be sent to the museum for study.

Given the lack of geographic specificity in the request for brains, embryos, fetuses, and skulls, this call was likely circulated to everyone in the Smithsonian's collecting network; after all, the museum was growing a global collection. Perhaps collectors gathering ethnographic materials from Native peoples in North America received this bulletin as well. While the bulletin does not specify where, exactly, these human specimens were to come from, the use of "tribe" and "pure-blood," and even the inclusion of "monkeys and animals or birds of any kind" alongside "brains of pure-bloods," makes clear that the Smithsonian wanted the brains and bones of nonwhite, non-Western people. I was unprepared for this, though I shouldn't have been. The ideas and attitudes that enabled this kind of collecting work, that rationalized grave robbing, that categorized people as parts waiting to be taken and studied, rather than ancestors who deserved to rest where they were interred, were pervasive.

In Mindanao, as elsewhere, the violence of the battlefield extended beyond the casualty count to include taking cultural objects and emptying graves. Mearns's itineraries for the spring of 1904 describe what he took from the battlefields and cemeteries he encountered during his Philippine service. In an entry for April 21, 1904, Mearns wrote, "Found graveyard. Skulls of natives abundant in boxes on surface. Obtained one good skull lacking lower jaw—Visayan (no. 5655)." He also gathered different kinds of local knives, as well as an unidentified haul of "Moro loot" that he sent to the National Museum.[81] The 1904–5 annual report of the Smithsonian's Department of Anthropology notes the significance not simply of what Mearns collected for them—they listed two skulls and 134 Moro artifacts—but also of how he labeled them: "He is an experienced collector, hence every piece will serve as a type in labeling a vast amount of valuable but hastily gathered material with little information."[82] Today's readers are left to wonder how Mearns was able to identify a looted skull as Visayan and what sorts of knowledge provided by local guides, scouts, and porters informed the labels and notes he added to the materials he sent to the Smithsonian. In the context of a later war Samuel Redman writes of Smithsonian curators speaking of "war opportunity" for uncovering and removing people from their resting places.[83]

Mearns gave the museum the cultural objects he took from the villages he moved through as part of General Wood's punitive expeditions in Mindanao, and many of these objects are still part of the Smithsonian's anthropological collections. The "war bag" that Mearns wrote about in his field book on August 20, 1903, has a catalog card that describes it as a "pouch with flap, made of colored pandanus strips covered with cotton cloth." The card also notes that this item was "taken from the body of the brother of Macabato, Sultan of Bacayanan at b[a]ttle of Lake Lanao."[84] The Department of Anthropology database lists 271 items as gifted by Edgar Mearns during his Philippine service: knives, baskets, swords, gourds, spoons, even copies of the Koran.[85]

Later soldiers serving in the Philippines in a different war collected skulls and other body parts, though not for any museum. Historian John Dower writes about the gruesome collecting done by some U.S. soldiers during World War II—skulls shipped to loved ones at home; ears, both dried and pickled; and gold teeth, a few gathered from still-alive enemies. These practices were widely discussed; that this kind of collecting targeted Japanese soldiers, rather than Axis soldiers from Germany or Italy, makes clear "the racial dimensions of the war."[86]

Half a century earlier the most famous skull of the Philippine-American War belonged, possibly, to David Fagen, an African American soldier who defected to fight on the side of Filipino revolutionaries. After two years of fighting the U.S. Army issued a reward for Fagen, and near the end of 1901 a severed head was delivered by a local hunter. It is unclear whether the head was Fagen's—competing reports cast doubt—but even this inverted example illustrates turn-of-the-century arguments about race, nationalism, and hierarchy: the head of a Black deserter was exchanged for a reward. It is unclear what the army did with it.[87] In 1906 the *Washington Post*, building on accounts suggesting that Fagen was still very much alive, cast the news this way: "Fagan Again on the Warpath."[88]

The Philippine Scientific Association

Mearns had a reputation for being a careful and detailed collector. His abilities, combined with the access his military assignments provided to environments bursting with potential specimens, made Mearns an ideal collector for the National Museum. And it supported him materially, with far more than friendship and advice on specimen preparation. In February 1904 the Smithsonian sent Mearns a substantial collecting outfit that contained the following:

300 loaded #12 shells #10 shot.
300 loaded #12 shells #6 shot.

1000 empty #12 shells good quality waterproof.
1000 loaded #32 (center fire) shells #10 shot (shells tha[t] can be reloaded).

2000 primers for #32 shells.
2000 wads for #12 shells.
    Wad cutter #32.
    2 sets reloading tools for #32 shells.
    1 shot gun (12 bore).
    225 loaded #12 shells #10 shot.
    225 loaded #12 shells #8 shot.
    25 loaded #12 shells #7 shot.
    50 loaded #12 shells #5 shot.
    50 loaded #12 shells #2 shot.
    200 loaded #12 shells #6 shot.
    250 loaded #12 shells #4 shot.
    75 loaded #12 shells #1 shot.
    100 loaded #12 shells BB shot.
        6 one lb. cans powder.
        14 oz. loose powder. 4 auxiliary barrels #32.
        1 reloading machine.
        35 lbs. shot assorted sizes.
        1 box No. 2 primers.
        1 doz. brass #12 shells.

2 ½ doz. Out o' sight rat traps.
4 ¾ doz. Out o' sight mouse traps.
18 doz. Cyclone mouse traps.
9 ⅓ doz. Schuyler mouse traps.
2 doz. Schuyler rat traps.
5 ¾ doz. B.&L. steel traps assorted sizes.

4 scalpels.
4 scissors.
4 forceps.
4 long stuffers.
4 dividers.
4 metric tapes.

25 lbs. tow.

50 lbs. wire assorted sizes.

10 lbs. alum.

4 lbs. moth balls.

10 lbs. arsenic.

20 lbs. cotton batting.

1000 standard labels.

1000 shell tags.

    8 balls twine (3 sizes).

    2 cyanide bottles.

    2 boxes small vials.

    2 bottles eternal ink.

    6 note books.

    1 package plant paper.

    12 packages pins.

    12 taxidermist needles.

    12 spools thread.

    10 yards cheesecloth.

    4 quarts formalin.

    8 quarts alcohol.

    ½ pound corrosive sublimate.[89]

When I first read that the Smithsonian had sent Mearns a collecting outfit, I imagined a small, portable set of supplies, something like a camping first-aid kit—certainly not anything of this size, scale, and specificity. Mearns had received support in the form of supplies from museum curators since his service in Apache and Yavapai homelands in the 1880s, but not like this. This list indicates not only the significance of the collecting possibilities in the Philippines for the Smithsonian but also the museum's enthusiasm for Mearns's efforts to support and mentor other collectors.

A few things stand out about this list. First, there is a lot of ammunition, in sizes suited for everything from small birds to larger mammals. (The higher the number, the smaller the ammunition.) The outfit contains the necessary tools for preparing and loading shells, as well as a twelve-bore shotgun.

Standard-issue military weapons were not necessarily ideal collecting weapons. Unlike a Krag-Jørgenson rifle, used earlier in the war, or a Mauser, the rifle adopted by the U.S. Army by the time Mearns was deployed to the Philippines, a shotgun could be loaded with ammunition of different sizes, making it possible to match ammunition with an intended future specimen. As an experienced hunter and collector Mearns would have brought his own shotgun with him to the Philippines.[90] As a medical officer rather than an infantryman, it is unlikely Mearns would have required—or even been issued—a standard rifle. This gun wasn't only for Mearns's use; it also enabled others to shoot and kill specimens, which could then be prepared and sent to the museum. The collecting outfit Mearns received contained four sets of scalpels, scissors, forceps, long stuffers, dividers, and metric tapes—sets that reflected curators' hope that Mearns would be able to find other soldiers to assist him in his scientific work.

On July 31, 1903, Gerrit Miller in the Division of Mammals received a letter from Mearns. Its contents were so exciting that Miller showed it to multiple people, who then mentioned having seen the news in their own letters to Mearns. In his letter Mearns seems to have outlined plans to form the Philippine Scientific Association, to be led by General Wood, with Mearns as its vice president. Miller's response affirms broad institutional enthusiasm for this new project, the news of which "spread a glow of delight on more faces than is usually the lot of letters." Miller's reply, on September 12 (the same day Mearns's letter arrived in Washington), is full of energy and support for what Mearns had begun: "The idea seems to me perfect in all respects, and all that remains is to work out the details of the relationships between the Society and the U.S.N.M." Miller's letter continues at a pace that feels almost like thinking out loud: the new association's secretary should send something official; Miller would go ahead and send one hundred sets of instructions for specimen collection; the museum would prepare a large collecting outfit for Mearns and the association; and so forth. "Of course it is premature to talk of all of this now, but you have set us thinking!" Miller exclaimed.[91]

Rathbun also responded with encouragement and approval: "It is very gratifying to us here in Washington to see the kindling of the scientific flame in our far off possessions, and especially so when I realize the fact that the Society in question was organized by you, and that you are the controlling force in its operations. We shall naturally expect great things after a while."[92] Miller, too, saw the potential of the Philippine Scientific Association, telling Mearns, "What we need is a representative in the Philippines, and one of the good things about your plan is that it seems to offer a means for establishing something of the kind."[93] In fact, the association sounds similar to what Mearns and True had once imagined. With the Smithsonian's encouragement and Wood's approval, Mearns organized existing and prospective collectors to support U.S. natural history work in the Philippines—work that would enable scientific knowledge production and U.S. advancement in this arena.

The Constitution of the Philippine Scientific Association was written on July 26, 1903, and adopted the following day. Article II of the constitution stated that "the object of the association is to promote and unite scientific effort in the Philippine Islands; to make known the physiographic features and products of the Islands; to gather collections for the enrichment of the museums of the United States government; and to collect such information as may contribute to a better knowledge of the Islands and their inhabitants."[94] Though the association was not expressly a military organization, its inaugural membership list included many army men and some army wives and daughters who had accompanied officers overseas. Richard McGregor of the Philippine Museum in Manila and Capt. George Ahern of the Philippine Bureau of Forestry were also on the list. Officers of the Seventeenth Infantry were particularly well represented in the list of fifty-nine members below Mearns's copy of the constitution.[95] Annual dues were one dollar, and Mearns's copy includes notes on those who had paid their membership fees. The association sent out requests to potential members, inviting them to join the organization and notifying those who wished to "become active workers" that they would receive more information soon.[96]

Meanwhile, Mearns began to build a library of materials and supplies for the association. Included in his Philippine Scientific Association correspondence file is a handwritten list of scientific papers and bird lists. In the margins Mearns scribbled his desires: "Want it"; "Want all"; and even "Want it! Mearns."[97] Smithsonian curators sent several duplicate copies of circulars with collecting instructions, and Miller made special mention of a "standard" field notebook included in the large collecting outfit sent to Mearns by the museum. He explained, "The pages can be detached and sent to us with the collections to which they refer, and when we get enough of them together we can have them bound for permanent record." Miller offered to include several of them for Mearns's "voluntary workers" and noted that he had included "several sets of skinning tools in the outfit" for the same purpose.[98]

While intended for the Philippine Scientific Association, it seems likely that some of these materials were also used by the local assistants Mearns recruited on his travels; for example, while on an expedition to collect materials from the Mount Apo region, Mearns wrote to his daughter that "Bogobos or one of the Moros were always out hunting and bringing in good birds and animals for food or specimens" and that he and his colleagues had "let them learn to use our guns."[99] Mearns was doing more than collecting: he was training new collectors. In a field book from March 1904, which opens with a note about two eggs a Moro boy brought to him, Mearns recorded that he "sent Nat. Mus. pamphlets giving directions for collecting Birds, nests + eggs, Mammals, Reptiles + Batrachians, Molusks and Shells, and Insects (6 pamphlets) to the officers' clubs at the following places": Marahui, Parang, Malabang, Zamboanga, Jolo, and Cotabato.[100] Notes like this help us trace the impact of Mearns's work as an advocate for the importance of natural history and scientific collection alongside military work. They also hint at the shape of the network Mearns was building. While Wood's leadership of the Philippine Scientific Association offered an important endorsement of this position, it seems Mearns was also developing relationships that extended beyond the community of U.S. colonial and military employees in the Philippines in the service of pursuing every available opportunity for scientific work.

"Fighting + Field Work"

Portions of Mearns's field books make it easy for a reader to forget his military assignment. His notes are focused on birds, and aside from the occasional local or Spanish words for birdsong and bird names, these pages are all science, no war. For example, consider this, from February 25: "After breakfast, walked down the rocky shore to the west, it being low tide. Saw plenty of little Blue Herons." And from later the same day: "After lunching + skinning a couple of birds I set out through coconut groves eastward. . . . At length we reached a stream and mangrove swamp in which a large herd of Monkeys was found. I shot a large male monkey that kept by himself." Mearns continued, "Green Parrots screamed everywhere towards night; and I heard the soft cooing of the little green pigeon in the swamp." The next day he noted, "Skinned mammals + birds until 2:30 P.M. Spent rest of day shooting."[101]

These entries aren't mixed together with military details; there's nothing here about colonial politics or shooting people. Still, they reflect Mearns's perspective and position as an agent of U.S. empire. In moments of relative calm, militarily speaking, Mearns's ability to move through Philippine landscapes, to observe and collect birds, was shaped by the access afforded him through his role as a major in the U.S. Army. Breaks in fighting enabled more collecting. Even when Mearns was actively engaged in military violence, his letters to his contacts at the Smithsonian do not say much about the work he'd been assigned to do. To Richmond, though, he acknowledged that there were military reasons for the delay in shipping more material: "I have a lot of stuff collected, but between the fighting + field work, can find little time for packing."[102]

In March 1904 Mearns participated in the Rio Grande Expedition, one of several punitive expeditions into Moro territory that marked the period of Wood's military governance of Moro Province.[103] With five companies of soldiers Wood started from Cotabato and headed up the river in search of a Moro leader named Datu Ali, the sultan of Buyuan.[104] Mearns's notes from this expedition again combine military, medical, and scientific work. For example, the entry for March 9 describes going on a scouting mission to within six hundred yards of Datu Ali's fort, then finishes with a list of birds preceded by, "Saw the following birds." That last line is underlined in pen, as if Mearns returned to these books to review the natural history of this expedition. The birds take up the rest of the page and all of the next one: "Black-throated Sunbird; Long-tailed Herinda; Plucky Swift; Gray Martin; Dendrocygna; Black Ibis; Carabao Bird, black legs; Great Blue Heron; Black Heron (or Bittern); Waterhen (Galli-nulau chlorppa); Kingfisher, blue, white-belly; Oriole, Necrops philippinus; Brown Java Sparrow; Whitish-gray Shrike; White-headed Hawk; Rain-crow, brown winged; Black (Barbet?); Soli-tary Tattler; Gallinggo, narrow-tailed; Crow; White + Gary bird in flocks; Little red + green Paroquet; Cockatoo; Large Green Parrot; Long-tailed Shrike; Porphyrio—Flying at evening night; Butorides; Dried green Tree Frog in botanical press."[105]

The entry for the following day describes shelling Datu Ali's fort—and more birds. The March 11 entry is about a morn-ing attack—and still more birds. Partway down, this day's list shifts from birds seen to weapons collected: brass and iron guns, "lantacas," and plenty of ammunition. Mearns wrote of "the white flag" appearing when they began to shell Sirinaya. "Then we marched over and looted the place."[106]

By March 14, after almost ten days in the Rio Grande estuary—which Wood biographer Jack McCallum calls "a morass of standing water covered with a mat of floating vege-tation thick enough to support small trees but porous enough to drop men, guns, and animals into the twenty-foot-deep liquid muck below"—Mearns was back on the *Ranger*.[107] The follow-ing day he was in Zamboanga, where he unpacked his belong-ings, skinned a few birds shot on the expedition, and met up with two other army doctors who had specimens to show him. In terms of Wood's military aims, the expedition had been a partial success: they had shelled Sirinaya heavily, confiscated weapons, and captured Datu Djimbangan, Datu Ali's brother. And in terms of scientific goals, Mearns's efforts had been successful. He'd collected both Moro cultural belongings and Philippine birds from the area around Datu Ali's fort. Here, at least, conquest and collection were compatible—for the colonizers. Still, the material victory was partial. Datu Ali, a key opponent of U.S. control of Mindanao, remained at large. In fact, Samuel Tan writes that it was Datu Ali's "exclusion by the American authorities from the St. Louis Exposition" that gave him "a reason to fight against American rule," suggesting that the U.S. military's work in Mindanao was always wrapped up in the larger circuits of U.S. empire.[108]

Wood planned another punitive expedition in the Lake Lanao region for April with the same basic plan: decimation. McCallum writes, "Wood's men went from cotta [village] to cotta, firing from the parapets until there was no sign of life then destroying the structures and everything in them."[109] Rather than attempt to solve issues in Mindanao peacefully, Wood pledged total war: "to go thoroughly over the whole valley, destroying all warlike supplies, and dispersing and destroying every hostile force, and also destroy every cota where there is the slightest resistance."[110] Some estimates suggest that twenty thousand Moros were displaced in 1904–5 by Wood's campaigns.[111] These practices resemble earlier parts of the U.S. Army's work in the Philippines—especially the destruction that followed instructions to make Samar into a "howling wilderness."[112]

The violence of Wood's expeditions in Mindanao—and Mearns's part in them—was never explicitly addressed by Mearns's museum colleagues. Their letters are focused on science, specifically the potential losses to science resulting from damaged or unlabeled specimens, rather than on tactics. For example, the correspondence between Mearns and Richmond contains much discussion of specimens arriving without labels. Richmond asked Mearns for information about specimens he couldn't label, and then, roughly six weeks later, Mearns wrote back with as much information as he could provide from his notes. It seems that most of these identification problems were eventually solved, though it is clear that the lack of information caused a little bit of exasperation. Miller began one letter, "Humbly, on my knees, in the dust, with ashes on my head, and with humility and the fear of God in my heart, I send you this prayer and supplication that you will not forward any more skins with mere numbers on them." I read this as an attempt at humor, but Miller's frustration was real: "It's such fine stuff and we need it so much that it makes me weep to see it in anything but first class shape."[113]

Without the information Mearns recorded about locality, appearance, and sometimes behavior, the work that museum scientists could do with these specimens was limited. These exchanges highlight all the harder-to-see steps between the field and the museum, as well as the ways that imperial pathways both hindered and enabled the study of specimens and the contributions of American scientists to broader systems of knowledge production.[114]

These requests for data went both ways: Mearns asked Richmond to share the names he'd assigned to the birds Mearns had sent to the museum but couldn't confidently identify. That way, Mearns would be able to update his notes and draw on the expertise of the museum curators, who could compare Mearns's birds with other specimens in their holdings, to build his own knowledge. This request would be "an advantage to [Mearns's] work" and also an advantage to the museum. Mearns noted that there were collectors for foreign museums in the Philippines; identifying Mearns's birds as they arrived "may save some types from going abroad." Furthermore, it would help the association. Mearns wrote that this information from Richmond would allow him "to make some reports of results of work and to identify specimens for the members of the Philippine Scientific Association at our meetings or when they come 'round to ask questions." Although he was getting information from McGregor at the museum in Manila, his bulletins did not cover much of what Mearns was encountering. "Besides," he wrote, "I am 'on the go' in the field much of the time."[115]

The field that Mearns was referring to was also sometimes a battlefield. If Mearns mentioned fighting, it was mostly in passing and only to Richmond. But on June 2, 1904, Mearns responded to a question from Richmond about a *Granculus* specimen with a bit more context for his collecting work: "A big battle was going on. A soldier near me was shot while I skinned the bird. I skinned a big Monkey at the same time but could not carry the skin away; but I saved the dark-gray bird and the skull of the Monkey. Bird size of Mourning Dove, not rare on Sulu but not seen elsewhere by me; my only specimen."[116] This image, of Mearns skinning a bird while a nearby soldier is shot, raises questions about the violence of both kinds of labor, about the connections between following orders, fighting Filipinos, and killing animals to collect them for science.

Preparing Soldiers

The letters between Mearns and the museum are centered on the logistics of collecting—what to collect, sending tools and materials to help with collecting, how to ship specimens halfway around the world, the challenges of making sense of the specimens and their identifying information once (or if) they arrived. But what about the logics of collecting? I have to imagine that Mearns thought about the work of war and the killing of collection. As a young man he described the sounds a night heron made as it suffered from a shot through the wing. Mearns had to chase the wounded bird and kill it with his hands: "I caught him, and ended his existence after no tame struggle on the bird's part, while I was nearly deafened by his screams."[117] The details in this description are striking—the scene is clear and vivid, as is the bird's distress. Mearns did not minimize the violence of this work; he simply explained what happened and owned his role in this bird's end. This is one of the few moments in Mearns's papers where he described not just the details of collection (place, date, time, or even shot used) but also the actual dying of creatures that would become specimens.

For him these deaths had purpose. He never came out and said so, but I see this in the care and attention he committed to the work of scientific collection and study, in the living record he built to document the specimens he killed and preserved.

But there is a section in one of Mearns's field books that contains a different sort of list: not of specimens but of soldiers. Still bodies but not of birds. And not bodies stolen from graves or described numerically in an enemy casualty count. These pages list fifteen U.S. soldiers from the Seventeenth Infantry by name, losses from a war already declared over. They had been ambushed, killed in a fight with Datu Ali's men earlier that month in what U.S. forces called the Simpitan Massacre.

MAY 25, 1904

1. Lieut. Woodruff
2. Lieut. Hall
3. Sergt. Wachter
4. Pvt. Eineit
5. Pvt. Osborn
6. Pvt. Molde
7. Musician Quillan
8. Pvt. Cole
9. Pvt. Smith
10. Sergt. Wallen
11. Pvt. Hughes
12. Pvt. Merredeth
13. Pvt. Litchens
14. Pvt. Gillam
15. Pvt. O'Connor[118]

Mearns prepared their bodies, too, and packed them in boxes for transport to a coastal town. The next page in Mearns's field book lists their contents: nine boxes, fifteen bodies. Mearns did not say anything about the condition of their bodies or about proper methods for preparing the bodies of the dead. His notes, however, indicate that he packed two men to a box and that Private Eineit's skull was separate from the rest of his body, "name written on skull and label attached."[119] From there the boxes were carried to Cotabato, where their contents were sealed into caskets and shipped home across the Pacific.

I haven't found many instances like this in my reading of Mearns's field books—the preparation of U.S. soldiers' bodies for transport home seems to have been rare, at least for Mearns—but here the resonance between his work with the bodies of birds and the bodies of people is impossible to ignore. As a surgeon Mearns's job was to heal—to dress wounds, treat illness, and respond to the trauma of war. As a scientist his primary task was to collect—to observe, shoot, skin, stuff, and preserve specimens for future study. And as a soldier the task was sometimes to fight, to take life, even if he was also trained to preserve it. These occupations—surgeon, scientist, and soldier—required many of the same tools and skills, all in the service of empire.

Mearns's papers are filled with painstakingly detailed instructions for how to get dead plants and animals from the Philippines to the United States without rotting or molding. The Smithsonian sent Mearns several chemical agents to aid in this process: arsenic, alum, formalin, formaldehyde. The Department of Anthropology had sent the circular requesting animal and human brains, along with instructions for preserving them. Those instructions were meant not for the brains and skulls of U.S. soldiers but rather for the bones and bodies of nonwhite people that collectors in the Smithsonian's network encountered in the field. Mearns answered this call, too, looting graves and sending the bones of those he uncovered to the museum. As he preserved the bodies of American soldiers for a final Pacific crossing, Mearns must have thought about what it meant to leave the field this way—in a box, prepared for a long journey home.

Though their letters gestured toward what might happen, toward the danger and uncertainty they lived with, soldiers rarely explained the structures (both military and civilian) for handling casualties of war and disease. But they knew something about it. While serving as a correspondent for the *Chicago Record*, John McCutcheon encountered a member of the

Quartermaster Burial Corps—an undertaker—aboard the *Helena*. He wrote, "There is one young fellow on board who has been something of a mystery to me. He wears a neat trim suit of tweed, a watch cap, eyeglasses, and has more the look of a tourist than either a soldier or a correspondent." McCutcheon asked about him, and "in a low tone" the ship's doctor told him, "He's the undertaker. He's a mighty nice fellow but if it is known what he's here for, the men would shun him and have nothing to do with him. We try to keep it quiet what his business is." McCutcheon observed that there were "a number of rough pine boxes on board—about six feet long by three wide and two and a half deep"—that were "now down in the hold, comparatively light for their size."[120]

Caskets like these housed the soldiers' bodies that Mearns prepared. Mearns described this work to Charles Richmond. He told Richmond that the officers who had been killed, Lieutenant Hall and Lieutenant Woodruff, had both been members of the Philippine Scientific Association. Mearns wrote that on May 25 he "packed the 15 bodies for transportation to Cottabato by native carriers and made a hard, hot march the same day + night."[121] Mearns said nothing about the local people impressed into service to carry the American dead and nothing about the other bodies he'd packed and shipped to the museum, looted from graveyards encountered on Wood's punitive expeditions. And Mearns said nothing to Richmond of the methods he used to prepare and pack the bodies of these men; some soldiers who died in the field were embalmed, using methods developed by Chaplain Charles Pierce, head of the U.S. Army Morgue and Office of Identification.[122] Perhaps Mearns followed guidelines handed down from this office. His inclusion of this list of bodies in his field notes helps make visible this other work of war—dealing with the dead. Mearns does not mention whether or how Moro casualties of war were treated.

As he read Mearns's letter Richmond, who had sent pages and pages of detailed instructions for specimen preparation and packing, may have been thinking about the resonances between Mearns's birds and soldiers' bodies. At the end of his letter Mearns asked Richmond, "How would you like to be a soldier?"[123]

The question, left hanging, asks to be turned around: how did Mearns like soldiering? There are brief private moments where Mearns mentioned leaving the army, but for the most part, the written record he left is silent about how he felt about this work and specifically about the imperial projects his service supported in both the U.S. West and the Philippines. The military enabled a scientific career, one that might not have been possible without the opportunities—and specimens—the U.S. Army placed in his field of vision. But at what cost? When Mearns looked at those birds later, when he pulled them out of their boxes and drawers to study them, compare them, did he see other bodies—those of the Moros he'd killed, the graves he'd looted, the soldiers he'd prepared and sent home? It is possible that Mearns recognized the echoes between the violence of war and the practices of imperial science. But perhaps the bodies of the birds he'd collected and prepared existed for him in a space beyond colonial collecting. Maybe he counted these bodies differently than he counted Filipino and American casualties; after all, for Mearns the birds added up to a fuller picture of avian life, to a collection that much closer to being complete.

"How would you like to be a soldier?" I wouldn't, I imagine Richmond responding as he read Mearns's letter about the soldiers killed at Simpitan, about the work Mearns did to prepare their bodies. I wouldn't, except for all the things I might see. Maybe Richmond, when he looked at Mearns's birds, saw more than just their beaks and their wings, more than their feet and feather patterns. Carefully labeled birds in boxes, men in pine caskets, all collected where they fell and shipped home across the Pacific—is this what empire looked like to its agents?

I have grappled with this question and whether it is the right question to ask. Why devote so much attention to how empire's agents saw and understood the world? What do their perspectives do for us now, more than a century after this mostly forgotten war? There are many more questions—and perspectives—to consider. But I keep returning to this question about how imperial agents understood their work, and here is why: ideas about what empire looked like, what it was supposed to look like, and who it was for did not stay in the minds of U.S. soldiers or the heads of U.S. colonial administrators. These ideas mingled with others—about science, about humanity, about the nature of the wider world—and together this tangle influenced how U.S. empire would be imagined, enacted, narrated, and displayed. To examine what "taking the field" meant in Mindanao is also to recognize the force deployed to do so and the range of shapes these actions took. Taking the field extended in many directions: U.S. soldiers took lives, removed resources, looted graves, collected natural history specimens, and even transported Filipino people across the Pacific for display at a world's fair where the United States would also take control of the story it told about itself and its empire.

Collecting the Philippines for the Fair

Raw materials, handcrafted artifacts, and Filipino people were deemed necessary to tell a story of U.S. imperial expansion— and success. Plans for a forty-seven-acre Philippine Exposition at the 1904 St. Louis World's Fair were set in motion years in advance; in fact, by the time the chief U.S. forester, Gifford Pinchot, arrived in Manila in October 1902, plans were already underway for a Philippine display at the fair.

Taft circulated a letter throughout the Philippines with instructions for collecting materials to display at the fair. From the beginning the emphasis was on the natural abundance of the archipelago—and on the financial opportunities available to those willing to invest in harnessing the resources of the Philippines. Taft wrote, "The visitors to the Philippine exhibition must see the possibility of good investments and successful enterprises in these Islands. All sources of wealth must be laid open to the world as a basis of future prosperity." The stakes were high. After all, "the purpose of the Philippine exhibit is not only to create interest and sympathy for the Philippine Islands, and to give confidence in the intelligence and capacity of the natives, but also to look for permanent profitable markets for the natural resources, in showing and in illustrating the fertility of soil and climate and the great wealth in forest, agricultural, fishing, mining, and other products."[124] Members from several bureaus of the U.S. colonial government in the Philippines were involved in the work of acquiring items for the fair. Secretary of the Interior Worcester, in his annual report for 1903, wrote that in preparation for the exposition, "each field party has been called upon to devote more or less time to the collection of material," including "logs for the forestry building" and "a botanical collection."[125]

As Pinchot traveled throughout the Philippines on Taft's gunboat in 1902, he began making notes about what should be included in the Philippine forestry display at the fair. Logs were first on Pinchot's list, "round + squared, sections polished," as well as "in house construction + specimens." He also wanted to display "logging methods," "tools + models in wood," and samples of "sawed lumber" in different sizes. In addition to the timber itself, Pinchot mapped out ideas for displaying wood products and handiwork, as well as samples of forest products beyond valuable timber: "gums + resins" that could be derived from the archipelago's myriad tree species, along with "dyestuff" and "fruits + seeds."[126]

Pinchot continued to refine his ideas about the display's content and approach, and at the conclusion of his Philippine trip he and Ahern wrote a set of recommendations for Taft. "The idea which should guide the formation of this exhibit," they suggested, "is that of making it striking at the expense of completeness." Pinchot and Ahern were emphatic about the goals of their exhibit and about the elements they perceived to be crucial to their success: "Unusual specimens and unusual yet suitable methods of installation will be necessary if the exhibit is to be remembered by those who see it."[127] The Philippines would be displayed as different—tropical and exotic, a spectacle capable of commanding the attention of fairgoers who would be stimulated on every side.

Though the forest resources of the Philippines were, for Pinchot and Ahern, a crucial dimension of how the Philippines would be represented at the fair, Taft's instructions for gathering materials for display encompassed far more than timber. He urged all branches of the U.S. colonial project to participate: "We trust that every provincial government and every municipality, without exception, will be proud to contribute, to show to the world the immense natural wealth, great fertility of soil, and enormous economical opportunities of these Islands and will not lose a moment's time in starting the highly appreciated work of collecting exhibits of all resources and conditions of their respective territories."[128]

This work of "collecting exhibits of all resources" included collecting people—this time, alive. Or at least alive initially. Robert Rydell describes a conversation among representatives of the Smithsonian, Columbia University, and the American Museum of Natural History about dividing up the bodies of those who died either on their way to or at the fair. While clear that at least one of the representatives understood the problematic optics, if not the inhumane ethics, of the arrangement, Rydell explains that the brains of three Filipinos who had died in St. Louis were sent to the Smithsonian after the fair.[129] Thus the looting as collecting conducted during military operations in the Philippines continued in the United States.

The U.S. military facilitated the collection and transport of people and artifacts from the Philippines to the fair, and in so doing it helped construct what—and whom—Americans would encounter at the fairgrounds in St. Louis. In fact, military arrangements had been made back in 1900 to assist Col. Frank Hilder (from the Smithsonian) and Penoyer Sherman (a photographer) as they collected materials from the Philippines for display at the 1901 Pan-American Exposition in Buffalo, New York.[130] Even with military support the two reported that the work of preparing an exhibit from a war zone was challenging. Not only were they attempting to gather materials that did not exist—villages, farms, and fields had been burned, the result of "hike" after "hike," and many farmers were also soldiers fighting against U.S. occupying forces—but Sherman and Hilder also found that they had competition. Soldiers collected souvenirs whenever they could ("curio crazy volunteers" is what Sherman called them), and other divisions of the federal government were interested in gathering relics from the war.[131]

Objects that might stand in for one's experiences in the service of the U.S. colonial project were especially desirable—recall the energy exerted by soldiers to retrieve pieces of Spanish ships. Bolo knives also captured soldiers' attention. Frank Dwight Baldwin held on to two boxes' and one crate's worth of Moro artifacts, the vast majority of them fitting under the heading "War Weapons and Implements Actually Used by the Malanao Moros." He donated them to the Michigan State Museum in 1920, accompanied by an inventory detailing which weapons had poisonous blades.[132]

Though they were not collecting expressly for the exposition, Mearns and the Philippine Scientific Association may have benefited from existing agreements between the Smithsonian and the government to use military pathways to move museum material intended for the fair. While the Philippine Exposition at the St. Louis Fair was coordinated by the Philippine Exposition Board, Smithsonian anthropologists, scientists, and curators were deeply involved in the preparation of the federal government's displays. Indeed, some of the individuals Mearns corresponded with were responsible for designing the federal government's exhibits at several fairs and expositions in the late nineteenth and early twentieth centuries. They coordinated exhibits centered on American nature and American science that demonstrated their vision of progress, celebrated particular forms of knowledge production, and implicitly argued for U.S. dominance on the world stage. The materials sent to the United States from the Philippines, some of which traveled farther to the fair, shaped popular ideas about nature and empire on both sides of the Pacific.

While stationed in Mindanao, Capt. Cornelius Cole Smith (an officer who later served as the superintendent of Sequoia and General Grant National Parks in 1908) wrote in his diary that on January 30, 1904, "fifty or sixty Moros, men, women, and children, came down from Lake Lanao . . . to await a steamer to take them to the United States where they were going to form a part of the great exposition at St. Louis." Smith wrote that he "saw much of them" while they were at Camp Overton "and found them more or less interesting," declaring that "no doubt they will be looked upon with much curiosity at the fair."[133] The same transport vessel that carried the Lake Lanao Moros to the United States also delivered John Muir to California at the end of his round-the-world trip. The naturalist and preservationist wrote in his diary that there were "45 Philippinos on board bound for St. Louis, a good looking set of men likely to exert favorable influence on their people on return."[134] These asides, brief thoughts preserved on the pages of a diary from Muir's botanizing journey, together with Pinchot's plans for exhibiting the timber potential of Philippine forests, suggest that for key environmental thinkers and policymakers like Muir and Pinchot, there was no contradiction between preservation and conservation and the work of U.S. empire.

The Lake Lanao Moros who shared the deck of a transport vessel with naturalist John Muir were on their way across the Pacific, following an imperial pathway that had also been traveled by U.S. soldiers and agents of the U.S. colonial government, as well as by the specimens that naturalists like Mearns had prepared and shipped to the Smithsonian. Preserved birds, looted bones, and casualties of war had traveled this route, as had specimen lists, love letters, and collecting tools. And now the Lake Lanao Moros were on their way across the Pacific and then overland through much of the U.S. West to St. Louis to participate in the 1904 St. Louis World's Fair. They traveled U.S. imperial pathways in reverse, part of a deeply uneven exchange in which they were to be displayed, positioned as part of a seamless narrative of U.S. imperial progress. That they refused to help tell this story reveals many of its holes.[135]

Interlude 2

Looking for Arrowhead Lake

THE LOUISIANA PURCHASE EXPOSITION COMPANY GENER-
ated an enormous record of the fair, including planning documents, company ledgers, meeting minutes, promotional items,
and even an official history written by David Francis, the exposition company's president. These materials are housed in the
Missouri Historical Society and Research Center, across from
present-day Forest Park and within the boundaries of the historical fairgrounds.

The fair's Publicity Department kept extensive records of the
exposition's exhibits—perhaps because the fair was designed
to be fleeting. From the beginning the company prioritized the
work of preserving it through photographs, stereographs, and
souvenir books. I'm grateful for these efforts; it wasn't until I
began looking through the company's albums and boxes filled
with photographs that I began to understand what it might have
been like to see the fair's "grand picture," to walk through the
palaces—to experience these spaces at scale.

These materials argue for the immensity of the undertaking, but what strikes me most about these Publicity Department photographs is their emptiness. Many of these images
were captured before the fair's opening day—the better to see
the details of each palace's design and each exhibit's components. But they reflect a fair without fairgoers. That doesn't
mean that all these exhibit photographs are without people. In
some cases people lived in exhibit spaces, and in other cases
people *were* the exhibits (fig. 23).

23. Photo labeled "Igorrote Village." Philippine Reservation, Department of Anthropology at the 1904 World's Fair. Photograph by Jessie Tarbox Beals, 1904. Missouri Historical Society, St. Louis.

I didn't figure this out at first. There are numbers on the back of these Publicity Department images. Some correspond to old slides and negatives, others to old boxes and outdated organizational schemes for the collection, but on each image there is also an exhibit number, identifiable as such because it is repeated on every photograph depicting a particular exhibit. Multiple photographs of Moro boats have the number #1316 (see fig. 24, for example), while images of the Moro village are labeled #1314.

But these exhibit numbers seem to have been used to label more than sections of ethnographic villages and discrete portions of displays, like Moro boats or houses. Individuals received exhibit numbers too. These Publicity Department files contain portraits of Geronimo at the fair. He stands in hat and jacket, holding a bow and arrow, likely his own handiwork. In one image he looks straight at the camera (fig. 25). In a second photograph he looks to his right. Both images are labeled

24. Moros in catamaran, St. Louis World's Fair. Photographer unknown, 1904. Missouri Historical Society, St. Louis.

"#1302—Chief Geronimo from Arizona, Dept. Anthropology." The label obscures the fact that Geronimo was never granted permission to return to Apache homelands in the Southwest; he came to the fair from Fort Sill, Oklahoma, where he remained a prisoner of war.

I've spent a lot of time looking at these portraits—at the flower pin attached to his jacket, at the way his fingers grasp the bow, at the clear-eyed gaze he aims directly at the camera lens and now at me. He is captivating—and, I remember, captive. He was not fixed in place, though he was accompanied by guards everywhere he went while at the fair. And despite repeated petitioning, he was not allowed to go home. Paige Raibmon writes about how some Native people on display at expositions "willingly participated in the public performance of their private lives, while others submitted somewhat more grudgingly to the public gaze."[1]

I don't know how Geronimo felt about the fair, about the role

25. Geronimo, Apache chief from Arizona, in the Department of Anthropology at the 1904 World's Fair. Official Photographic Company, 1904. Missouri Historical Society, St. Louis.

he'd been assigned in St. Louis. I know he was able to use expositions like this one to sell his likeness and signature, to commodify parts of the story Americans had been telling themselves about him since at least the 1870s. Alexia Kosmider describes how, for a price, he would cut a button off of his jacket or part with the hat on his head, only to immediately replace the missing item. His "perception of the colonizers' desires," writes Kosmider, "seems uncanny." At an earlier fair he'd been required to wear his military uniform alongside other enlisted Native scouts; at Omaha in 1898 he and other Apaches incarcerated at Fort Sill lived in military tents.[2] Here he is in civilian clothes, items of his own making in his hands. The Filipinos in the other Publicity Department photos are captured at a wide angle, framed as part of the scenery, but Geronimo fills this frame. I can't tell where in the fairgrounds he is in this portrait.

So I went looking for Geronimo—or, rather, for where he would have been positioned, according to the fair's official guidebook—on one of my trips to St. Louis. To find him I first had to locate Arrowhead Lake, named for its shape and to signal the heavy-handed narrative visitors were supposed to take in as they crossed over it. The Philippine Exposition was separated from the rest of the fairgrounds by Arrowhead Lake; the ethnographic displays of Indigenous North Americans, Geronimo among them, were positioned on the other side of this constructed reservoir in the anthropology exhibit. The story being told at the fair was clear: visitors could experience remnants of the old West before walking across the replica of the Bridge of Spain to the living exhibits containing Filipinos, residents of the new Pacific frontier.

Though assigned a number and treated as an exhibit by the Louisiana Purchase Exposition Company, Geronimo had some opportunities to move through the fairgrounds. In an account of his life told to S. M. Barrett through Asa Daklugie the following year, he described seeing "some little brown people at the Fair that United States troops captured recently on some islands far away from here."[3] To see the Igorot Village, he would have crossed over Arrowhead Lake to visit the Philippine Exposition.

Arrowhead Lake doesn't exist anymore. But I'm pretty sure it used to be at the curved intersection of Wydown Boulevard and De Mun Avenue.[4] So I parked there, let my dog out of the car, and tucked a map of the 1904 fairgrounds into my back pocket. We walked up and down the block, looking for anything that might help orient us. And then we cut into the neighborhood, through what might have been the lake and toward the Philippine Exposition. Most of the smaller streets off the main blocks were gated. The yards were lush and green, in stark contrast to the public spaces, which had been scorched by the summer sun. And suddenly we were on the grounds of Concordia Seminary, heading up a carefully landscaped and gently rolling hill. Were we in the old walled city at the center of Manila? We wandered the campus and found a place to sit and rest. I made some notes while my dog settled down in a small patch of shade.

From our perch I wondered what someone here in the Philippine Exposition would have been able to see of the rest of the fair. Could the Filipinos brought to live here for the fair's duration see across the lake to Geronimo, to the Indigenous North Americans on display? Was the fair's narrative about the nation's imperial past and future visible from this spot?

It's hard to tell now, more than a century later. Today the space between these two parts of the fair is filled with homes. And the fair is just a memory. Forest Park was once on the western edge of the city; now it sits at city center. And St. Louis, once the gateway to Native homelands framed as the frontier West, is now understood as part of America's heartland. An arch stands tall, signaling the city's place in a particular narrative of U.S. history—and when I was first there, learning about the Louisiana Purchase Exposition, I noticed its form mowed into the green grass beneath the St. Louis Art Museum. The building, the only palace from the fair constructed to outlive the exposition, sits atop a hill at the center of Forest Park, the arch a green shadow beneath it.

Not everyone who came to St. Louis left or did so on their own terms. Janna Añonuevo Langholz is an interdisciplinary artist and researcher who is working to locate the gravesites of Filipino and Indigenous people who died at the fair—and to honor their memory by advocating for more acknowledgment of the most unsettling parts of the exposition. Langholz serves as the caretaker of the Philippine Village Historical Site in Clayton, Missouri, an ongoing effort to mark and to remember the Philippine Exposition.[5] Her work links the dead to the living: she has created a contemporary directory of 1,200 Filipino American artists, an echo of the 1,200 Filipino people brought to participate in the fair's living exhibits. Paired with this emphasis on present-day artists "exhibiting their work . . . as opposed to being exhibited" is the task of excavating the past, and Langholz shares online the work she does to connect newspaper mentions of those who died at the fair with their likely burial sites so far from home.[6] In a recent interview Langholz said, "I want peace for those who died here, and once that is achieved I feel that I can have peace myself too."[7]

It might be hard to see in fancy neighborhoods, in college campuses and city streets, and even in the wrought-iron bird cage (now a part of the St. Louis Zoo) designed by the Smithsonian to house more than eight hundred avian bird species so long ago, but the fair is still here, even if most of its structures are long gone. The fair lives on in stories—in the role it played in repeating a still-familiar narrative about American progress as expressed through expansion and conquest, and in the faint outlines of the shadow stories visible to those who look for them.

5

The Frontier in Miniature

THE CENTRAL FEATURE OF THE LOUISIANA PURCHASE EXPO-
sition in St. Louis was the Grand Basin (fig. 26); by entering at
the Lindell Boulevard gate, fairgoers could walk through the
plaza of St. Louis and find themselves looking up the basin to
the Palace of Fine Arts—the only palace built to survive the
exposition. The Grand Basin was flanked by four palaces on
each side: to the east were the Palaces of Education, Manufactures, Mines and Metallurgy, and Liberal Arts, with the U.S.
Government Building and the exhibits of many individual states
stretching out beyond it; to the west were the Palaces of Electricity, Varied Industries, Machinery, and Transportation, with the
international and remaining state exhibits wrapping around to
their south and west. Farther west were those requiring more
room: the Palaces of Horticulture, Agriculture, and Forestry,
Fish and Game were allocated large swaths of indoor and outdoor space, complemented by plant nurseries, parade grounds,
athletic fields, and even an aeronautic concourse. Farther west
still was the forty-seven-acre Philippine Exposition, on the
other side of Arrowhead Lake from the Anthropology Department. The Pike, home to private concessions intended to daz-
zle, shock, and entertain, stretched along the fair's north side.

All told the 1904 St. Louis World's Fair offered visitors more
than 1,200 acres to explore across both day and evening hours.
The palaces were illuminated at night, transforming the day-
time scene into a shimmering expanse. Sam Hyde, an Illinois
bookkeeper who made multiple visits, wrote, "Many an hour

26. Forest Park's Grand Basin, 2012. Author photo.

I sat watching these lights as one who hates to be awakened from a pleasant dream."[1]

The official histories documenting the Louisiana Purchase Exposition are encyclopedic, perhaps designed to provide their readers a sense of its scale. Accounts from visitors, including those who made repeat trips to see its many palaces and exhibits, affirm the fair's immensity and the impossibility of taking it all in. Edmund Philibert, a local carpenter, carefully described his twenty-eight visits in great detail. We learn where he went, what he saw, and who accompanied him, and on the final page of his fair record are his daily expenses, carefully itemized for each visit.[2] The scrapbook of Mary McKittrick Markham, whose husband, Daniel, was named chief of the Bureau of Music at the exposition, suggests that the social events attended by many of the city's wealthiest families migrated to the fairgrounds while the fair was open. While Philibert tracked each ticket purchase and train ride, the invitations, place cards, dinner menus, and event programs Mary Markham preserved offer a contrasting view.[3] St. Louis attorney Edward V. P. Schneiderhahn carefully chronicled much of his adult life across several handwritten volumes; he later distilled his fair experiences into a memoir. On opening day he wrote, "The picture is grand. The scale immense. The distances enormous."[4]

And yet when compared with the distance, the reach, the scale of American empire, they weren't. The Louisiana Purchase Exposition reproduced U.S. conquest and colonialism in miniature, over 1,200 acres, rather than across the continent and around the globe. It collected—and displayed—together objects and peoples from lands under U.S. control and invited the nations of the world to participate in this celebration of "progress." Despite filling the fairgrounds with exhibits, with people, with buildings, with material objects, the planners of the exposition repeatedly emphasized that process was on display too. Louisiana Purchase Exposition Company president David Francis wrote that the collection "was not a dead array. Color and life, infinite variety and activity, process as well as product exhibits characterized every section."[5]

Even the processes of conquest were explicitly signaled. Near the base of the hill at the center of the Main Picture were equestrian statues depicting "the people from who this region was taken, the Indians as first possessors of the soil," part of narrating, in the words of Department of Sculpture chief Karl Bitter, "the story of the Indians' disappearance."[6] And fairgoers who walked from the central palaces to the Colonnade of States encountered "the effigies of the white men who traversed the [Louisiana Territory] and first made known its resources and possibilities"—Lewis, Clark, Boone, Renault, Laclede, Marquette—all of whom stood, sculpted, "like sentinels of progress in the pioneering period."[7] The master narrative of American imperial expansion was retold in many forms at the Louisiana Purchase Exposition, but before it was put on display for fairgoers, it was reenacted in miniature—and in metaphor—on the land itself.

Visitors encountered this narrative when they came to St. Louis, but its construction and presentation required the work of thousands, including exposition staff and those recruited or compelled to work in the living exhibits the fair's planners tirelessly promoted. Though their labor built a vision of American empire in St. Louis, they sometimes worked against it—or, rather, they worked in the service of their own aims and not for the goals of the exposition's planners. The lived experiences of Indigenous North Americans and Filipinos at the St. Louis Fair reveal some of the cracks in the exposition's "grand picture" and remind us to look beyond the ornate facades of the fair's temporary buildings for our own encounter with U.S. empire in St. Louis.

The Louisiana Purchase and the Exposition

The 1904 St. Louis World's Fair was supposed to happen in 1903. Officially designated the Louisiana Purchase Exposition, the fair was framed as a centennial commemoration of Jefferson's 1803 decision to buy from France territory that would nearly double the size of the nation. Though the transaction was at first an abstract exchange that took place far from the already-occupied territory changing hands, it enabled the settler-colonial extension of U.S. power across the continent.[8]

The city of St. Louis had, in fact, also bid to host the 1893 World's Columbian Exposition, so named because it commemorated the four hundredth anniversary of Columbus's supposed "discovery" of America in 1492—then was delayed a year—and the success of the Chicago spectacle smarted. But the St. Louis elite were determined that their city should have the opportunity to host a world's fair, and in 1899, against the backdrop of war in the Philippines, key players in Missouri politics and business set in motion plans to convince the people of St. Louis that they should invest in a bid to host another exposition. Other cities meanwhile had hosted smaller expositions in the years since Chicago: Atlanta, Omaha, Buffalo. But St. Louis wanted a world's fair, an exposition that would surpass Chicago's, a victory that would land a decisive blow in the rivalry between these midwestern centers of American capital.[9]

The Louisiana Purchase became a central feature of the case fair boosters made, both to potential supporters in St. Louis and to the federal government. The Louisiana Purchase, they argued, occupied a central place in the context of the whole of American history and in the establishment of the city of St. Louis as the gateway to the West.[10] Standing before the House of Representatives on February 5, 1901, Chairman James Tawney, speaking on behalf of proposed legislation that would authorize the exposition and provide the project with federal support, argued that the Louisiana Purchase ranked alongside the American Revolution and the Civil War as a defining moment in the nation's history and that "the glory of this achievement . . . deserve[s] to be commemorated in a manner befitting a nation which by that acquisition has become the greatest nation on earth."[11] Echoing Frederick Jackson Turner's argument for the frontier experience as a critical element of American democracy (an argument Turner had voiced at the 1893 American Historical Association meeting at the World's Columbian Exposition in Chicago), Tawney continued:

> At the time of this purchase nineteen-twentieths of the territory embraced in it was unpeopled save by wild beasts and savages. The rivers flowed unvexed by the fretting wheels of commerce; on the broad prairies the flowers bloomed and died with none to note their beauty or enjoy their fragrance; luxuriant grasses ripened in summer airs, rotted and enriched a soil on which no harvest waved. In less than

half a century all this was changed. The strong hand of the pioneer was laid upon the mighty forces of nature, bringing them under his complete control.[12]

"The strong hand of the pioneer," but not the strong hand of the soldier, apparently. Though so central to the work of transforming the West and occupying the Philippines, soldiers quickly lost their places in the exposition's version of the national story. In Chairman Tawney's telling, soldiers' labor—and thus their work in the service of U.S. empire—was practically invisible. President Theodore Roosevelt described the people of the states formed from the Louisiana Purchase as both "mighty in war" and "mighty in strength to tame the rugged wilderness," saying, "They could not thus have conquered the forest and the prairie, the mountains and the desert, had they not possessed the great fighting virtues, the qualities which enable a people to overcome the forces of hostile men and hostile nature."[13] The people who settled the West, tamed the wilderness, and formed state governments were, for Roosevelt, heroes. Soldiers—agents of the federal government sent to fight, dispossess, and then manage both Native people and newly occupied land—weren't mentioned. But even though soldiers' actions became harder to see in the narratives offered by exposition planners and politicians, the results of their labor—all that their work in the West and the Philippines had yielded—became focal points of the St. Louis World's Fair.

Roosevelt's remarks echoed those of Frederick Jackson Turner, and the connection wasn't a coincidence. Turner's arguments about the frontier as central to the formation of American identity fit perfectly with the way exposition planners were positioning the significance of the Louisiana Purchase—and thus the significance of their proposed exposition—in American history. Early in the planning process the president of the Louisiana Purchase Exposition Company, David Francis, shared the stage of the Contemporary Club in St. Louis with Turner, who seems to have outlined ideas published in 1903 as "The Significance of the Louisiana Purchase," ten years after he presented "The Significance of the Frontier in American History" at an earlier world's fair. Francis told the audience that after hearing Professor Turner's speech, they would "be deeply impressed with the importance of celebrating so great an event in our history."[14]

Still, the argument that the Louisiana Purchase was a significant moment wasn't new. It had been used by Brig. Gen. Francis Vinton Greene on board the *China* to inspire the ranks as they steamed across the Pacific to the Philippines on the Fourth of July in 1899. Based on Jefferson's decision to acquire Louisiana, Greene imagined that if faced with the choice to take the Philippines, the man who had doubled the size of the continental United States would be on the side of empire and of course would be eager to occupy the Philippines.[15] Civilian voices, too, used the history of the Louisiana Purchase as a frame for understanding American empire in the Pacific. Senator Henry Cabot Lodge of Massachusetts positioned the acquisition of the Philippines as consistent with both Jefferson's expansionist views and his decision to acquire Louisiana. To the Senate Lodge declared, "In 1804 the party which opposed expansion went down in utter wreck before the man who, interpreting aright the instincts, the hopes, and the spirit of the American people, made the Louisiana Purchase. We make the same appeal in behalf of our American policies. We have made the appeal before, and won, as we deserved to win. We shall not fail now."[16]

Others argued that the case of the Philippines was completely different from the Louisiana Purchase. Representative W. Bourke Cockran claimed that while the Louisiana Purchase was a means to achieve peace, taking ownership of the Philippines was an act of empire inconsistent with the values of American democracy.[17] Cockran's framing suggests he saw key differences between continental expansion and overseas empire; while "peace" justified the genocide and dispossession of Native people that followed the abstract extension of U.S. control over the Louisiana Purchase, more starkly ambitious goals—profit, prosperity, better access to Asian markets—did not reflect American values.

Others disagreed. President McKinley, as he campaigned for reelection in the West, publicly thanked Jefferson: "I never travel through this mighty West, a part of the Louisiana purchase, Iowa, part of Minnesota, and the Dakotas, that I do not feel like offering my gratitude to Thomas Jefferson and his wisdom and foresight in acquiring this vast territory, to be peopled by men and women such as I have seen before me as I have journeyed through these states."[18] Here McKinley narrated the West as empty and unpeopled, waiting for American settlement. McKinley offered "gratitude to Jefferson" before suggesting a similar pathway for the Philippines. Articles and letters to the editor in a range of newspapers demonstrate the frequency—and perceived utility—of this connection: the imperialists used it to position the acquisition of the Philippines as a logical step in a Jeffersonian view of the nation; the anti-imperialists, to suggest the difference between the two cases.[19] Politicians and concerned citizens both linked the future of the Philippines with the history of the North American West—and while sometimes the connection was a cautionary tale, for fair planners it was more of a rallying cry.

So when Chairman Tawney, David Francis, and even, apparently, Frederick Jackson Turner spoke of the Louisiana Purchase in the same breath as they did the proposed Louisiana Purchase Exposition, the contemporary relevance of this long-past event and the modern political value of celebrating its centennial not only would have made perfect sense but would have been especially appealing. The fair, a business venture for the people of St. Louis, could—and would—strengthen a particular narrative about U.S. empire in both the West and the Pacific.

Part of this story was about scale. The Louisiana Purchase had doubled the size of the nation, and the leadership of the Louisiana Purchase Exposition Company, the businessmen behind the St. Louis World's Fair, planned an exposition that would both surpass the Chicago fair in size and reflect the expansion they were commemorating in the physical landscape of the fairgrounds. At 1,270 acres the Louisiana Purchase Exposition would almost be larger than the fairs at Philadelphia, Chicago,

Omaha, and Buffalo combined.[20] Though the emphasis would be "both national and international in its character," the planners wrote, the fair would "present, in a special degree, and in the most comprehensive manner, the history, the resources, and the development of the states and territories lying within the boundaries of the Louisiana Purchase, showing what it was and what it is; what it contained and produced in 1803; what it contains and produces now." Furthermore, their exhibit would "make plain that the prophecy of 1803 has been more than fulfilled, and show that a veritable empire now lies between the Gulf of Mexico and Puget Sound, within the limits of the territory Jefferson obtained by the Louisiana Purchase." This fair would showcase "the history, resources, and development of the possessions of the United States."[21] To do this exposition planners needed space, and after considering the options, the Louisiana Purchase Exposition Company settled on Forest Park.

Formally established in 1876 after much debate and several land transactions, the 1,200 acres of Forest Park became a destination for picnickers, horseback riders, young athletes, bicyclists, even boaters and winter tobogganers. Before 1876 the land that became Forest Park had contained forests and fields, planted orchards, common lands, a dairy farm, and coal mines. And still earlier, the region had been a site of constant encounter, with the Mississippi River linking Indigenous and Anglo networks of power and commerce.[22] Just fifteen miles east of St. Louis stands Cahokia Mounds, the site of a major urban center of Mississippian culture, where a city larger than London had bustled at its peak in 1250 AD.[23] In the late nineteenth century, to create the park, laborers took down fences, shacks, and barns and even pulled trees to disrupt the area's ordered rows. Artificial lakes were constructed, and in the Wilderness, the western section of the park, "men cleared trees from the virgin forest that had given the park its name, to make room for roads and to open scenic vistas." The first streetcar line to Forest Park was completed in 1885, and by 1896 seven streetcar lines were bringing more than 2.5 million visitors through its gates.[24]

The city of St. Louis granted the Louisiana Purchase Exposition Company permission to use the western half of Forest Park, an area of 657 acres at the edge of the city, and as Francis recounts, the planners began discussions about "the annexation of additional territory for exposition purposes."[25] Local property owners, including Washington University, leased the rest to the Louisiana Purchase Exposition Company, and in the case of the university the agreement included the use of its new campus buildings. Though all these arrangements were temporary—from negotiations in 1901 through the conclusion of the fair and the cleanup afterward—the planners began an involved process of imagining and then transforming the landscapes that would host their fair, an exposition that would "gather the products of the soil, mine, forest and sea from the whole earth."[26] But first they had to prepare the grounds.

Transforming Forest Park

A ceremony to "driv[e] the first stake" and begin "the physical work" of the exposition was scheduled for September 3, 1901. More than two thousand people gathered to witness this formal beginning to the project, but the ceremony was delayed because the official party, comprising President Francis and the other World's Fair directors, was lost. Apparently "the geography and topography of Forest Park were not so familiar to the World's Fair Directors as they afterward became." The chief civil engineer found the group "wandering in what was known as the wilderness."[27] This wasn't just a descriptive label for undeveloped terrain in a portion of the park; this is how the western portion of Forest Park was labeled on the map (fig. 27).

The directors of the Louisiana Purchase Exposition saw only potential in the Wilderness of Forest Park: it was to become the center of the expansive exposition (fig. 28). The directors marked the beginning of the process of remaking the landscape by burying in the ground a two-foot stake, "hewn out of a stout, young oak which grew upon the Worlds' Fair grounds" and that had been "polished and varnished" for the occasion.[28]

An official groundbreaking ceremony was scheduled a few

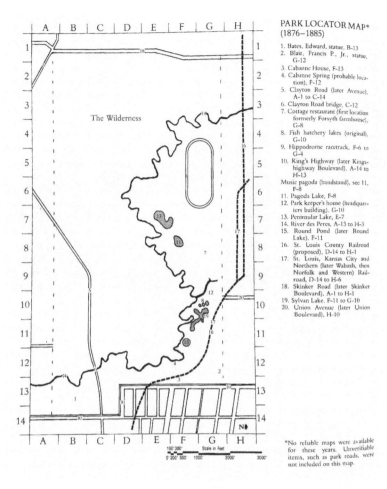

27. Map of Forest Park, ca. 1876–85. Loughlin and Anderson note that there are no reliable maps from the period before 1885; this map is their reconstruction of verifiable details. "Park Locator Map," Loughlin and Anderson, *Forest Park*, 20.

months after the first stake had been driven into the ground with "a new ax."[29] This time all involved found their way to the designated place. The directors of the Louisiana Purchase Exposition never wasted an opportunity to connect their project to the moment it commemorated and its significance in American history, and thus they carefully dug into the soil of Forest Park with a shovel from 1803. Reflecting on this moment in the history he authored of the fair, David Francis wrote, "These simple

28. Scene at the site of the World's Fair in Forest Park before construction. Photographer unknown, ca. 1900. Missouri Historical Society, St. Louis.

tools were in strange contrast to the powerful tractor excavators, the steam shovels, and twenty-horse plows with long trains of dump wagons which in a few months were to move a million cubic yards of earth and bring the site to building levels." Despite the natural beauty of Forest Park's grounds, celebrated repeatedly in the fair's promotional materials, the vision of Isaac Taylor, director of public works, and his commission of architects required substantial changes to this Wilderness to make it suitable for the fair, and Francis's words describe the process witnessed by planners, laborers, and early fairgoers alike. When Taylor looked at Forest Park, he saw wild woods. "This northern portion was sparsely grown with trees at its eastern end; at its western end there was a tangle of wild woods, with trees of large dimensions and a dense undergrowth, the ground being swampy in places, while in others it rose in elevations twenty to thirty feet in height, divided by deep ravines; this portion was commonly known as the Wilderness."[30]

Sam Hyde, a bookkeeper from Illinois, wrote, "Our first visit was just after the surveyors had finished their preliminary work and the hills and valleys bristled with their stakes. I am told that much annoyance was caused by some of these stakes being carried off by souvenir fiends. We did not get one. Many trees were tagged—some for felling and others for transplanting."[31] Hyde carefully inked these words into an album filled with beautifully crafted sentences that swirl around photographs and sketches from the months he spent at the fair. He began collecting memories of the exposition long before the palaces were constructed. When Hyde first visited Forest Park two years before opening day, he already saw signs of the transformations planned.

James Buel, author of a ten-volume history of the Louisiana Purchase Exposition, saw nature's beauty, describing Forest Park as "the largest public ground of the kind in the world, as well as being one of the most beautiful, diversified as it is by hills, ravines, graceful prospects, charming lakes, level expanses of sward, and a lovely natural forest." He knew the rest of the story, though, and he could see the possibilities: "Beautiful as it was to visit, that part of the park selected for Exposition purposes required an immense amount of grading, filling, clearing, excavating and replanting."[32]

Sam Hyde saw those changes taking place: "We went again," he wrote, "when the hills and valleys were disappearing before the dredge and scraper and the face of the landscape was changing every day. And again, when the sights of the vast buildings had been marked and long trains of cars were unloading lumber and iron and sewer pipe and rock and sand and cinders. And we were there when the skeletons of the buildings began to rise from the broad acres that had been leveled by the hand of man."[33]

Hyde was among the estimated one hundred thousand visitors who came to Forest Park before the exposition opened to observe the preparation of the fairgrounds. A fence dividing the eastern portion of Forest Park from the section allocated for the Louisiana Purchase Exposition was constructed, though visitors were free to wander throughout the grounds of both landscapes.[34]

29. Field of stumps with the Administration Building in the distance during construction phase of the 1904 World's Fair. Photograph by George Stark, 1902. Missouri Historical Society, St. Louis.

George Stark, a photographer assigned to capture the transformation of Forest Park in 1901, took several photographs of the clearing of this Wilderness.[35] To capture the image in figure 29, Stark pointed his camera westward across an expanse of stumps and stakes. One tree stands off to the left—saved for some special purpose or simply not yet removed? The new buildings of Washington University emerge from the hazy background. This is not the work of David Francis's commemorative shovel but of forces far more powerful and operating on a larger scale: steam shovels, tractors, concession contracts, city boosterism.

Stark's photograph looks like a battlefield. Branches and limbs lie strewn across the landscape, and a trench in the foreground offers mirror images of nearby stumps. The scene is grim. There appear to be wagons and perhaps laborers in the distance, but it is difficult to separate them from what remains of the forest. One of the workmen told a *Globe-Democrat* reporter that some of the trees had seen three centuries go by. Interviews conducted by reporters reveal ambivalence about this transformation of the Wilderness: remorse one week and anticipation the next. There is something in this anticipation, even in the face of stump-strewn acreage, that captures a critical element of the spirit of the fair: it is the sense that anything is possible, that the future is as yet unknown. Yes, much of what had existed on the site was cut down, destroyed, removed. Even the park's river was forced underground.[36] Edward Schneiderhahn, in his 1904 memoir about visiting the fair, wrote, "It was a pity to see giant monarchs of the forest fall before the woodman's ax to make room for the exhibit palaces." But despite describing "a whole plain that had been swept bare of patriarchs of the forest," Schneiderhahn paid many compliments to the "graceful outline and splendid proportions" of the exhibit palaces.[37]

All this labor was in service to a particular design aesthetic: "In no matter what direction he looks, the view obtained will be ample reward for the longest journey to the World's Fair." This reward would be imparted through the "absolute harmony" of architecture and landscaping: "The conception is one of grand display, calculated to fill the spectator with admiration and completely occupy his vision."[38] The approach was different from those for previous expositions: in searching for ways to set the St. Louis fair apart from the legacy of Chicago and its White City, planners highlighted Forest Park as one of the Louisiana Purchase Exposition's unique features. In fact, the *Official Guidebook of the Louisiana Purchase Exposition* played up the diversity of the Forest Park landscape to fair visitors: "Surrounded on three sides with primeval forests, and embracing hill and valley, plateau and lowlands, precipitous ravine and gently undulating slope, the ground on which the Louisiana Purchase was built afforded the architects opportunity for beautiful effects such as were denied the builders of former Expositions."[39] This slip—the guidebook describes "the ground on which the Louisiana Purchase was built," not "the ground on which the Louisiana Purchase *Exposition* was

30. View west from the balcony of the German Pavilion looking toward the East Restaurant Pavilion and Festival Hall on the left and the Palace of Electricity on the right at the 1904 World's Fair. Photograph by F. J. Koster, 1904. Missouri Historical Society, St. Louis.

built"—further conflated the work of remaking both the U.S. West and Forest Park.

The exposition's Publicity Department made much of these "beautiful effects." Despite (or because of) the substantial modifications made to the Wilderness of Forest Park, the fair was praised repeatedly for its attention to the "natural landscape." Newspaper articles leading up to and during the fair emphasized the site again and again: "No exposition of the past has had a situation so naturally attractive. Its hills and shallow valleys give it many landscape features. Portions of the ground are covered with tall trees, and the delightful groves will serve as restful retreats for tired visitors who seek diversion from sight-seeing."[40] Professor Victor Wilker wrote in the *Christian Advocate*, "This ideal arrangement was made possible by the natural condition of the ground. So beautiful a location has never been witnessed before at any world's fair."[41] These voices nar-

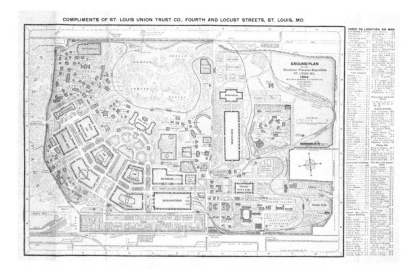

31. Ground plan of the Louisiana Purchase Exposition. Compliments of St. Louis Union Trust Company. (1904 World's Fair.) Map by Buxton & Skinner, 1904. Missouri Historical Society, St. Louis.

rated the exposition planners' vision into being just as workers materially transformed the fairgrounds, not unlike the work soldiers had performed in the landscapes of their service with both their words and their labor.

While the architecture of the St. Louis World's Fair mostly maintained the Beaux-Arts style of the 1893 World's Columbian Exposition, the fan-shaped layout and the integration of Forest Park's ravine invited the viewer to take in the fair from all angles (fig. 30). The Main Picture consisted of "eight big exhibit palaces and a mile and a half of lagoon, [and] is on a level area surrounded on two sides by hills that rise to a height of 65 feet."[42]

These palaces were oriented around the semi-circular Grand Basin (fig. 31). "No handsomer artificial basin can be found anywhere in the world," reported the guidebook.[43] David Francis commented that visitors to world's fairs were sick of symmetry. "You never tire of Forest Park," he said.[44] James Buel echoed this sentiment in his history of the fair: "The gorgeous scene had as many different points of view as there was standing room in the vast area. The slightest change in the angle of vision

32. *The St. Louis World's Fair Site, Forest Park.* Image taken by Ferd Ruhland for the *World's Fair Bulletin* 3, no. 1 (1901–2): 8. Courtesy of the University of Missouri, MU Libraries.

revealed an effect different from all the rest and equally wonderful."[45] Buel was pointing to how the view changed depending on the viewer's perspective.

This focus on looking emphasized appearances. Beneath their gleaming exteriors, after all, the palaces were just temporary buildings, masterfully sculpted staff (a plaster of paris mixture) on a wooden frame. But the finished grounds, shiny palaces, and sparkling lagoons that constituted the Main Picture did more than hide their temporary status; the view also managed to obscure the labor that constructed it.

This is part of what makes the *World's Fair Bulletin*, a monthly promotional magazine, so interesting. Though most of its pages were devoted to other sorts of exposition details—commitments from foreign governments, press coverage, profiles of the directors, architects' renderings of the palaces and grounds—in its coverage of the progress toward opening day, the *World's Fair*

33. *The Grand Work of Transformation in Forest Park.* Image taken by Ferd Ruhland for the *World's Fair Bulletin* 3, no. 1 (1901–2): 4. Courtesy of the University of Missouri, MU Libraries.

Bulletin also tracked the physical work that occurred at Forest Park (fig. 32).

For example, in the November 1901 issue, under the heading "Scenes on the World's Fair Site: Transforming the Wilderness of Forest Park into an Exposition Landscape," the *World's Fair Bulletin* made the link between the remaking of the American West and the remaking of Forest Park explicit. The author described the "beautiful, undulating forest of unculled timber and tangled undergrowth" of Forest Park as a "cherished" piece of the "unsettled Louisiana Purchase," then suggested that the Wilderness of Forest Park had "passed through the various stages of a pioneer 'clearing,' presenting scenes of timber destruction and burning brush-piles, now almost as novel as the untouched forest itself."[46] So not only was Forest Park being transformed into the Louisiana Purchase Exposition, but the Wilderness of the park became a stand-in for the wilderness of the U.S. West. Just as the West had been cleared, settled, and planted, so too was the Wilderness of Forest Park transformed (fig. 33). But in this analogy, who were the pioneers?

Well, according to the *World's Fair Bulletin*, they were an "army," one "nearly as large as the American force that stormed and took Manila." This "World's Fair army" of "graders and teamsters from all sections of the country" streamed into the city, ready to do the work of clearing trees, digging channels, and regrading the Wilderness and the leased land beyond it.[47] And like the pioneers, they set up temporary camps, or "colonies," on the fairgrounds with names such as Camperstown and Graders' Home.[48]

The work was backbreaking. Sometimes workers were hacking through frozen ground; other times they were digging up roots and stumps loosened by dynamite. Once the stumps were removed by men wielding axes, next came plows, and after that grading machines. Even this progression mirrored the settlement of the West—or one version of it. But just as the transformation of the West—a violent, uneven, genocidal process of dispossessing Native people and confining them to reservations—had been turned into a simpler story of preparing an empty waiting landscape, of building homesteads and planting fields to fulfill a Jeffersonian vision of an American continent, the remaking of Forest Park was more complicated than this story of untouched Wilderness might have us believe.

For Forest Park contained "Indian mounds," evidence of deep and persistent human history. When a local archaeologist pointed them out, the Louisiana Purchase Exposition Company approved an excavation and assigned several workmen to assist. The *World's Fair Bulletin* reported, "The mounds that were on land to be graded were carefully opened up and the examination resulted in the finding of one almost complete skeleton, three skulls, fragments of pottery, and numerous flint arrowheads, besides bones too much decomposed for preservation."[49] The archaeologist supervising the excavation was careful to point out that these ancestors and cultural belongings were not from the Mississippian culture that built Cahokia, but

34. *Looking West from Varied Industry Building.* Dr. J. Perry Worden for the *World's Fair Bulletin* 3, no. 10 (1902–3): 33. Courtesy of the University of Missouri, MU Libraries.

from the more recent past: these were Omaha tools and graves. Omahas had interacted with Lewis and Clark after the Louisiana Purchase and traded along the Missouri River in the nineteenth century.[50] These findings did not fit neatly with the way fair planners intended to frame Native people—as remnants from the continent's deep past. Perhaps this is why the *World's Fair Bulletin* ended its coverage there. It is unclear whether these ancestors and cultural belongings were ever returned to their descendants.

Once the terrain had been graded to the specifications of Isaac Taylor and his team of planners, work began on the buildings, and the *World's Fair Bulletin* shifted its focus accordingly. Its issues are filled with images of palace scaffolding, and I can understand why: the wooden shells of the palaces—what Hyde called "skeletons"—are lovely, haunting against the backdrop of the recently emptied Wilderness (fig. 34).

With the Wilderness cleared, the grounds prepared, and the main palaces rising, the next step was the exhibits. What would be displayed inside the palaces? Which governments, of both foreign nations and U.S. states, would commit to constructing buildings and exhibits on the fairgrounds? The *World's Fair*

Bulletin reported every detail of these developments, even noting when foreign newspapers were using space in their pages (and how much) to cover the coming exposition. The planners sent delegates around the world, and David Francis, the president of the Louisiana Purchase Exposition Company, traveled abroad to generate interest in the fair and secure commitments to participate.

This was critical, because while world's fairs received government support, federal money did not drive these expositions. Boosters and businessmen put up the initial funds and made their bids, and once a site had been selected, the leaders of that city's efforts began to assign roles and divide up the tasks: choose a location and negotiate for its use; hire people to manage exhibits and departments; recruit participation from the global community; keep raising money and interest. This meant a lot of traveling, a lot of lectures, and a lot of promotional coverage. And it's why the *World's Fair Bulletin* exists.

As early as February 1902 Francis was in Boston, making the pitch for New England to be well represented at the fair: "Send your representatives as ou[r] guests to the scene of the Exposition and we will show you a landscape of a thousand acres, dotted with primeval forests, through which courses a natural water-way, a location for an Exposition which is beautiful beyond compare, and which is accessible from the heart of Saint Louis within twenty minutes for electric or steam lines of transportation." He was careful to stress both the beauty and the accessibility of the fairgrounds. At a banquet the same evening Francis continued to argue for New England participation in St. Louis. His strategy? To highlight the significance of the Louisiana Purchase and remind Bostonians of the place of New England men in the making of the West: "The progress of which we are so proud is due in great measure to the industry of the sons of New England, who left the homes of their youth to settle in the West." He continued: "The capital which you have furnished has enabled us to bridge rivers, tunnel mountains, build cities, open mines, enrich lands, establish manufactories and extend commerce." The efforts of those in the East transformed a region critics of Jefferson labeled a "boundless waste" into "the seat of productive power of the nation."[51] Francis was good at this, moving seamlessly from the West owing everything to New England to being the country's engine of growth. Now, would they please commit to a large showing at the fair?

These speeches and banquets led to promises of participation, which led to boards of commissioners, who then traveled to St. Louis for ceremonies commemorating the future sites of their buildings at the fair. The ceremonies and details about the size and style of each of the planned buildings (and commentary on what might be displayed inside) received extensive coverage in the *World's Fair Bulletin*, which contains numerous photographs featuring groups of people standing on their assigned plots of land while work on the grounds occurs around them. This was the work taking place in St. Louis—the large-scale coordination and actual construction of the exposition. A version of the world was being re-created, albeit in miniature, in St. Louis. And most of the pieces came from somewhere else.

Louisiana Purchase Exposition employees and ambassadors traveled the country, and the globe, to find exhibits and persuade exhibitors—American states and territories, foreign governments, corporations, individuals—to contribute materials for the fair. The goal was for the exposition to be universal. David Francis called it a success: "So thoroughly did it represent the world's civilization that if all man's other works were by some unspeakable catastrophe blotted out the records established at this Exposition by the assembled nations would afford the necessary standards for the rebuilding of our entire civilization."[52] Or at least what the exposition company's planners deemed significant or representative. This effort to craft a spectacle that, in the minds of its creators, could stand in for the world itself might be the perfect example of U.S. empire in action.

To enact their vision the exposition's planners did not have to start from scratch. A long history of world's fairs had come before their attempt, and they were able to turn to past expositions for inspiration, artifacts, and collecting networks. As with previous fairs, the Louisiana Purchase Exposition expected the federal government to supply exhibits showcasing U.S. resources and achievements. And as it had done before, the U.S. government turned to the Smithsonian Institution and its United States National Museum to procure many exposition needs (and wants).

Collecting and Preparing for the Fair

The Smithsonian had played a significant role in world's fair exhibits from the beginning; in fact, the national museum owed its existence (at least in part) to the first world's fair held on U.S. soil, the 1876 Centennial Exposition in Philadelphia. At its founding in 1846 the Smithsonian's shape and form remained unclear. The bequest from James Smithson was supposed to go toward "the increase and diffusion of knowledge."[53] But exactly how to do that was up for debate, and not everyone was convinced that the Smithsonian needed a museum. Enter the 1876 Exposition. The Smithsonian's exhibit in Philadelphia attracted plenty of interest and contributed to the overall success of the fair. Afterward the Smithsonian made arrangements for significant portions of the fair's varied displays to find permanent homes in its collections.[54] The upward momentum from the exposition, paired with the practical need for a place to store and display the Smithsonian's latest acquisitions, resulted in the formal establishment of the Smithsonian's United States National Museum—as well as the go-ahead on plans to construct a building where the museum would be housed.[55]

Thus established, the Smithsonian continued to play a significant role in U.S. government exhibits at world's fairs and expositions.[56] And although its ever-growing holdings provided a strong base to work from, Smithsonian curators used their extensive networks to collect specific items for their world's fair displays. If existing records are any indication, Smithsonian staff spent a significant amount of time working to acquire desired specimens and artifacts, plan exhibits, transport materials, and construct exposition displays. And by the time preparation began for the 1904 World's Fair in St. Louis, curators who had been at the Smithsonian for even just a few years had helped plan government exhibits at the 1901 Pan-American Exposition in Buffalo. Still, St. Louis was going to be bigger, and the Smithsonian's efforts, which included a wrought-iron birdcage the size of a football field and the skeleton of a sulphur-bottom whale from Newfoundland, appear to have been an attempt to outdo itself yet again.

Preparation began early. Public Act No. 192, approved on June 26, 1902, authorized the appropriation of $800,000 for the "selection, purchase, preparation, transportation, arrangement, installation, safe-keeping, exhibition, and return of such articles and materials as the heads of the several Executive Departments, the Smithsonian Institution, the National Museum, the United States Fish Commission, the Department of Labor, and the Library of Congress may respectively decide shall be embraced in the Government exhibit," as well as for the physical installation of the exhibit and to cover the salaries of those involved in the undertaking. An additional sum of $200,000 was appropriated for the construction of the buildings that would house the federal government's exhibits.[57] Though the government exhibits represented more than the contributions from the Smithsonian and the National Museum, these entities received the largest funding allocations from the appropriations bill—as well as the largest allocations of physical space at the fair: 15,275 feet combined for the Smithsonian and the National Museum.[58]

It took a lot of work to fill this space. From the sheer volume of exposition-related correspondence, it seems that many Smithsonian staffers did nothing but write letters in the service of acquiring and preparing materials for the fair. Incoming letters were organized by the last name of the sender, so a systematic review of these records covers A to Z (or almost), from fair-related correspondence from J. A. Allen at the American Museum in New York to letters about alligator acquisition from Charles K. Worthen. Commercial collectors, furriers, and taxidermists offered to provide birds and bird eggs, reptiles, grizzly bears, fish, even ostriches.[59] There's an exchange between the Smithsonian's special agent, Dr. Marcus Lyon Jr., and a young man who claimed he could provide a large elk. The conversation broadened to include the game warden of the state of Washington, once it became clear that the young man had broken state game laws to shoot the elk in question.[60] The records also include an invoice for a Mongolian tiger skin and a note from a shipping company about the transport of two live cobras, warning that the company "cannot of course accept risk of mortality of the snakes, and would ask you to meet the amount of our Bill whether the snakes arrive alive or dead."[61]

New structures and exhibit concepts were designed to display the objects and specimens the Smithsonian worked to acquire. For example, the National Zoological Park planned a football-field-size birdcage.[62] It was to be filled with more than eight hundred varieties of birds, "notable for their brilliant colors, sweet songs or peculiar forms." A passageway built through the cage allowed visitors to watch as the different species flew all around them. The cage included "trees and shrubs, pools and running streams, where the perching birds can find shelter and the aquatic birds proper exercise."[63] The *World's Fair Bulletin* explained that in constructing the birdcage, it was "the aim to counterfeit nature as near as possible"; "there will be trees, brush and rocks that will give it the appearance of a miniature forest."[64] And that forest would be filled with birds from around the world, both reflecting global biodiversity and hinting at the imperial reach required to bring them all to St. Louis.

The Smithsonian searched for far more than birds, and its exposition records reveal efforts to procure and exhibit a series of mounted large game—including a hippopotamus, wild sheep, deer, caribou, and "an exceptionally fine example" of a giraffe.[65] In 1902 the Smithsonian also requested an elk from the herds at Yellowstone National Park—using as its go-between Edgar Mearns, who was stationed at Fort Yellowstone at the time. But one of the biggest projects undertaken by the Department of Biology for the 1904 St. Louis World's Fair was the acquisition of a sulphur-bottom whale.

The effort was enormous—and so was the whale. The

sulphur-bottom whale, or blue whale, is the largest animal on the planet, and it was the perfect animal to display at the world's largest exposition. F. A. Lucas, a zoologist and curator at the National Museum, traveled to Newfoundland and coordinated the work of inspecting whales brought in during the whaling season. He was looking for the biggest whale—one over seventy feet—and it could have no injuries to its vertebrae or defects in its overall shape; the museum also wanted to make a plaster mold of the whale so that his team could construct a full-scale model for the fair and, later, the museum.

Once Lucas selected his whale, he and the men he'd hired through Ward's Natural Science Establishment in Rochester, New York—a business centered on natural history specimens—made a cast. After the molds hardened, Lucas and the preparators from Ward's built a temporary maceration plant on site in Newfoundland and began the work of preparing and packing the bones, which Lucas described as "a greasy, laborious, and puzzling piece of work." Lucas commented on both the difficulty of the work—"there isn't much fun in working with one's fingers bleeding"—and the particular challenges of moving a whale: "A box as large as a room and weighing four tons is not an easy thing to handle."[66] Still, they managed to get the bones into thirteen packages, which were loaded onto ss *Silvia* and transported to New York. Here they were placed onto two different railcars, weighing 26,550 pounds in total, bound for Ward's in Rochester.[67] It was quite a feat.

Ward's handled the work of getting the whale skeleton and cast ready for the fair, but other commercial establishments were contracted to help with the government exhibits. The Smithsonian's records reveal a significant network of natural history firms, collectors, furriers, and taxidermists supporting (for fees, of course) the work of the museum.[68] The fair was not simply an opportunity to construct the finest exhibit imaginable; it was also a business opportunity for those in the business of natural history.[69] Firms offered their services, sent their price lists, described their most exciting stock. Some made donations, no doubt hoping for future business. Other companies benefited from the opportunity to display their commissioned handiwork in the Smithsonian exhibit. For example, the newest addition to the Department of Geology's display was a (not quite) walking advertisement for the Milwaukee Papier Mache Works in the form of a stegosaurus model. Extensive correspondence details the work of constructing this model, with letters about the bracing inside the dinosaur, the coloring of different parts of the back and belly, even the texture of the skin.[70] Getting it right, as it were, mattered, not just to meticulous museum curators but also for the impact of the exposition's broader arguments about the success—and perhaps even the superiority—of the American project in all realms, among them democracy, empire, and science.

That authenticity mattered to Smithsonian curators is evident in their correspondence. William Henry Holmes of the Bureau of American Ethnology wrote to ask Frederick True if they could simply put Smithsonian ethnologists already in the field on the payroll for the exposition instead of hiring other people to aid in gathering materials for the department's display at the fair: "It will be apparent to all that these experienced ethnologists are better qualified than any other persons to undertake the assemblage of collections that will represent the operations of the Bureau." (Written on True's copy of the correspondence: "Approved.")[71] This strategy of using anthropologists already in the museum's network to collect materials for expositions was not new. Frederic Ward Putnam, who had led the anthropology division at the Chicago World's Fair in 1893, had contracted with some of the same anthropologists to purchase materials for the exhibits under his direction. Putnam also coordinated directly with Native collectors—Cornelius C. Cusick (Tuscarora), George Hunt (Fort Rupert), and Odille Morison (Tsimshian)—and David Beck suggests that the exhibits featuring materials acquired by these collectors, who could draw on existing connections and community relationships, were among Putnam's most successful displays.[72] Once these cultural belongings were collected, they often continued along the exposition circuit before being placed in museums, where they would shore up settlers and their science.[73]

Though the states and territories of the U.S. West had their own spaces at the fair, the Smithsonian's exhibits emphasized the peoples and resources of the territory acquired through the Louisiana Purchase. Materials from the U.S. West made up a significant portion of the Smithsonian's oldest collections; the survey expeditions led by army men and scientists to explore the continent throughout the nineteenth century had brought back material to be studied, described, and displayed.[74] Exhibits focused on biology, geology, and anthropology featured western specimens, art, and artifacts alongside models of Mayan ruins, the giant whale skeleton, and replicas of ancient art from around the world.

Indigenous People at the Fair

In addition to displaying objects and cultural belongings from the West's Native people, the government exhibit was to include "representatives of almost every tribe of American Indians." W J McGee, chief of the fair's Department of Anthropology, explained that the Native groups at the fair would "typify aboriginal life" and that "both special students and general visitors [would] find in them an index to the inner life of the Red Race whose rise and passing form the opening epic of American history."[75] Indigenous people were placed "before" in the story exposition planners wanted to tell; they were present to illustrate an incredibly tidy tale about U.S. expansion and cultural dominance that moved through the West and across the Pacific to the Philippines.[76]

As emissaries from the "opening epic of American history," Native people would, according to the World's Fair Bulletin, "give their dances and illustrate their sports and modes of primitive and modern life." Unlike at other world's fairs, there would be no additional admission fee for this part of the exposition. The government exhibit would give visitors to the St. Louis fair a special opportunity—the chance to see "a real, live midway show for nothing."[77] The fair's own mouthpiece, then, framed Indigenous peoples as spectacle, as entertainment.

Focusing only on how Indigenous people were framed or seen by visitors to the fair risks reproducing the narratives that exposition planners chose to tell and suggests that what was planned was exactly what happened. But Native people did not simply agree to McGee's framing; their participation was motivated by a multitude of factors, including the opportunity to travel, to work, to earn income, and even to share elements of their arts and cultures with others from around the world. And once at the fair Native people participated on their own terms. Bonnie Miller emphasizes that although fair planners had decided how those in living exhibits should be understood, expositions were not "closed ideological system[s]." In her work on the visual culture of the 1898 Trans-Mississippi and International Exposition in Omaha, she reminds those focusing on how empire was displayed that "the improvisational performances of 'living' exhibits, the unpredictability of crowds, and the contingency of foreign events prevented organizers from maintaining tight control over cultural content."[78]

In some ways experiences at previous fairs helped shape the heavy-handedness of the progress narrative on display at St. Louis, but despite all attempts to direct fairgoers' encounters with imperial subjects from both sides of the Pacific, Indigenous people who participated in the fair chose whether, when, and how to engage. Planners' attempts at presenting what they imagined to be authentic displays of Native life were compromised almost immediately when it became clear that the people in their living exhibits were also interested in seeing the fair, purchasing souvenirs, and interacting with the diverse range of people the event had gathered together. Despite promotional articles promising exhibits featuring "remnants" who would "return . . . to their picturesque life of a hundred years ago," McGee had to settle for "request[ing] authenticity from 9:00 to 11:00 a.m. and 2:00 to 4:00 p.m., when groups were officially demonstrating."[79]

Still, exposition planners limited which Native people could participate. A decade earlier, when planning the Chicago fair, Putnam had "turned away those he thought to be too civilized or advanced to portray the ancient lifeways of the Americas." Those Indigenous people who participated in the 1893 Chicago World's Fair were intended to represent the "before" part of a story of U.S. power, progress, and modernity. But as David Beck points out, these same people were active agents in a "modern" economy at the fair: they were participating in the living exhibits as workers on contract or as entrepreneurs selling their goods to fairgoers for a profit.[80]

Geronimo, in particular, used his presence at the St. Louis fair for his own purposes. After negotiating for a monthly salary, as well as to select other Chiricahuas imprisoned at Fort Sill to join him, Geronimo agreed to participate in the Louisiana Purchase Exposition.[81] He made and sold bows, arrows, and canes for fair attendees who wanted souvenirs. He also sold his own picture for a quarter; he was allowed to keep ten cents per portrait, along with whatever amount he could generate from signing his name. He later said that after the fair, "I had plenty of money—more than I had ever owned before."[82] Visitors were happy to pay him for his wares—and for their chance to see the man who had been framed as one of the nation's most terrifying and capable enemies just a few decades earlier.[83]

Many of the fair's Indigenous participants made items to sell: Acoma and Santa Clara women made pottery, while men made souvenir adobe bricks; Lakotas made pipes, bows, arrows, and beadwork; Wichitas made moccasins. There was Navajo weaving and silverwork, Kickapoo beading, and Pima basketry. The fair's oldest Indigenous participant, Mon-e-do-wats (Anishinabe, Leech Lake band), made birchbark canoes in miniature. And Pomo artists Mary and William Benson sold all that they had brought with them and as much as they could make (basketry, stonework) while in St. Louis.[84] All told, the St. Louis fair had representatives from at least twenty-two different Indigenous North American groups.[85] While some of the fair's Native participants made and sold their goods from their assigned spots in the Anthropology Village and Indian Village, many demonstrated their crafts at booths inside the fair's Indian School.

If the ethnographic village exhibits and the people who lived in them were intended to embody the nation's past, its future was signaled by the "modern Indian School" in the federal government's display at the fair. Though the instruction occurring within its walls supposedly reflected the civilizing impact of U.S. control, the building did not demonstrate the benefits of modern life: the roof leaked, grading issues caused flooding, and the budget was blown so early that students, teachers, and exhibitors had to bring their own bedding. Native students completed the necessary carpentry, electrical and plumbing work after Samuel McGowan, the Indian School's superintendent, negotiated with the fair and with local labor unions for permission to use the students as workers.[86]

Once the building was complete, the school, perched atop one of the fairgrounds' hills, became a focal point: visitors came to purchase Native art from artists who would rotate through the school's booths and to observe recitations, performances, and classroom activities involving approximately 150 students from the Chilocco, Haskell, Fort Shaw, Sacaton, and Genoa schools over the course of the fair's seven-month run. While exposition planners intended to demonstrate the supposed difference between "older" Native people and students in the boarding school system, with the adults representing the "before" portion of the planners' narrative timeline of apparent progress, Native artists—and their art—also fit into different narratives. Nancy Parezo and Don Fowler note that Native artists "were the producers of beautiful, handmade, nonmechanized objects for which many Americans longed" and that their work connected well with the turn-of-the-century U.S. Arts and Crafts Movement.[87]

The students, too, moved beyond the frameworks that had been created for them at the fair. For example, the Fort Shaw Blues, a women's basketball team with members from a range of Native nations, beat every team they played; even specially constituted teams of former all-stars were no match for them, and they won victories over men's teams too. Their dominance did not quite fit with the arguments on display at the Indian School; after all, their victories were evidence that they were already better than U.S. high school, college, and alumni teams. Their achievements were downplayed by McGowan and exposition leadership, with McGowan saying that they "were nice girls and made a good record"; however, historians have clarified that the Blues were actually world champions.[88]

The fair's Indian School, which was intended to show the supposed progress made by Native children as they learned assimilation, could also be interpreted, according to W J McGee, "as a prophecy" and "as a guide to the future." McGee wrote, "Over against the Indian on the grounds, just beyond Arrowhead Lake, will stand the Filipino, even as over against the Red Man on the continent, just beyond the Pacific, stands the brown man of the nearer Orient."[89] McGee's celebration of the damaging and traumatic system of assimilationist boarding schools in the United States as a model for a similar type of "uplift" for Filipino children reflects not just dominant ideas about turn-of-the-century "civilizing" practices but also the pervasive influence of the hierarchical vision of human societies advocated almost everywhere at the fair.[90]

The Philippine Exposition

At the 1901 Pan-American Exposition in Buffalo, the Philippines had been part of the government exhibits; in fact, the Smithsonian Institution had sent Col. Frank Hilder to the Philippines in 1899 to collect items for the fair at Buffalo. As Frederick True described it, the Philippine Exhibit, included in the fair's Government Building, displayed to visitors "how the Filipinos live, what kind of houses they live in, what clothes they wear, what they eat, how they cultivate the soil, their fisheries, their industries, their trades and manufactures, their games and amusements, and the thousand and one things that make up their home environment." True explained how the Government Board, despite the lack of specifically designated funding for a separate Philippine display, "took steps at an early day to represent in an adequate manner the life of these new wards of the nation."[91] The plan was different for St. Louis. This time there would be a separate Philippine Exposition, with exhibits gathered from all over the archipelago at the urging of Governor-General Taft.

"I can assure you that our people feel the Philippine Exhibit will be one of the leading, if not the overshadowing feature of the Exposition," wrote David Francis to Taft. "You can depend on our hearty co-operation. Your statement to us of the far-reaching influence and value of a thorough and complete representation from the Archipelago has not only aroused great interest here, but has been widely and favorably commented upon by the press of the country."[92] Taft came to St. Louis in 1902 to meet with Francis and the other members of the Louisiana Purchase Exposition Company Board about plans—and support—for a Philippine exhibit at the fair. At a luncheon given in his honor he articulated the importance of the St. Louis Fair for the work taking place in the Philippines: "Nothing, I think, can bring the two peoples together to promote friendly and trade relations between the States and the Archipelago so well as such an exhibit as I hope we will be able to make at your exposition." With the financial support of the Exposition Company and its backers, Taft explained, he could "go back to the Filipinos and say that the Louisiana Purchase Exposition was willing to help us, and this will have a deep effect in demonstrating to the Filipinos the friendliness and sympathy of the United States toward them."[93]

The Exposition Company gave Taft $100,000 to begin putting together a Philippine exhibit, and once back in Manila Taft issued a circular that encouraged people throughout the archipelago to aid in preparing materials for St. Louis.[94] After all, the fair was to be an opportunity "to create interest and sympathy for the Philippine Islands," "to give confidence in the intelligence and capacity of the native," and perhaps most important, "to look for permanent profitable markets" for Philippine natural resources.[95] While a compelling Philippine Exposition would help guarantee a successful venture for those on the St.

Louis side, the economic possibilities it might open up in the Pacific could have significant financial benefits for the U.S. colonial project.

Taft's visit—and the funds from the Louisiana Purchase Exposition Company—set several processes in motion. The Philippine Exposition Board was established, with Dr. W. P. Wilson of the Philadelphia Commercial Museum at the helm and Dr. Gustavo Niederlein as the director of exhibits. On his way to the Philippines Niederlein traveled to St. Louis. The *World's Fair Bulletin* reported that "the Skinker tract, a dense primeval forest, thick with tangled underbrush and oak and other forest trees of various sizes, pleased the doctor greatly."[96] This section of the grounds, even farther west of what had been the Forest Park Wilderness, was to be the site of the Philippine Exposition: forty-seven acres, to be exact. Niederlein asked that the trees be preserved; they could be useful in keeping the different exhibit villages, and the people who would be brought to St. Louis to live in them, separated from each other. Not long after Niederlein headed overseas, Gifford Pinchot began the trip that would take him across Siberia and to the Philippines. Before leaving, Pinchot agreed to serve as honorary chief of the Department of Forestry for the Louisiana Purchase Exposition.[97] The *Bulletin* reported on Pinchot's participation and on the ways his trip to the Philippines would benefit the exposition: "While in the islands, he will also assist in arranging plans for securing an elaborate collection of specimens of timber, illustrating the wonderful variety of hardwood and other species of trees found in that region, where nearly 700 valuable varieties have already been found."[98]

Forestry was a focal point of the Philippine Exposition. Forest products from the Philippines were not simply displayed throughout the exhibit; they were used in the exhibit's physical construction.[99] The Forestry Building was to be made out of one hundred varieties of Philippine wood and, once complete, would feature samples of these tree species in various forms, from raw materials to finished products. The houses for the Filipinos joining the exhibit were to be made from materials transported across the Pacific for this purpose. Filipino workmen from various ethnic groups, all of them "experts in the construction of the thatched bamboo houses common in their country," escorted "2,000 tons of bamboo poles, palm leaves for use in thatching, and much other building material, including some very fine woods and a big canoe sixty feet long, hollowed out of one 'madera' log."[100] The construction on the Philippine "reservation," as many called it, was to be as authentic as possible, as close a replica of homes and living conditions as could be constructed in a Missouri forest halfway around the world. And the echo with the reservation system central to federal Indian policy was part of a broader set of comparisons played up by exposition planners. The *World's Fair Bulletin* reported that over eight thousand tons of building material was on its way, all of it necessary for the construction of homes for almost three thousand Filipinos who would be living on these forty-seven acres at the fair.[101]

According to the *Bulletin*, the Philippine exhibit was to be "the garden spot of the Exposition," a place where Filipinos from "some twenty tribes" would "live under the same surroundings as in their Island home." The *Bulletin* editorialized that "the people of the United States owe a vote of thanks" to the Philippine Exposition Board "for the striking miniature of the Philippine Islands and their inhabitants" that had been re-created in St. Louis.[102] These lines were delivered earnestly and with no acknowledgment that the tropical archipelago on the other side of the world was wildly different from the forty-seven acres set aside for the Philippine Exposition in a land-locked state in the middle of the North American continent. "Perhaps the most striking feature of the display is its naturalness. There is no attempt at artificiality, no straining after effect," asserted the fair's official guidebook, even though the exhibit was filled with constructed replicas of "life" on the other side of the world.[103] Paige Raibmon has analyzed the ways colonial viewers turned Native domestic spaces into spectacle and how fairgoers' fascination with what Filipino—especially Igorot and Moro—homes were like reflected their own ideas about what constituted "civilization."[104]

This emphasis on naturalness evoked the broader anthropological framing of the Louisiana Purchase Exposition. The fair was organized according to an elaborate system of taxonomy, grounded in a carefully articulated set of ideas about the evolution and progress of man, as espoused by W J McGee. This particular brand of anthropology looked at the processes of the past to "predict the future and legitimate the rapid societal and technological changes" that had occurred. According to this logic, all that had happened in the past made possible the pathways to progress that white, Western, industrial, imperial powers had followed.[105] The "naturalness" of the Philippine Exposition also naturalized the framing of Filipino groups as more primitive examples on the supposed spectrum of savagery to civilization, with the world's white, Western, industrialized nations representing the peak of progress, the top of the evolutionary hierarchy.

The physical organization of many of the fair's ethnographic villages reflected the racial hierarchies that the fair's planners believed in and actively espoused. Arrowhead Lake was at the outer edge of the acreage designated for the Philippine Exposition. Representatives of a range of Indigenous North American nations were given space on the other side of Arrowhead Lake. According to Robert Rydell, the arrangement of Native Americans and Filipinos "made explicit the connection between America's imperial past and imperial future."[106] Much like the Anthropology and Indian Villages and the model Indian School, the living exhibits within the Philippine Exposition were planned to display specific arguments about the benefits of U.S. colonialism. In fact, the children living in the Philippine Exposition had a model school of their own to attend, where they learned rhymes and songs in English. The Igorot students even performed a chorus of "My Country 'Tis of Thee" for President Theodore Roosevelt, who marveled at their rapid progress.[107]

The most popular exhibits of the Philippine Exposition were the Filipinos themselves. Cast as existing along a spectrum of development or "civilization," the five groups brought to the fair (Visayans, Moros, Igorots, Negritos, and Bagobos) occupied their own encampments, or "villages." Each group constructed homes using the materials transported from the Philippines to meet planners' goals of an authentic representation of life there. Visitors were also expected to interpret the "naturalness" of the exhibit as an actual analogue for the presumed virgin landscape of the Philippines. One of the fair's official histories described the Philippines as containing "50,000,000 acres of untouched and unsurpassed forest."[108] And *The Official Handbook of the Philippines and Catalogue of the Philippine Exhibit* described the mountains of the Philippines as "forest clothed." It continued, "In the higher elevation are found large pine trees, with open spaces between carpeted with pine needles, but lower down huge trees tower to an enormous height. These mighty forest monarchs are draped and festooned with fantastic creepers and beautified with graceful ferns and exquisite orchids. Vegetation runs riot."[109]

This language—trees as "monarchs," ferns as "graceful," mountains as "forest clothed"—calls up an earlier moment of imagined abundance and evokes visions of a New World, a new landscape, as yet unspoiled, filled to overflowing with plant and animal species divinely provided for colonists to use.[110] It also sounds a lot like the way U.S. soldiers described the landscapes of their Philippine service a few years before, suggesting that soldiers' impressions of the Philippines had circulated widely, contributing to broader American ideas about the landscapes the United States occupied in the Pacific.

Preparing exhibits that would effectively represent such abundant, undeveloped resources was an extensive undertaking. Mark Bennitt noted in his exposition history that the artifacts and specimens on display at the fair had come "from more than a thousand islands populated by a hundred different tribes, speaking different dialects." Bennitt praised all who did this labor: "In the prosecution of their work, the agents of the Exposition Board had to penetrate mountain fastnesses accompanied only by guides and interpreters, and often to visit districts previously unexplored."[111] This sounds similar to the work soldiers had been doing, only in this example, exposition agents were hiking deep into the hills to gather materials for the fair instead of cached weapons and supplies. Bennitt extended the pioneer metaphor deployed throughout the *World's Fair Bulletin*, linking a popular narrative of U.S. expansion in both the West and the Philippines to the collecting work carried out by the contractors of the Louisiana Purchase Exposition Company.

But the agents of the Exposition Board weren't the only ones with Philippine items to display. Frederick True received a letter from the National Army and Navy Spanish War Veterans asking if there might be "space in the Government exhibit to display souvenirs and relics of our service."[112] And early in the fair planning process the *World's Fair Bulletin* pointed to "a widely spread desire among soldiers and ex-soldiers to utilize the World's Fair . . . for national soldiers' re-unions and military pageants."[113] There were even soldiers inside the Philippine Exposition: among the representatives of the different Filipino groups were a battalion of Philippine Scouts, led by twelve U.S. officers, and the Philippine Constabulary Band.[114] So although soldiers—and the work of empire they carried out—weren't emphasized in the story of the Louisiana Purchase and the settling of the West that fair planners chose to tell, soldiers themselves were very much present at the Louisiana Purchase Exposition. They understood their role in the conquest of the U.S. West and in the occupation of the Philippines, and they wanted evidence of their service displayed too.

Dedication Ceremonies

Though the exposition was not slated to open until April 1904, the fair's dedication ceremonies took place on April 30–May 2, 1903. St. Louis pulled out all the stops to introduce its fair to the world: a massive military parade, speeches from honored guests, and an extensive series of celebratory fireworks. The Centennial Day display included "gigantic fire portraits of Washington, Jefferson, Napoleon, and McKinley" and "One hundred The Eagle Screams rockets," from which emanated "the national bird's screech realistically produced."[115]

Everything was coming together, and the dedication ceremonies were meant to share this with the rest of the nation, to send forth "a host of competent witnesses" who could testify that the fairgrounds would be ready, that the fair would open as scheduled in 1904. The *World's Fair Bulletin* editorialized that the transformation of the North American West, "this marvelous development of a mighty, prosperous, and happy civilization, in what was so recently a savage wild, is the proudest human achievement of the century of the world's grandest forward strides in every line of progress."[116] And the fair would display all that progress to the world.

The dedication ceremonies began with the entrance of the president of the United States, Theodore Roosevelt. A parade of U.S. soldiers and members of the National Guard followed. Gen. Nelson A. Miles, now the commanding general of the U.S. Army, was in attendance.[117] Celebratory speeches were presented, alternating with choral performances of songs titled "The Heavens Proclaiming," "Unfold, Ye Portals," and simply "America."[118] The Honorable Thomas H. Carter described "the conquest of space, forests, streams, and deserts, and the founding of cities and States in waste places within this territory," as "an advance unsurpassed in the history of human endeavor." And while President Roosevelt highlighted qualities associated with masculinity and conquest, "the qualities which enable a people to overcome the forces of hostile men and hostile nature," former president Grover Cleveland told the assembled crowds, "Every feature of our celebration should remind us that we memorialize a peaceful acquisition of territory for truly American uses and purposes."[119]

This idea of a "peaceful acquisition" ran throughout the Louisiana Purchase Exposition Company's version of the event it was commemorating. The *World's Fair Bulletin*, in one of its many overviews of the history of the Louisiana Purchase, highlighted this very angle, writing that the exposition "celebrates the centennial of the first extension of the boundaries of the United States and the peaceful acquisition of a wilderness that has yielded up its riches generously as a reward for the unceasing toil of the pioneer and home-builder. Where the savage dwelt and herds of bison roamed a few decades ago are now the cultivated farms and the flourishing cities of a progressive people."[120] A later issue of the *Bulletin* editorialized about what a wonderful time it was for attending an exposition, calling the present moment "a prolonged season of peace, a remarkably prolonged series of prosperous years for all industrial nations."[121]

This selective storytelling was belied by the visibility of soldiers at the fair's dedication ceremonies—soldiers who had worked in the service of the United States to establish control of the Louisiana Territory and the Mexican cession and who had most recently fought first to oust the Spanish from the Philippines and then against Filipinos battling for self-determination in the Philippines. Despite the violent work of expansion and empire, some continued to characterize the acquisition of California, New Mexico, Arizona, and the Philippines as "peaceful" processes, even as the fighting continued in Mindanao and as Native people across the United States persisted in their efforts to navigate and resist the structures of settler colonialism.

This insistence on the peacefulness of U.S. expansion and domination did not preclude the militaristic celebration of American empire, and the extensive pyrotechnic display on the first night of the dedication ceremonies had significant imperial overtones. The program described each kind of firework in detail. Number 40, named "Our Empire," was particularly impressive: "This unique novelty is produced by mammoth combination shells, which at 1,000 feet release a large bomb with red, green, blue and white stars, representing the United States, followed by a gold shell representing Hawaii, followed by a silver shell for Porto Rico, and finishing with a number of smaller shells for the Philippines." A bomb filled with shells representing American empire sounds fitting. It was accompanied by a "pyrotechnic cuttlefish, produced by the electrical discharge of 100 30-inch repeating bombs, filling the sky with long, radiating, fiery tentacles."[122] These literal tools of war were transformed into a crowd-pleasing spectacle, at least for those fond of cuttlefish. Or maybe the "long, radiating, fiery tentacles" signified the literal reach of American imperialism.

Along with the parades and the fireworks, visitors to the fair's dedication ceremonies were able to see the progress made on the fair's construction and to get a first look at the overall structure of the exposition. As the director of exhibits explained, "A modern universal exposition is a collection of the wisdom and achievements of the world, for the inspection of the world." He continued, "Such a universal exposition might well be called an encyclopedia of society, and it contains, in highly specialized array, society's words and works. It constitutes a classified, compact, indexed compendium (available for ready reference) of the achievements and ideas of society."[123] While fair planners promoted the exposition's exhibits as representative of all the world had to offer, in practice what was displayed represented a complex back and forth among potential exhibitors, Louisiana Purchase Exposition Company directors, foreign nations, domestic states, and federal institutions, all attempting to participate in this "encyclopedia of society" while highlighting their own place in it. Thus world's fairs tell us much more about their creators than about the range of people, places, and products on display. And this particular fair, with its dual focus on the U.S. West and the Philippines, amplified a narrative arc that positioned American conquest and colonialism as continuous, stretching from the Louisiana Purchase to the Pacific and beyond.

This reach—of the exposition and the nation—was emphasized over and over again in the way the fair's planning, construction, and execution were narrated. David Francis even highlighted the reach of the fair's agents as collectors, using military language to celebrate that "the campaign of preparation was vigorously pushed in every part of the globe."[124] Edgar Mearns, though never explicitly tasked with collecting for the fair, was one of those agents, working in the service of both colonial conquest and imperial science. And during the fair's seven-month run he recrossed the Pacific.

Mearns at the Fair

On September 15, 1904, Maj. Edgar Alexander Mearns boarded a navy transport vessel bound for San Francisco. He had been granted sick leave, and he was headed back to the United States to rest and recover. Mearns kept detailed notes about his journey back across the Pacific, beginning with how he got from the hospital in Manila to USAT *Logan*. True to form, he spent two hours at Jesuit College in Manila looking at specimens in its museum collection before boarding the ship. As the *Logan* left Manila Harbor Mearns again watched for birds. At first he saw only fish. But then he began to see them—boobies, terns, kites, and later an albatross. Mearns wrote that the *Logan's* first officer told him that birds sometimes, but not always, came on board while the ship was traversing the Pacific.[125]

In early October a large petrel appeared on board, and the next details Mearns documented were its measurements. He collected it, prepared it, and gave it the number 13737.[126] A shearwater alighted on the deck, and Mearns killed, skinned, and stuffed it too. The soldiers saw white terns as they approached Honolulu, and as they sailed toward California a golden plover flew with them, following, circling, whistling. As the ship neared San Francisco it was escorted by "about a dozen black-footed albatrosses."[127]

Mearns had followed birds first across the U.S. West and then across the Pacific, and now they were following him home. They appeared at different moments of the journey back, helping him mark his place in the ocean; certain birds were visible closer to or farther from land, so Mearns's focus on the sky served also to track his progress across the sea. He did far more watching than collecting, but even from the deck of a military transport vessel he still collected and prepared what he could.

Once back on land Mearns spent a month in San Francisco. Then, with an extension of his sick leave approved, he began traveling eastward to his family—and to his friends and his specimens at the Smithsonian. But first he visited St. Louis.

Mearns boarded an eastbound train on November 19, 1904. His notes describe what he saw out the window: prairie dogs, a hawk, long-crested jays, "magpies and nests on both sides of [the] Rocky Mtn. divide." His entry for November 24 reads, "Crossed Missouri from Kansas City to St. Louis. Saw a shrike,

Bobwhites, Bluebirds, Juncos, Crows, English Sparrows, Red-tailed Hawk." And then there's a local address in his field book. The next entry is written from Ohio, where his wife's family lived: "At Circleville, Ohio, Nov. 30 to Dec 5, 1904."[128]

It did not take a week to get from St. Louis to Circleville, and I am certain Mearns went to the Louisiana Purchase Exposition. The evidence isn't incontrovertible; I haven't found a ticket stub, as I did for one frontier army soldier who managed to make it to the 1893 World's Columbian Exposition in Chicago. But that address, for the intersection of "McPherson Ave. + King's Highway," sounded familiar.[129] I'd encountered a road called Kingshighway on maps of the exposition; it's still the name of a street running along the eastern boundary of today's Forest Park. It intersects with McPherson Avenue about half a mile north of Lindell Boulevard, Forest Park's northern boundary. The auto shop that was at that intersection when I first started searching this address is closed now, but whatever it was in 1904, it was also an easy walk from the Louisiana Purchase Exposition.

It makes sense that Mearns would go to the exposition. His letters include several references to world's fairs—a mention of visiting Philadelphia in 1876; an acknowledgment that his wife, Ella, was headed to the World's Columbian Exposition in Chicago in 1893 while he was working on the U.S.-Mexico Boundary Survey; even a reference to the St. Louis Exposition in July 1904 to his daughter, Lillian, while he was in the Philippines.[130]

Furthermore, Mearns's Smithsonian contacts—people who had become important colleagues and collaborators throughout his military service—were deeply involved in planning the federal government's displays at the fair, and Mearns had been sending material to the museum for decades. Perhaps he wanted to see their work or how the museum might represent the landscapes of his service.

If Mearns did walk through the gates of Forest Park in November 1904, he would have come in through the Lindell Boulevard Entrance. Entering here, alongside a throng of excited fairgoers, Mearns would have first marveled at the fair's Main

Picture—the Grand Basin and its surrounding lagoons, the palaces fanned out around the fair's central feature. Maybe he would have explored the Horticulture and Agriculture Buildings, which bordered Arrowhead Lake and the Philippine Exposition. To get into the Philippine Exposition, Mearns would have paid the entrance fee and walked over a replica of the Bridge of Spain, a bridge he'd certainly encountered in Manila. It led into a replica of Manila's Walled City, or *intramuros*, the inner core of the capital city. I imagine it would have been strange to see a place he'd experienced so recently in person replicated here for fairgoers.

Mearns was too late for Philippine Day at the fair, a day complete with a military parade and sham battle that amplified the military dimensions of a supposedly peaceful conquest. Celebrated on August 13, 1904, this day brought former governor-general and current secretary of war Taft to St. Louis. Jose Fermin describes how Taft was accompanied by a massive military escort of more than six thousand soldiers. Other decorated veterans of the Philippine-American War were in attendance, including the now-retired "Howling" Jake Smith, so nicknamed for the way he carried out orders to make a "howling wilderness" on the island of Samar in 1902.[131]

The fair represented a peaceful Philippines, already conquered, at least according to the exposition, but Mearns would have known otherwise. Just a few months earlier he'd been shooting his collecting shotgun at Moros resisting U.S. colonial rule, looting Moro graveyards, and preparing dead U.S. soldiers for their journey home. Did he wonder at an exhibit that affirmed that the Philippines had been won and the war was over—especially given that he was only home on sick leave and would soon return to the field?

Just as Governor Taft and the exposition planners had hoped, the Philippine Exposition was one of the most popular destinations at the fair, attracting more visitors than the spectacles of the Pike, the Anthropology Department, and many of the fair's palaces. Admission to this fair within a fair was set first at a quarter and later fifty cents. The revenue brought in at the gate,

in these increments, totaled between $3,000 and $5,000 daily.[132]
Once inside, visitors could explore the exhibits in the main
buildings, which were surrounded by "villages typical of Philippine life from the lowest grade to the better class," according
to one of several official histories of the fair.[133] A report filed by
several of the men involved in preparing the Philippine Exposition expressed their satisfaction with the impact of the displays: "While the expenditure for the exhibit far exceeded the
amount original contemplated by the Philippine commission . . .
the consensus of opinion as gathered from visitors was that it
was worth all it cost and more in giving to the people of the
United States a more intimate knowledge of the resources and
possibilities of the Philippines than they could acquire except
by an actual and extended visit."[134] Despite the emphasis on the
people of the Philippines, at least in the popular press, these
men highlighted the resources of the islands, rather than the
opportunity for cultural exchange.

Of the Philippine Exposition, the official guidebook of the
Louisiana Purchase Exposition declared, "In scope, thorough-
ness and general interest, it far exceeds any other display on
the grounds."[135] Edmund Philibert would have agreed. In his
account of November 19, 1904, he described the impressive
range of exhibits he encountered after crossing the Bridge of
Spain: the Constabulary exhibit was filled with "knives, bolos,
guns and cannon that had been captured from insurgents";
the Fisheries and Game Building had "snake skins twenty six
feet long, stuffed reptiles and birds of all kinds"; the Education Building displayed the students' writing and composition
skills, as well as "grand" linen embroidery with "very fine single threads running through it like cobwebs"; and the Government Building allowed him to observe "a specimen of the work
of some insect which gets in books and eats them destroying
them completely."[136] With his eye for detail and penchant for
description, Philibert transports his modern readers to the displays he marveled at, but his account offers no commentary
on either the subtext or the broader context of these exhibits.
Perhaps to Philibert the broader argument on display about

the benefits—and beneficence—of U.S. empire was obvious. Or maybe reckoning with the violence that had preceded this display and continued on the other side of the globe during the fair was harder to explain on the page.

Photographs of the fair, especially those taken by Jesse Tarbox Beals, emphasize the domestic, ordinary ways of life on display and, as Laura Wexler has argued, make Beals, and others like her, "complicit in keeping offstage any vision of the violence of the pacification of a people."[137] The highlight of the Philippine Exposition, most visitors and official histories seem to agree, was the living exhibits depicting the so-called daily life of different Filipino groups. Florence McCallion, Philibert's sister, joined him to see the fair and wrote to her husband about their visit to the Igorot Village, where Bontocs, Suyocs, and Tinguans lived during the exposition. McCallion described them as looking "like bronze statues." She continued, "A great many women were weaving and some men were blacksmithing. One of the women gave me her autograph. I had my white shawl on my arm. She said, 'puty, puty,' meaning pretty. Just think they charge fifty cents a person now to go in there."[138] Newspaper coverage focused on concerns about whether the Igorots were wearing enough clothes and on the "barbarity" of a dog-eating ceremony that exposition planners encouraged and organized several times a week, likely placing press and profits over accuracy.[139]

The interest some women fairgoers took in members of the Philippine Scouts and Constabulary heightened anxieties about race, class, and masculinity—and led to actual violence, with marines and guards threatening and then scuffling with Filipino soldiers.[140] The actual work of war—work that exposition planners tried to keep out of the fair itself, preferring instead to highlight peace, progress, and civilization as outcomes of U.S. conquest—turned out to be difficult to hide.

These encounters with Filipinos were new for most fairgoers, who seem to have been at times intrigued, at times appalled, and certainly entertained by the practices of people that the fair presented to them as savage, as primitive, but also as worthy of—and capable of—being "civilized."[141] Some residents of the Filipino villages welcomed visitors—and the chance to earn income and interact with people from other places. But not all Filipinos at the fair were interested in cross-cultural encounters. Little has been written about the detachment of Lake Lanao Moros from Mindanao, possibly because they "refused to perform for the amusement of visitors, and as a result, fair organizers considered them a disappointment."[142]

It seems likely that Mearns would have been particularly interested in how the peoples and resources of the southern Philippines were displayed in St. Louis; after all, he had just come from Mindanao. I don't imagine the Lake Lanao Moros at the fair would have been at all interested in Mearns, though, given his direct role in the ongoing violence toward Moro communities across the province. They would have noticed inconsistencies between the narrative on display in St. Louis of a conquered, colonized Philippines and what both they and Mearns understood as a continuing struggle for control of Mindanao.

Maybe when Mearns crossed back over Arrowhead Lake, he wandered toward the Indian School or the Anthropology Department, toward where Native people from the U.S. West, along with Indigenous peoples from all over the world, had assigned spaces to live and work. It is possible that he visited Geronimo, a man he would have remembered from his first military assignment in Apache homelands.[143] They might have met before, on one of the trips Mearns had taken with General Crook to reservation lands under army control. Did Mearns see the connections between the West and the Philippines, American frontiers on both sides of the Pacific? I wonder if Mearns recognized that he—and men like him—served to link these distant places and the violent projects of empire conducted in them.

If Major Mearns did indeed attend the fair between November 24 and November 30, 1904, he would have arrived just in time. December 1 was the exposition's last day, decreed David Francis Day in honor of Francis's efforts to bring the fair to St. Louis and orchestrate such a spectacular event. Edward Schneiderhahn, writing to himself in his diary, described the final moments this way: "There were many about you but your thoughts were your own, and you hardly know whether you could give them aptly and accurately.... At promptly 12 o'clock President Francis turned the switch that controlled the power and the light. The flood of light grew fainter and fainter and of a sudden all was darkness. The Cascades were silent. The scene was dead. Passed into history forever."[144]

Schneiderhahn wasn't wrong; the scale, the spectacle, the scenery—this particular combination of artifacts, specimens, people, and palaces—would never again be illuminated in quite this way. But although the fair "was dead," "passed into history forever," the ideas on display were very much alive. And the landscapes of the U.S. West and the Philippines, with their natural and human histories, their unknown futures, were very real. Edgar Mearns knew that as well as anybody. Despite the stories on display at St. Louis to the contrary, the fighting in the Philippines continued. The vision constructed and displayed at St. Louis was a facade, all bright lights obscuring the temporary nature of a world made of staff and plaster. If one looked closely, the cracks became visible—in these fleeting structures, perhaps, but also in the strategies deployed by those on display.

A few months after the close of the fair Mearns made his way back through the West and across the Pacific to report for another tour of duty in Mindanao, drawing another line, building another link between frontiers west and farther west, between nature and empire, between the varied landscapes where he labored in the service of both the United States and natural history.

Taking Mountains

In 1905, after six months medical leave in the United States, Mearns returned for a second tour of duty. Now the chief surgeon of the Department of Mindanao, he used his position to conduct multiple scientific expeditions. This might suggest a period of relative calm, but if that were the case for Mearns, it was not true for the rest of what soldiers called Moroland.

Just a few weeks before Mearns launched his Mount Malindang expedition, several hundred Taosug Muslims, including many women and children, were slaughtered by American soldiers in a four-day massacre at Bud Dajo, a volcano on the island of Jolo.[145] To avoid local leaders and U.S. colonial policies, the Taosugs had fled to the volcano, taking refuge inside the crater. In response Gen. Leonard Wood ordered soldiers up to the mouth of the volcano, where their guns and grenades were supported by shelling from American gunboats. Images of several U.S. soldiers standing over the dead, who lay piled in trenches at the soldiers' feet, conveyed what words could not about the continuing brutality in the southern Philippines.[146]

When news of the massacre reached the United States, President Roosevelt congratulated General Wood. The president of the Anti-Imperialist League, Moorfield Storey, wrote a stinging condemnation of the massacre and how it was being represented to the American people. Storey quoted Wood's official report, which said that "six hundred bodies were found on the field," and challenged his readers to "suppose . . . even that 600 song birds had been slaughtered for their plumage, would not our papers have been filled with protests and expressions of horror?"[147]

An image that accompanies most discussions of the massacre at Bud Dajo began to circulate in the United States a few months afterward. In it U.S. soldiers stand over a trench piled with bodies. It is difficult to look at. Oliver Charbonneau points first to the soldiers' faces, "haunted, battle-weary," and then to the woman, dead, in the center of the photograph. The light pulls the viewer's attention to a wound beneath her throat, a hole made by a bayonet or bullet. Once I see it, it is all I can look at.[148]

Mearns's field books do not mention Bud Dajo, but his military paperwork does. In a list detailing his absences from his assigned post at Zamboanga, one of the entries reads, "Absent March 8th at Jolo, P.I. in answer to emergency call for medical assistance from Commanding Officer, Jolo, Jolo, on account of numerous casualties resulting from engagement of troops with hostile Moros at Bud-Dajo, P.I."[149] The trip to Jolo took about nine hours, and once he arrived, Mearns "dressed wounded until 12 midnight and brought 34 wounded soldiers" back to Zamboanga.[150] There were twenty-one American casualties.[151]

A few weeks later, in northeastern Mindanao, Mearns moved forward with what he called a "biological and geographical reconnoissance of Mt. Malindang." Mearns wanted "to spend twenty days as high on the mountain as water can be found, gathering specimens to illustrate the gross surface geology, fauna, and flora of the mountain region; also to roughly determine the altitude of Mt. Malindang and the extent of its vertical life zones."[152] While there were military benefits to having a better idea of the topography of Mindanao, this undertaking was framed more as a biodiversity survey than a route-finding expedition.

One sergeant and three privates were assigned to the expedition, which called itself the Malindang Mountain Group, along with their "usual field equipment": rifle, ammunition, and long underwear for the conditions at higher elevations. It was also specified, in correspondence from the Department of Mindanao's military secretary, that a Sergeant Leakins was to "bring [a] National Museum shot-gun in addition to his equipment."[153] Beyond the army men, the expedition members included a representative from the Philippine Bureau of Forestry, members of the U.S. Engineers Corps, and a member of the Hospital Corps, as well as representatives from the Philippine Constabulary, twenty-eight Moro porters, and a man named Weneslao Estrellas, who had been assigned the role of "bird shooter" for Mearns.[154] The basic plan was this: establish a base camp at Catagan and from there take trips in smaller groups to the surrounding peaks and rivers. While gathering information about how to climb Mount Malindang, the group would collect specimens.

The letters that survive from this expedition cover quite a bit of ground: they show that the Moro porters, or cargadores, did not want to work for U.S. soldiers (one letter says they "bucked"); they detail directions for returning borrowed (stolen?) carabao (water buffalo used for transporting supplies) to their owner with payment for services rendered; and they deliver news of orders for two of the group's military members to report for duty in

Zamboanga, even though the expedition was only partway complete.[155] The reassigned soldiers sent Mearns their best guesses for how to approach the summit of Malindang: "I believe the top can be reached from Jimenez in three to four days. . . . The trail is very rough, and in some places passes over ravines on logs which the Subano, with whom we talked, said could not be crossed by men wearing shoes, but I think it can be done."[156] These expedition members both reproduced existing ideas about the suitability of white men for tropical exploration and challenged them by suggesting that they were up to the task—framing that runs throughout narrative accounts of "hikes" and expeditions undertaken by U.S. soldiers in the Philippines.

What's left of these letters can be difficult to decipher. The group encountered plenty of rain, and one letter describes sending a telegram to Major Mearns only after it had been dried "by the fire" and "wrapped" in "dry paper."[157] The letters between members in the field and the expedition's established base camp are mostly logistical. In one a group requested rice for a certain number of days; another alerted the recipient that specimens were on their way down the mountain: "I am sending one deer skin and skull to be taken care of. The Major regards it as the most valuable specimen secured on this trip as it is intirely new."[158]

Despite false starts and attempts that ended on different mountaintops or were impeded by impassable obstacles, the group eventually found a workable route up Grand Malindang (fig. 35). Expedition members took and recorded scientific readings of many kinds and collected a significant number of specimens from the summit, and the expedition was pronounced a triumph. One member, Robert Schroeder, said that from the summit he saw "a view too grand for description." And then he described it: "Down before our eyes lay Mindanao like one great miniature; mountains 3000 feet high looking like small hills, and beyond them from the coast very clearly defined, stretched the ocean in its calm magnificence to the very horizon, many miles away." "This sight alone," wrote Schroeder, "was worth the climbing of grand old Malindang."[159]

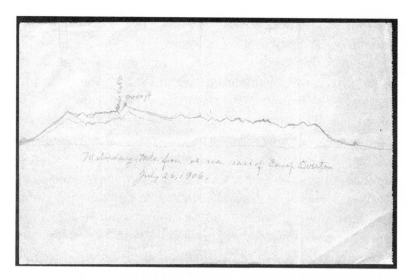

35. Terrain sketches and heights of summits in Malindang Group.
Edgar Alexander Mearns Papers, Smithsonian Institution Archives,
Record Unit 7083, image no. MODSI3287.

The memo sent to Gen. Tasker Bliss, under whose authority this expedition was carried out, focused on the expedition's
deliverables: "A monument was placed upon the highest peak,
known as Grand Malindang; and a map and a report embodying photographs and topographical drawings, klinometer sight-
ings, altitudes of peaks, barometric and thermometric readings
is being prepared." As for natural history, "Major Mearns and
Mr. Hutchinson collected 1000 good Botanical specimens. . . .
Major Mearns, for the U. S. National Museum, made a large
general collection in zoology, including 240 birds and 80 mammals, with new genera and species."[160]

Expeditions like this one reenacted the U.S. conquest narrative over and over again in miniature. Unknown territory
was surveyed, the flag was planted, specimens were collected,
and reports were written. Massacres, like the one at Bud Dajo,
weren't part of this story. Though not only for show—unlike
the massive temporary constellation of exhibits in St. Louis—
reaching the summit, placing the monument, and taking all
sorts of measurements were certainly a kind of performance.
Mearns and the Malindang Mountain Group asserted U.S. con-

trol over yet another part of Mindanao—over its land and natural history specimens, if not directly over its people.

The expeditions Mearns led to mountaintops across Mindanao produced valuable information for both the U.S. military and U.S. science and natural history. They reproduced the mechanics of conquest but also demonstrated, through their repetition, the incompleteness of U.S. colonialism. Though the story on display at St. Louis asserted total U.S. control over the Philippines, the military and scientific work conducted by Mearns and his peers, at Bud Dajo and on expeditions to multiple Mindanao mountains, tells a different story—a story of imperial work as ongoing and unfinished. Years after the United States declared its war in the Philippines over, flags were still being planted, measurements taken, and specimens collected and preserved. As U.S. soldiers continued this violent work, the specimens, artifacts, and information they collected followed pathways back to the United States.

Conclusion

Unnatural History

THE PLANNERS AND CURATORS CRAFTING THE NARRATIVES
on display at the 1904 St. Louis World's Fair worked hard to
naturalize the relationship between the Louisiana Purchase
and the acquisition of the Philippines, to tell a story that made
one follow, almost inevitably, from the other. That story was
peaceful, the very picture of steady progress. But soldiers like
Mearns—and Ovenshine, Bowen, Baldwin, Steele, Lawton, and
so many others—had lived these linkages, had crossed from
the U.S. West to the Philippines and returned home again after
laboring on both frontiers in the service of empire. Their stories, too, yoke the U.S. West to the Philippines, but theirs are
stories of claimed conquest, stories written in public and private prose, in the tasks of transforming landscapes, in the labor
done to remove people, dead and alive, from their homes. U.S.
soldiers constructed and collected American frontiers, work
that demanded that they use their bodies and their skills to
enact a vision of violence, dispossession, and occupation on
both sides of the Pacific. From the plains and the desert to the
Philippine coastline and the mountains of Mindanao, U.S. soldiers fought Indigenous and local people, struggled to master
and marveled at new environments, and captured these experiences in words. Some soldiers took more than their official
assignments instructed them to. Mearns, in particular, drew
from the landscapes of his service to provide an incredible
record, not just of nature on American frontiers but also of

36. Rufous hornbill, *Buceros hydrocorax mindanensis*. NMNH 200923, NHB2013-00982, Donald E. Hurlbert and Brittany M. Hance, Smithsonian Institution.

the tangled work of U.S. empire and environmental knowledge production.

This record takes many forms: it exists in the confluence of rivers and on school grounds that used to be fairgrounds, in letters sent to and from the field on both sides of the Pacific, in military tactics, in museum annual reports, and in exposition planning and execution. We can also read this record in the bodies of birds. Consider, for example, a rufous hornbill collected by Edgar Mearns during the Malindang Mountain Group's 1906 army-approved expedition to summit the mountain—an opportunity made possible by the U.S. occupation of the Philippines (fig. 36).

I am absolutely captivated by this bird. It is *Buceros hydrocorax mindanensis*, a stunning creature whose life and death opened up a window into the nature of empire—and the empire of nature. This hornbill lies in its assigned Smithsonian drawer in profile to protect the feature for which it was named. It has been dead more than a hundred years, and yet there is something about this study skin that makes me pause every time I look at this image, convinced that the bird is only sleeping. It's in the eye, I think—or, since I know the eye was removed as part of this bird's preparation, in the way each lash lies down neatly over it.[1]

"Bill red, tipped with yellow," reads the description of this specimen, alongside its number in Mearns's list of birds collected on the Malindang Mountain Expedition. The hornbill's feet were red, too, but "yellowish on underside of toes."[2] These colors fade once blood stops circulating in the body, so when I look at this spectacular specimen, I know that in life, more than a century ago, this bird was even more brilliant. A closer look at the bill reveals three tiny holes, left by the birdshot that probably caused the hornbill's unnatural death.

Mearns didn't shoot this bird, though anyone requesting to view it wouldn't know this from the tag. But alongside Mearns's documentation of several details about this specimen in his collecting list, including the brilliant colors of this bird's soft parts, he wrote, "Shot by Estrellas."[3] Elsewhere in the records of the expedition, Weneslao Estrellas is listed as "Dr. Mearns bird shooter."[4] Alongside the officers, enlisted men, and representatives from various colonial and military divisions assigned to the Malindang Mountain Group, as well as twenty-eight Moro porters, was Estrellas, accompanying the expedition to aid in collecting birds. It is likely that Estrellas brought more than gun skills to the table; Mearns's thousands of specimens suggest that Mearns himself was a good shot, practiced at shooting a bird to kill cleanly, rather than destroy or obliterate. Estrellas's presence suggests that he had expertise Mearns valued, knowledge that enabled the expedition's success. Though legible as a named member of this expedition in Mearns's papers, Estrellas's role as part of the Malindang Mountain Group is harder to track. Mearns credited him with shooting the hornbill in his specimen entry, a practice he repeated across his field books and specimen lists whenever anyone else shot or skinned a specimen. But Estrellas's other contributions do not appear to have been documented. His role in this hornbill's pathway from Catagan, Mindanao, to the Smithsonian's National Museum of

Natural History has been obscured from view, hidden in those three small holes.

Harder to see, too, are the Subano names written in the field book descriptions for many of the specimens collected during the Malindang Mountain Expedition. Did they come from Estrellas, from the porters the expedition hired, or from other people they encountered along the way? The source of these names is unclear. But that Mearns asked about them and phonetically transcribed them signals that they carried some value for him and for the structures of scientific knowledge production he was invested in as a naturalist. The names written on the tags were sometimes brand new, given to species deemed "discovered" on this and other expeditions and then described in official publications. Many were revised by later naturalists whose examination of scientific study skins side by side prompted new realizations about the boundaries between species and subspecies. Reconnecting the birds with the notes describing their collection reveals details that are useful for both bird specialists and historians; taken together, these materials situate these seemingly timeless birds in time, in place, and in relation to their collectors and their contexts, showing us more than exists on the tags, while perhaps also revealing a pattern of erasure.

This hornbill is one example among thousands collected by Mearns and among hundreds of thousands in the Smithsonian's collection, and its story suggests that bird specimens can tell us about far more than their own identities, behaviors, and ranges. They tell us about the people, patterns, and structures that shaped their collection, preparation, and circulation as specimens in networks connecting soldiers with local collaborators and museum curators. These networks are imperial in nature: built around the goal of extracting resources from one place and accumulating them elsewhere. But they also show us how empire works and how the imperial work of soldiers like Mearns helped generate museum collections of great range and depth. Museum collections have a history; in this case, the breadth of the Smithsonian's collections is deeply tangled together with the work of U.S. empire.

The enthusiasm about Mearns's reassignment to the Philippines expressed by museum curators was in part tied to the lack of Philippine specimens in the Smithsonian's holdings. Mearns's work as both army surgeon and naturalist, together with the thousands of soldiers constituting an invading army and occupying force, grew museum collections and reinforced interest in collecting natural history specimens and in looting villages for bones and cultural belongings. The Philippine-American War facilitated the growth of museum holdings and created opportunities for formal museum collaborators like Mearns, as well as for novice souvenir hunters to take from the fields in which they were deployed.

Mearns's collecting work centered on birds but extended to include other kinds of animals and artifacts. Mearns recorded how he excavated and emptied ancestral Puebloan sites in the Southwest and wrote in one of his Philippine field books how he shot Filipinos with his collecting gun and looted graves in a village he helped attack. This violence, though harder to see, accompanied material to the museum. Mearns's extensive collecting work is represented in the museum by thousands of specimens and artifacts, but they combine to tell not only his story, reflecting twenty-five years of military assignments and some postretirement collecting expeditions, but also a story of U.S. empire and the removal, dispossession, and occupation that it wrought. While U.S. empire did not look the same on both sides of the Pacific, it shared agents and tactics, of which the work of natural history was part.

This was not a new development; soldiers had already been taking, whether from the Indigenous people they fought to remove from their homelands in what is currently the U.S. West or from the battlefields of the U.S. Civil War. But reconstituting much of what they collected in museums like the Smithsonian creates a particular kind of imperial archive—an archive of vast and varied material collections that reflect an army of collectors who were embedded in a vision that linked U.S. empire with U.S. progress. These soldiers collected for many reasons— personal desire, professional obligation, institutional interest, scientific curiosity. In doing so they reinforced one of the central logics of settler colonialism: removal.

Collecting while soldiering was not just a historical practice; soldiers still collect, for themselves and for institutions. Even in the much more recent past, military needs and scientific knowledge production have continued to align. For example, when I first visited the Smithsonian's National Museum of Natural History, I took a tour of the various departments; the people I encountered in the preparation lab were working on jirds, small rodents that had been cleared from runways on U.S military bases in the Middle East. I didn't think much of it then; I was still getting my bearings. But now I see this activity as an extension of the intersection of military and scientific work that Mearns and his colleagues were invested in so long ago. The museum's mammals database includes several jirds and a few foxes taken from Ali Al Salem Air Base in Al Jahra, Kuwait.[5] Animals on or near runways are a safety concern for pilots and soldiers; risk mitigation measures to minimize danger are both necessary and not unusual.[6] What interests me is the resonance with earlier connections between military work and the preparation of specimens for scientific study. After removal from U.S. Air Force bases, these mammals were examined, measured, skinned, and prepared. They are now part of the Smithsonian's collections, a result of the material, imperial presence of the United States in the wider world.

Just as soldiers still collect for the museum, scientific knowledge generated at the museum has meaning for soldiers—and potentially for the birds they encounter in the (air)field. For example, members of the 332nd Air Expeditionary Wing Safety Office at Balad Air Base began collecting and shipping local birds to the Smithsonian's Feather Identification Lab in May 2006. The idea was that researchers could prepare and study these specimens to extend scientific understanding of Iraqi bird species and their migration habits. While reducing local bird populations is one strategy for managing the risk of bird strikes for military aircraft, a piece published by the U.S. Air Force suggests that more information about "peak hours of bird activity" could influence flight scheduling, perhaps reducing the need to limit local bird populations, "if mission requirements permit."[7] What is learned in the museum, then, matters for what happens in the field. This work requires a set of specimens to study. The air force article notes that this collecting work would substantially grow the Smithsonian's holdings in Iraqi birds; when this project began there were only four species (eight specimens) in the Division of Birds.[8] As I write this the National Museum of Natural History birds database lists 147 entries for Iraqi bird specimens, most of them collected between 2006 and 2010.[9]

Birds collected by the U.S. Army traveled imperial pathways from the landscapes of soldiers' service to the Smithsonian in the late nineteenth and early twentieth centuries. Though the routes have changed, specimens travel these pathways still, evidence of the ongoing tangle of military labor and the production of scientific knowledge. These routes reveal the role of empire in shaping how collections are built, how cabinets are filled, and in particular, how the relationships between military priorities and natural history possibilities have structured the collecting work of soldiers in the past and in the present.

The birds, thousands of them, of Lieutenant Colonel Mearns reflect a career spent going mostly where he was ordered to go.[10] In the service of the U.S. Army Mearns contributed to imperial projects on both sides of the Pacific: he shored up the work of containing Apache and Yavapai people on reservations in the Southwest, and he participated in punitive expeditions that decimated Moro villages in Mindanao. What he took from these places—in the service of natural history, ethnography, and scientific knowledge production—can tell the story of the imperial work that he and so many others performed on multiple frontiers.

U.S. soldiers have continued collecting from the sites of their service, but the practice of birding while soldiering outlasted Mearns and his colleagues too. Sgt. Jonathan Trouern-Trend of the 118th Area Support Medical Battalion, who served in Iraq starting in 2004, kept a blog that he later adapted into a short book, detailing the birds he encountered during his deployment. He wasn't alone. In the preface to *Birding Babylon* Trouern-Trend notes, "I know of at least a dozen marines, soldiers, airmen, and civilians from several countries who brought their binoculars to war."[11] In sentences that sound as though they could have come from a letter written by Paul Fletcher in the Philippines to his wife, Hughine, in St. Louis, or from a field book entry describing a day's activities from Mearns's assignments in either the U.S. Southwest or Mindanao, Trouern-Trend writes of Camp Anaconda, north of Baghdad: "Though it was a hive of military activity and a target of almost daily rocket and mortar attacks, it was also a refuge of sublime natural beauty to those who looked."[12]

A medic, not unlike Mearns or Fletcher, Trouern-Trend participated in missions beyond his base to unnamed locations—missions that presented at least the possibility of seeing more birds, of adding new species to his life list. And once, while facing an uptick in "rocket and mortar attacks" requiring everyone "to go everywhere in body armor and helmet," he spent a Saturday "birding in 'full battle rattle,' weapon included, of course." Trouern-Trend's narrative centers the birds he sees and emphasizes birding as a strategy for embracing the "resiliency of life, of both birds and people." But his military work is present throughout—work he is committed to, even as he imagines returning someday "with binoculars but without a weapon."[13]

EVEN AS U.S. SOLDIERS PERFORMED THE WORK OF EMPIRE, they sometimes questioned that labor and its implications. Their critiques were typically quiet; they were more likely to share their thoughts in private letters than to offer them out loud to commanding officers or publish them for a wider public. Still, these rumblings suggest that soldiers have more to tell us: about the violence of their work, about their experiences of new environments, and about how their service shaped their understanding of the United States and the wider world.

After a decade of studying a particular set of soldiers and their ideas about nature and empire, I continue to grapple with what it means to write a history that centers empire's agents. I am a white woman, a historian, a settler. I am writing another book mostly about white men, who mostly embraced a settler-colonial and imperial vision, and who mostly worked to carry it out. They invaded Native homelands and occupied the Philippines in the service of this vision—a vision that shaped how they made sense of the people and environments they encountered. When they took the field, they also took things—ancestors, cultural belongings, and natural history specimens—from those fields, further contributing to a form of science that ranked and categorized the world's peoples and cultures just as it ordered and named its plants and animals.

Lately I've been thinking about how I am taking too. My collecting work looks different from the work of someone like Mearns. I'm not preparing birds (well, except for that blackbird). Instead, I'm reading letters never meant for me, shooting pictures of materials in archives, walking through mostly forgotten landscapes and squinting to see what once was there. I'm collecting what empire produced: the writing of its agents, the specimens and artifacts they took, the residue of their work on multiple frontiers. Once collected this material feels as if it needs curation: description, organization, interpretation.

In some strange way, then, this book is my display case, a set of stories organized not by taxonomy but by some other logic: by pathways and ideas shaped by imperial labor, bookended by my blackbird and Mearns's hornbill. Here, following soldiers connects the U.S. West with the Philippines, places with environments and histories too often studied separately. Linking these landscapes—and the wars fought in them—as soldiers did reveals exactly how tangled the histories of nature and empire actually are: the language of wilderness appreciation creeps into the varied, violent work of war; natural history collecting practices are visible in the techniques used to manage Apache people; and soldiers' ideas about the imperial work of emptying frontier landscapes inform the ways they describe the beauty and possibility of these landscapes to their families and to broader audiences as well.

The pieces of my display case do not tell the same stories soldiers told. Rather, together they reveal how soldiers' stories came to be, how linked encounters with the natural world in the service of empire structured a story of continuity, a story of the reach of imperial thinking, of the embeddedness of notions of nature in experiences of empire on both sides of the Pacific. These pieces—preserved by naturalists and curators, by the recipients of letters and the keepers of archives, by the natural world itself, in the confluence of rivers and the echoes of exposition grounds—combine here to offer a story of conquest and continuity, of soldiers who moved along circuits of empire, whose encounters with the natural world and with imperial work shaped and revised their understandings of both. There are other ways to curate these pieces, I'm sure; other ways to tell this story. But these pieces, ordered in this way, have preserved a story of conquest, a tangled web of empire that stretches across oceans and across fields.

This story also stretches into the present. I keep returning to that hornbill, shot by Estrellas, prepared by Mearns, and shipped to the Smithsonian from Mindanao. I have watched in wonder as specialists, scientists, and curators use their expertise to translate what birds like this hornbill can reveal. Measurements, stomach contents, feather patterns, range: these details help us understand how and where the birds lived. There is still much for us to learn, though, and this specimen, like those near it in the collection's drawers and cabinets, might contain leads to follow—lingering genetic material, perhaps, that might be extracted from a claw; evidence to assist in understanding species variation; or even data that might prompt a reconsideration of the bird's name. All this to me feels like what I understand natural history to be: the study of plants and animals through observation and description in order to better understand their lives, their relationships, and their habitats.

But what of the hornbill's "unnatural" history? By this I mean all the human forces that brought this bird from the mountains of Mindanao to the drawers of the Smithsonian. This hornbill is positioned within the broad reach of American empire. Its path crossed with that of the Malindang Mountain Expedition of 1906, a venture enabled by an ongoing war already declared over, shored up by museum curators a world away, and built on a lifetime of scientific collecting made possible by the U.S. Army. It is but one bird in a collection with immense depth and range, but its mere presence in a drawer invites a set of questions that have less to do with natural history and more with a set of processes that are, well, unnatural—or at the very least, deeply human. In suggesting that there is more to study about what I am calling the unnatural history of this hornbill and its comrades in museum cabinets, I am not trying to say that we humans are not natural, not part of the natural world. But the structures that continue to shape scientific knowledge production cannot be understood without this realm we might call the unnatural—namely, the imperial.

The extraordinary specimens in natural history collections can tell us about far more than their own lifeways: they can also teach us about the people who encountered, collected, and prepared them. From the bird shot holes in this hornbill's beak to the care with which its claws were crossed and its belly sown up, there are clues here that animate something bigger about the context of this bird's death, collection, and preparation. This hornbill represents the collision of nature and empire, its very existence—now, still—an outcome of a set of interlocking imperial histories, histories that soldiers help us see.

ACKNOWLEDGMENTS

WHEN I BEGAN GRADUATE SCHOOL, I NEVER IMAGINED that my dissertation—now this book—would cross the Pacific. And while I've remained in the United States to conduct my research, the soldiers I study have led me to some surprising places: the surgeon's quarters at Fort Verde State Historic Park and the old wagon ruts that run alongside the road heading east out of town; the Smithsonian National Museum of Natural History, where an army surgeon's papers brought me to an archive of birds; the Beef Creek Apache Cemetery at Fort Sill, where the boom of artillery practice sounded around me; and St. Louis, where, 1904 World's Fair map in hand, I wandered present-day Forest Park and the surrounding neighborhoods searching for what had once been Arrowhead Lake.

I found the soldiers I study in a range of archives: the U.S. Army Heritage and Education Center, Smithsonian Institution Archives, Newberry Library, Library of Congress, National Archives, Missouri History Museum Library and Research Center, Huntington Library, and New York Public Library. I am grateful to the staff at these institutions; they make research possible. In particular, I thank Dennis Northcott, Jaime Bourassa, Molly Kodner, and Lauren Sallwasser at the Missouri History Museum Library and Research Center for advice during my first research trip and for help with image permissions more than a decade later. Peter Blodgett took the time to share ideas for further research in the Huntington's collections, and Paul Harrison helped me navigate military records at the National

Archives. And at the U.S. Army Heritage and Education Center I learned the meaning of "Hooah!" Ranger Sheila Stubler gave me a tour of Fort Verde State Historic Park and shared research materials gathered by past park employees. At Fort Sill Lt. Jonathan Peters was kind enough to talk with me about the rhythms of life on a military post. And I owe an enormous thank-you to Christina Gebhard, Brian Schmidt, and everyone at the Smithsonian National Museum of Natural History's Division of Birds. The project we collaborated on connecting the papers of Edgar Mearns with the birds he collected (supported by the Smithsonian's Web Advisory Group and the Coypu Foundation) shaped my understanding of natural history practice, past and present. You made me a bird person!

I am grateful to several institutions for providing significant financial support for this project. At Cornell University I received funding from the History and American Studies Departments, John S. Knight Institute for Writing in the Disciplines, Society for the Humanities (which, in addition to supporting a dissertation writing group, funded me to take a birding course at the Cornell Lab of Ornithology), and Graduate School. I also received support from the Michael and Carol Kammen Fellowship, Walter LaFeber Research Assistance Fund, and Joel and Rosemary Silbey Fellowship. A Newberry Consortium on American Indian Studies Graduate Student Fellowship provided me with the time to examine and think with collections that are central to this project. At Colorado College I have benefited from research support from the History Department and the Social Science Executive Committee; a Dean's Office Mrachek Fellowship and a Southwest Studies Jackson Fellowship gave me valuable summer funding to research, write, and revise the book manuscript.

This book exists because of the extraordinary support—intellectual, emotional, and material—I have received from so many people. Aaron Sachs chaired my dissertation committee, and this project owes so much to his encouragement, offered over fourteen years of lunches, walks, and phone calls, and his advice to follow my questions wherever they took me, especially when they pointed in unexpected directions. Whatever kind of teacher and scholar I am, I am because of Aaron. Sara Pritchard's influence—on this project and in my life—is clear to me too. As mentor, writing buddy, and now dear friend, she continues to model what it means, and what it takes, to keep pushing the academy to live up to our values for it. In many ways Eric Tagliacozzo is responsible for the reach of this project: in a course on modern Southeast Asia he pushed me to write something connected to my research interests, rather than a one-off essay. I wrote about nature on display at the 1904 St. Louis World's Fair. And here we are. Many members of the Cornell History Department offered encouragement and constructive feedback along the way, whether in colloquium sessions or more informal conversations.

I called Ithaca, New York, home for seven years, and I remain so appreciative of my graduate school community—formed over beers at the Chapter House after colloquium and through coursework, teaching, reading groups, and writing groups—for making it feel like one. Daegan and Talia Miller, Mari Crabtree, Maeve Kane, Josi Ward, Heather Furnas, Kate Horning, Sarah Ensor, Tom Balcerski, Jackie Reynoso, Catherine Biba, Susana Romero, Ryan Edwards: I miss being in the same place as you all. In particular, I thank Historians Are Writers!, the reading and writing group at the center of my graduate school intellectual community. You helped me find my voice as a writer. I also appreciate the folks behind *The Appendix*—Chris Heaney, Brian Jones, Ben Breen, and Felipe Cruz—for creating a space for experimental historical writing and for inviting me to join them. I'm proud of the work we did together. Jenna Tonn and Megan Shields Formato included me in a panel they put together for the 2013 History of Science Society meeting, which led to an accountability spreadsheet and a writing retreat in the Berkshires. Can we do that again, please?

After graduate school I worked as a visiting assistant professor of environmental humanities at Davidson College. I'd be lying if I said I worked on this book during my first year of full-time teaching, but the kindness of the Environmental Studies and

History Departments there deserves mention. In 2016 I joined the Colorado College community. I am so grateful to my History Department colleagues for cultivating such a kind and energizing space to teach, research, and write. I am lucky to learn from all of you. Thank you especially to Jane Murphy, for our ongoing Slack chat about all of the things, and to Jake Smith, for afternoon dog time and reading really rough drafts. To my colleagues in environmental studies, Southwest studies, and museum studies at cc, the interdisciplinary work we do together continues to influence my scholarship and my teaching. Thank you.

The Colorado College Crown Faculty Center funded a manuscript workshop that allowed me to invite Anne Hyde and Doug Sackman to read a draft of the book and come to campus in October 2019 to discuss it with me. They helped me scrap the sixth chapter and think about the book's structure—and "Taking" in the title was Doug's idea. Christine DeLucia read drafts of chapters 1 and 2; among her many helpful suggestions was to think more about countercollecting. Maurice Crandall read a draft of chapter 2 and encouraged me to be mindful of the experiences of Yavapais as well as Apaches in the nineteenth-century Southwest.

The week before a global pandemic shut down our campus, I traveled to Penn State for a manuscript workshop sponsored by the University of Nebraska Press's Many Wests series and hosted by the George and Ann Richards Civil War Era Center, expertly coordinated by Barby Singer; there I benefited from the insights of a whole room full of generous colleagues and readers: Thomas Andrews, Ari Kelman, Amy Lonetree, and Christina Snyder, editors for the Many Wests series, as well as Cathleen Cahill, Amira Rose Davis, Amy Greenberg, Chris Heaney, Julie Reed, Honor Sachs, Amanda Scott, Rachel Shelden, Ellen Stroud, Sam Davis, Edward Green, ShaVonte Mills, A. J. Perez, Christopher Thrasher, and Kenneth West. Thank you especially to Susan Johnson for serving as the press's invited reader at this workshop and for her careful comments on the full manuscript. I flew home, encouraged and a little overwhelmed, not realizing it would be years before I'd get on another plane.

I was lucky, though, to be welcomed into another scholarly community in the summer of 2020, when I joined the Clements Center for Southwest Studies at Southern Methodist University as the David J. Weber Fellow for the Study of Southwestern America. Though I participated remotely, I cannot say a big enough thank-you to Andrew Graybill, Neil Foley, and Ruth Ann Elmore for the community they built during an uncertain and challenging time. My fellowship year began with a manuscript workshop on Zoom. I am grateful to the Clements Center's invited readers, Christopher Capozzola and David Igler, who pushed me to think more deeply about empire and imperial work, as well as to the scholars who agreed to participate in a lively conversation about soldiers serving on multiple frontiers: Andrew Graybill, Neil Foley, and Ruth Ann Elmore; Tatiana Seijas, Brennan Rivas, and Sean Harvey (my fellow fellows for 2020–21); and Maurice Crandall, Julian Lim, Katherine Morrissey, and Megan Kate Nelson.

I regularly tell the students in our history capstone course that a lot less of the work of scholarly writing happens by ourselves than we might imagine, that actually it is in talking and thinking with other people that our ideas become clear. Standing writing dates with Sara Pritchard, Chris Heaney, Mari Crabtree, and Jackie Reynoso helped me keep going, keep writing, against the backdrop of a global pandemic. We jokingly called this practice of working together over Zoom "soft surveillance." But it was also a lifeline. In addition to reading the full draft at my Penn State workshop, Chris commented on drafts of the book's conclusion. And Mari read and talked through drafts of many of the book's chapters, helping me strengthen their through lines and tighten their arguments. Thank you, Sara, Chris, Mari, and Jackie for making time to talk and to write—together.

I have shared portions of this project, in various stages of development, at the Cornell History Department Colloquium, Cornell Science and Technology Studies Research Group, Colorado College History Department Seminar, George and Ann Richards Civil War Era Center, Pueblo Archaeological and Historical Society, and Lost Museums Symposium at Brown

University, as well as at meetings of the American Society of Environmental History, History of Science Society, North American Labor History Conference, Western History Association, and Pacific Coast Branch of the American Historical Association. The feedback I have received from chairs, fellow panelists, and attendees has been generous and generative. In particular, the 2020 PCB-AHA panel I chaired featuring Ashanti Shih, Kathleen Gutierrez, Christine Peralta, and Josh McGuffie created space for a discussion of U.S. empire and the history of science that has stayed with me. And I appreciate the detailed and thoughtful comments from the anonymous readers who read the manuscript for the University of Nebraska Press. Thank you also to my editor Bridget Barry, for conversations that began long before there was a book proposal and for shepherding this project into an actual book, together with project editor Sara Springsteen and copyeditor Joyce Bond.

As I hope is clear, this project has benefited from the generosity of many readers. I'm grateful for their ideas, their questions, and their critiques; the book is better because of them. Any errors are my own.

Over the last many years several people helped make the financial support I have received stretch further. It's possible that the Bribriesco family's move to St. Louis started this whole project in motion. Thank you for enthusiastically hosting me on multiple visits. Jill and Scott MacVicar, Ali and David Scrymgeour, and Dan Nugent also hosted me during research travel. Josh Champagne has my gratitude for hosting me for whole weeks at a time (and for powering my archival work with homemade rice-based energy bars), but the prize goes to Maddy Fleisher and Matt McKenzie, who let me stay for two months in 2013. Joan Jacobs Brumberg and David Brumberg offered their Ithaca home (and the company of their pup, Malcolm MacDuff) for three weeks in fall 2019, which made for the perfect sabbatical writing retreat. And my parents, Charles and Mary Kohout, and my brother, James Kohout, have stepped in many times—not just with love but also with much appreciated dog-sitting.

Many others have freely given of their time, advice, and

encouragement, including my colleagues in the History Department at Colorado College, past and present: Paul Adler, Susan Ashley, Peter Blasenheim, John Marquez, Purvi Mehta, Doug Monroy, Jane Murphy, Carol Neel, Ulices Piña, Tip Ragan, Jamal Ratchford, Bryan Rommel-Ruiz, Danielle Sanchez, Jake Smith, and John Williams, as well as Joanna Popiel and Thecla Shubert. My thanks also go to Dwanna McKay, Rebecca Tucker, Genny Love, Dylan Nelson, Eric Perramond, Tyler Cornelius, Lynne Gratz, Becca Barnes, and Scott Ingram. Beyond the college, I am grateful to Ari Kelman, Leah Davis Witherow, Megan Kate Nelson, Annie Merrill, Roman Utkin, Rob Vanderlan, Daegan Miller, Jenna Tonn, Tom Balcerski, Chris Cantwell, Mary Mendoza, Megan Raby, Rebecca Onion, Maddy Fleisher, Josh Champagne, Steve Pepe, Kate Lambert, and Dorian Needham.

MY 2015 DISSERTATION WAS DEDICATED TO NANNY, MY grandmother on my father's side. She died the following year. As I sit here writing these acknowledgments, her engagement ring glitters on my finger. It was given to her by my grandfather Pop-Pop, whom she married after he returned home from serving as a bombardier in the Philippines during World War II.

Nanny grew up in Highland Falls, New York, in the caretaker's house on the grounds of the West Point Cemetery. Sometimes I think about how she would have played there, running between the stones marking the graves of some of the soldiers I write about in this book. Her brother, shot down over Germany in 1944, is buried there now. I never intended to become a military historian, but the questions that interested me about notions of nature and experiences of empire led me to soldiers. And only once I was deep into this project did it hit me that Pop-Pop served in the Philippines and that his story, and Nanny's, too, is tangled up in the long history that links the United States with the Pacific world.

Wearing Nanny's ring reminds me of these uncanny resonances and of all the memories I have of going through family albums and old photographs at our kitchen table. This was our thing, especially once she had trouble sustaining a conversation, and I delighted in the spark of recognition for her younger self, for the man she loved, even when the words were jumbled.

This ring isn't just a reminder of Nanny and Pop-Pop, though; it is now also my engagement ring, and together with my wedding band, it symbolizes the love and commitment I share with Cory Johnston. Nanny isn't here to see her ring on my finger or to hold this book in her hands. But Cory is, and this book is dedicated to him. Cory, thank you—for your love and support but also for bike rides, bear hugs, and Boomer walks. I'm the luckiest.

NOTES

Introduction

1. Severing wings, legs, and tail from the body is necessary to be able to remove the organs and musculature from the skin, enabling an almost full separation of the bird's insides from its outside. My description of this process is drawn from my own experience and from a series of PowerPoint presentations shared with me by Christina Gebhard at the Smithsonian National Museum of Natural History's Division of Birds. For an updated version of these materials, see Ildiko Szabo, "How to Prepare Bird Specimens: Part 2, Skinning Your First Bird," Beaty Biodiversity Museum, October 10, 2019, https://beatymuseum.sites.olt.ubc.ca/files/2019/10/part2.pdf. Any errors are my own.

2. Taxonomy is dynamic; careful study and comparison often lead to renaming and recategorizing, as well as to animated discussion of where the boundaries between species should be set. This means that even as specimens, birds might still move, if only to a different drawer or cabinet, to reflect contemporary scientific thought. Many of the birds Mearns collected have different names from those he gave them, but the older tags are still attached, allowing twenty-first-century viewers the opportunity to see these changes. On debates in nomenclature and taxonomy, see Lewis, *Feathery Tribe*; Barrow, *Passion for Birds*.

3. The basic process is the same, even if different materials are used. For example, preparators no longer use arsenic as a preservative.

4. Partway through the research for this project I encountered Kirsten Greer's wonderful work on British military officers who pursued ornithological collecting. *Red Coats and Wild Birds* uses biographies or "life geographies" of both officers and birds "as a means of capturing the circuitry of empire in the production of British imperial knowledge, territory, and identity" (5). Though our work is centered on different subjects, I take much encouragement from Greer's project and especially appreciate her thinking on what she calls the "avian imperial archive" (12).

5. On the visual culture of the nineteenth-century U.S. West, see, for example, Hyde, *American Vision*; Sandweiss, *Print the Legend*; Nash, *Wilderness*.

6. Some academic fields have been grappling with this history longer, but it seems as though the work of water protectors at Standing Rock and public debates over the future of Bears Ears National Monument have brought renewed and necessary attention to both Indigenous history and contemporary Native sovereignty. For environmental historians writing on Native dispossession and the formation of U.S. national parks, see Spence, *Dispossessing the Wilderness*; Jacoby, *Crimes against Nature*. For broader histories of the national park idea, see Runte, *National Parks*; Nash, *Wilderness*.

7. Many of the soldiers who used "hiking" to describe military excursions placed the word in quotation marks.

8. Williams, "United States Indian Policy," 826–27.

9. Blackhawk, *Violence over the Land*, 3.

10. Williams also notes overlaps in military personnel deployed to serve in both continental and Pacific imperial contexts to further shore up his argument about continuity between the West and the Philippines. "United States Indian Policy," 827–28.

11. It seems impossible—or at least irresponsible—to frame a project about the continuities of U.S. empire without engaging with Kramer's expansive essay on empire and the imperial in U.S. history, "Power and Connection." While in some ways my project is an example of the kind of "methodological nationalism" that Kramer describes when discussing the impacts of the turn toward grappling with U.S. imperialism in American studies (1363–64), I hope that it succeeds in some of the other areas Kramer outlines as exciting possibilities for scholars of imperial history. In particular, *Taking the Field* joins other scholars in arguing against an exceptionalist framing of U.S. empire as an aberration, situating what many of us learned about as "formal" U.S. empire in the Philippines as part of an ongoing set of imperial processes with much deeper roots. Second, it pushes against some of the temporal and geographic boundaries that have become naturalized in the study of U.S. history—the hard break at 1890, reifying the "end of the frontier" outlined by Frederick Jackson Turner—and the exclusion of U.S. empire in the Pacific from many narratives of the nation's history. See Kramer, "Power and Connection," 1350.

12. Bender and Lipman, "Introduction," 2.

13. Hoganson and Sexton, introduction to *Crossing Empires*, 5, 11. For an earlier push to move beyond empires as "things" and instead center "imperial formations," see Stoler and McGranahan, "Refiguring Imperial Terrain," 8.

14. Here I am borrowing from Bender and Lipman, whose edited volume, *Making the Empire Work*, offers much encouragement to scholars interested in the intersection of labor and imperialism.

15. Nash, "Furthering the Environmental Turn," 134. Nash is not wrong; the environmental history scholarship that engages with American empire is rather limited, though it is growing. Of particular relevance to my project are Anderson, *Colonial Pathologies*; Sutter, "Nature's Agents?"; Miller,

Nature of the Beasts; Tyrell, *Crisis*; Bankoff, "First Impressions"; Bankoff, "Breaking New Ground?"

16. Renda, *Taking Haiti*, 181.

17. Stoler, *Haunted by Empire*, 1. Moyd, too, in her examination in *Violent Intermediaries* of the askari, African men who served in the German colonial army in East Africa in World War I, emphasizes what she calls "everyday colonialism" (30).

18. In the realm of empire studies Grandin's *End of the Myth* and Immerwahr's *How to Hide an Empire* examine the persistent interplay of frontier thinking and U.S. imperialism. While Grandin stresses the impact of frontier rhetoric on U.S. foreign policy, saying, "No myth in American history has been more powerful" (2), Immerwahr demonstrates, by reading the "logo map" (what most people picture when asked to visualize the geographic shape of the United States), how quickly the sites of U.S. colonial rule vanish from view, even as they remain critical for understanding the whole of U.S. history (8–15).

19. In fact, Civil War historians have led the charge, as it were, to apply environmental questions to military contexts. See, for example, Nelson, *Ruin Nation*; Brady, *War upon the Land*; Meier, *Nature's Civil War*; Drake, *Blue, the Gray, and the Green*.

20. Wolfe, "Settler Colonialism," 387. On settler colonialism, see also Veracini, *Settler Colonialism*; Hixson, *American Settler Colonialism*. On using genocide to describe U.S. actions toward Indigenous nations, see Ostler, *Surviving Genocide*.

21. Nostalgia shaped how soldiers remembered their service and also, more broadly, how American culture framed notions of masculinity in the late nineteenth century. See Johnson, "'Memory Sweet to Soldiers.'" On late nineteenth- and early twentieth-century masculinity, see Bederman, *Manliness and Civilization*.

22. This is not to suggest that moving through western landscapes was not challenging for others who chose to make these journeys, only that soldiers' perspectives about the West were also shaped by their work. For earlier approaches centered on cultural elites, see, for example, Nash, *Wilderness*, especially chaps. 3 and 4, "Romantic Wilderness" and "American Wilderness," as well as the frontier narrative included in Cronon's foundational essay, "Trouble with Wilderness."

23. Samuel Ovenshine to Sallie Ovenshine, July 25, 1876, SOP, Personal Correspondence, 1874, 1876.

24. In focusing on soldiers' writing I take inspiration from Valenčius's work, especially *"Health of the Country"* and *Lost History*. In both, Valenčius takes seriously how ordinary people made sense of where they were and demonstrates how valuable it is to pursue cultural history with sources written by everyday people about the nature in their daily lives. I think, too, of Morrissey's work on the Inland Empire as a "perceptual region," in which

she draws on a range of perspectives to trace how a particular sense of place emerged and was contested. Morrissey, *Mental Territories*, 8.

25. While U.S. empire across the North American continent and into the Pacific was settler-colonial, in the Philippines it looked more like other European projects, focused more on control and exploitation than on dispossession and elimination. In "Wages of Empire," Greene cautions historians against equating U.S. empire in the North American West with its empire in the Pacific, noting that "transformations of class, racial, and gender ideologies changed the ways subject groups were conceptualized and managed in the early twentieth century" (41). I agree that we need to be careful not to suggest that ideas, assumptions, and ideologies remained fixed across these dynamic decades; still, examining agents of empire whose lived experiences link these landscapes makes visible which ideas were transported and which were transformed through imperial encounters. There is much to gain from thinking about the forms and iterations of U.S. empire on both sides of the Pacific together. See Greene, "Wages of Empire," 40–42. This is not to say that settler-colonial projects were not possibilities in the Philippines; they just were not the dominant strategies employed by the United States there. For more on these attempts, see Charbonneau, "'New West in Mindanao.'" On U.S. colonialism, see also Goldstein, *Formations of U.S. Colonialism.*

26. I am by no means the first to suggest that continuities across sites of U.S. imperialism warrant more study; J. Kēhaulani Kauanui and other American studies scholars have emphasized the significance of the Pacific world, especially for "understanding multidimensions of U.S. domination." Kauanui, "Imperial Ocean," 625.

27. O'Brien, *Firsting and Lasting*, xxi.

28. See Hicks, *Brutish Museums*. For contemporary organizing and activism, see Decolonize This Place, accessed July 7, 2021, https://decolonizethisplace .org/. And for a foundational piece examining narratives of display, see Haraway, "Teddy Bear Patriarchy."

29. "Division of Birds," Smithsonian National Museum of Natural History, accessed July 7, 2021, https://naturalhistory.si.edu/research/vertebrate -zoology/birds.

30. On this transformation from animal to specimen, see Alberti, "Objects and the Museum."

1. The Nature of Frontier Army Work

1. Samuel Ovenshine to Sallie Ovenshine, August 11, 1876, SOP, Personal Correspondence, 1874, 1876.

2. Frank Dwight Baldwin to Alice Blackwood Baldwin, July 17 and August 4, 1876, FDBP, box 11, folder "1876." Quoted material is reproduced here without any corrections to grammar, spelling, syntax, or punctuation. These details are part of the work of reading letters from the field!

3. In Roberts's work on the California Gold Rush, *American Alchemy*, he urges readers to recognize that the way we view correspondence between men far away from home, doing something unusual and perhaps extraordinary, and their wives and families, at home doing far more ordinary things, is often "ideological." Roberts proposes that we look at gold rush letters as "literary creations," texts that "contain elements of style, writers' decisions on metaphor, tone, and subject, attentiveness to audiences imagined and real," instead of assuming that what they say is true (8–10). We should read soldiers' letters the same way.

4. Ovenshine to Sallie, August 11, 1876.

5. Wyckoff, *How to Read*, 3.

6. Ovenshine to Sallie, August 11, 1876.

7. Miller, *This Radical Land*, 6.

8. Schama, *Landscape and Memory*, 10.

9. For more on the army and labor, and on soldiers as workers, see Freeman and Field, "Labor and the Military"; McGrath, "'Army of Working Men.'" For a fascinating look at the U.S. Army's reliance on Native scouts in the Southwest, see Lahti, "Colonized Labor." For an overview of western labor history and historiography that demonstrates the range of laborers earning attention in more recent decades, see Gregory, "West and the Workers."

10. For more on the U.S. Army during Reconstruction, see Downs, *After Appomattox*. For connections between the U.S. Army in the South and the West, see McGrath, "'Army of Working Men,'" especially 16–87. See also Murolo, "Wars of Civilization," in which the author considers how members of the U.S. Army made comparisons between Native people, striking workers, and Philippine "insurrectos."

11. See, for example, Hahn, *Nation without Borders*; White, *Republic for Which It Stands*; Lears, *Rebirth of a Nation*.

12. In "Still Walking, Still Brave," Karen Leong discusses how this imaginary has shaped scholarly conversations in the history and historiography of the U.S. West—stressing especially its limits. Here I am interested, in part, in how nineteenth-century soldiers contributed to its construction.

13. The same can be said for their wives. The letters, diaries, and memoirs of army wives demonstrate complex and sometimes contradictory ideas about frontier army life—and about Native people. See Smith, *View from Officers' Row*; Myres, *Westering Women*; Myres, "Romance and Reality"; Eales, *Army Wives*; Nacy, *Members of the Regiment*; Dichamp, *Let Them Speak*.

14. Ovenshine to Sallie, July 25, 1876.

15. McChristian, *Regular Army O!*, 431.

16. McChristian, *Regular Army O!*, 431–32.

17. Sandweiss, *Print the Legend*, 3.

18. See Miller, *Empire of the Eye*, 22, 39, 48–49.

19. See, for example, Albert Bierstadt, *Emigrants Crossing the Plains*, 1869, oil on canvas, Butler Institute of American Art, Youngstown OH.

20. On the construction of American ideas about western nature, see Hyde, *American Vision*.

21. United States Statutes at Large, 1872, quoted in Nash, *Wilderness*, 108.

22. In 1864 Yosemite had been set aside as a state park in California, but Yellowstone was the first park to receive federal protection. On the history of national parks, see Runte, *National Parks*; Nash, *Wilderness*; Spence, *Dispossessing the Wilderness*.

23. Langford's words reached an audience beyond the *Scribner's Monthly* readership. Other publications reported on his account in *Scribner's* and described portions to their subscribers. For example, pieces were published in the *Ohio Farmer*, *New England Farmer and Horticultural Register*, and *Maine Farmer*. The *Overland Monthly* also published coverage of the expedition. For a compilation of documents pertaining to early Yellowstone expeditions and the formation of the park, see Crampton, *Early History of Yellowstone*; of particular interest is the "Yellowstone Bibliography" (69–75), which details newspaper coverage, lectures, reports, and congressional discussion on the Yellowstone region.

24. Langford, "Wonders of the Yellowstone."

25. Langford, "Wonders of the Yellowstone."

26. Doane, *Letter from the Secretary of War*, 29, 13, 3–4.

27. Doane, *Letter from the Secretary of War*, 6. Even the fish were better. Doane celebrated the trout of the Yellowstone region with these words: "They do not bite with the spiteful greediness of eastern brook trout, but amount to much more in the way of subsistence when caught. Their flesh is of a bright yellow color on the inside of the body, and of a flavor unsurpassed" (3). For more on the sublime, see Nash, *Wilderness*, 44–66; Nye, *American Technological Sublime*, 1–43.

28. Langford, "Wonders of the Yellowstone"; Nash, *Wilderness*, 111. Anne Farrar Hyde juxtaposes Langford's "struggle for words" with Hayden's approach to describing Yellowstone. Hayden, according to Hyde, "rarely used architectural terms of the language of the sublime"; instead "the language of science now served him well." See Hyde, *American Vision*, 195–97.

29. For a discussion of the bill's introduction and passage through Congress, see Haines, *Yellowstone Story*, especially chap. 6, "New Creation."

30. See Nash's discussion of the motivations underlying the creation of Yellowstone National Park and of the ways that later actions by Congress to limit railroad development through the park helped to establish Yellowstone as a wilderness worthy of protection. *Wilderness*, chap. 7, "Wilderness Preserved."

31. Doane, *Letter from the Secretary of War*, 37.

32. Doane, *Letter from the Secretary of War*, 40.

33. Sheridan and Sherman, *Reports of Inspection*, 34–36.

34. Doane, *Letter from the Secretary of War*, 26.

35. Writes Jacoby, "What this ideology of dispossession overlooked was that Indian migratory patterns were not a series of random wanderings but

rather a complex set of annual cycles, closely tied to seasonal variations in game and other wild foodstuffs." *Crimes against Nature*, 85.

36. For more on the army at Yellowstone and what Jacoby calls "the militarization of conservation," see Jacoby, *Crimes against Nature*; Spence, *Dispossessing the Wilderness*.

37. For a detailed social history of Yellowstone military service, see Rust, *Watching over Yellowstone*, especially 17–54 and 133–58. Rust offers the example of Herbert Angelo, who enlisted in 1901 because he wanted to serve in the Philippines but instead found himself assigned to Yellowstone. Rust writes, "The army did little to help persuade the more reluctant soldiers to shift their identity from imperialist agents of America to a constabulary force for nature" (143), but I would argue that soldiers policing Yellowstone were also engaged in imperial work in Native homelands, even if by 1901 most of the fighting done by the U.S. Army was happening in the Philippines.

38. Ovenshine to Sallie, August 1, 1876.

39. Ovenshine to Sallie, August 1, 1876. On reading letters between men far from home and their wives at home, see Roberts, *American Alchemy*, 8–10.

40. Ovenshine's papers do not include any more letters from that fall or winter. In fact, the next folder in his papers at the United States Army Heritage and Education Center contains materials pertaining to his service in the Philippines in 1898–99. There aren't any letters from his earlier service either, though there is a document that outlines particular milestones in his career, such as his presence at the surrender of Sitting Bull at Fort Buford in 1881. See "Grandpa Ovenshine's Indian Campaigns," sop, Autobiographical and Biographical Outlines of His Military Career.

41. Ovenshine to Sallie, August 8 and 11, 1876.

42. Karuka defines countersovereignty as "a position of reaction to distinct Indigenous protocols governing life in the spaces the United States claims as its national interior." *Empire's Tracks*, xii.

43. On the army's "dual missions," see McChristian, *Regular Army O!*, 7–10. "Indian Wars" has become a kind of shorthand for U.S. military violence against Indigenous people, especially in the nineteenth century. This label combines a series of campaigns against different Native groups into a singular extended episode. In thinking about U.S. settler colonialism and its reach, there are perhaps several reasons to combine these military campaigns under a single heading, to think about the shared ideological perspective underneath them. But to use this label without pause is also to perpetuate the flattening of all Indigenous peoples into one category and to see them as the U.S. Army did, rather than to recognize the diversity of nations, cultures, and languages of Indigenous North Americans. The Indian Wars represent both the singular framing of Native people by the U.S. Army and also the army's repeated incursions into many different peoples' homelands.

44. Adams, *Class and Race*, 12–13. These numbers reflect what was on the rolls but not necessarily who was in the field. Several historians have written

about desertion rates in the frontier army. McChristian devotes a chapter of *Regular Army O!* to desertion, in which he examines a range of possible motivations, as well as the existing data. While acknowledging that some deserters were "repeaters," McChristian states that the desertion rate in the early 1870s was about 30 percent. See chap. 12, in particular, 406. See also Utley, *Frontier Regulars*, 23, which identifies a 25–40 percent loss due to "death, desertion, and discharge" annually during the Indian Wars.

45. For a demographic profile of the frontier army's officers and enlisted men in the second half of the nineteenth century, see Utley, *Frontier Regulars*, chap. 2, "The Postwar Army: Command, Staff, and Line," 10–43. See also Coffman, "Army Life on the Frontier"; McChristian, *Regular Army O!*; Adams, *Class and Race*. On Black soldiers in the U.S. Army, see Dobak and Phillips, *Black Regulars*.

46. McChristian, *Regular Army O!*, 16–22; Utley, *Frontier Regulars*, 22–23.

47. Smith, *View from Officers' Row*, xiv. This book focuses on what officers and their wives wrote about Native people and federal Indian policy, limiting its scope to "the comments the officers made in the context of their work as soldiers rather than as explorers, scientists, agents, or other roles they sometimes took on" (xv).

48. On the western theater of the Civil War, see Nelson, *Three-Cornered War*.

49. The pay wasn't wonderful for most officers or enlisted men, but the differences were significant. Field officers like Ovenshine could earn $1,400–$3,500 annually, depending on their rank (for context, Utley notes that civilians in roughly equivalent jobs had higher salaries), while enlisted men made $13–$22 per month. Furthermore, soldiers were paid in person by the paymaster, who did not make it to each post monthly. Once paid, they needed to convert the paper currency they received into the coins used in the West, often at a loss, which could be up to 40 percent. *Frontier Regulars*, 19–22.

50. Names matter. One of the challenges of working with these sources is that the names soldiers use to describe Native people are often not the names Native people would use to describe themselves; here Ovenshine uses "Sioux" to describe those he is tasked with pursuing, but as many scholars have pointed out, this was not a word Lakota (or Dakota or Nakota) nations used to self-identify. Estes notes that Sioux "derives from an abbreviation of 'Nadouessioux,' a French adoption of the Ojibwe word for 'little snakes,' denoting the Ojibwe's enemies to its west. Instead, they simply call themselves the 'Oyate,' the 'Nation,' or the 'People,' and sometimes the 'Oyate Luta,' (the Red Nation); as a political confederacy, they called themselves the 'Oceti Sakowin Oyate' (the Nation of the Seven Council Fires)." *Our History*, 69–70.

51. Estes, *Our History*, 115.

52. Ovenshine, "S. Ovenshine's Diary, 1876," entries for July 12 and 21, SOP.

53. Ovenshine to Sallie, August 2 and 3, 1876.

54. Baldwin to Alice, 11 PM, November 5, 1876.

55. For more on the Civil War in the West—an area of growing scholarly attention—see Arenson and Graybill, *Civil War Wests*, as well as Nelson, *Three-Cornered War*.

56. Utley, *Indian Frontier*, 41.

57. Ovenshine to Sallie, August 9, 1876.

58. McChristian, *Regular Army O!*, 452.

59. For more on Civil War route building, see Nelson, *Ruin Nation*, 103–59.

60. Utley, *Frontier Regulars*, 267–95. For other accounts of what is sometimes called the Great Sioux War or Black Hills War, see Ostler, *Lakotas and the Black Hills*; Cozzens, *Earth Is Weeping*, 249–312. For Lakota perspectives, see Waggoner, *Witness*, 102–76; Greene, *Lakota and Cheyenne*.

61. Ovenshine to Sallie, August 2, 1876.

62. For histories of settlement that both draw on and engage with nineteenth-century epistolary and writing practices, see Kolodny, *Land before Her*; West, *Contested Plains*; Faragher, *Sugar Creek*; Valenčius, "Health of the Country"; Roberts, *American Alchemy*.

63. Fred H. Tobey, "Scraps from the Yellowstone Expedition," especially entries for August 14, September 9 and 17, July 24, and August 3–10, 1876, FHTP.

64. Utley and McChristian both make this observation in the introductions to their books about enlisted men in the frontier army. See Utley, *Frontier Regulars*; McChristian, *Regular Army, O!*

65. For discussion of the terms and interpretations of the 1868 Fort Laramie Treaty, see Ostler, *Lakotas and the Black Hills*, 38–68; Hämäläinen, *Lakota America*, 290–93, 310–11.

66. Bourke, *On the Border*, 241–42.

67. Hämäläinen describes Custer's 1874 expedition this way in *Lakota America*, 343, figure 46.

68. Dodge, *Black Hills Journals*, 39.

69. Kime, *Colonel Richard Irving Dodge*, 195.

70. Kime, introduction to Dodge, *Black Hills Journals*, 13, 23.

71. The Black Hills, known to Lakotas as Puha Sapa or He Sapa (Black Hills or Black Mountains), are home to Wind Cave, where, according to Lakota beliefs, the earth's first humans and buffalo emerged from below the ground. See Ostler, *Lakotas and the Black Hills*, 3–6.

72. See Estes, *Our History*, 8, 72.

73. Black Elk and Neihardt, *Black Elk Speaks*, 63, 62.

74. Dodge, *Black Hills Journals*, 52, 81.

75. Dodge, "Black Hills Journal #2," RIDP, box 1, folder 2. Published in Dodge, *Black Hills Journals*, 83.

76. Dodge, *Black Hills Journals*, 83.

77. Dodge, *Black Hills Journals*, 105.

78. Dodge, *Black Hills Journals*, 107.

79. For more on the assumptions white Americans held about Native people, see Blackhawk, *Violence over the Land*; Jacobs, *White Mother*; Conn, *History's Shadow*.

80. Dodge, *Black Hills Journals*, 206–8.

81. Dodge, *Black Hills*, 28. Note the difference between Dodge's *Black Hills* and Dodge's journals, edited by Kime and published as *Black Hills Journals*.

82. Robinson, *Diaries of John Gregory Bourke*, 1:171.

83. Dodge, *Black Hills*, 25. This quotation seems to be drawn almost directly from Dodge's journal entry of June 9, 1875. See *Black Hills Journals*, 72.

84. Dodge, *Black Hills*, 49.

85. Dodge, *Black Hills*, 28.

86. Parkman, *Oregon Trail*, 227, 228.

87. Twain, *Roughing It*, 75.

88. Dodge, *Black Hills Journals*, 83.

89. "Council between Heads of the Interior Department and the Sioux Chiefs: Characteristic Speech by Spotted Tail; The Indians Object to Leaving the Black Hills," *Daily Alta California*, May 28, 1875, California Digital Newspaper Collection at UC-Riverside. Pekka Hämäläinen's *Lakota America* pointed me to this article about Spotted Tail's speech.

90. On the nineteenth-century language of improvement, see Stoll, *Larding the Lean Earth*, 13–66.

91. Ostler, *Lakotas and the Black Hills*, 88. Ostler cites the writings of Col. Richard Irving Dodge, geologist Walter Jenney, and botanist A. B. Donaldson to develop the idea that the Lakotas did not actually live in or use the Black Hills. *Lakotas and the Black Hills*, 88–90.

92. Robinson, *Diaries of John Gregory Bourke*, 1:179.

93. "After some natural hesitation the blanket was appropriated as the Indian contribution to science," wrote Dodge. *Black Hills*, 19–20.

94. Colwell, *Plundered Skulls*, 5, 85–86.

95. Dodge, *Black Hills Journals*, 58. McGillycuddy, though trained as a medical doctor, also had experience as a topographer, and it was in this capacity that he served on the Black Hills Expedition. For a narrative of McGillycuddy's experiences in the Black Hills, see Moulton, *Valentine T. McGillycuddy*, 43–65. (Moulton's account does not mention the jawbone.)

96. On this practice of looting Native graves for bones to study, see Fabian, *Skull Collectors*, 165–204; Redman, *Bone Rooms*, 16–68.

97. Dodge, *Black Hills*, 101–2.

98. Dodge, *Black Hills*, 136.

99. Robinson, *Diaries of John Gregory Bourke*, 1:185, 171–72.

100. Robinson, *Diaries of John Gregory Bourke*, 1:188.

101. Ostler, *Lakotas and the Black Hills*, 94–97.

102. For images and a transcription of the 1868 Treaty of Fort Laramie, see "Treaty of Fort Laramie (1868)," National Archives, last reviewed February 8, 2022, https://www.archives.gov/milestone-documents/fort-laramie-treaty.

103. LaDuke, *All Our Relations*, 78. Lame Deer, Montana, is the tribal head-quarters for the Northern Cheyenne Nation.

104. Ostler describes "an angry Congress" that demanded the Lakotas relinquish their rights to all territory outside a permanent reservation assigned to them. If they did not agree, Congress would stop allocating resources for the Lakotas, regardless of prior arrangements. Ostler continues, "Although Congress had abolished treaty making in 1871, most of its members thought it would be unseemly to authorize a unilateral seizure of the Black Hills. They preferred to foster the illusion of assent." *Lakotas and the Black Hills*, 98. For a discussion of the terms proposed and the process by which the Manypenny Commission secured Lakota "support," see *Lakotas and the Black Hills*, 98–103.

105. On the construction of "wilderness," see Cronon, "Trouble with Wilderness," which offers a compelling history of the development of the American wilderness idea. But his discussion of the shift that took place in the nineteenth century—the transition from the frontier itself to the pursuit of a frontier experience in the West—centers on elite tourists escaping cities for an authentic wilderness vacation. I'm interested in how soldiers participated in this process of constructing an idea of the West that others—their families, their eastern readers—then encountered. These wilderness ideas weren't shaped only by elites, explorers, and gentlemen tourists; soldiers also contributed to cultural ideas about American wilderness even as they labored in these landscapes.

106. On the rhetoric of this mythology of the West as a garden, see Kolodny, *Land before Her*.

107. Dodge, *Black Hills*, 150.

108. Dodge, *Hunting Grounds*, 2.

109. In her study of elite hunters and their fascination with the U.S. West, Monica Rico describes how a "community of hunters committed to documenting, regulating, and celebrating the pursuit of big game" formed on both sides of the Atlantic. *Nature's Noblemen*, 4. Blackmore, though not one of Rico's subjects, reflects the pathways and the values of the community she describes: he was an English investor and philanthropist with an affinity for hunting who encouraged Dodge to write his book and helped see it through to publication.

110. Dodge, *Hunting Grounds*, 2.

111. Rico, *Nature's Noblemen*, 173–74. Rico writes that sport hunting "generated a whole cultural language" on both sides of the Atlantic. *Nature's Noblemen*, 173.

112. Rico points out that Theodore Roosevelt published two books on hunting and ranching in the 1880s that contributed to the genre produced by elite masculine hunting culture: *Hunting Trips of a Ranchman* (1885) and *Ranch Life and the Hunting Trail* (1888). *Nature's Noblemen*, 184.

113. Dodge, *Hunting Grounds*, 99.

114. Dodge, *Hunting Grounds*, 99.

115. Rosaldo, "Imperialist Nostalgia," 108. Rosaldo explores this idea in the context of his own fieldwork among the Ilongots in the Philippines and examines his own letters, field journals, and memories to think through moments of imperial nostalgia in his own experience. He writes, "The memories that evoke moods of imperialist nostalgia both reproduce and disrupt ideologies" (121).

116. Rosaldo describes talking with a missionary who expressed sadness over the ways Ilongot practices have changed—they wear T-shirts now, no one threatens head-hunting, they no longer sing traditional songs—even though these changes were part of her broader religious agenda. And for his part, Rosaldo reads letters he wrote and finds evidence of his own imperial nostalgia. The piece is a thoughtful reflection on what it means to have these feelings. "Imperialist Nostalgia," 121. Cronon also highlights the importance of "frontier nostalgia" in his examination of the origins of the wilderness idea. "Trouble with Wilderness," 77–79.

117. William H. C. Bowen, "One Trip," w h c b p, box 1.

118. See, for example, the papers of Charles Rhodes (c d r p), Eli Helmick (e c h p), and Cornelius Cole Smith (s c f p), all at the U.S. Army Heritage and Education Center, Carlisle p a.

119. Dodge offered abstract "truths" grounded in anecdotes from his experiences in the West; the focus is on what Native people do. Dodge often spoke of the generic "Indian" rather than the cultural practices of particular people, though he sometimes used specific examples from his experiences to illustrate his points. See "Indians," part 3 in Dodge, *Plains of the Great West*.

120. Dodge, *Our Wild Indians*, xi.

121. William Tecumseh Sherman, "General Sherman's Introduction," in Dodge, *Our Wild Indians*, xxxix. My goal here is not to rehabilitate Dodge; his solutions (if they can be called that) were racist and paternalistic, and they were consistent with what other white reformers proposed as a way forward for the United States and its dealings with Native people. Dodge advocated assimilation and "civilization" (implying that Indigenous cultures had none) and characterized Native peoples as primitive.

122. On the framing of Native people as "primitive" and even "ahistorical," see Blackhawk, *Violence over the Land*, especially chaps. 5–7, on Great Basin peoples, and the epilogue; Conn, *History's Shadow*.

123. For the Dodge correspondence, see r i d p, box 3, folders 26, 30, 35.

124. Gruber, "Ethnographic Salvage," 1293. Gruber makes this particular statement after giving evidence of similar ideas about the urgency of ethnographic collecting in the nineteenth-century U.S. West from Joseph Henry, Henry Rowe Schoolcraft, Samuel Morton, and John Wesley Powell.

125. O'Brien, *Firsting and Lasting*, xiii.

126. Conn, *History's Shadow*, 30.

127. Garrick Mallery to Col. Richard Irving Dodge, July? 1880, r i d p, box 3, folder 31, Correspondence.

128. Spencer Baird to Richard Irving Dodge, March 22, 1880, RIDP, box 3, folder 25, Correspondence. See also letters dated October, 25, 1880, and August 31, 1881.

129. Of particular significance were the world's fairs, which became critical spaces for the United States to display ideas about its past and future, to represent its pathway to "progress"—and to empire. On America's world's fairs, beginning in the same year that Samuel Ovenshine was writing to Sallie from the Yellowstone River, see Rydell, *All the World's a Fair*. On Progressive Era anthropology, American notions of nature and modernity, and anthropologists' study and display of Native people, see Sackman, *Wild Men*. On museums, display, and the contemporary representation of Native people, see Lonetree, *Decolonizing Museums*. On memory, place, and the history of objects, see DeLucia, *Memory Lands*. On the history of ethnography, see Kline, *Frontiers of Historical Imagination*; Fabian, *Skull Collectors*; Mitchell, *Witnesses*.

130. On the history of removing Native ancestors from their homelands for institutional collections and scientific study, see Redman, *Bone Rooms*, 16–68. On the complex and collaborative work of repatriating ancestors and cultural belongings, see Colwell, *Plundered Skulls*.

131. Bourke also collected artifacts for the Smithsonian Institution, including some particularly gruesome souvenirs of war. See Porter, *Paper Medicine Man*, 56, 63.

132. Porter, *Paper Medicine Man*, 59.

133. Porter, *Paper Medicine Man*, 35, 51; Ovenshine to Sallie, August 11, 1876.

134. For a detailed narrative of the attack on the camp of Morning Star/ Dull Knife, see Greene, *Morning Star Dawn*, 106–40.

135. Greene, *Lakota and Cheyenne*, 114.

136. Utley, *Frontier Regulars*, 275. See Utley's narrative of the fight at Morning Star/Dull Knife's village in *Frontier Regulars*, 275–76.

137. Bourke, *Mackenzie's Last Fight*, 36. Both Jerome Greene and Sherry L. Smith quote this line from Bourke's narrative of the aftermath of the attack on Morning Star's village. Greene, *Morning Star Dawn*, 137; Smith, *Sagebrush Soldier*, 83.

138. Wheeler, *Frontier Trail*, 187.

139. Caption of a photographic print titled "Necklace Belonging to High Wolf," rg2955.ph000060-b, rg2955, John Gregory Bourke, 1846–1896, Nebraska State Historical Society, Omaha.

140. Bourke, "Medicine-Men," 481.

141. Greene, *Lakota and Cheyenne*, 113.

142. Greene, *Lakota and Cheyenne*, 114.

143. Greene, *Morning Star Dawn*, 160–61, 190–91.

144. Robinson, *Diaries of John Gregory Bourke*, 4:78.

145. Robinson, *Diaries of John Gregory Bourke*, 4:87.

146. Wheeler, *Buffalo Days*, 169.

147. It appears that Bourke collected a souvenir from this battlefield too: the feet of "the horse supposed to have been ridden by Custer." According to Col. Homer W. Wheeler, who collected horse feet of his own, "Bourke had his pair made into ink-stands and gave one of them to a Philadelphia museum." Wheeler, *Buffalo Days*, 184.

148. Christine DeLucia read an earlier draft of this chapter and encouraged me to think more about this practice of countercollecting.

149. Wooden Leg, *Wooden Leg*, 258–67.

150. See identical articles about this exhibit published in two different newspapers with different feature photographs: Lorna Thackeray, "Meticulous Collection from Little Bighorn Fight Goes on Display at museum," *Billings Gazette*, May 10, 2010, https://billingsgazette.com/news/state-and-regional /montana/meticulous-collection-from-little-bighorn-fight-goes-on-display -at/article_ee888d88-5997-11df-82e9-001cc4c002e0.html; and Lorna Thackeray, "Relics from Little Bighorn Battle on Display," *Gillette News Record*, May 22, 2010, https://www.gillettenewsrecord.com/news/article_9cacb8e4 -06d5-5e44-abeb-3035b57c5ef8.html.

151. For details on Bourke and Powell, see Porter, *Paper Medicine Man*, 71– 73. For a description of Bourke's travels and research between March 1881 and September 1882, see 89–141.

152. Porter, *Paper Medicine Man*, 146. Bourke was promoted to the rank of captain in 1882.

153. Bourke's first assignment after graduating from West Point was in the Southwest. (He'd served in the Civil War before attending the academy.) Bourke reported for duty in September 1869. Crook was assigned to Arizona Territory in 1871, and in September Bourke became his aide-de-camp. See Porter, *Paper Medicine Man*, 9–12.

154. Bourke, "Medicine-Men," 481; author correspondence with Smithsonian Department of Anthropology, July 16, 2020.

2. Collecting the West

1. Edgar Alexander Mearns, "The Collecting List of Edgar A. Mearns," entry for March 13, 1884, EAMP, box 8, folder 7. The finding aid for this collection lists twenty-seven boxes; boxes 1–7 are at the Smithsonian Institution Archives, while boxes 8–27, as listed in the finding aid, are currently held at the Smithsonian National Museum of Natural History's Division of Birds, where they are numbered 1–20. I have chosen to follow the numbering system of the finding aid. Note that when matching my citations to the finding aid, box 8, Record Unit 7083, NMNH, is physically labeled as box 1 on the shelves in the National Museum of Natural History Division of Birds. Much of this collection has been digitized; in instances where I point to a particular page number of a "scan," I am referring to the page number of the relevant digital document.

2. Mearns, "Collecting List," March 17, 1884.

3. Richmond, "In Memoriam," 2.

4. Richmond, "In Memoriam," 2.

5. Hume, *Ornithologists*, 52–89. For a detailed account of the founding of the American Ornithologists' Union, see Lewis, *Feathery Tribe*, 70–113. For more on the development of American ornithology, see Barrow, *Passion for Birds*.

6. Bendire is an example of a soldier who began his career as an enlisted man and was promoted into the officer ranks during the Civil War. Born Karl Emil, he changed his name to Charles when he enlisted. He retired at the rank of major in 1886.

7. Bendire's private collection of eight thousand specimens is a key part of the Smithsonian's zoological collection. See Hume, *Ornithologists*, 22–37.

8. Mearns, "Collecting List," March 20, 1884.

9. For more on Coues, see Hume, *Ornithologists*, 52–89.

10. Mearns, "Collecting List," March 20, 1884.

11. See Lewis, *Feathery Tribe*, 1–34.

12. Worster notes that after a trip with a military escort to the Badlands went poorly, Powell stopped requesting escorts. *River Running West*, 271.

13. Simpson, *As We Have Always Done*, 154, 40–41.

14. For a nuanced discussion of Yavapai and Apache histories in what the United States called Arizona Territory, see Herman, *Rim Country Exodus*, especially chap. 1, "Kinship, History, Home." For contemporary information about tribal governments and tribal land, one place to start is the Inter Tribal Council of Arizona (http://itcaonline.com/). See also the websites for the Yavapai-Apache Nation (https://yavapai-apache.org/) and the Chiricahua Apache Nation (https://chiricahuaapachenation.org/) for maps and descriptions of Apache homelands and treaties.

15. Historically, "Apache" referred to seven different tribes: Plains-Apache, Lipan, Jicarilla, Navajo, Western Apache, Chiricahua, and Mescalero. Today Navajos are often excluded from this grouping. As head of the U.S. Department of Arizona, Crook would have been assigned responsibility by the United States for territory that included the homelands of Western Apache and Chiricahua Apache people, in addition to some groups of Yavapai people. The Western Apache prereservation groups and subgroupings that scholars agree on today seem to be grounded in the ethnographic fieldwork of Grenville Goodwin in the 1930s. The Western Apaches were divided into four subtribal groups: White Mountain, Cibecue, San Carlos, and Dilzhe'e (Tonto). Some Yavapais from the Kwevkepaya (Southeastern Yavapai) also lived in the Tonto Basin area and intermarried with Dilzhe'e people. These families were bilingual and often had both Dilzhe'e and Yavapai names, though not all gave equal weight to these identities. Farther south the Chiricahuas were divided in four or five subtribal groups: Chihenne (Warm Springs) and Mimbrenos (sometimes grouped together with Chihenne), Bedonkohe, Chokonen, and Nednhi. For historical context, see Herman, *Rim Country Exodus*, especially chap. 1; Sweeney, *From Cochise to Geronimo*; Basso, *Wisdom Sits in Places*; Basso,

Western Apache Witchcraft; Goodwin, *Social Organization*; Debo, *Geronimo*. On Grenville Goodwin's fieldwork—and its limits—see Maurice Crandall, "Reflections on *The Social Organization of the Western Apache* and *Grenville Goodwin among the Western Apache: Letters from the Field*," Open Arizona, University of Arizona Press, 2020, https://open.uapress.arizona.edu/read/reflections-on-grenville-goodwin-essay/section/fd2cb1ea-1e59-4cec-8006-57466af33a49.

16. Crook, *General George Crook*, 179.

17. For a detailed discussion of the meaning of these homelands, see the website for the Chiracahua Apache Nation, https://chiricahuaapachenation.org/.

18. Basso, *Wisdom Sits in Places*, chap. 1, "Quoting the Ancestors," and 32.

19. DeLucia, *Memory Lands*, xv.

20. Herman, *Rim Country Exodus*, 169.

21. Estes describes the "carceral reservation world" established by the United States in his discussion of Oceti Sakowin resistance on the Plains in the 1870s. *Our History*, 115.

22. Herman, *Rim Country Exodus*, 43.

23. Herman, *Rim Country Exodus*, 43.

24. This narrative is drawn from Herman, *Rim Country Exodus*, 43–44.

25. For Crook's orders, see Crook, *General George Crook*, 160. Both Karl Jacoby and Chip Colwell have done extensive research on the Camp Grant Massacre and questions around historical memory and meaning making from multiple perspectives. See Jacoby, *Shadows at Dawn*; Colwell-Chanthaponh, *Massacre at Camp Grant*.

26. For survivors of the Camp Grant Massacre at San Carlos, see Jacoby, *Shadows at Dawn*, 255; Colwell-Chanthaphonh, *Massacre at Camp Grant*, 37, 73–74.

27. Herman, *Rim Country Exodus*, 75.

28. Burns, *Only One Living*, 6. This description of the Skeleton Cave Massacre is drawn from Herman, *Rim Country Exodus*, 78–80. See also Norm Tessman, "Skeleton Cave through the Haze of 133 Years," *Verde Independent*, January 11, 2006, https://www.verdenews.com/news/2006/jan/11/skeleton-cave-through-the-haze-of-133-years/. Tessman relies on site visits and archaeological information to contextualize Bourke's descriptions of the massacre at Skeleton Cave.

29. Herman, *Rim Country Exodus*, 81.

30. Herman writes, "The soldiers and scouts—many of them Dilzhe'es and Yavapais—ringed Tonto Basin, riding across some of the hardest terrain in the territory. In the seven months from November 1873 to May 1874, they killed perhaps 250 Indians." *Rim Country Exodus*, 84.

31. Summerhayes, *Vanished Arizona*, 80.

32. The title of chapter 2 of *Vanished Arizona* is "I Joined the Army"; this is also the phrase she used before explaining that she and Jack, then a second lieutenant, got married. See Summerhayes, *Vanished Arizona*, 19–20.

33. Bourke, *Apache Campaign*, 83.

34. Tate uses the term "multipurpose army" to highlight the varied work of soldiers on the frontier. In *Frontier Army*, he returns to arguments made by Prucha in *Broadax and Bayonet* about the centrality of the army for the development of the West and broadens his focus to cover a fuller swath of the "frontier" throughout the nineteenth century.

35. Mearns, "Collecting List," March 25, 1884. Mearns later changed his mind about the supposedly Aztec origins of the ruins in the Verde Valley.

36. The story of Fort Verde State Historic Park is complicated and involves the hard work of many Camp Verde citizens, most notably Harold and Margaret Hallett. The fort's land and outbuildings were privately owned for eighty years before the state of Arizona acquired and preserved them. For more information, see the Fort Verde Historic Park website, https://azstateparks .com/fort-verde.

37. For more on early modern collecting practices, see Bleichmar and Mancall, *Collecting across Cultures*, especially the introduction, 1–11.

38. Mearns, "Collecting List," March 28, 1884.

39. As a surgeon Mearns was detailed to a specific place, rather than assigned to a regiment, company, and troop, like most officers and enlisted men, or to a particular command detail, like Bourke, who was assigned to Crook.

40. Mearns to Mr. Robert Donald, March 16, 1885, quoted in Richmond, "In Memoriam," 7. Mearns's notes from these expeditions are filled with observations on Crook's skill as both a hunter and a naturalist. Take, for example, this anecdote from Mearns's journal: "In the evening Gen'l Crook called out to me as I sat talking to Dr. Davis 'Say, Doctor, did you hear that note? That was the Gila Woodpecker!' I snatched up my gun and after waiting among the scattered cottonwoods a little while I Shot the first specimen I ever saw." "Journal of the Natural History of the Expedition Conducted by Brig. General George A. Crook, Whipple Barracks, Prescott, to San Carlos Indian Agency, October 1–October 27, 1884," entry for October 15, EAMP, box 12, folder 2.

41. For a more detailed treatment of the Sierra Madre campaign and the eight months between Crook's meeting with Geronimo and Geronimo's arrival at San Carlos in 1884, see Utley, *Geronimo*, 134–48; Bourke, *On the Border*, 433–64.

42. Mearns, "Journal of the Natural History," October 13, 1884.

43. Edgar Alexander Mearns, "Notes on the Natural History of the Expedition conducted by Brig. General George A. Crook, U.S.A., commanding the Department of Arizona from Whipple Barracks, Prescott, A[rizona] T[erritory], to San Carlos Indian Agency, via Forrest Dale and Fort Apache, and thence back to Whipple Barracks via Globe City, Fossil Creek, etc., between the dates of October 1st and October 27th, inclusive, 1884," entry for October 3, EAMP, box 12, folder 1.

44. I began birding while in graduate school in Ithaca, New York, and now I watch mostly red-tailed hawks and northern flickers in my Colorado Springs neighborhood.

45. Mearns, "Notes on the Natural History," October 3, 1884.

46. In the context of the British empire, geographer Greer's work *Red Coats and Wild Birds* also brings together soldiers and birds (and the "life geographies" of both) to explore the ways that ornithological practice shaped understandings of the British Mediterranean and the linkages between Europe and Northern Africa. Ornithological practice, for the soldiers Greer studies, was imperial work.

47. On getting lost, see Solnit, *Field Guide to Getting Lost.*

48. Mearns, "Notes on the Natural History," October 4, 1884.

49. Summerhayes, *Vanished Arizona,* 80.

50. Sheila Stubler, a ranger at Fort Verde State Historic Park, kindly gave me a tour of the grounds and shared some staff research files when I visited in 2012. She pointed me to where I could see the ruts along General Crook Trail Road.

51. Mearns, "Notes on the Natural History," October 8, 1884.

52. Mearns, "Notes on the Natural History," October 8, 1884.

53. On Indigenous refusal, see Simpson, *As We Have Always Done,* 33. Leanne Simpson's discussion pointed me to Audra Simpson, *Mohawk Interruptus.*

54. Mearns, "Notes on the Natural History," October 4, 1884.

55. Missionaries, anthropologists, and trading-post operators collected the materials in the Guenther and Goodwin collections at the Arizona State Museum, though army men collected cultural belongings from Native people across the U.S. West as well. For object images and discussion of their construction, meaning, and collection, see Ferg, *Western Apache Material Culture,* 87–152.

56. I am grateful to Christina Gebhard at the Smithsonian National Museum of Natural History's Division of Birds for inviting me into the lab to watch specimen preparation, answering my questions, and providing me with the following guides: Szabo, "Preparing Bird Specimens"; Sergei V. Drovetski, "Preparation of Avian Specimens for Research Collections," 2007, http:// fabioschunck.com.br/site/wp-content/uploads/2016/11/Drovetski_2007.pdf; Winker, "Obtaining, Preserving, and Preparing Bird Specimens."

57. Many thanks to Brian Schmidt at the Smithsonian National Museum of Natural History's Division of Birds for talking me through the guns and ammunition Mearns would have used. Any errors are my own.

58. For a beautiful exposition on loss as viewed through the history (and reanimation) of the Jenks Museum at Brown University, see Lubar, *Inside the Lost Museum.*

59. Email correspondence with Christina Gebhard at the Smithsonian's Division of Birds, July 23, 2020.

60. Edgar Alexander Mearns to Ella Wittich Mearns, April 18, 1885, EAM-PLC, box 1, folder "Correspondence—Family 1885." While Mearns doesn't give Lieutenant Vogdes's first name in his field books, I believe him to be Lt.

Charles B. Vogdes, who, according to an 1884 report of the secretary of war, served as both second lieutenant with the First Infantry and acting assistant quartermaster at Fort Verde. *Report of the Secretary of War*, 350.

61. Mearns, "Notes and Journal Taken on Trip from Fort Verde, Arizona, to the Havasupai Indian Village, to Peach Springs, and Return to Fort Verde, November 4–November 26, 1884," EAMP, box 12, folder 4, 20–21.

62. Mearns's specimen register for the Havasupai village trip indicates that several of his prepared specimens were shot by General Crook. Surgeon General's Office to Edgar Mearns, April 3, 1888, EAMPLC, box 10, folder "Military Correspondence, 1888." While Crook's support seems to have been grounded in his personal interests and values, and not necessarily the army's overall goals, Greer suggests in *Red Coats and Wild Birds* that in the British imperial context (during the Crimean War), the British Army stressed the importance of natural science and encouraged the development of what she calls the "military-scientific hero" (7).

63. George Crook to Edgar Alexander Mearns, January 28, 1885, EAMPLC, box 4, folder "Correspondence—January 1885."

64. Spencer F. Baird to Edgar Alexander Mearns, March 25, 1885, EAMPLC, box 4, folder "Correspondence—March 1885."

65. On the network cultivated by Baird and the Smithsonian, as well as for a discussion of amateur and professional naturalists—and arguments for interrogating these categories—see Goldstein, "Yours for Science"; Keeney, *Botanizers*.

66. On the professionalization of science in the second half of the nineteenth century, see Pauly, *Biologists and the Promise*.

67. Annual and Monthly Reports for 1881–89, USNMCR, boxes 6, 7, and 8.

68. For a consideration of evolving U.S. practices around death and dying during the U.S. Civil War, see Faust, *This Republic of Suffering*. For the history of the Army Medical Museum and its collectors, see Fabian, *Skull Collectors*.

69. John S. Billings to Edgar Alexander Mearns, September 17, 1885, EAMPLC, box 10, folder "Military Correspondence—1885."

70. John S. Billings to Edgar Alexander Mearns, July 17, 1885, EAMP, box 12, folder 6.

71. For more on the role of museums in building collections and studying human differences, see Redman, *Bone Rooms*.

72. See Otis, *List of the Specimens*.

73. On settlers' ideas about Aztec connections to the region, see Herman, *Rim Country Exodus*, 23.

74. On "specimen-soldiers" and on the collection of corpses and limbs for the Army Medical Museum, see Tuggle, "Afterlives of Specimens."

75. See Fabian, *Skull Collectors*, 182–83. The late nineteenth century was certainly the peak of the Army Medical Museum's collection in terms of size and range. Between 1900 and 1904 the museum refocused its emphasis on pathological specimens. The institution transferred over three thousand sets

of skeletal remains to the Smithsonian, keeping primarily materials useful for studying pathology or traumatic injury. See "Repatriation at the National Museum of Health and Medicine," National Museum of Health and Medicine, last modified December 16, 2013, http://www.medicalmuseum.mil/index.cfm ?p=collections.anatomical.repatriation.index.

76. Fabian, *Skull Collectors*, 176. For more on dealing with death, dying, and the dead during and after the Civil War, see Faust, *This Republic of Suffering*.

77. Fabian, *Skull Collectors*, 171.

78. See Conn, *History's Shadow*, 176–80, 193–94.

79. See, for example, Goetzmann, *Exploration and Empire*; Bartlett, *Great Surveys*.

80. For work in the history of American scientific practice that theorizes "the field," particularly in relationship to the museum and later the lab, see Kohler, *Landscapes and Labscapes*; Vetter, "Cowboys, Scientists, and Fossils"; Vetter, *Field Life*.

81. Merrill, "In Memoriam."

82. Charles E. Bendire to Mearns, May 28, 1886, EAMPLC, box 4, folder "Correspondence Jan–June 1886."

83. Hume, *Ornithologists*, 68.

84. Hume, *Ornithologists*, 31, 68.

85. Mearns, "Some Birds of Arizona," 65.

86. Mearns, "Ancient Dwellings," 763, 747, 751. For more information on what is now the National Park Service site called Montezuma Castle National Monument, see https://www.nps.gov/moca/index.htm.

87. Herman, *Rim Country Exodus*, 22.

88. Mearns, "Ancient Dwellings," 760, 763.

89. Surgeon General's Office to Mearns, March 15 and April 3, 1888, EAMPLC, box 10, folder "Military Correspondence, 1888."

90. Bendire to Mearns, May 28, 1886.

91. The historiography of the Apache campaigns is extensive and filled with minute details. For a clear overview, see the introduction to Cozzens, *Eyewitnesses*, xvi–xxxiv. For a more detailed narrative account, see Sweeney, *From Cochise to Geronimo*.

92. Utley, *Geronimo*, 220.

93. Bourke, "With Crook in the Sierra Madre," diary excerpt quoted in Cozzens, *Eyewitnesses*, 361. Not everyone resorted to animal imagery to describe Apache skills. William Shipp used the language of maturity: "Small and unable to compete with white men in any athletic sports, yet they made us feel like babies when it came to mountain work." Shipp then explains these skills further: "Their knowledge of country; their powers of observation and deduction; their watchfulness, endurance, and ability to take care of themselves under all circumstances made them seem at times like superior beings from another world." William E. Shipp, "Captain Crawford's Last Expedition," *Jour-*

nal of the United States Cavalry Association 5, no. 19 (December 1892): 343–61, quoted in Cozzens, Eyewitnesses, 519.

94. Crook to Sheridan, telegram dated March 28, 1886, quoted in Cozzens, Eyewitnesses, 575–76.

95. Faulk, Geronimo Campaign, 32; Burns, Only One Living, 70, 98.

96. L. Y. Loring, "Report on [the] Coyotero Apaches," Hubert H. Bancroft Collection, Bancroft Library, quoted in Cozzens, Eyewitnesses, 195.

97. Miles Powell has investigated the linkages between nineteenth-century attitudes about race and notions of nature; some of the theorists he studies made comparisons between Native people and animals in their discussions about what each culture or species required to survive. He writes in Vanishing America, "When pundits justified restricting Indians to reserves or enslaving African Americans on the grounds that these peoples would otherwise vanish like untamable animals, they further entrenched a pervasive conviction that wildlife was beyond saving. At the same time, by comparing Indians to moribund creatures of the wild, commentators provided a convenient pretext for horrific acts of cruelty towards the nation's indigenous peoples" (44). See also Jacoby's discussion of language, and of animal comparisons, in "'Broad Platform of Extermination,'" on settler-colonial violence toward Apache people—and Apache responses to settler demands for their extermination.

98. Lahti, Cultural Construction of Empire, 144–45.

99. Bourke, On the Border, 219.

100. Herman, Rim Country Exodus, 163.

101. Bourke, On the Border, 219.

102. For examples of the use of tags or passes in other contexts, see Hadden, Slave Patrols, on the regulation of enslaved people's movements. For a discussion of the use of slave badges, copper tags issued annually and engraved with a number, the year, and the enslaved person's profession, as well as the laws governing this practice in South Carolina, see Greene and Hutchins, Slave Badges. Many examples of these badges have been uncovered in excavations, and the Charleston Museum's Slave Badge Collection can be viewed at https://www.charlestonmuseum.org/research/collection/?group_by=object _id&collection=Slave+Badge+Collection&category=Communication+Artifact &sub_category=Personal+Symbol&object_name=Badges&redirected=1&page =3. The Lancashire Mining Museum describes the use of pit checks, metal tokens used to record work attendance and document how many miners were in a mine for rescue purposes. See "Miners Tally Checks," Lancashire Mining Museum, August 11, 2017, https://lancashireminingmuseum.org/2017/08/11 /miners-tally-checks. Issuing dog tags to U.S. soldiers, identification tags they were expected to wear around the neck, did not become standard practice until World War I, though it was first recommended by Chaplain Charles C. Pierce, who led the U.S. Army Morgue and Office of Identification in the Philippines before retiring in 1908. See Hirrel, "Beginnings"; Katie Lange, "Dog

Tag History: How the Tradition & Nickname Started," U.S. Department of Defense, September 9, 2020, https://www.defense.gov/Explore/Inside-DOD /Blog/Article/2340760/dog-tag-history-how-the-tradition-nickname-started/. Conrad writes in *Apache Diaspora* that Spanish soldiers in the eighteenth century had assigned Apache prisoners numbers to keep track of them, and that later U.S. soldiers, tasked with guarding Apache prisoners and lacking an interpreter, gave their charges numbers as well (253).

103. Charles P. Elliott, "An Indian Reservation under General George Crook," *Military Affairs* (Summer 1948): 91–102, quoted in Cozzens, *Eyewitnesses*, 408, 411.

104. Merritt likened these Apache men to "snakes ready to strike." Wesley Merritt, "Incidents of Indian Campaigning in Arizona," *Harper's New Monthly Magazine* 80, no. 459 (April 1890), quoted in Cozzens, *Eyewitnesses*, 156–57. Cozzens notes that the practice of tagging was instituted by Crook in the spring of 1873 (660n5).

105. U. S. Grant et al., "Where Is Crook?" *El Paso Times*, May 20, 1883, quoted in Cozzens, *Eyewitnesses*, 386–87. This piece responded to an interview in the *El Paso Times* with General Raguero about Crook's borderlands campaign in pursuit of three hundred Apache people.

106. Merritt, "Incidents of Indian Campaigning."

107. In a section of Crook's autobiography, *General George Crook*, tracing his life after the account written by Crook ends, editor Martin Schmitt describes this practice: "As in the old days, every male Indian able to bear arms was to wear a tag. Roll calls would be held often to make sure that everyone was still on the reservation" (244). Schmitt goes on to describe a council meeting in November 1882 (it is unclear with whom) in which Crook said that a regular roll call at the agency was not necessary, meaning that people could choose to live anywhere on the reservation; instead, Captain Crawford at San Carlos and Lieutenant Gatewood at Apache would be in charge (244). This does not appear to have ended the system but just to have changed where and to whom Apache people were expected to report.

108. Haley writes in *Apaches*, "The dehumanizing census method was not done away with officially until 1913, and continued in some cases for forty years past that date" (358).

109. Murat Masterson, "General Crook's Return," *Prescott Arizona Democrat*, November 25, 1882, quoted in Cozzens, *Eyewitnesses*, 316.

110. Bourke, *Apache Campaign*, 41. Here Bourke is describing tagging at San Carlos.

111. See, for example, Welch, Colwell-Chanthaphonh, and Altaha, "Retracing the Battle."

112. The tag has catalog number E151969-0, and its accession date is March 26, 1891. It was donated by Capt. John G. Bourke, Department of Anthropology, Smithsonian National Museum of Natural History.

113. "Company 'A' 2nd Battalion, Indian Scouts, commanded by 1st Lieut. M. P. Maus, 1st Infantry" and "Company 'B' 2nd Battalion, Indian Scouts, commanded by 1st Lieut. M. P. Maus, 1st Infantry," Record Group 393: Records of the United States Army Continental Commands, 1821–1920, NARA, part 1, entry 182, box 1.

114. The counts recorded in this document suggest that there were approximately one thousand Native men at San Carlos during the fall of 1882.

115. "San Carlos Census of Reservation Indians," October–November 1882, Record Group 393: Records of the United States Army Continental Commands, 1821–1920, NARA, part 5, entry 406-27.

116. For more on this history and its relationship to political formation and sovereignty, see Crandall, *These People*, as well as the website for the Yavapai-Apache Nation, https://yavapai-apache.org/history/. For discussion of how the army's tag-band system did not reflect the complex system of clans and kinship for Cibecue Apaches, see Kaut, *Western Apache Clan System*, 60–62.

117. Goodwin, *Social Organization*, 189. Goodwin goes on to describe how some tag-band chiefs functioned as "true chiefs," but by 1895 "there was less and less room for chiefs" (190).

118. Watt, *Don't Let the Sun*, 16, 220, 16. In "Edgar and Minnie Guenther," an essay about the history of the Guenther family and the Western Apache collection they donated to the Arizona State Museum, Kessel describes a friendship between the Guenthers, who were missionaries, and "an Apache woman known by the identification number B-3, a Chiricahua Apache of Geronimo's band" (14–15). Materials at the Arizona State Museum collected between 1919 and 1924 contain an aluminum comb with "A-19" stamped into one side, which could be a tag-band ID number. This item, labeled EEG 231, can be found in Ferg, *Western Apache Material Culture*, 99 and as color illustration no. 14. Beyond these examples, this book contains several mentions of individuals who are identified by their tag-band ID numbers.

119. In the notes accompanying Watt's narrative, anthropologist Keith Basso mentions that tag-band identifiers were sometimes repurposed as livestock brands. Basso does not elaborate on the origins of the tagging practice, describing them simply as a tool "to facilitate record keeping by reservation administrators." *Don't Let the Sun*, 306n8.

120. In *Shadows at Dawn*, Jacoby mentions the tags Crook made Apache men wear and links the practice to Scott's analysis of "state simplification" in *Seeing like a State* (229, 315n21).

121. If the male and female of a species are especially different, an allotype of the opposite sex from the holotype will be identified and described. See "Just Our Types: A Short Guide to Type Specimens," *From the Collections Posts* (blog), American Museum of Natural History, February 26, 2015, https://www.amnh.org/explore/news-blogs/from-the-collections-posts/just-our-types-a-short-guide-to-type-specimens/. On the history of type specimens in botanical practice, see Datson, "Type Specimens."

122. G. Gordon Adam, "Resolution Adopted at Meeting of Residents of Cochise County, Arizona, Regarding Outbreak of Indians from San Carlos Reservation," quoted in Cozzens, *Eyewitnesses*, 420–21.

123. Hernández argues in *City of Inmates* that incarceration is a form of elimination (9–10). Here I am suggesting that "tagging," a kind of emptying, operated in a similar way.

124. General Crook, report dated April 12, 1884, written from Whipple Barracks, Arizona Territory, Record Group 393: Records of the United States Army Continental Commands, 1821–1920, NARA, part 1, entry 182, Records of the Department of Arizona, Apache Campaign, 1886, box 5.

125. Estes, *Our History*, 115.

126. Hernández, *City of Inmates*, 2.

127. Sweeney, *From Cochise to Geronimo*, table on p. 406. Sweeney says that he "pieced together, from several sources of information, a compilation by band of those men who left the reservation and those who remained, most of whom served as scouts for Crook in the upcoming campaigns" (406).

128. Bourke, *Apache Campaign*, 102.

129. In *View from Officers' Row*, Smith demonstrates the complexity of frontier officers' ideas about and relationships with Native people in the nineteenth century.

130. Parker, *Old Army*, 152.

131. Henry W. Daly, "The Capture of Geronimo," *Winners of the West* 11, no. 1 (December 1933): 1, 3, quoted in Cozzens, *Eyewitnesses*, 448.

132. Marietta told the soldiers that the Apaches had gone up the road, which was partially true. But after about two hundred yards, they'd turned off the road and went up a steep hill. She failed to mention this final change in direction to the soldiers who visited her family's camp. Oral history interview with Mrs. Marietta Wetherill, 1953, tape 424, transcript, PHOHC.

133. George Crook, "Apache Affairs: An Interview with George Crook," *New York Herald*, July 9, 1883, quoted in Cozzens, *Eyewitnesses*, 402.

134. Robinson, *General Crook*, 279–82. For Chiricahua numbers, see Utley, *Geronimo*, 186.

135. Crook, *General George Crook*, 264–65.

136. Jack Lane, the editor of Wood's published journal of this campaign, calls Lawton's letters to Mary "lugubrious." Wood, *Chasing Geronimo*, 11.

137. Henry Ware Lawton to Mary "Mame" Craig Lawton, June 30, July 7, July 22, July 16, and June 26, 1886, HWLP, box 1, folders 6 and 7.

138. Debo, *Geronimo*, 287.

139. Lawton to "Mame," August 26, 1886, folder 9.

140. For more on this meeting between Miles and Geronimo, see Utley, *Geronimo*, 217–25; Debo, *Geronimo*, 293–308.

141. In Barrett's account of Geronimo's story (which he told to Barrett with the help of Asa Daklugie in 1904), Geronimo described Miles as offering this deal: "'There is plenty of timber, water, and grass in the land to which I will

send you. You will live with your tribe and with your family. If you agree to this treaty you shall see your family within five days.'" Geronimo and Barrett, *Geronimo*, 146.

142. Geronimo and Barrett, *Geronimo*, 147.

143. Chihuahua's band, who had surrendered to Crook in March 1886, had already made the trip to Fort Marion in St. Augustine, Florida. For the conditions of the journey, see Debo, *Geronimo*, 300; Sweeney, *From Cochise to Geronimo*, 575.

144. In his personal papers reflecting on his military career, William H. C. Bowen described how Geronimo "rendered portions of Arizona uninhabitable." WHCBP, box 2, folder 5, "Mount Vernon Barracks Alabama."

145. Utley, *Geronimo*, 228.

146. Mearns, "Field Notes and Specimen Lists, September 1, 1885–June 5, 1886," EAMP, box 13, folder 1; Mearns, "Field Notes and Specimen Lists, June 10, 1885–January 20, 1888," EAMP, box 13, folder 2; Mearns, "A Journal of a Journey from Fort Verde, Arizona, to Deming, New Mexico," March 25, 1885–May 20, 1895, EAMP, box 12, folder 6.

147. Edgar Mearns, copy of "The Natural History of the Mexican Boundary Line," to be presented to the president and members of the Newport Natural History Society, n.d., EAMP, box 16, folder 3.

148. The women and children of Geronimo's band had been sent to Fort Marion, on Florida's eastern coast. In April 1887 Geronimo's family members were transferred to Fort Pickens, and the rest of the Chiricahuas at Fort Marion were moved to Mount Vernon Barracks in Alabama. In May 1888 Geronimo's band was transferred to Alabama. See Utley, *Geronimo*, 226–35.

149. Conrad, *Apache Diaspora*, 266.

150. Utley, *Geronimo*, 234.

151. In *Geronimo*, Debo acknowledges the possibility that many of the Chiricahuas' health problems (particularly consumption) originated during their train travel east under brutal conditions—closed windows and doors, intense heat (300). See Conrad, *Apache Diaspora*, 251–66, for a discussion of the conditions Apache people endured and the violence of this practice of exile, as well as a discussion of the strategies Apache prisoners developed and employed to survive and to bring attention to the conditions they were enduring.

152. See Debo, *Geronimo*, 313–57, for a discussion of the multiple transfers of the imprisoned Apache people. Several different people, including their supervisors at various forts, members of associations interested in the treatment of Native people, Crook and Bourke, and even army surgeon Walter Reed, weighed in on what constituted proper treatment for these prisoners of war. Crook and Bourke, in particular, advocated on behalf of former scouts who had been sent to Florida along with Geronimo.

153. Bowen, "Mount Vernon Barracks Alabama," WHCBP, box 2, folder 5.

154. See Utley, *Geronimo*, 257–58; Geronimo and Barrett, *Geronimo*, 167–70; Debo, *Geronimo*, 420–22.

Interlude 1

1. Fletcher, September 21, 1900, PRFP, box 2, vol. 1 (letterbook).

2. For a description of Baldwin's Lake Lanao Expedition and the ensuing Battle of Bayan, see Arnold, *Moro War*, 28–39.

3. Martínez, *Front Lines*, 32.

3. The Nature of the Philippine Frontier

1. Harper, *Just outside of Manila*, 71, 75, 93–94. For an examination of ideas about water, health, and disease under U.S. occupation and colonialism, including at Mariquina, see Peralta, "Medical Modernity," especially 31–56.

2. On the construction of the idea of the tropics, Sutter writes in "Tropics" that we should "appreciate the several centuries of imperial history that have shaped the use of the category, and question the purposes that bifurcating the world at the tropic lines have served and continue to serve" (198).

3. Gonzales, *Securing Paradise*, 8, 9.

4. "Epitome of Matt Steele's Record" and "Biography of Lieutenant Colonel Matthew Forney Steele," MSP, box 1, folder 1.

5. Matthew Steele to Stella Folsom Steele, September 8, 1899, 6:30 a.m and 8 p.m., MSP, box 8, folder 3.

6. Munroe, *Painted Desert*, 3, 10.

7. Daly to Fannie, November 15, 1903, BCDP, box 1, folder 8.

8. Fletcher's wife, Hughine, carefully transcribed portions of these letters into a single volume, PRFP, box 2, vol. 1 (letterbook).

9. Paul Fletcher to Hughine Fletcher, August 23, 1900. Today visitors to Cañon City, Colorado, can take a train that follows this same route, which includes a hanging bridge where the canyon narrows and its rock walls steepen. See https://www.royalgorgeroute.com/.

10. George Telfer [to Lottie Telfer?], May 28, 1898, in Telfer, *Manila Envelopes*, 9. Editor Sara Bunnett notes that Telfer formatted the letters between May 28 and June 1 "as a shipboard diary" (172n29).

11. Telfer to Family, June 3, 1898; Telfer to son Willis, June 6, 1898; Telfer, in diary form (ostensibly to Family), June 16, 1898, all in Telfer, *Manila Envelopes*, 13–17, 19.

12. Fletcher to Hughine, September 21, 1900.

13. Robinson, *Diaries of John Gregory Bourke*, 1:171.

14. Beverly Daly to his mother, June 5, 1899, BCDP, box 1, folder 3. Clearly, Daly loved commas.

15. Fletcher to Hughine, September 21, 1900.

16. Fletcher to Hughine, October 1, 1900.

17. For U.S. domestic and foreign policy and the Philippines, see Welch, *Response to Imperialism*; Zwick, *Mark Twain's Weapons*; Karnow, *In Our Image*; Miller, "*Benevolent Assimilation*"; Stanley, *Reappraising an Empire*; Brands, *Bound to Empire*.

18. See Linn, *Guardians of Empire*; Linn, *Philippine War*; Cosmas, *Army for Empire*; Linn, "Long Twilight."

19. The same might be said of some scholarship in the history of North American frontiers—in particular, the work of Richard Drinnon and Richard Slotkin. See Drinnon, *Facing West*; Slotkin, *Fatal Environment*; Slotkin, *Gunfighter Nation*.

20. See, for recent examples, Immerwahr, *How to Hide an Empire*; Grandin, *End of the Myth*.

21. See, for example, Hoganson, *Fighting for American Manhood*; Kramer, *Blood of Government*; Harris, *God's Arbiters*; Love, *Race over Empire*; Wexler, *Tender Violence*; Silbey, *War of Frontier and Empire*; McCoy and Scarano, *Colonial Crucible*; Capozzola, *Bound by War*. On settler colonialism in the Philippines, see Charbonneau, "'New West in Mindanao'"; McKenna, "Igorot Squatters."

22. An exciting exception is *Prairie Imperialists*, in which Bjork traces how "the historical experience of domestic Indian Country shaped efforts to bring new areas where sovereignty was contested under American control following the war with Spain" (4). She follows three army officers—Hugh Lenox Scott, Robert Lee Bullard, and John Pershing—from their frontier service to assignments in Cuba, the Philippines, and later Mexico. Despite making similar arguments about the importance of studying soldiers' experiences on multiple frontiers, we study almost entirely different groups of soldiers, suggesting that this is an incredibly fruitful area for scholars to pursue.

23. Daly to his mother, June 19, 1899.

24. McCutcheon, January–May 1898, no. 14, p. 69, JTMP, box 33, folder 869. This volume is a reporter's notebook, and the numbering scheme for the pages suggests that the user should write only on the facing side of each page and then flip the book over and work backward. Revised versions of the entries McCutcheon drafted in his tiny notebooks made it into the *Chicago Record* the following week. The *Record* printed them in diary format, the firsthand observations of their man in Manila Bay. Excerpts of these newspaper pieces, as well as edited selections from McCutcheon's diary, appear in Feuer, *America at War*.

25. McCutcheon, January–May 1898, p. 69.

26. McCutcheon, January–May 1898, p. 124.

27. Karnow, *In Our Image*, 102–5. See also Kramer, *Blood of Government*, 93.

28. McCutcheon, January–May 1898, pp. 108, 107.

29. Edward C. Veberhagen to Friend Burt (possibly Floyd Dessery), October 25, 1898, FDP.

30. Nelson, *Ruin Nation*, 220.

31. McCutcheon, January–May 1898, p. 94.

32. For a helpful discussion of both the archipelago's geography and its diverse peoples, see Francia, *History of the Philippines*, 23–25, 46–48.

33. Linn, *Philippine War*, 5–6.

34. Linn, *Philippine War*, 6–12.

35. Linn, *Philippine War*, 6–7.

36. Telfer [to Lottie?], June 30, 1898, in Telfer, *Manila Envelopes*, 22. While the letter isn't addressed to anyone, the sign-off is consistent with letters to Lottie.

37. This notion—that the next step after conquest was colonization, in the Pacific as it had been in the West—was articulated beyond soldiers' letters. McEnroe writes in "Painting the Philippines," "The *Oregonian* often presented the idea that the annexation of the Philippines would reenact the settlement of Oregon" (31).

38. Telfer to Family, July 8, 1898, in Telfer, *Manila Envelopes*, 23.

39. Wilcox, *Harper's History*, 50. The waiting that Telfer described in his letters sounds plenty challenging, with sickness, heat, and lots of rain. He also wrote, "We cannot go into the sea water on account of poisonous fish." Telfer to Lottie, July 24, 1898, in Telfer, *Manila Envelopes*, 33.

40. Nielsen, *Inside the Fighting First*, 77.

41. Greene, "Address by Brigadier-General F. V. Greene, U.S. Volunteers, commanding 2nd Philippine Expedition on Steamship China, Pacific Ocean, Longitude 166° East, Latitude 19° North. July 4, 1898," FVGP, box 4, folder 11.

42. Lt. Charles Henry Hilton of the First Colorado Regiment mentioned that the speeches by Greene and Colonel Hale included "advice to the men to obey orders," but he also noted, "Altogether we had a good 4th particularly as we were the first Americans in the world to celebrate it," owing to their place in the Pacific. Harper, *Just outside of Manila*, 12.

43. Welch, *Response to Imperialism*, 43–46.

44. Jacobson, *Barbarian Virtues*, 228–30. Kramer discusses this as well in *Blood of Government*, 117–20.

45. Anti-Imperialist League, *Soldiers' Letters*, 4.

46. Berudo, *Import of the Archive*, 52, 51.

47. For a discussion of newspaper and magazine editorials, see Welch, *Response to Imperialism*, 105–9, 130. In "Water Cure," Kramer notes Herbert Welsh's "Indian Rights" advocacy—which took the form of championing assimilationist policies, rather than Native sovereignty.

48. See Brands, *Bound to Empire*, especially 3–35.

49. Ventura, "'I Am Already Annexed,'" 427.

50. Welch, *Response to Imperialism*, 57.

51. While outside the scope of this book, it is important to recognize resistance to U.S. imperialism and occupation in Hawai'i in both the past and the present. See, for example, Silva, *Aloha Betrayed*; Kauanui, *Paradoxes of Hawaiian Sovereignty*.

52. On Hawaiian resistance to the U.S. occupation of Hawai'i, see Silva, *Aloha Betrayed*, especially 123–63.

53. For a timeline of the events of the summer of 1898, see "The World of 1898: The Spanish-American War," Library of Congress, June 22, 2011, http://www.loc.gov/rr/hispanic/1898/chronology.html.

54. Samuel Ovenshine, August 15, 1898, SOP, box 1, folder 11. It isn't clear whether this narrative was part of a letter. It is dated but there is no addressee, and the text includes none of the conversational moments or interjections common in his earlier letters to his wife, Sallie.

55. Karnow, *In Our Image*, 130.

56. Owen, Chandler, and Roff, *Emergence of Modern Southeast Asia*, 284–85.

57. For a clear overview of the complexities of the 1896 revolution and the relationships among the Spanish, Filipino, and American forces and interests, see May, *Battle for Batangas*, especially part 1, "Before the Battle." For a discussion of the structure of the Philippine Republic formed at Malolos, see Angeles, "As Our Might Grows Less," 108–77. On the framing of the revolution, see Ileto, *Filipinos and Their Revolution*.

58. On Tagalog colonial experiences and the relationships between Spanish colonialism and conversion, see Rafael, *Contracting Colonialism*.

59. This discussion of the mission to occupy Iloilo City is drawn from Linn, *Philippine War*, 38–41. The Melliza quotation comes from military correspondence housed at the National Archives and is quoted in Linn, *Philippine War*, 40. For an even finer-grained discussion of the negotiations between the Malolos government of the Philippine Republic and those in Iloilo City, and the negotiations between General Miller on the *Baltimore* and local Filipino forces, see Funtecha, "'Iloilo Fiasco.'"

60. Silbey, *War of Frontier and Empire*, 64.

61. See Harris, *God's Arbiters*, 33; Francia, *History of the Philippines*, 144; Miller, "*Benevolent Assimilation*," 57–66. Linn includes a more detailed narration of individual troop movements, but his interpretation is mostly in line with Silbey's. See *Philippine War*, 42–46.

62. Nielsen, *Inside the Fighting First*, 98–99.

63. For an account of the battle focused on the Philippine perspective, see Angeles, "As Our Might Grows Less," 178–239. Angeles offers both rich context and a detailed narrative of the Philippine side of the Philippine-American War, reconstructed from the Philippine Insurgent Records and a range of additional primary materials.

64. Nielsen, *Inside the Fighting First*, 98.

65. This distinction between "war" and "insurrection" is included in "The Philippine-American War, 1899–1902," U.S. Office of the Historian (site retired May 9, 2017, but still accessible as of this writing), https://history.state.gov/milestones/1899-1913/war.

66. President McKinley, campaign speech, Pittsburgh, August 28, 1899, Record Group 350: Bureau of Insular Affairs: Special Records Relating to the Philippine Islands, NA, box 1, entry 33.

67. Renda, *Taking Haiti*, 64–65.

68. Nielson, *Inside the Fighting First*, 101.

69. A. A. Barnes to his brother, March 20, 1899, quoted in Anti-Imperialist League, *Soldiers' Letters*, 15. This letter was published in the *Standard* in Greensburg, Indiana, on May 8, 1899, according to the Stanford History Education Group.

70. Telfer to Lottie, April 7, 1899, in Telfer, *Manila Envelopes*, 151.

71. Frank Loucks to George Loucks, October 2, 1898, Camp Dewey, Manila, Philippines, FLL.

72. Barnes to his brother, March 20, 1899.

73. Matthew Steele to Stella Folsom Steele, October 24, 1899, 2 p.m., MSP, box 8, folder 4.

74. Mary Lawton to Mr. Craig, August 10, 1899, HWLP, box 2, folder 3. It looks as though the letter has been lightly edited, with a word underlined here, commas added there.

75. Lawton to Mr. Craig, August 10, 1899. Characterizing Filipino people, especially men, as "little" runs throughout the political rhetoric of the Philippine-American War. On gender and masculinity in this context, see Hoganson, *Fighting for American Manhood*.

76. Berkey, "Splendid Little Papers," 161.

77. Walter L. Cutter, Scrapbook, WLCP, box 1. The image is a loose clipping marked with the number Acc 1898-w-160 (8). All the clippings in Cutter's papers are either loose or carefully pasted into a scrapbook—without the header information that would reveal which newspaper(s) he wrote for.

78. C. L. Clark, "From the Philippines: C. L. Clark Writes Another Interesting Letter," September 30, 1899, Scrapbook, WLCP, box 1. Clark's rank isn't listed anywhere in the scrapbook, though it seems likely that he, like Cutter, was a private.

79. Cutter, "Soldiers in Luzon: Company H Nicely Situated at San Carlos," February 6, 1900, Scrapbook, WLCP, box 1. A reference to the people of Milford, combined with the address to "Editor FARMERS' CABINET," suggests that Cutter was serving as a correspondent for the *Farmers' Cabinet* (now the *Cabinet Press*) in Amherst, New Hampshire.

80. Cutter, "In the Philippines: Walter L. Cutter Describes an Execution in Luzon," December 28, 1900, Scrapbook, WLCP, box 1.

81. Faust, *Campaigning in the Philippines*, 133, 139, 144, 311. These volumes were customized with supplements describing the specific work of individual states' volunteer regiments. The version I looked at contained a supplement on the First Nebraska Infantry, complete with officer biographies and lists of soldiers by company.

82. Faust, *Campaigning in the Philippines*, 314.

83. Cutter, "In the Philippines: Correspondent Cutter Writes from Jolo City," December 14, 1901, Scrapbook, WLCP, box 1.

84. Daly to his brother Arthur, September 18, 1899, BCDP, box 1, folder 3.

85. See, for example, Cronon, *Changes in the Land,* for how colonists framed the possibilities of New England.

86. Freeman, *Soldier in the Philippines,* 65.

87. Fletcher to Hughine, April 17, 1901.

88. William H. C. Bowen to Mr. T. H. Goodman, September 26, 1905, describing his 1902 service in the Cagayan Valley, WHCBP, box 4, folder 7, "Governor Philippines Newspaper Correspondence 1899–1908."

89. Matthew Batson, small volume from the field, April 1899, MABP, box 3.

90. In "Ideology of Empire," Tuason observes a shift toward emphasizing "moral responsibility" later in the decade she studies here (40).

91. McKenna, *American Imperial Pastoral,* 23.

92. McKenna, *American Imperial Pastoral,* 144.

93. Freeman, *Soldier in the Philippines,* 63–65.

94. Cutter, "In the Philippines," December 14, 1901. "Moro" is a label deployed to describe Muslim people in the southern part of the Philippines; the term has Spanish origins and bundles different communities into a single category (note the similarities between Moor and Moro). Charbonneau traces the Spanish origin for the word in "'New West in Mindanao'" and notes that the "Muslim peoples of Mindanao-Sulu have reclaimed the name in recent decades" (14n4). "Moro" was the word used by soldiers to describe the people they encountered in Mindanao.

95. Gatewood, *"Smoked Yankees,"* a collection of letters written by Black soldiers who served in Cuba and the Philippines, provides opportunities to examine how Black soldiers experienced the Philippines and made sense of the American colonial project. For Gatewood's discussion of African American newspapers and their editors' responses to war coverage, see 16–18. On Black soldiers' experiences in the Philippines, see also Ontal, "Fagen and Other Ghosts."

96. Gatewood, *"Smoked Yankees,"* 258–59. Rank from Marasigan, "'Between the Devil and the Deep Sea,'" 68.

97. Gatewood, *"Smoked Yankees,"* 269–71.

98. Gatewood, *"Smoked Yankees,"* 255–56. Rank from Donaldson, *Duty beyond the Battlefield,* 58.

99. For more on race and masculinity, especially as navigated by Black soldiers in the U.S. Army, see Donaldson, *Duty beyond the Battlefield.* For more on Indigenous, Black, and Filipino experiences in the U.S. Army, as scouts, enlisted men, and members of constabulary forces, see Krueger, "'To Hold What the U.S. Has Taken.'"

100. Marasigan, "'Between the Devil and the Deep Sea,'" 18. See also 99–173, 502.

101. Gatewood, *"Smoked Yankees,"* 279–81.

102. Fletcher to Hughine, February 27, 1901.

103. For example, Charles Rhodes found a weapons cache in a local cemetery. Charles D. Rhodes, "1901–1903 Diary of the Philippines Insurrection," entry for February 11, 1901, CDRP, box 1.

104. Leslie Dennison, memoir excerpt, n.d., CMP, box 2.

105. Nash, *Wilderness*, 131–33.

106. *Articles of Association, Articles of Incorporation, By-Laws, and List of Charter Members of the Sierra Club*, quoted in Nash, *Wilderness*, 132.

107. See Solnit, *Wanderlust*, 148–55.

108. Solnit, *Wanderlust*, 150.

109. E. A. Brininstool, "City Fables: Albert's Camping Trip," *Los Angeles Times*, August 10, 1901, 15, ProQuest Historical Newspapers.

110. *Oxford English Dictionary*, s.v. "hike." The dictionary cites the first usage as a verb in 1809 (noun 1865). Last modified March 2022. https://www .oed.com/view/Entry/86975?result=2&rskey=bF2PNT&.

111. Jenks, *Death Stalks*, 80.

112. Fulton, *Moroland*, 253.

113. Rhodes, foreword to "1901–1903 Diary."

114. Harper, *Just outside of Manila*, 96.

115. Lewis, *Foot Soldier*, 90.

116. Matthew Batson to Florence Batson, November 10, 1899, MABP, box 1, folder "Matthew A. Batson, 4th U.S. Cav, Correspondence."

117. Daly to Arthur, September 18, 1899.

118. McCutcheon, *Chicago Record's Stories*, 40–41.

119. Batson to Florence, October 14, 1900, and following undated letter (unclear if a continuation of previous letter), MABP, box 2, Correspondence.

120. Capt. Frank Russell to Adjt., May 19, 1900, CMP, box 1, folder "US Army 34th Infantry (Volunteer)."

121. Frank Dwight Baldwin, "Report of Lake Lanao Expedition," FDBP, box 5 (folder contains many drafts).

122. "Short History of F Company, 34th, Infty, U.S, V.," CMP, box 2; Baldwin, "Report of Lake Lanao Expedition." McGrath describes the labor and management challenges Lt. Col. Robert Bullard faced at the helm of a challenging roadbuilding project in Mindanao. See McGrath, "'Army of Working Men,'" 204–83.

123. Fletcher to Hughine, January 20, February 16 and 18, March 12, 1901.

124. Fletcher to Hughine, March 27, 1901. A month earlier Fletcher was already reflecting on his age and life experience: "The world has as many sides and phases as the myriad stars above and I, who am yet a boy, have seen many of them. My life has not been of much length as yet, yet it has since my seventeenth year, been an active one." Fletcher to Hughine, February 16, 1901.

125. Fletcher to Hughine, January 22, 1901.

126. For a military summary of this expedition, see Kobbé, "Report."

127. McCutcheon, "1900–Jan 17–31, Detail[?] Journal, Opening the Hemp Ports, Sketches Also, 24," entry for January 21, JTMP, box 34, folder 872.

128. McCutcheon, *Chicago* Record's *Stories*, 47. I had hoped to see this for myself, to compare McCutcheon's sketches at the turn of the twentieth century with my own reactions early in the twenty-first, but State Department travel warnings for Mindanao and later a global pandemic got in the way.

129. McCutcheon, *Chicago* Record's *Stories*, 51.

130. Silbey, *War of Frontier and Empire*, 135.

131. McCutcheon, *Chicago* Record's *Stories*, 52.

132. McCutcheon's depictions of Mayon are surprisingly accurate, despite being ink drawings in a tiny notebook. Contemporary images of Mayon bear this out; photographs of the volcano were immediately recognizable to me after poring over McCutcheon's Mayon sketches.

133. McCutcheon, "1900–Jan 17–31, Opening the Hemp Ports," entry for January 23.

134. Fletcher to Hughine, November 13, 1900, and April 24, 1901.

135. Fletcher to Hughine, December 9, 1900. See also May, *Battle for Batangas*, for descriptions of similar practices under J. Franklin Bell, especially 254–56. May describes two expeditions, one lasting seven days and the other eight, at the beginning of 1902.

136. Fletcher to Hughine, December 9, 1900, February 13, 1901, and October 1, 1900.

137. Trafton, *We Thought We Could Whip Them*, 64, 53, 67, 76, 66, 52. Trafton's narrative was written in 1934, three decades after he returned from the Philippines. While we can't treat his account in the same way we would read letters and narratives written during the Philippine-American War, the consistency of Trafton's description, his mention of his commanding officer's service with Custer, and the many ways his story squares with other accounts from the period all lead me to think that his descriptive language was not added to his storytelling solely after the fact. William Henry Scott, the editor of Trafton's papers, comments on Trafton's language choices and comparisons to Native people throughout the text.

138. McEnroe, "Painting the Philippines," 47, 26.

139. Roth, *Muddy Glory*, 46. See also Bowe's memoir, *With the 13th Minnesota*.

140. Anti-Imperialist League, *Soldiers' Letters*, 10. This letter was published in the *Kansas City Journal* on April 22, 1899, according to the Stanford History Education Group.

141. Silbey, *War of Frontier and Empire*, 184.

142. Gatewood, *"Smoked Yankees,"* 277–79. No rank is given.

143. In *Blood of Government*, Kramer frames the Philippine-American War as a "race war"; the care and nuance he employs to unpack how U.S. "racial-imperial ideologies took shape" is a model for anyone working to think about this war in both U.S. and Philippines history. See 87–158.

144. See Robert Carter, "Henry Ware Lawton Scrapbook," EDGC.

145. These headlines do not oversell the article's content. It begins, "At the head of the 5,000 regulars now in the Philippine islands is a modern fighting machine. Its name is Lawton—Henry W. Lawton—and for nearly forty years it has worn the uniform of the United States army." Later on we learn that "headaches are not known to him, except through hearsay." For the full article, see "Lawton, Fighting Machine," *American*, May 6, 1899, pasted into Carter, "Henry Ware Lawton Scrapbook."

146. Faust, *Campaigning in the Philippines*, 234.

147. The terminology "Indian-fighters" or "Indian-fighting" is used—even if in passing—in almost every history of the Philippine-American War I have encountered, whether scholarly or popular. (I also include in this category lightly edited volumes containing the papers of a particular soldier or company.)

148. See, for example, the arguments made in Paulet, "Only Good Indian"; Bruno, "Violent End of Insurgency"; Gedacht, "'Mohammedan Religion.'"

149. Bjork, *Prairie Imperialists*, 173–74. For a discussion of scouting as a technique, see especially chaps. 6 and 7. For an examination of comparisons between Indigenous North Americans and Moros in the southern Philippines, see McGrath, "'Army of Working Men,'" 376–84. McGrath also notes an instance where officers made comparisons between the Ghost Dance as practiced by Lakotas in 1890 and a religious dance movement occurring in Davao in 1906 (344–47).

150. Aune, "Indian Fighters."

151. Miller, *From Liberation to Conquest*, 195, 190.

152. Harper, *Just outside of Manila*, 90.

153. Batson, Field Journal, entry dated April 23, 1899, MABP, box 3.

154. Batson, May 21, 1899, quoted in Coffman, "Batson," 69–70.

155. Batson to Florence, December 23, 1899 (typed copy of original letter), MABP, box 3.

156. Batson had previously served with Black soldiers in the U.S. Army known as "buffalo soldiers." For more on Batson, see Capozzola, *Bound by War*, 13–16.

157. Batson to Florence, February 3, 1901 (typed copy of original letter).

158. The travels of Henry Lawton's body across the Pacific, home to Indiana, and then to his final resting place at Arlington were national news. See, for example, "Funeral of General Lawton: Services at Manila in Which Army, Navy, Civilians, and Natives Take a Part. Impressive Funeral Procession; Crowds Watch Departure," *Chicago Daily Tribune*, December 31, 1899, 3; and "Funeral of Gen. Lawton: Body Is Expected about Feb. 1—Details Await Its Arrival," *New York Times*, January 21, 1900, 6.

159. Fletcher to Hughine, February 27, 1901.

160. Fletcher to Hughine, June 30, 1901.

161. On "improvement" and "improvers," and especially on farmers in the early American republic who used this language as part of a vision that

"enabled land to be cultivated in the most prosperous possible way over the longest possible time," see Stoll, *Larding the Lean Earth*, 20–21. For a treatment of improvers in the context of both the history of science and the history of capitalism, see Pawley, *Nature of the Future*.

162. See Silbey, *War of Frontier and Empire*, 185.

163. Fletcher to Hughine, July 12, 1901.

164. Fletcher to Hughine, July 18, 1901.

165. For a discussion of some of the historiographical disagreements about the degree of brutality exercised by American forces in Batangas specifically, see May, *Battle for Batangas*, 242–44.

166. Fletcher Diary, entry dated June 22, 1901, PRFP, box 2, vol. 2.

167. *Los Angeles Herald*, April 9, 1902, California Digital Newspaper Collection, http://cdnc.ucr.edu/cgi-bin/cdnc?a=d&d=LAH19020409. Miller, "*Benevolent Assimilation*," describes the "KILL ALL" *New York Journal* headline as taking up most of the front page (230).

168. Karnow, *In Our Image*, 191.

169. For a detailed narrative of the expedition that resulted in this order, see Linn, *Philippine War*, 306–21.

170. Linn notes in *Philippine War* that Samar, "for generations, has been associated in the public mind as typifying the Philippine War" (321). In *War of Frontier and Empire*, Silbey also acknowledges the attention Samar received and characterizes it as an "aberration," while pointing out that even if the American campaign on Samar was not representative, that fact "does not excuse it" (196). During the proceedings the *Atlanta Constitution* reported that Senator John Spooner linked Smith's order to the Fort Pillow Massacre, in which Union soldiers, many of them Black troops, were massacred after surrendering to Confederate forces. "Guns Trained on Gen. Smith," *Atlanta Constitution*, April 30, 1902, 10, ProQuest Historical Newspapers.

171. Silbey, *War of Frontier and Empire*, highlights the implications of calling this attack a "massacre" (189–95). Massacre suggests "a sly, wanton, treacherous assault by ungrateful natives" instead of a planned attack by a military opponent—an attack that seemed to be a direct response to particularly harsh treatment of Samar residents by the post commander, Thomas Connell (193). For the events that prompted this attack on U.S. forces, see Capozzola, *Bound by War*, 56–57.

172. See Fritz, "Before the 'Howling Wilderness.'"

173. Bruno, "Violent End of Insurgency," 36.

174. Silbey, *War of Frontier and Empire*, 195.

175. Silbey, *War of Frontier and Empire*, 195; Bruno, "Violent End of Insurgency," 34.

176. Silbey, *War of Frontier and Empire*, 196.

177. Waller occupies a curious place in the historical record. Some accounts seem to depict him as speaking truth to power (Karnow, *In Our Image*; Miller, "*Benevolent Assimilation*"), others as a criminal or at least a poor soldier

(Linn, *Philippine War*; Silbey, *War of Frontier and Empire*). For a detailed accounting of the courts-martial of the spring of 1902, see Miller, *"Benevolent Assimilation,"* 219–52.

178. Linn, *Philippine War*, 319. Waller also testified that Smith told him "to 'kill and burn,' take no prisoners . . . and regard every male over ten as a combatant" (315).

179. Bruno, "Violent End of Insurgency," 32. Here Bruno is quoting Andrew Birtle's analysis of an earlier campaign in Marinduque. Bruno uses this phrase to describe the American military strategy in campaigns against Indigenous people in the U.S. West and says the components of this "triple press" were "a guide for the later campaign on Samar" (32). Bruno also points out that in the aftermath of Waller's and Smith's testimonies, the military did not condemn Smith's orders or approach: "Not one of the opinions published in the *Army and Navy Journal* in 1902 was critical of Smith" (43). See also Birtle, "U.S. Army's Pacification of Marinduque." Furthermore, Waller later found himself the ranking U.S. officer in Haiti. See Renda, *Taking Haiti*, 101.

180. See Silbey, *War of Frontier and Empire*, 195–96.

181. To support the Chaffee theory, Bruno, in "Violent End of Insurgency," points to a letter Chaffee wrote in response to American efforts in Batangas using similar language: "can't say how long it will take us to make a wilderness of that country" (46n53). Linn, in *Philippine War*, points to slightly different language: "orders to 'make a desert of Balangiga'" (312). Here Linn is quoting military correspondence from Robert P. Hughes to Issac [Isaac] DeRussy, September 29, 1901. Linn also notes that no hard copy of Smith's order has ever been located (398n37).

182. Linn, *Philippine War*, 313.

183. Miller, *"Benevolent Assimilation,"* 236. Karnow, *In Our Image*, reports the nickname as "Howling Wilderness" Smith (191).

184. This is not hyperbole. In fact, as historian Reynaldo C. Ileto notes, U.S. forces had already been deploying these tactics elsewhere in the archipelago—often as part of the "hikes" many soldiers described in their letters home. "To be precise," writes Ileto in "Philippine-American War," over twelve days "a total of 540 houses, 5500 bushels of rice, 87 native ponies, 70 cattle, 14 carabaos, and 115 hogs were either confiscated or destroyed" by a cavalry troop led by Lt. H. Richmond (14).

185. For more on the American idea of wilderness, see Nash, *Wilderness*; Cronon, "Trouble with Wilderness." For settler experience in the West, see Smith, *Virgin Land*; Kolodny, *Lay of the Land*; Kolodny, *Land before Her*.

186. For more on supposed wildernesses as gardens cultivated by Indigenous communities, see Solnit, *Savage Dreams*, 294–308. For more on the relationship between Native people and environmental change, see Cronon, *Changes in the Land*; Smalley, *Wild by Nature*.

187. Miller, in *This Radical Land*, demonstrates that free Black pioneers (their word) in the antebellum Adirondacks also imagined the wilderness as a place where people might thrive—and work (47–96).

188. I'm thinking in particular of work on Black ecology and environmental history, as well as work in Native and Indigenous studies that offers more ways of being in and with the natural world. These projects make clear the narrowness of the white settler notion of wilderness. See, for example, Dungy, *Black Nature*; Finney, *Black Faces, White Spaces*; Savoy, *Trace*; McCammack, *Landscapes of Hope*; Miller, *This Radical Land*; Yusoff, *Billion Black Anthropocenes*; Kimmerer, *Braiding Sweetgrass*; Hoover, *River Is in Us*; Estes and Dhillon, *Standing with Standing Rock*.

189. On soldiers serving in national parks, see Meyerson, *Nature's Army*; Rust, *Watching over Yellowstone*.

190. Muir, *Our National Parks*, 1.

191. Muir, *Our National Parks*, 13, 15.

192. Muir, *Our National Parks*, 40.

193. "Buffalo Soldiers," National Park Service, last updated May 10, 2021, https://www.nps.gov/yose/learn/historyculture/buffalo-soldiers.htm.

194. On Young, see Donaldson, *Duty beyond the Battlefield*, 126–49.

195. "Moro Rock," *Atlas Obscura*, November 6, 2015, https://www.atlasobscura.com/places/moro-rock.

196. See, for example, Nash, *Wilderness*; Worster, *Passion for Nature*; Hyde, *American Vision*; Sandweiss, *Print the Legend*.

197. See Brady, *War upon the Land*, 93–126.

4. Collecting the Philippines

1. For more on Ahern's military career and his trajectory at the helm of the Philippine Department of Forestry, see Rakestraw, "George Patrick Ahern."

2. Unfortunately for Ahern, it seems this species has probably been renamed. I found this scientific name in Ahern, *Tree Species*, a list he assembled in 1901.

3. George Patrick Ahern to Gifford Pinchot, February 28, 1901, GPP, box 640, folder "1902 XII Philippines."

4. Tagalog Dictionary, s.v. "ilang," accessed March 27, 2022, http://www.tagalog-dictionary.com/cgi-bin/search.pl?s=ilang.

5. On what she calls "linguistic imperialism," see Schiebinger, *Plants and Empire*, 194–225. For more on botany and the visibility (or not) of empire, see Bleichmar, *Visible Empire*. And for more on Latin naming and Philippine botany, see Gutierrez, "What's in a Latin Name?"; Gutierrez, "Region of Imperial Strategy."

6. Capozzola, *Bound by War*, 64. Capozzola notes that while there are disagreements about the numbers, the "devastation" is clear. The numbers he offers are 4,200 U.S. soldiers and between 15,000 and 20,000 Filipino soldiers

killed, with civilian casualties numbering 100,000 to 300,000, a result of the destructive tactics employed by U.S. officers like Smith (64).

7. Ahern to Pinchot, September 5, 1899, GPP, box 966, folder "Gifford Pinchot, Speech, Article, Book File, Breaking New Ground, Correspondence (Selected), 1899."

8. Gifford Pinchot to James Pinchot, October 26, 1902, GPP, box 62, folder "Gifford Pinchot, Family Correspondence, Oct 1902."

9. Pinchot, *Breaking New Ground*, 233.

10. Gifford Pinchot to Gertrude Pinchot, November 8, 1902, GPP, box 62, folder "Gifford Pinchot, Family Correspondence, Nov 1902."

11. Pinchot to James, November 6, 1902, GPP, box 640, folder "1902 XII Philippines."

12. On the work of the U.S. Forest Service, see Williams, *Americans and Their Forests*, 393–424. On imperial forestry, see Bankoff, "Breaking New Ground?"; Barton, "Empire Forestry."

13. Pinchot, *Fight for Conservation*, 48. For an overview, see Worster, *Passion for Nature*; Miller, *Gifford Pinchot*.

14. Describing their relationship in the 1890s, Nash writes that "their common interest had definite limits." He describes Pinchot as caring most about "civilization and forestry," while Muir was primarily concerned with "wilderness and preservation." *Wilderness*, 135.

15. On Muir's 1903–4 round-the-world trip, see Worster, *Passion for Nature*, 377–86.

16. John Muir, "January–May 1904, World Tour, Part V," entries for April 17 and 21, 1904, JMP.

17. Muir, "World Tour," entry for April 19, 1904.

18. In "Breaking New Ground?" Bankoff characterizes this trip as "forestry from the deck of a ship" (371). It isn't clear whether this mileage includes only the sea miles traveled or whether Pinchot factored all his hiking through Philippine forests into this estimate.

19. Pinchot, "Philippine Islands," typed and bound narrative of his Philippine trip, GPP, box 640.

20. Pinchot, "Philippine Islands."

21. Pinchot to James, November 6, 1902.

22. Pinchot, "Philippine Islands."

23. Gifford Pinchot to Theodore Roosevelt, November 22, 1902, GPP, box 640.

24. Rakestraw, "George Patrick Ahern," 143. On Ahern's pathway to the helm of the Philippine Bureau of Forestry, see Roberts, "U.S. Forestry," 37–93.

25. Roberts, "U.S. Forestry," 77–78.

26. Charles Richmond to Edgar Mearns, March 5, 1898, EAMPLC, box 5, "Correspondence—March 1898."

27. F. W. True to Mearns, April 13, 1903, EAMPLC, box 7, "Correspondence, April, 1903." For more on the relationship between the Smithsonian and Yel-

lowstone National Park (including the role of the U.S. cavalry), see Smith, *Yellowstone and the Smithsonian.*

28. Edgar Mearns to Family ("Dear Ones All"), November 7, 1900, EAMPLC, box 1, "Correspondence—Family, 1900."

29. Edgar Mearns to Ella Mearns, January 27, 1901, EAMPLC, box 1, "Correspondence—Family, 1901."

30. Though the Smithsonian had limited materials from the Philippines, its curators were certainly aware of the possibilities the archipelago held for its collections. In *Western Impressions of Nature*, Savage offers an extensive survey of the ways Western travelers wrote about what they saw in this region in the eighteenth and nineteenth centuries. Significant nineteenth-century naturalists like Alfred Wallace, Albert Bickmore, William Hornaday, and Carl Bock traveled, observed, and collected in Southeast Asia, and it is likely that Smithsonian scientists were aware of their findings.

31. Gerrit S. Miller Jr. to Mearns, April 15, 1903, EAMPLC, box 7, "Correspondence, April 1903." For more on curators' perspectives on what Mearns's Philippine service could mean for the museum, see Kohout, "More Than Birds."

32. True to Mearns, April 13, 1903. On the relationship between climate and health as understood by Mearns's contemporaries, see Anderson, *Colonial Pathologies*, 37–44. On the notion of the "tropics" and on increasing scientific interest in both tropical environments and the establishment of tropical field stations, see Raby, *American Tropics*, 1–56.

33. True to Mearns, May 14, 1903, EAMPLC, box 13, "Correspondence—Botanical and Ornithology, 1903."

34. Leonhard Stejneger to Mearns, September 12, 1903, EAMPLC, box 7, "Correspondence—September 1903"; E. J. Brown to Mearns, May 23, 1903, EAMPLC, box 7, "Correspondence, May, 1903."

35. Mary was the sister of Richard Rathbun, who was the assistant secretary of the Smithsonian Institution and in charge of the National Museum. On the relationship between museum collecting and U.S. imperialism, see Quintero, "Trading in Birds." Quintero focuses on the relationship between American and Colombian ornithologists in the first half of the twentieth century. Though his focus is later than mine, the networks (and power dynamics) he describes grew out of turn-of-the-century collecting. His work, like much of the scholarship on the history of science and imperialism, explores government surveys and museum-sponsored expeditions, rather than the kinds of collecting that Mearns was doing alongside his military work. This focus on institutional or government collecting expeditions that are necessarily embedded in imperial relationships and networks of power pairs nicely with my examination of Mearns. After all, though his collecting was far less structured, he was part of an imperial occupation. See also Quintero Toro, *Birds of Empire*, for further elaboration of the ways that scientific imperialism and nationalism worked together in the U.S.-Colombian context.

36. Mary Rathbun to Mearns, February 17, 1904, EAMPLC, box 13, "Correspondence—Botanical and Ornithology, 1904."

37. True to Mearns, April 13, 1903, EAMPLC, box 7, "Correspondence, April 1903."

38. Mearns, Field Book, 1902–3, EAMP, box 17, folder 8, pp. 49, 53, 54 of digital scan of this volume (not page numbers in volume itself). Nothing else in Mearns's papers indicates that he already knew Ahern, but it is possible they had met before.

39. Richard MacGregor to Mearns, August 1, 1903, EAMPLC, box 7, "Correspondence August 1903."

40. McCallum writes in *Leonard Wood* that Moros held roughly 40 percent of the territory in the Philippines, despite being only 5 percent of the archipelago's population (205).

41. On the Organic Act of 1902, see Kramer, *Blood of Government*, 165–66.

42. Military governance of Moro Province continued until 1914. See Kramer, *Blood of Government*, 217.

43. Kramer, *Blood of Government*, 154–55.

44. On Worcester, see Rice, *Dean Worcester's Fantasy Islands*; Christopher Capozzola, "Photography and Power in the Colonial Philippines–2," Visualizing Cultures, Massachusetts Institute of Technology, 2012, https://visualizingcultures.mit.edu/photography_and_power_02/index.html. For a history of the U.S. Department of the Interior that tracks its long history of outward-facing, imperial work, see Black, *Global Interior*, including a discussion of the department's role in the Philippines on 39–50.

45. Adas, *Dominance by Design*, 144.

46. For a detailed explanation of the political structures operating in Mindanao and the Sulu islands, as well as a careful and nuanced consideration of how ideas about slavery and nationalism figured into U.S. colonialism in the Philippines, especially in Mindanao, see Salman, *Embarrassment of Slavery*. See also Paredes, *Mountain of Difference*, for an explanation of the role of a datu (28–29). Some soldiers spelled the word as "datto."

47. On the importance of telling histories of the Philippines that are differently oriented (and centered not only on or from Manila), see both Paredes, *Mountain of Difference*, and Abinales, "American Colonial State." While Paredes is focused on a much different moment (early Spanish colonialism), she notes the importance of thinking about *lumad* peoples in the history of Mindanao, rather than only Muslim Mindanao. Abinales, too, suggests that "scholars with Manila-centered and Manila-driven politics" overlook especially the south and the particular conditions of American military administration of "Moroland" (108). See also Charbonneau, *Civilizational Imperatives*, for a history of Moros and Americans in the southern part of the Philippines that emphasizes this often-overlooked region's connections to the wider world and pays special attention to the nature of U.S. empire. For a narrative of the Moro War, see Arnold, *Moro War*, in which Leonard Wood's tenure as the gov-

ernor of Moro Province is described in chaps. 6–12. See also Hawkins, *Making Moros*, for a consideration of the co-construction of Moro identity through a consideration of U.S. colonialism centered in the southern Philippines.

48. Charbonneau's *Civilizational Imperatives* highlights thirteen Moro groups in the southern part of the archipelago (xvi), but the army men I'm examining here tend to use the colonial imposed category of "Moro."

49. McCallum calls Wood an "architect of American imperialism" in the subtitle of his biography. For more on Wood's leadership in Cuba, see McCallum, *Leonard Wood*, 147–96.

50. Hagedorn, *Leonard Wood*, 2:1.

51. Hagedorn, *Leonard Wood*, 2:1–2.

52. Hagedorn, *Leonard Wood*, 2:3.

53. Hagedorn, *Leonard Wood*, 2:4.

54. Mearns to F. W. True, November 15, 1899, USNMAS, box 82, folder 1.

55. Mearns to True, November 15, 1899.

56. Mearns, Field Book, 1902–3, p. 55 of scan. These items are in the Smithsonian's collections, according to the Division of Anthropology's database.

57. Mearns, "Itinerary," entry for August 20, 1903, EAMP, box 22, folder 1.

58. McCallum, *Leonard Wood*, 217.

59. McCallum, *Leonard Wood*, 217–18.

60. Mearns, Field Book, 1903–4, entry for November 12, 1903, EAMP, box 17, folder 10, p. 3 of scan.

61. Mearns, Field Book, 1903–4, entry for November 16, 1903, p. 5 of scan.

62. Mearns, Field Book, 1903–4, entry for November 16, 1903, p. 5 of scan. I am not sure that I have correctly transcribed "sirge" before "flavipes" in the fifth line from the end of the list.

63. Mearns, "Itinerary of the Simpitan Expedition, May 17–29, 1904," EAMP, box 21, folder 22.

64. Mearns, "Itinerary of the Simpitan Expedition."

65. For a discussion of military intelligence work and Moro ethnography, see Charbonneau, *Civilizational Imperatives*, 33–35.

66. Mearns, Field Book, 1903–4, entry for December 2, 1903, p. 11 of scan.

67. Mearns, Field Book, 1903–4, entry for December 7, 1903, p. 14 of scan.

68. Richmond to Mearns, May 16, 1903, EAMPLC, box 13, "Correspondence—Botanical and Ornithology, 1903."

69. Mearns to Richmond, May 27, 1903, USNMDOB, box 22, folder 8. Mearns also wrote in this letter, "At Frisco will run out doors somewhere and shoot some birds just so you'll know I got there safely."

70. Richmond to Mearns, May 16, 1903.

71. See Goldberg, "History of Pest Control," 23–24. On arsenic poisoning experienced by naturalists, see Lewis, *Feathery Tribe*, 134.

72. Richmond to Mearns, May 16, 1903.

73. For more on both the mechanics and politics of collecting and empire (in a different empire) over great distances, see Endersby, *Imperial Nature*.

74. Leonhard Stejneger to Mearns, September 12, 1903, EAMPLC, box 7, "Correspondence—September 1903." He included additional instructions for snakes: "Cut all snakes, even small ones, open along the middle of the belly to whole length."

75. Frederick Coville to Mearns, October 21, 1903, EAMPLC, box 13, "Correspondence—Botanical and Ornithology, 1903."

76. Miller to Mearns, February 8, 1904, EAMPLC, box 13, "Correspondence—Botanical and Ornithology, 1904."

77. Richmond to Mearns, December 3, 1903, USNMDOB, box 7, folder 3.

78. Richard Rathbun to Mearns, February 13, 1904, EAMPLC, box 13, "Correspondence—Botanical and Ornithology, 1904."

79. Memo written by Charles Richmond accompanying letter from Rathbun to Mearns, February 13, 1904.

80. "Information," n.d., EAMPLC, box 13, "Correspondence—Botanical and Ornithology, 1903."

81. Mearns, "Itinerary," April 21, March 11, and April 4, 1904, EAMP, box 22, folder 1. "Visayan" refers to one of the three main ethnolinguistic groups of the Philippines.

82. Otis T. Mason, "Report on the Department of Anthropology for the Year 1904–1905," USNMCR, box 26, folder 16.

83. Redman, *Bone Rooms*, 91–94. He also mentions coverage of the arrival of the skeletons of "black dwarfs" from the Philippines to the Smithsonian in the *Chicago Daily Tribune* and notes the racist language in the piece, representative of dominant cultural attitudes about racial hierarchy at the beginning of the twentieth century (78).

84. Catalog card describing Moro ammunition bag from Lake Lanao, Philippine Islands, January 27, 1904, cat. no. E229436, Smithsonian NMNH Department of Anthropology, http://n2t.net/ark:/65665/m3a18d4a18-2dde-4904 -8982-a8142a85b793.

85. Search conducted using the NMNH Anthropology Collections database. "Search the Department of Anthropology Collections," NMNH, accessed June 10, 2021, https://collections.nmnh.si.edu/search/anth/.

86. Dower, *War without Mercy*, 64–66.

87. Robinson and Schubert, "David Fagen." For a detailed look at Fagen's service in both the U.S. Army and the Philippine Army, see Marasigan, "Between the Devil and the Deep Sea," 80–81, 184–87, 321–25, 351–53; Ontal, "Fagen and Other Ghosts."

88. Morey, *Fagen*, 287. It seems the *Washington Post* misspelled Fagen's name.

89. List appended to letter from Rathbun to Mearns, February 13, 1904. For clarity, I have written out the words where Rathbun used ditto marks to indicate the same words in successive entries.

90. Recall that Mearns noted that he used his shotgun to kill three people during a fight. "Itinerary," entry for August 20, 1903.

91. Gerrit S. Miller Jr. to Mearns, September 12, 1903, EAMPLC, box 13, "Correspondence—Botanical and Ornithology, 1903."

92. Rathbun to Mearns, September 18, 1903, EAMPLC, box 13, "Correspondence—Botanical and Ornithology, 1903."

93. Miller to Mearns, September 12, 1903.

94. Constitution of the Philippine Scientific Association, July 26, 1903, EAMPLC, box 15, "Correspondence, Philippine Scientific Assoc., 1904."

95. Constitution of the Philippine Scientific Association.

96. Form letter appended to Constitution of the Philippine Scientific Association.

97. Annotated list of scientific papers and bird lists, EAMPLC, box 15, "Correspondence, Philippine Scientific Assoc., 1904." While there is no indication that this list of papers is unrelated to Mearns's Philippine Scientific Association work, it is a partial list, so I cannot be completely sure that these annotations are for the association.

98. Miller to Mearns, February 27, 1904, EAMPLC, box 13, "Correspondence—Botanical and Ornithology, 1904."

99. Edgar Mearns to Lillian Mearns, July 22, 1904, EAMP, box 21, folder 1.

100. Mearns, Field Book, March 1–3, 1904, EAMP, box 17, folder 11.

101. Mearns, Field Book, 1903–4, entries for February 25–26, 1904, EAMP, box 17, folder 10, pp. 56–65 of scan.

102. Mearns to Richmond, February 19, 1903, USNMDOB, box 22, folder 8. Mearns's itinerary for this week confirms that he and his colleagues were busy with military work. Mearns noted "several hundred" Moro casualties, one dead American soldier, and several wounded after a fight on February 21. Mearns, "Itinerary," February 21, 1904, EAMP, box 22, folder 1.

103. For more on punitive expeditions, see Bjork's discussion of this tactic in Prairie Imperialists, 180–94. Bjork names Leonard Wood as "the greatest—and most disastrous—exponent of punitive lessons" (181).

104. For more on this expedition, see McCallum, Leonard Wood, 219–20.

105. Mearns, Field Book, March 4–15, 1904, entry for March 9, EAMP, box 17, folder 12.

106. Mearns, Field Book, March 4–15, 1904, entries for March 10 and 11. Tan writes in Filipino-American War that Wood's forces killed hundreds of Moros at Sirinaya (171).

107. McCallum, Leonard Wood, 219.

108. Tan, Filipino-American War, 171. Carlo Jones Velayo identifies some of the local and familial politics that tie into Datu Ali's relationship with the United States. See Velayo, "The Good, the Bad and the Friendly." Charbonneau writes in Civilizational Imperatives that Ali's opposition to the U.S. stemmed from "antislavery measures, economic constraints, and a rescinded offer to participate in the 1904 St. Louis World's Fair" (104).

109. McCallum, Leonard Wood, 220.

110. Wood Diary, entry for April 7, 1904, quoted in McCallum, *Leonard Wood*, 220.

111. Charbonneau, *Civilizational Imperatives*, 104.

112. See chapter 3 of this volume for an extended discussion of these orders and their cultural resonance with shifting American notions of wilderness.

113. Miller to Mearns, March 25, 1904.

114. There is a rich body of literature on the relationship between the field and the museum, and the field and the lab, in the history of science. As the questions asked by historians of science have broadened over the last several decades, scholars have begun asking questions about a larger set of scientific practices and practitioners. With this expansion has come greater attention on field sites and field workers. This work takes seriously issues of power, expertise, and knowledge production. But much of it, understandably, gets at these questions through planned surveys and collecting expeditions by scientists, universities, museums, and governments. Actors like Mearns—collectors who were incorporating collecting work into military obligations—don't quite fit into these frameworks for understanding the place of the lab and the field in scientific practices. For an excellent overview of the questions that studying the field can help us think about, see the introduction by Kuklick and Kohler to a special volume of *Osiris* on "Science in the Field." See also Kohler, *Landscapes and Labscapes*; Vetter, "Cowboys, Scientists, and Fossils"; Endersby, *Imperial Nature*; Jardine, Secord, and Spary, *Cultures of Natural History*; Quintero Toro, *Birds of Empire*.

115. Mearns to Richmond, June 2, 1904, USNMDOB, box 22, folder 8.

116. Mearns to Richmond, June 2, 1904.

117. Mearns, "An Ornithological Journal and Register, 1874–1886," entry for May 23, 1877, EAMP, box 8, folder 6, p. 172 of scan.

118. Mearns, Field Book, May 17–29, 1904, entry for May 25, EAMP, box 17, folder 13.

119. Mearns, Field Book, May 17–29, 1904, entry for May 25.

120. McCutcheon, "1900–Jan 17–31, Detail[?] Journal, Opening the Hemp Ports, Sketches Also, 24," entry for January 19, JTMP, box 34, folder 872.

121. Mearns to Richmond, June 2, 1904.

122. As many U.S. casualties as possible were repatriated through the combined effort of Pierce's office and the Quartermaster Burial Corps. During the Spanish-American War, the Quartermaster Burial Corps consisted of contract morticians who were civilians employed by the U.S. Army. See Hirrel, "Beginnings"; Potter and Deeben, "Care for the Military Dead," 1035; Sledge, *Soldier Dead*. The mention of Pierce's experimentation with embalming techniques occurs in Hirrel, "Beginnings," 65.

123. Mearns to Richmond, June 2, 1904.

124. Taft and Philippine Exposition Board, *Circular Letter*, 29–30.

125. "Fourth Annual Report of the Philippine Commission, 1903," War Department: Government Printing Office, 1904, Library Materials, Record

Group 350: Bureau of Insular Affairs: Special Records Relating to the Philippine Islands, NA, volume 1368 (Forestry Information), entry 95.

126. Pinchot, Forestry notebook, 1902, GPP, box 37, folder 5.

127. Pinchot and Ahern, "Philippine Forest Exhibit," GPP, box 1010, Gifford Pinchot Book File, Breaking New Ground, Philippine Islands, Miscellany.

128. Taft and Philippine Exposition Board, *Circular Letter*, 15.

129. Rydell, *All the World's a Fair*, 164–65.

130. Kramer, *Blood of Government*, 233–42.

131. Kramer, *Blood of Government*, 235.

132. Frank Dwight Baldwin to Mrs. M. B. Ferry, June 3, 1920, FDBP, box 3, folder "Melaker–Mile High Club, Correspondence."

133. Cornelius Cole Smith Diary, Part 2, SCFP, box 1, folder 4. For more on Cornelius Cole Smith, see Smith, *Don't Settle for Second*.

134. Muir, "World Tour," April 23, 1904.

135. On the refusal of the Lake Lanao Moros to "perform for the amusement of visitors," see Parezo and Fowler, *Anthropology*, 185.

Interlude 2

1. Raibmon, "Living on Display," 71.

2. Kosmider, "Refracting the Imperial Gaze," 328, 324.

3. Geronimo and Barrett, *His Own Story*, 160.

4. My detective work is now much more easily confirmed with an incredible online overlay of the 1904 World's Fair map onto contemporary digital maps of St. Louis. See "Louisiana Purchase Exposition, St. Louis, Missouri, 1904 (Raster Image)," Harvard Map Collection, Harvard College Library, accessed March 29, 2022, https://maps.princeton.edu/catalog/harvard-g4164 -s4q48-1904-b8.

5. For more on Janna Añonuevo Langholz's work, see her website at https:// www.jannalangholz.com.

6. On Langholz's Filipino American Artist Directory, see the About page at https://www.filamartistdirectory.com/about.

7. Megan Cattel, "1904 World's Fair Revised: One Artist Memorializes Filipino and Indigenous People," St. Louis Public Radio, May 16, 2021, https:// news.stlpublicradio.org/2021-05-16/1904-worlds-fair-revised-one-artist -memorializes-filipino-and-indigenous-people. Parezo and Fowler assembled an appendix of Indigenous and Filipino participants in the anthropology exhibits at the fair in *Anthropology*, 405–16.

5. The Frontier in Miniature

1. Clevenger, *Indescribably Grand*, 146. See also Sam Hyde Album, MHS Photographs and Prints Collection, Missouri Historical Society Archives, St. Louis.

2. Edmund Philibert, "Account of 28 Visits to World's Fair," PFP. See also Clevenger, *Indescribably Grand*, 74–118.

3. Mary McKittrick Markham, Record Book 1897–1909, vol. 1, MMMDS.

4. Edward Schneiderhahn Diary, vol. 6, EVPSD. This diary is also excerpted in Clevenger, *Indescribably Grand*, 40–72. I cite the published version where possible for accessibility.

5. Francis, *Universal Exposition of 1904*, 189.

6. Francis, *Universal Exposition of 1904*, 201.

7. Francis, *Universal Exposition of 1904*, 199. Francis wrote that each sculptor "presented his subject with historic accuracy" (199).

8. On the Louisiana Purchase and the abstraction of the transfer of power, see Hyde, *Empires, Nations, and Families*, 1–24.

9. See both Barnes, *Standing on a Volcano*, and Francis, *Universal Exposition of 1904*, for more on the endless work required to generate support for the city's bid.

10. See, in particular, the 1899 speech made by the chairman of the executive committee of the Committee of Two Hundred, in which he traces the booming growth of St. Louis: "What was the St. Louis of 1890 compared with the St. Louis of 1899? We have thirty per cent more people than we had then, and the assessed value of our taxable property has almost doubled. Our railroad facilities have increased, our tributary territory has been enlarged by the opening of Oklahoma to settlement, and the rapid immigration to that productive region has contributed no little to the large growth of the city's trade." Francis, *Universal Exposition of 1904*, 28.

11. Francis, *Universal Exposition of 1904*, 34.

12. Francis, *Universal Exposition of 1904*, 35.

13. Francis, *Universal Exposition of 1904*, 145.

14. "President D. R. Francis before Contemporary Club, at St. Louis on Evening of Oct 26, 1901, the Principal Speakers of the Evening Being Mr. W. I. Buchanan, Director General of the Pan American Exposition, and Prof. Turner, of the Wisconsin University," DRFP, box 10, folder 11. Francis and the other boosters worked to make the link between the Louisiana Purchase and their proposed fair meaningful by centering it in their planning—including featuring Frederick Jackson Turner at this event.

15. Francis Vinton Greene, "Address by Brigadier-General F. V. Greene, U.S. Volunteers, Commanding 2nd Philippine Expedition on Steamship China, Pacific Ocean, Longitude 166° East, Latitude 19° North. July 4, 1898," FVGP, box 4, folder 11.

16. Lodge, *Retention*, 5.

17. "Mr. Cockran in Chicago: Addresses over 12,000 People in the Coliseum. 'McKinley Making War to Take Territory'—Jefferson's Policy of Expansion Defined and Upheld," *New York Times*, September 30, 1900, 2.

18. "The Trip through Iowa: The President, in His Speeches, Devotes the Greater Part of His Time to the Philippines," *New York Times*, October 17, 1899, 5.

19. See, for example, the letters to the editor about the Philippines in the Sunday *New York Times*, January 15, 1899.

20. The Louisiana Purchase Exposition Company did the math—the area of those four fairs combined totaled 1,319 acres—and it used this fact to promote its project. See Francis, *Universal Exposition of 1904*, 46.

21. Francis, *Universal Exposition of 1904*, 50.

22. Hyde, *Empires, Nations, and Families*, 1–24.

23. DuVal, *Native Ground*. See also "Explore Cahokia Mounds," Cahokia Mounds Museum Society, accessed March 29, 2022, https://cahokiamounds .org/explore/.

24. Loughlin and Anderson, *Forest Park*, 16, 17, 32.

25. Francis, *Universal Exposition of 1904*, 46. The eastern half of Forest Park was not an option; it already contained several heavily used community resources, including a boathouse, a zoo, greenhouses, picnic grounds, and a police substation. See the incredibly detailed park history in Loughlin and Anderson, *Forest Park*, for debates over the fair site. One of the concerns articulated about the selected site was that "there would be damage to 'that glorious gift of nature,' Forest Park" (64–65). See also 40–50 and map on 59.

26. Francis, *Universal Exposition of 1904*, 50.

27. Francis, *Universal Exposition of 1904*, 66. The detour taken by some members of the group was not mentioned in the write-up of the ceremony in the *World's Fair Bulletin*.

28. Francis, *Universal Exposition of 1904*, 67.

29. Francis, *Universal Exposition of 1904*, 67. Both the stake and the ax were later "preserved among the souvenirs of the Exposition" (67).

30. Francis, *Universal Exposition of 1904*, 69, 83.

31. Hyde Album. Text of memoir, along with some illustrations, excerpted in Clevenger, *Indescribably Grand*, 128–46.

32. Buel, *Louisiana and the Fair*, 1298.

33. Hyde Album; Clevenger, *Indescribably Grand*, 130.

34. Loughlin and Anderson, *Forest Park*, 70–71.

35. Fox and Sneddeker, *From the Palaces*, 260.

36. Loughlin and Anderson, *Forest Park*, 71–72.

37. Schneiderhahn memoir, quoted in Clevenger, *Indescribably Grand*, 54–55.

38. Publicity Department Materials, GEKP, box 1, folder 3.

39. Lowenstein, *Official Guide*, 36.

40. "The Louisiana Purchase Exposition," *Current Literature* (1888–1912), June 1, 1903, 670, ProQuest Historical Newspapers.

41. Victor Wilker, "The Louisiana Purchase Exposition: How It Differs from Former World's Fairs," *Christian Advocate* (1866–1905), August 25, 1904, 1386, ProQuest Historical Newspapers.

42. Lowenstein, *Official Guide*, 21.

43. Lowenstein, *Official Guide*, 40.

44. *World's Fair Bulletin*, August 1901, quoted in Fox and Sneddeker, *From the Palaces*, 8.

45. Buel, *Louisiana and the Fair*, 1393.

46. "Scenes on the World's Fair Site: Transforming the Wilderness of Forest Park into an Exposition Landscape," WFB 3, no. 1 (1901–2): 8.

47. "The Largest Employer," WFB 3, no. 4 (1901–2): 5; "Work at World's Fair Site," WFB 3, no. 4 (1901–2): 4.

48. "Sunday in Camperstown" and "Sunday at Graders' Home," WFB 3, no. 4 (1901–2): 10.

49. "Indian Mounds in Forest Park," WFB 3, no. 2 (1901–2): 9.

50. For archaeologist identifying Omaha artifacts, see "Indian Mounds in Forest Park," WFB 3, no. 2 (1901–2): 9. For more on Mississippian culture, see DuVal, *Native Ground*, especially 13–28. For contemporary information on the Omaha Tribe of Nebraska, see the nation's website at https://www.omahatribe.com/.

51. David Francis, Boston speech, February 27, 1902, DRFP, box 11, folder 4.

52. Francis, *Universal Exposition of 1904*, vi.

53. Henson, "'Objects of Curious Research,'" s249.

54. In 1858 the Smithsonian had assumed supervision of the thousands of specimens and artifacts collected by the United States Exploring Expedition (1838–42), or U.S. Ex. Ex., so it was not starting from scratch; still, world's fairs created an expanding and enduring venue for the development of exhibits and the acquisition of new material. On the U.S. Ex. Ex. and the Smithsonian, see Nathaniel Philbrick, "The Scientific Legacy of the U.S. Exploring Expedition," Smithsonian Libraries, January 2004, https://www.sil.si.edu/DigitalCollections/usexex/learn/Philbrick.htm.

55. Yochelson and Jarrett, *National Museum*, 15–16.

56. The Smithsonian also participated in smaller fairs and expositions, such as the South Carolina Inter-State and West Indian Exposition in Charleston in 1901–2. A part-time employee in the Smithsonian's Philippine Exhibit in Charleston wrote to ask if there might be work for him in St. Louis. Letter from W. S. Senteney to F. W. True, May 30, 1902, USNMER, box 61, folder 7.

57. Extract from Public Act No. 182, USNMER, box 62, folder 26.

58. "Uncle Sam at the World's Fair," reprinted from the *St. Louis Globe-Democrat* in WFB 4, no. 4 (1902–3): 28.

59. "The cost of a full grown, live male ostrich would be at least $350." Edwin Cawston to M. Lyon, May 14, 1903, USNMER, box 61, folder 23.

60. Correspondence between Lyon and Roy M. Cabot and between Lyon and Game Warden H. Reif, USNMER, box 61, folder 24.

61. You can guess how that turned out, right? Eastern Landing, Clearing, & Forwarding Company, August 28, 1903, to F. W. True, USNMER, box 61, folder 38. For Mongolian tiger skin invoice, see USNMER, box 62, folder 1.

62. "Dimensions of Bird-Cage at St. Louis" and correspondence between Lyon and Frank Baker, Superintendent of the National Zoological Park, USNMER, box 61, folder 9.

63. Drafts of "Exhibit of the Smithsonian Institution and National Museum at the St. Louis Exposition," USNMER, box 70, folder 3.

64. "Uncle Sam," 28.

65. "Uncle Sam," 28.

66. F. A. Lucas to F. W. True, March 23, June 24 and 16, 1903, USNMER, box 62, folder 27.

67. Memo from George O. Cornelius, U.S. Consular Service, July 15, 1903, USNMER, box 61, folder 23; Henry Davis, Lehigh Valley Railroad Agent, to Mr. S. C. Brown at the Smithsonian, July 29, 1903, USNMER, box 62, folder 27.

68. For the list, see "Articles and Property Purchased by Smithsonian Institution and U.S. National Museum, Louisiana Purchase Exposition, St. Louis, Missouri, 1904," USNMER, box 62, folder 7.

69. For more on natural history firms in the second half of the nineteenth century, see Barrow, "Specimen Dealer."

70. The modeler at the Milwaukee Papier Mache Works wanted to get it just right and cited his previous experience "in scientific studies," including "a good deal with Edward Cope and one time with Major Powell on the Green and Colorado Expedition," to indicate his attention to detail and concern for authenticity. Milwaukee Papier Mache Works to F. A. Lucas, August 10, 1903, USNMER, box 63, folder 5.

71. W. H. Holmes to F. W. True, November 10, 1903, USNMER, box 62, folder 16.

72. Beck, *Unfair Labor?*, 51–67.

73. This is a corollary to what Beck highlights in *Unfair Labor?*—that while some Native people benefited in the short term from exposition collecting, in the form of payment to alleviate settler-caused hardships, white anthropologists made a healthy living from their collecting work. Beck writes, "This followed a longtime colonial pattern of settler society people benefiting from indigenous people's resources" (101).

74. On these earlier surveys, see Sachs, *Humboldt Current*; Goetzmann, *Exploration and Empire*; Bartlett, *Great Surveys*.

75. "Anthropology by W J McGee, Chief of Department," WFB 5, no. 4 (1903–4): 5.

76. While these living expositions were different from the sorts of productions that Phillips examines in *Staging Indigeneity*, they seem to reflect elements of what she calls "salvage tourism," which "builds on ideas of a nostalgic past through the nation-building practices of tourism and the creation of a distinctly American identity—one that can only really be achieved with Indians" (7).

77. "Uncle Sam," 28.

78. Miller, "Incoherencies of Empire," 41.

79. W. C. M'Carty, "The Tribes' Last Stand," *Bridgeport Herald*, December 6, 1903; Parezo and Fowler, *Anthropology*, 100.

80. Beck, *Unfair Labor?*, 170, 106.

81. Beck, *Unfair Labor?*, 96.

82. Geronimo and Barrett, *Geronimo*, 155.

83. Parezo and Fowler, *Anthropology*, 113.

84. Parezo and Fowler, *Anthropology*, 100–134.

85. An official list does not seem to exist, but Parezo and Fowler put together a register of all the Indigenous North American participants they could locate in *Anthropology*, appendix 2, 404–8.

86. Parezo and Fowler, *Anthropology*, 62–63.

87. Parezo and Fowler, *Anthropology*, 140–42.

88. Parezo and Fowler, *Anthropology*, 160; see also Peavy and Smith, "World Champions."

89. "Anthropology by W J McGee," 6–7.

90. On the practice of removing Native children from their homes and taking them to boarding schools, see Child, *Boarding School Seasons*; Jacobs, *White Mother*.

91. F. W. True, handwritten draft of "The Philippine Exhibit in the Government Building," [1901?], USNMER, box 52, folder 23. Later published in the *Buffalo Courier*, April 1901.

92. David Francis to William Taft, May 15, 1902, DRFP, box 11, folder 8.

93. "The Philippine Display," WFB 3, no. 7 (1901–2): 20–21.

94. Financing the Philippine Exposition involved extensive negotiations during the lead-up to the fair. See Executive Committee Minutes, LPEC, series 11, subseries 3, folders 10 and 14, February 14–March 31, 1903, and September 1–December 1, 1903.

95. Taft and Philippine Exposition Board, *Circular Letter*, 29–30.

96. "Dr. Gustavo Neiderlein," WFB 3, no. 12 (1902–3): 30.

97. Gifford Pinchot to Frederick Skiff, Director of Exhibits, August 8, 1902, DRFP, box 12, folder 1.

98. "Eminent in Science and Letters," WFB 3, no. 11 (1902–3): 34.

99. On the emphasis on forest products for export at the fair, see Roberts, "U.S. Forestry," 212.

100. John C. Lebens, "Philippine Exhibit: Forty Acres of Ground Covered with Native Buildings," WFB 4, no. 12 (1903–4): 7; "Arrival of Filipino Workmen," WFB 4, no. 12 (1903–4): 43.

101. This number was a bit of an exaggeration; the final number of residents in the Philippine Exposition ended up being closer to 1,100. See the untitled editorial on the first page of WFB 5, no. 8 (1903–4): 1. In *Anthropology*, Parezo and Fowler use an estimate of 1,250 Filipinos living on the fairgrounds during the exposition (165).

102. Untitled editorial, WFB 5, no. 8 (1903–4): 1.

103. Lowenstein, *Official Guide*, 117.

104. Raibmon, "Living on Display."

105. Parezo and Fowler, *Anthropology*, 10.

106. Rydell, *All the World's a Fair*, 167.

107. Parezo and Fowler, *Anthropology*, 174.

108. Bennitt, *History*, 469.

109. *Official Handbook*, 26.

110. For more on the rhetoric of abundance used by colonists in early America, see Cronon, *Changes in the Land*; Nash, *Wilderness*.

111. Bennitt, *History*, 472–73.

112. L. Dyer, Adjutant General of the National Army and Navy Spanish War Veterans, to F. W. True, March 16, 1903, USNMER, box 61, folder 29.

113. "Soldiers at World's Fair," WFB 3, no. 2 (1901–2): 13.

114. For an explanation of the structure and assignments of the Philippine Scouts and the Philippine Constabulary, see Capozzola, *Bound by War*, 35–41, 50–54. In *Anthropology*, Parezo and Fowler say there were twelve officers, 420 Filipino enlisted men, and forty-five band members (172). For a rich discussion of the Philippine Constabulary Band and its leader, Walter Loving, see Marasigan, "Between the Devil and the Deep Sea," 369–428.

115. "Official Program of the Great Dedication," WFB 4, no. 7 (1902–3): 5, 7.

116. Untitled editorial, WFB 4, no. 7 (1902–3): 3.

117. General Miles was in attendance as an honored guest. WFB 4, no. 8 (1903–4): 25. Miles retired later that year at sixty-four, the mandatory retirement age. "Commanding General of the United States Army," Wikipedia, last modified February 16, 2022, https://en.wikipedia.org/wiki/Commanding _General_of_the_United_States_Army.

118. "Official Program of the Great Dedication," WFB 4, no. 7 (1902–3): 5.

119. "Dedicated by the President," WFB 4, no. 8 (1903–4): 13, 18, 20.

120. "World's Fair, St. Louis, U.S.A., 1904: Commemorating the Acquisition of Louisiana Territory: Its Story and Purpose," WFB 4, no. 7 (1902–3): 15–16.

121. Untitled editorial, WFB 5, no. 3 (1903–4): 1.

122. "Official Program," 7.

123. Frederick J. V. Skiff, Director of Exhibits, "The Universal Exposition: An Encyclopedia of Society," WFB 5, no. 2 (1903–4): 2.

124. Francis, *Universal Exposition of 1904*, v.

125. Mearns, "Itinerary, Manila to San Francisco, September 15–October 16, 1904," EAMP, box 21, folder 25.

126. There is a note here that Mearns gave this bird to the California Academy of Sciences in San Francisco; it was lost in the earthquake of 1906. Mearns, "Itinerary, Manila to San Francisco."

127. Mearns, "Itinerary, Manila to San Francisco."

128. Mearns, Field Book, October–December 1904, EAMP, box 17, folder 14.

129. Mearns, Field Book, October–December 1904.

130. Mearns, "An Ornithological Journal and Register, 1874–1886," entry for October 8, 1876, EAMP, box 8, folder 6; Edgar Mearns to Ella Mearns, October 15, 1893, EAMPLC, box 1, folder 18, "Family Correspondence—1893"; Edgar Mearns to Lillian Mearns, July 22, 1904, EAMP, box 21, folder 1.

131. Fermin, *1904 World's Fair*, 34–35. See also Marasigan, "Between the Devil and the Blue Sea," 406–8.

132. Parezo and Fowler, *Anthropology*, 192.

133. Francis, *Universal Exposition of 1904*, 565.

134. Report written by Mr. Lawshe, Mr. Niederlein, Mr. Stone, and Mr. Guerrero at the close of the exposition, quoted in Bennitt, *History*, 564.

135. Lowenstein, *Official Guide*, 117.

136. Clevenger, *Indescribably Grand*, 102–3.

137. Wexler, *Tender Violence*, 282. For photographs—and wonderfully insightful commentary on the place of photography, anthropology, subjects, and objects at the fair—see Breitbart, *World on Display*.

138. Florence McCallion to Frank McCallion, October 6, 1904, PFP, Correspondence of Florence McCallion.

139. On dog eating, see Parezo and Fowler, *Anthropology*, 181–84. This particular tradition was supposed to have been a "one-time event to celebrate their safe arrival and dedicate a shrine" (181). Parezo and Fowler point to anthropologist Albert Jenks's early twentieth-century work as evidence that dog eating was not a daily practice—but also to the fact that Jenks did not counter the framing of those in the Igorot Village advanced by the fair (183–84). See also Fermin, *1904 World's Fair*, 20.

140. Rydell, *All the World's a Fair*, 177.

141. See Kramer, *Blood of Government*, 229–94.

142. Parezo and Fowler, *Anthropology*, 185.

143. On the representation of Native people at world's fairs, and in particular on the range of arguments about empire conveyed through these representations (e.g., "living" exhibits, staged battles, an Indian Congress) at the Omaha Trans-Mississippi and International Expositions in 1898 and 1899, see Miller, "Incoherencies of Empire."

144. Edward Schneiderhahn, EVPSD, vol. 6. Reprinted in Clevenger, *Indescribably Grand*, 50.

145. Estimates for the number of Taosug casualties at Bud Dajo vary: between six hundred and one thousand dead. For a discussion of these estimates, see Charbonneau, *Civilizational Imperatives*, 106.

146. For more on the Bud Dajo massacre, see Kramer, *Blood of Government*, 218–19; Capozzola, *Bound by War*, 67; McCallum, *Leonard Wood*, 227–31; Hagedorn, *Leonard Wood*, 2:63–69. Hagedorn's 1931 biography refused to judge Wood's actions beyond acknowledging that "the killing of women and children had indeed an ugly sound" (66).

147. Storey, *Moro Massacre*. Charbonneau's *Civilizational Imperatives* pointed me to this source.

148. Charbonneau, *Civilizational Imperatives*, 108–9.

149. Mearns, "Statement of Absences from Zamboanga, Mindanao, P.I., of Major Edgar A. Mearns, Chief Surgeon, Department of Mindanao, from December 27th, 1905 to August 9th 1906," EAMP, box 23, folder 15.

150. Mearns, "Itinerary," March 8, 1906, EAMP, box 22, folder 1.

151. For this number, see Charbonneau, *Civilizational Imperatives*, 106.

152. "Proposed Itinerary for Mt. Malindang Expedition," Mearns to Brig. Gen. Bliss, April 14, 1906, EAMP, box 21, folder 3, p. 13 of scan.

153. J. R. Williams to Edgar Mearns, April 25, 1906, EAMP, box 21, folder 3.

154. List of expedition members appended to Robert Schroeder's letter to Military Secretary of the Department of Mindanao, July 10, 1906, EAMP, box 22, folder 10; Mearns, "Malindang Notes," EAMP, box 17, folder 21, p. 9 of scan.

155. "Bucked" in letter to Colonel Steerer, May 28, 1906, EAMP, box 21, folder 3.

156. J. P. Jervey to Major Mearns, June 5, 1906, EAMP, box 21, folder 3.

157. Pvt. West to Major Mearns, June 5, 1906, EAMP, box 21, folder 5.

158. West to Mearns, June 4, 1906.

159. Robert Schroeder to the Military Secretary, Department of Mindanao, July 10, 1906, EAMP, box 22, folder 10.

160. Mearns, "Memorandum for General Bliss," EAMP, box 22, folder 10.

Conclusion

1. I cannot help but think of Rachel Poliquin's stunning project on taxidermy, *Breathless Zoo*, which I encountered early in my natural history research.

2. Hydrocorax mindanensis, entry 14147, "Birds Collected on Malindang Expedition," EAMP, box 21, folder 33.

3. Hydrocorax mindanensis, entry 14147, "Birds Collected."

4. For "Dr. Mearns bird shooter," see Mearns, "Malindang Notes," EAMP, box 17, folder 21, p. 9 of scan. Given the variations in the spelling of Weneslao Estrellas's name throughout Mearns's records, he may also appear in an "estimate of personnel and materials" Mearns put together for an expedition to Mount Halcon. For the Mount Halcon expedition roster, which includes the heading "2 Native Assistants from Zamboanga (Names: Estrellus and Abdarre)," see Mearns to Maj. Gen. Leonard Wood, October 24, 1906, EAMP, box 21, folder 7.

5. "Search the Division of Birds Collections," NMNH, accessed April 19, 2022, https://collections.nmnh.si.edu/search/mammals/.

6. On bird strike accidents, the founding of forensic ornithology, and the extraordinary career of ornithologist Roxie Laybourne, see Chris Sweeney, "The Remarkable Life of Roxie Laybourne," National Audubon Society, October 5, 2020, https://www.audubon.org/news/the-remarkable-life-roxie-laybourne.

7. Lisa Spilinek, "Study of Iraqi Birds to Help Reduce Aircraft Mishaps," U.S. Air Force, May 6, 2008, https://www.af.mil/News/Article-Display/Article/123649/study-of-iraqi-birds-to-help-reduce-aircraft-mishaps/.

8. Spilinek, "Study of Iraqi Birds."

9. A search conducted using the Division of Birds database with "Iraq" in the country field yielded 147 entries. Not all these entries are for whole skins; some are for skeletons and others for loose feathers. Just as with Mearns a

century earlier, some specimens arrived in poor condition. "Search the Division of Birds Collections," NMNH, accessed June 23, 2021, https://collections .nmnh.si.edu/search/birds/.

10. Mearns earned this rank on his retirement from the U.S. Army in 1909. Pilcher, *Military Surgeon*, 491.

11. Trouern-Trend, *Birding Babylon*, 11.

12. Trouern-Trend, *Birding Babylon*, 9–10.

13. Trouern-Trend, *Birding Babylon*, 26, 12, 64.

BIBLIOGRAPHY

Archives and Manuscript Materials

BCDP. Beverly C. Daly Papers. U.S. Army Heritage and Education Center, Carlisle PA.

CDRP. Charles D. Rhodes Papers. U.S. Army Heritage and Education Center, Carlisle PA.

CMP. Charles Manahan Papers. Huntington Library, San Marino CA.

DRFP. David Rowland Francis Papers. Missouri Historical Society Archives, St. Louis.

EAMP. Edgar Alexander Mearns Papers. Smithsonian Institution Archives, Record Unit 7083, Washington DC.

EAMPLC. Edgar Alexander Mearns Papers. Manuscript Division, Library of Congress, Washington DC.

ECHP. Eli and Charles Helmick Papers. U.S. Army Heritage and Education Center, Carlisle PA.

EDGC. Everett D. Graff Collection of Western Americana. Newberry Library, Chicago.

EVPSD. Edward V. P. Schneiderhahn Diaries. Missouri Historical Society Archives, St. Louis.

FDBP. Frank Dwight Baldwin Papers. Huntington Library, San Marino CA.

FDP. Floyd Dessery Papers. Huntington Library, San Marino CA.

FHTP. Fred H. Tobey Papers. Huntington Library, San Marino CA.

FLL. Frank Loucks Letters. Huntington Library, San Marino CA.

FVGP. Francis Vinton Greene Papers. Manuscripts and Archives Division, New York Public Library, New York.

GEKP. George E. Kessler Papers. Missouri Historical Society Archives, St. Louis.

GPP. Gifford Pinchot Papers. Manuscript Division, Library of Congress, Washington DC.

HWLP. Henry Ware Lawton Papers. Manuscript Division, Library of Congress, Washington DC.

JMP. John Muir Papers. Holt-Atherton Special Collections and Archives, University of the Pacific Library, © 1984 Muir-Hanna Trust.

JTMP. John T. McCutcheon Papers. Newberry Library, Chicago.

LPEC. Louisiana Purchase Exposition Company Records. Missouri Historical Society Archives, St. Louis.

LPECPP. Louisiana Purchase Exposition Company Records, Prints and Photographs. Missouri Historical Society Archives, St. Louis.

MABP. Matthew A. Batson Papers. U.S. Army Heritage and Education Center, Carlisle PA.

MMMDS. Mary McKittrick Markham Diaries and Scrapbooks. Missouri Historical Society Archives, St. Louis.

MSP. Matthew Steele Papers. U.S. Army Heritage and Education Center, Carlisle PA.

NA. National Archives, College Park MD.

NARA. National Archives and Records Administration (Archives I), Washington DC.

NMNH. National Museum of Natural History, Smithsonian, Washington DC.

PFOHC. Pioneers Foundation (New Mexico) Oral History Collection (MSS 123). Center for Southwest Research and Special Collections, University Libraries, University of New Mexico, Albuquerque.

PFP. Philibert Family Papers. Missouri Historical Society Archives, St. Louis.

PRFP. Paul R. Fletcher Papers. Missouri Historical Society Archives, St. Louis.

RIDP. Richard Irving Dodge Papers. Newberry Library, Chicago.

SCFP. Smith-Cole Family Papers. U.S. Army Heritage and Education Center, Carlisle PA.

SOP. Samuel Ovenshine Papers. U.S. Army Heritage and Education Center, Carlisle PA.

USNMAS. Smithsonian Institution Assistant Secretary in Charge of the United States National Museum, Correspondence and Memoranda, 1860–1908. Smithsonian Institution Archives, Record Unit 189, Washington DC.

USNMCR. United States National Museum Annual Curators' Reports, 1881–1964. Smithsonian Institution Archives, Record Unit 158, Washington DC.

USNMDOB. United States National Museum Division of Birds, Records, ca. 1854–1959. Smithsonian Institution Archives, Record Unit 105, Washington DC.

USNMER. Exposition Records of the Smithsonian Institution and the United States National Museum, 1867–1940. Smithsonian Institution Archives, Record Unit 70, Washington DC.

WFB. *World's Fair Bulletin.* 6 vols., Bradford Publishing, Digital Collection at the University of Missouri Library System's Digital Library.

WHCBP. William H. C. Bowen Papers. U.S. Army Heritage and Education Center, Carlisle PA.

WLCP. Walter L. Cutter Papers. U.S. Army Heritage and Education Center, Carlisle PA.

Published Works

Abinales, Patricio. "An American Colonial State: Authority and Structure in Southern Mindanao." In *Vestiges of War: The Philippine-American War and the Aftermath of an Imperial Dream, 1899–1999*, edited by Angel Velasco Shaw and Luis Francia, 89–117. New York: New York University Press, 2002.

Adams, Kevin. *Class and Race in the Frontier Army: Military Life in the West, 1870–1890*. Norman: University of Oklahoma Press, 2009.

Adas, Michael. *Dominance by Design: Technological Imperatives and America's Civilizing Mission*. Cambridge MA: Belknap Press of Harvard University Press, 2006.

Ahern, George Patrick. *Tree Species of the Philippine Islands*. Manila: Forestry Bureau, 1901.

Alberti, Samuel J. M. M. "Objects and the Museum." *Isis* 96, no. 4 (December 2005): 559–71.

Anderson, Warwick. *Colonial Pathologies: American Tropical Medicine, Race, and Hygiene in the Philippines*. Durham NC: Duke University Press, 2006.

Angeles, Jose Amiel P. "As Our Might Grows Less: The Philippine-American War in Context." PhD diss., University of Oregon, 2013.

Anti-Imperialist League. *Soldiers' Letters: Being Materials for the History of a War of Criminal Aggression*. Boston: Rockwell and Churchill Press, 1899.

Arenson, Adam, and Andrew Graybill, eds. *Civil War Wests: Testing the Limits of the United States*. Berkeley: University of California Press, 2015.

Arnold, James. *The Moro War: How America Battled a Muslim Insurgency in the Philippine Jungle, 1902–1913*. London: Bloomsbury Press, 2011.

Aune, Stefan. "Indian Fighters in the Philippines: Imperial Culture and Military Violence in the Philippine-American War." *Pacific Historical Review* 90, no. 4 (2021): 419–47.

Bankoff, Greg. "Breaking New Ground? Gifford Pinchot and the Birth of 'Empire Forestry' in the Philippines, 1900–1905." *Environment and History* 15, no. 3 (2009): 369–93.

———. "First Impressions: Diarists, Scientists, Imperialists and the Management of the Environment in the American Pacific, 1899–1902." *Journal of Pacific History* 44, no. 3 (2009): 261–80.

Barnes, Harper. *Standing on a Volcano: The Life and Times of David Rowland Francis*. St. Louis: Missouri Historical Society Press, 2001.

Barrow, Mark. *A Passion for Birds: American Ornithology after Audubon*. Princeton NJ: Princeton University Press, 1998.

———. "The Specimen Dealer: Entrepreneurial Natural History in America's Gilded Age." *Journal of the History of Biology* 33, no. 3 (Winter 2000): 493–534.

Bartlett, Richard A. *Great Surveys of the American West*. Norman: University of Oklahoma, 1962.

Barton, Gregory. "Empire Forestry and American Environmentalism." *Environment and History* 6 (2000): 187–203.

Basso, Keith. *Western Apache Witchcraft*. Tucson: University of Arizona Press, 1969.

———. *Wisdom Sits in Places: Landscape and Language among the Western Apache*. Albuquerque: University of New Mexico Press, 1996.

Beck, David. *Unfair Labor? American Indians and the 1893 World's Columbian Exposition in Chicago*. Lincoln: University of Nebraska Press, 2019.

Bederman, Gail. *Manliness and Civilization: A Cultural History of Gender and Race in the United States, 1880–1917*. Chicago: University of Chicago Press, 1995.

Bender, Daniel E., and Jana K. Lipman. "Introduction: Through the Looking Glass: U.S. Empire through the Lens of Labor History." In *Making the Empire Work: Labor and United States Imperialism*, edited by Daniel E. Bender and Jana K. Lipman, 1–34. New York: New York University Press, 2015.

———, eds. *Making the Empire Work: Labor and United States Imperialism*. New York: New York University Press, 2015.

Bennitt, Mark. *History of the Louisiana Purchase Exposition: Comprising the History of the Louisiana Territory [. . .]*. 1905. Reprint, New York: Arno, 1976.

Berkey, James. "Splendid Little Papers from the 'Splendid Little War': Mapping Empire in the Soldier Newspapers of the Spanish-American War." *Journal of Modern Periodical Studies* 3, no. 2 (2012): 158–74.

Berudo, Cheryl. *Import of the Archive: U.S. Colonial Rule of the Philippines and the Making of American Archival History*. Sacramento CA: Litwin Books, 2013.

Birtle, Andrew J. "The U.S. Army's Pacification of Marinduque, Philippine Islands, April 1900–April 1901." *Journal of Military History* 61, no. 2 (April 1997): 255–82.

Bjork, Katharine. *Prairie Imperialists: The Indian Country Origins of American Empire*. Philadelphia: University of Pennsylvania Press, 2019.

Black, Megan. *The Global Interior: Mineral Frontiers and American Power*. Cambridge MA: Harvard University Press, 2018.

Black Elk and John Neihardt. *Black Elk Speaks: Being the Life Story of a Holy Man of the Oglala Sioux*. 1932. Reprint, Albany: SUNY Press, 2008.

Blackhawk, Ned. *Violence over the Land: Indians and Empires in the Early American West* Cambridge MA: Harvard University Press, 2006.

Bleichmar, Daniela. *Visible Empire: Botanical Expeditions and Visual Culture in the Hispanic Enlightenment*. Chicago: University of Chicago Press, 2012.

Bleichmar, Daniela, and Peter Mancall, eds. *Collecting across Cultures: Material Exchanges in the Early Modern Atlantic World*. Philadelphia: University of Pennsylvania Press, 2011.

Bourke, John Gregory. *An Apache Campaign in the Sierra Madre: An Account of the Expedition in Pursuit of the Hostile Chiricahua Apaches in the Spring of 1883*. New York: Charles Scribner's Sons, 1958.

———. *Mackenzie's Last Fight with the Cheyennes: A Winter Campaign in Wyoming and Montana*. 1890. Reprint, Bellevue NE: Old Army Press, 1970.

———. "The Medicine-Men of the Apache." In *Ninth Annual Report of the Bureau of Ethnology to the Secretary of the Smithsonian Institution, 1887–88*, edited by J. W. Powell, 443–604. Washington DC: Government Printing Office, 1892.

———. *On the Border with Crook*. Lincoln: University of Nebraska Press, 1971.

Bowe, John. *With the 13th Minnesota in the Philippines*. Minneapolis: A. B. Farnham, 1905.

Brady, Lisa M. *War upon the Land: Military Strategy and the Transformation of Southern Landscapes during the American Civil War*. Athens: University of Georgia Press, 2012.

Brands, H. W. *Bound to Empire: The United States and the Philippines*. New York: Oxford University Press, 1992.

Breitbart, Eric. *A World on Display: Photographs from the 1904 St. Louis World's Fair*. Albuquerque: University of New Mexico Press, 1997.

Bruno, Thomas A. "The Violent End of Insurgency on Samar, 1901–1902." *Army History* (Spring 2011): 30–46.

Buel, James. *Louisiana and the Fair: An Exposition of the World, Its People and Their Achievements*. Vol. 4. St. Louis: World's Progress, 1904.

Burns, Mike. *The Only One Living to Tell: The Autobiography of a Yavapai Indian*. Edited by Gregory McNamee. Tucson: University of Arizona Press, 2012.

Capozzola, Christopher. *Bound by War: How the United States and the Philippines Built America's First Pacific Century*. New York: Basic Books, 2020.

Charbonneau, Oliver. *Civilizational Imperatives: Americans, Moros, and the Colonial World*. Ithaca NY: Cornell University Press, 2020.

———. "'A New West in Mindanao': Settler Fantasies on the U.S. Imperial Fringe." *Journal of the Gilded Age and Progressive Era* 18, no. 3 (2019): 304–23.

Child, Brenda. *Boarding School Seasons: American Indian Families, 1900–1940*. Lincoln: University of Nebraska Press, 1998.

Clevenger, Martha. *Indescribably Grand: Diaries and Letters from the 1904 World's Fair*. St. Louis: Missouri Historical Society Press, 1996.

Coffman, Edward M. "Army Life on the Frontier, 1865–1898." *Military Affairs* 20, no. 4 (Winter 1956): 193–201.

———. "Batson of the Philippine Scouts." *Parameters: Journal of the Army War College* (1977): 68–72.

Colwell, Chip. *Plundered Skulls and Stolen Spirits: Inside the Fight to Reclaim Native America's Culture*. Chicago: University of Chicago Press, 2017.

Colwell-Chanthaponh, Chip. *Massacre at Camp Grant: Forgetting and Remembering Apache History*. Tucson: University of Arizona Press, 2007.

Conn, Steven. *History's Shadow: Native Americans and Historical Conscious-ness in the Nineteenth Century*. Chicago: University of Chicago, 2004.

Conrad, Paul. *The Apache Diaspora: Four Centuries of Displacement and Sur-vival*. Philadelphia: University of Pennsylvania Press, 2021.

Cosmas, Graham A. *An Army for Empire: The United States Army in the Spanish-American War*. 2nd ed. College Station: Texas A&M University Press, 1994.

Cozzens, Peter. *The Earth Is Weeping: The Epic Story of the Indian Wars for the American West*. New York: Vintage, 2016.

————. *Eyewitnesses to the Indian Wars, 1865–1890*. Vol. 1, *The Struggle for Apacheria*. Mechanicsburg PA: Stackpole Books, 2001.

Crampton, Louis. *Early History of Yellowstone National Park and Its Relation to National Park Policies*. Washington DC: Government Printing Office, 1932.

Crandall, Maurice. *These People Have Always Been a Republic: Indigenous Electorates in the U.S.-Mexico Borderlands, 1598–1912*. Chapel Hill: University of North Carolina Press, 2019.

Cronon, William. *Changes in the Land: Indians, Colonists, and the Ecology of New England*. New York: Hill and Wang, 1983.

————. "The Trouble with Wilderness, or Getting Back to the Wrong Nature." In *Uncommon Ground: Rethinking the Human Place in Nature*, edited by William Cronon, 69–90. New York: W. W. Norton, 1996.

Crook, George. *General George Crook: His Autobiography*. Edited by Martin Schmitt. Norman: University of Oklahoma Press, 1986.

Datson, Lorraine. "Type Specimens and Scientific Memory." *Critical Inquiry* 31, no. 1 (Autumn 2004): 153–82.

Debo, Angie. *Geronimo: The Man, His Time, His Place*. Norman: University of Oklahoma Press, 1976.

DeLucia, Christine. *Memory Lands: King Philip's War and the Place of Violence in the Northeast*. New Haven CT: Yale University Press, 2018.

Dichamp, Christiane Fischer. *Let Them Speak for Themselves: Women in the American West, 1849–1900*. Hamden CT: Archon Books, 1977.

Doane, Gustavas C. *Letter from the Secretary of War, Communicating the Report of Lieutenant Gustavus C. Doane upon the So-Called Yellowstone Expedition of 1870*. Washington DC: Government Printing Office, [1871?]. http://hdl.handle.net/2027/njp.32101079825236.

Dobak, William A., and Thomas D. Phillips. *The Black Regulars, 1866–1898*. Norman: University of Oklahoma Press, 2001.

Dodge, Richard Irving. *The Black Hills: A Minute Description of the Routes, Scenery, Soil, Climate, Timber, Gold, Geology, Zoölogy, Etc.* New York: J. Miller, 1876.

————. *The Black Hills Journals of Colonel Richard Irving Dodge*. Edited by Wayne Kime. Norman: University of Oklahoma Press, 1996.

————. *The Hunting Grounds of the Great West: A Description of the Plains, Game, and Indians of the Great North American Desert [. . .]*. With an introduction by William Blackmore. London: Chatto and Windus, 1877.

———. *Our Wild Indians: Thirty-Three Years' Personal Experience among the Red Men of the Great West; A Popular Account of Their Social Life, Religion, Habits, Traits, Customs, Exploits, Etc. [. . .].* With an introduction by William Tecumseh Sherman. 1882. Reprint, Hartford CT: A. D. Worthington, 1890.

———. *The Plains of the Great West and Their Inhabitants, Being a Description of the Plains, Game, Indians, &c., of the Great North American Desert.* New York: G. P. Putnam's Sons, 1877.

Donaldson, Le'Trice D. *Duty beyond the Battlefield: African American Soldiers Fight for Racial Uplift, Citizenship, and Manhood, 1870–1920.* Carbondale: Southern Illinois University Press, 2020.

Dower, John. *War without Mercy: Race and Power in the Pacific War.* New York: Pantheon, 1986.

Downs, Gregory. *After Appomattox: Military Occupation and the Ends of War.* Cambridge MA: Harvard University Press, 2015.

Drake, Brian Allen, ed. *The Blue, the Gray, and the Green: Toward an Environmental History of the Civil War.* Athens: University of Georgia, 2015.

Drinnon, Richard. *Facing West: The Metaphysics of Indian-Hating and Empire-Building.* Norman: University of Oklahoma Press, 1997.

Dungy, Camille. *Black Nature: Four Centuries of African American Nature Poetry.* Athens: University of Georgia Press, 2009.

DuVal, Kathleen. *The Native Ground: Indians and Colonists in the Heart of the Continent.* Philadelphia: University of Pennsylvania, 2006.

Eales, Anne Bruner. *Army Wives on the American Frontier: Living by the Bugles.* Boulder CO: Johnson Books, 1996.

Endersby, Jim. *Imperial Nature: Joseph Hooker and the Practices of Victorian Science.* Chicago: University of Chicago Press, 2008.

Estes, Nick. *Our History Is the Future: Standing Rock versus the Dakota Access Pipeline, and the Long Tradition of Indigenous Resistance.* New York: Verso, 2019.

Estes, Nick, and Jaskiran Dhillon, eds. *Standing with Standing Rock: Voices from the #NoDAPL Movement.* Minneapolis: University of Minnesota Press, 2019.

Fabian, Ann. *The Skull Collectors: Race, Science, and America's Unburied Dead.* Chicago: University of Chicago Press, 2010.

Faragher, John. *Sugar Creek: Life on the Illinois Prairie.* New Haven CT: Yale University Press, 1986.

Faulk, Odie. *The Geronimo Campaign.* Oxford: Oxford University Press, 1969.

Faust, Drew Gilpin. *This Republic of Suffering: Death and the American Civil War.* New York: Knopf, 2008.

Faust, Karl Irving. *Campaigning in the Philippines: Illustrated.* San Francisco: Hicks-Judd, 1899.

Ferg, Alan, ed. *Western Apache Material Culture: The Goodwin and Guenther Collections.* Tucson: University of Arizona Press, 1987.

Fermin, Jose D. *1904 World's Fair: The Filipino Experience*. West Conshohocken PA: Infinity, 2004.

Feuer, A. B., ed. *America at War: The Philippines, 1898–1913*. Westport CT: Praeger, 2002.

Finney, Carolyn. *Black Faces, White Spaces: Reimagining the Relationship of African Americans to the Great Outdoors*. Chapel Hill: University of North Carolina Press, 2014.

Fox, Timothy, and Duane Sneddeker. *From the Palaces to the Pike: Visions of the 1904 World's Fair*. St. Louis: Missouri Historical Society Press, 1997.

Francia, Luis. *A History of the Philippines: From Indios Bravos to Filipinos*. New York: Overlook Press, 2014.

Francis, David R. *The Universal Exposition of 1904*. St. Louis: Louisiana Purchase Exposition Company, 1913.

Freeman, Joshua, and Geoffrey Field. "Labor and the Military: Introduction." *International Labor and Working-Class History* 80, no. 1 (Fall 2011): 3–5.

Freeman, N. N. *A Soldier in the Philippines*. New York: F. Tennyson Neely, 1901.

Fritz, David L. "Before the 'Howling Wilderness': The Military Career of Jacob Hurd Smith, 1862–1902." *Military Affairs* 43, no. 4 (December 1979): 186–90.

Fulton, Robert A. *Moroland: The History of Uncle Sam and the Moros, 1899–1920*. Bend OR: Tumalo Creek Press, 2009.

Funtecha, Henry F. "The 'Iloilo Fiasco.'" *Philippine Quarterly of Culture and Society* 14, no. 2 (June 1986): 75–85.

Gatewood, Willard B., Jr. *"Smoked Yankees" and the Struggle for Empire: Letters from Negro Soldiers, 1898–1902*. Fayetteville: University of Arkansas Press, 1987.

Gedacht, Joshua. "'Mohammedan Religion Made It Necessary to Fire': Massacres on the American Imperial Frontier from South Dakota to the Southern Philippines." In *Colonial Crucible: Empire in the Making of the Modern American State*, edited by Alfred McCoy and Francisco Scarano, 397–409. Madison: University of Wisconsin Press, 2009.

Geronimo and S. M. Barrett. *Geronimo: His Own Story*. 1906. Reprint, New York: Meridian, 1996.

Goetzmann, William. *Exploration and Empire: The Explorer and the Scientist in the Winning of the American West*. New York: Knopf, 1966.

Goldberg, Lisa. "A History of Pest Control Measures in the Anthropology Collections, National Museum of Natural History, Smithsonian Institution." *Journal of the American Institute for Conservation* 35, no. 1 (1996): 23–43.

Goldstein, Alyosha, ed. *Formations of U.S. Colonialism*. Durham NC: Duke University Press, 2014.

Goldstein, Daniel. "Yours for Science: The Smithsonian Institution's Correspondence and the Shape of Scientific Community in Nineteenth-Century America." *Isis* 85, no. 4 (December 1994): 573–99.

Gonzales, Vernadette Vicuña. *Securing Paradise: Tourism and Militarism in Hawai'i and the Philippines.* Durham NC: Duke University Press, 2013.

Goodwin, Grenville. *The Social Organization of the Western Apache.* Chicago: University of Chicago Press, 1942.

Grandin, Greg. *The End of the Myth: From the Frontier to the Border Wall in the Mind of America.* New York: Metropolitan Books, 2019.

Greene, Harlan, and Harry S. Hutchins Jr. *Slave Badges and the Slave-Hire System in Charleston, South Carolina, 1783–1865.* With the assistance of Brian E. Hutchins. Jefferson NC: McFarland, 2004.

Greene, Jerome, ed. *Lakota and Cheyenne: Indian Views of the Great Sioux War, 1876–1877.* Norman: University of Oklahoma Press, 1994.

——— . *Morning Star Dawn: The Powder River Expedition and the Northern Cheyennes, 1876.* Norman: University of Oklahoma Press, 2003.

Greene, Julie. "The Wages of Empire: Capitalism, Expansionism, and Working-Class Formation." In *Making the Empire Work: Labor and United States Imperialism,* edited by Daniel E. Bender and Jana K. Lipman, 35–58. New York: New York University Press, 2015.

Greer, Kirsten. *Red Coats and Wild Birds: How Military Ornithologists and Migrant Birds Shaped Empire.* Chapel Hill: University of North Carolina Press, 2020.

Gregory, James. "The West and the Workers, 1870–1930." In *A Companion to the American West,* edited by William Deverell, 240–55. Hoboken NJ: Wiley-Blackwell, 2007.

Gruber, Jacob W. "Ethnographic Salvage and the Shaping of Anthropology." *American Anthropologist* 72, no. 6 (1970): 1289–99.

Gutierrez, Kathleen Cruz. "The Region of Imperial Strategy: Regino García, Sebastián Vidal, Mary Clemens, and the Consolidation of International Botany in the Philippines, 1858–1936." PhD diss., University of California–Berkeley, 2020.

——— . "What's in a Latin Name? *Cycas wadei* and the Politics of Nomenclature." *Philippine Journal of Systematic Biology* 12, no. 2 (2018): 24–35.

Hadden, Sally. *Slave Patrols: Law and Violence in Virginia and the Carolinas.* Cambridge MA: Harvard University Press, 2001.

Hagedorn, Hermann. *Leonard Wood: A Biography.* 2 vols. 1931. Reprint, New York: Kraus, 1969.

Hahn, Steven. *A Nation without Borders: The United States and Its World in an Age of Civil Wars, 1830–1910.* New York: Penguin, 2016.

Haines, Aubrey L. *The Yellowstone Story: A History of Our First National Park.* Vol. 1. Boulder: University Press of Colorado, 1999.

Haley, James L. *Apaches: A History and Cultural Portrait.* New York: Doubleday, 1981.

Hämäläinen, Pekka. *Lakota America: A New History of Indigenous Power.* New Haven CT: Yale University Press, 2019.

Haraway, Donna. "Teddy Bear Patriarchy: Taxidermy in the Garden of Eden, New York City, 1908–1936." *Social Text*, no. 11 (Winter 1984–85): 20–64.

Harper, Frank, ed. *Just outside of Manila: Letters of Members of the First Colorado Regiment in the Spanish-American and Philippine-American Wars*. Denver: Colorado Historical Society, 1991.

Harris, Susan K. *God's Arbiters: Americans and the Philippines, 1898–1902*. New York: Oxford University Press, 2011.

Hawkins, Michael C. *Making Moros: Imperial Historicism and American Rule in the Philippine's Muslim South*. DeKalb: Northern Illinois University Press, 2013.

Henson, Pamela. "'Objects of Curious Research': The History of Science and Technology and the Smithsonian." *Isis* 90, no. s2 (1999): s249–69.

Herman, Daniel. *Rim Country Exodus: A Story of Conquest, Renewal, and Race in the Making*. Tucson: University of Arizona Press, 2012.

Hernández, Kelly Lytle. *City of Inmates: Conquest, Rebellion, and the Rise of Human Caging in Los Angeles, 1771–1965*. Chapel Hill: University of North Carolina Press, 2017.

Hicks, Dan. *The Brutish Museums: The Benin Bronzes, Colonial Violence, and Cultural Restitution*. London: Pluto Press, 2020.

Hirrel, Leo P. "The Beginnings of the Quartermaster Graves Registration Service." *Army Sustainment* (July–August 2014): 64–67. https://alu.army .mil/alog/2014/JulAug14/PDF/128693.pdf.

Hixson, Walter. *American Settler Colonialism: A History*. New York: Palgrave Macmillan, 2013.

Hoganson, Kristin L. *Fighting for American Manhood: How Gender Politics Provoked the Spanish-American and Philippine-American Wars*. New Haven CT: Yale University Press, 1998.

Hoganson, Kristin L., and Jay Sexton. Introduction to *Crossing Empires: Taking U.S. History into Transimperial Terrain*, 1–22. Edited by Kristin L. Hoganson and Jay Sexton. Durham NC: Duke University Press, 2020.

Hoover, Elizabeth. *The River Is in Us: Fighting Toxics in a Mohawk Community*. Minneapolis: University of Minnesota Press, 2017.

Hume, Edgar Erskine. *Ornithologists of the United States Army Medical Corps*. Baltimore: Johns Hopkins Press, 1942.

Hyde, Anne Farrar. *An American Vision: Far Western Landscape and National Culture, 1820–1920*. New York: New York University Press, 1990.

———. *Empires, Nations, and Families: A History of the North American West, 1800–1860*. Lincoln: University of Nebraska Press, 2011.

Ileto, Reynaldo C. *Filipinos and Their Revolution: Event, Discourse, and Historiography*. Manila: Ateneo de Manila University Press, 1999.

———. "The Philippine-American War: Friendship and Forgetting." In *Vestiges of War: The Philippine-American War and the Aftermath of an Imperial Dream 1899–1999*, edited by Angel Velasco Shaw and Luis Francia, 3–21. New York: New York University Press, 2002.

Immerwahr, Daniel. *How to Hide an Empire: A History of the Greater United States*. New York: Farrar, Straus and Giroux, 2019.

Jacobs, Margaret. *White Mother to a Dark Race: Settler Colonialism, Maternalism, and the Removal of Indigenous Children in the American West and Australia, 1880–1940*. Lincoln: University of Nebraska Press, 2011.

Jacobson, Matthew Frye. *Barbarian Virtues: The United States Encounters Foreign Peoples at Home and Abroad, 1876–1917*. New York: Hill and Wang, 2001.

Jacoby, Karl. "'The Broad Platform of Extermination': Nature and Violence in the Nineteenth-Century North American Borderlands." *Journal of Genocide Research* 10, no. 2 (June 2008): 249–67.

———. *Crimes against Nature: Squatters, Poachers, Thieves, and the Hidden History of American Conservation*. Berkeley: University of California Press, 2001.

———. *Shadows at Dawn: A Borderlands Massacre and the Violence of History*. New York: Penguin, 2008.

Jardine, Nicholas, James A. Secord, and E. C. Spary. *Cultures of Natural History*. Cambridge: Cambridge University Press, 1996.

Jenks, Maud Huntley. *Death Stalks the Philippine Wilds*. Edited by Carmen Nelson Richards. Minneapolis: Lund Press, 1951.

Johnson, Susan Lee. "'A Memory Sweet to Soldiers': The Significance of Gender in the History of the 'American West.'" *Western Historical Quarterly* 24, no. 4 (November 1993): 495–517.

Karnow, Stanley. *In Our Image: America's Empire in the Philippines*. New York: Ballantine Books, 1989.

Karuka, Manu. *Empire's Tracks: Indigenous Nations, Chinese Workers, and the Transcontinental Railroad*. Berkeley: University of California Press, 2019.

Kauanui, J. Kēhaulani. "Imperial Ocean: The Pacific as a Critical Site for American Studies." *American Quarterly* 67, no. 3 (September 2015): 625–36.

———. *Paradoxes of Hawaiian Sovereignty: Land, Sex, and the Colonial Politics of State Nationalism*. Durham NC: Duke University Press, 2018.

Kaut, Charles R. *The Western Apache Clan System: Its Origins and Development*. Albuquerque: University of New Mexico Publications in Anthropology, 1957.

Keeney, Elizabeth. *The Botanizers: Amateur Scientists in Nineteenth-Century America*. Chapel Hill: University of North Carolina Press, 1992.

Kessel, William B. "Edgar and Minnie Guenther." In *Western Apache Material Culture: The Goodwin and Guenther Collections*, edited by Alan Ferg, 9–26. Tucson: University of Arizona Press, 1987.

Kime, Wayne R. *Colonel Richard Irving Dodge: The Life and Times of a Career Army Officer*. Norman: University of Oklahoma Press, 2006.

Kimmerer, Robin Wall. *Braiding Sweetgrass: Indigenous Wisdom, Scientific Knowledge, and the Teachings of Plants*. Minneapolis: Milkweed, 2015.

Kline, Kerwin. *Frontiers of Historical Imagination: Narrating the European Conquest of North America, 1890–1990.* Berkeley: University of California Press, 1997.

Kobbé, W. A. "Report of Brig. Gen. W. A. Kobbé, U.S.V., of an Expedition to Occupy and Open Hemp Ports in the Philippine Islands, January 18 to April 8, 1900." In *Annual Reports of the War Department for the Fiscal Year Ended June 30, 1900,* 7–64. Washington DC: Government Printing Office, 1900.

Kohler, Robert E. *Landscapes and Labscapes: Exploring the Lab-Field Border in Biology.* Chicago: University of Chicago Press, 2002.

Kohout, Amy. "More Than Birds: Loss and Reconnection at the National Museum of Natural History." *Museum History Journal* 10, no. 1 (2017): 83–96.

Kolodny, Annette. *The Land before Her: Fantasy and Experience of the American Frontiers, 1630–1860.* Chapel Hill: University of North Carolina Press, 1984.

————. *The Lay of the Land: Metaphor as Experience and History in American Land and Letters.* Chapel Hill: University of North Carolina Press, 1975.

Kosmider, Alexia. "Refracting the Imperial Gaze onto the Colonizers: Geronimo Poses for the Empire." *American Transcendental Quarterly* 15 (December 2001): 317–32.

Kramer, Paul A. *The Blood of Government: Race, Empire, the United States, and the Philippines.* Chapel Hill: University of North Carolina Press, 2006.

————. "Power and Connection: Imperial Histories of the United States in the World." *American Historical Review* 116, no. 5 (December 2011): 1348–91.

————. "The Water Cure." *New Yorker,* February 25, 2008. https://www.newyorker.com/magazine/2008/02/25/the-water-cure.

Krueger, David. "'To Hold What the U.S. Has Taken in Conquest': The United States Army and Colonial Ethnic Forces, 1866–1914." PhD diss., Harvard University, 2020.

Kuklick, Henrika, and Robert E. Kohler. "Introduction." *Osiris* 11 (1996): 1–14.

LaDuke, Winona. *All Our Relations: Native Struggles for Land and Life.* Cambridge MA: South End Press, 1999.

Lahti, Janne. "Colonized Labor: Apaches and Pawnees as Army Workers." *Western Historical Quarterly* 39, no. 3 (Autumn 2008): 283–302.

————. *Cultural Construction of Empire: The U.S. Army in Arizona and New Mexico.* Lincoln: University of Nebraska, 2012.

Langford, Nathaniel Pitt. "The Wonders of the Yellowstone." *Scribner's Monthly* 2, no. 1–2 (1871).

Lears, Jackson. *Rebirth of a Nation: The Making of Modern America, 1877–1920.* New York: Harper Perennial, 2009.

Leong, Karen. "Still Walking, Still Brave: Mapping Gender, Race, and Power in U.S. Western History." *Pacific Historical Review* 79, no. 4 (November 2010): 618–28.

Lewis, Daniel. *The Feathery Tribe: Robert Ridgway and the Modern Study of Birds*. New Haven CT: Yale University Press, 2012.

Lewis, Peter. *Foot Soldier in an Occupation Force: The Letters of Peter Lewis, 1899–1902*. Compiled by H. R. Kells. Manila: De La Salle University, 1999.

Linn, Brian McAllister. *Guardians of Empire: The U.S. Army and the Pacific, 1902–1940*. Chapel Hill: University of North Carolina Press, 1997.

———. "The Long Twilight of the Frontier Army." *Western Historical Quarterly* 27, no. 2 (Summer 1996): 141–67.

———. *The Philippine War, 1899–1902*. Lawrence: University Press of Kansas, 2000.

Lodge, Henry Cabot. *The Retention of the Philippine Islands: Speech of Hon. Henry Cabot Lodge, of Massachusetts, in the Senate of the United States, March 7, 1900*. Washington DC: Government Printing Office, 1900.

Lonetree, Amy. *Decolonizing Museums: Representing Native America in National and Tribal Museums*. Chapel Hill: University of North Carolina Press, 2012.

Loughlin, Caroline, and Catherine B. Anderson. *Forest Park*. Columbia MO: Junior League of St. Louis, 1986.

Love, Eric T. L. *Race over Empire: Racism and U.S. Imperialism, 1865–1900*. Chapel Hill: University of North Carolina Press, 2004.

Lowenstein, M. J., comp. *Official Guide to the Louisiana Purchase Exposition at the City of St. Louis, State of Missouri, April 30th to December 1st, 1904 [. . .]*. St. Louis: Official Guide, 1904.

Lubar, Steven. *Inside the Lost Museum: Curating, Past and Present*. Cambridge MA: Harvard University Press, 2017.

Marasigan, Cynthia. "'Between the Devil and the Deep Sea': Ambivalence, Violence, and African American Soldiers in the Philippine-American War and Its Aftermath." PhD diss., University of Michigan, 2010.

Martínez, Miguel. *Front Lines: Soldiers' Writing in the Early Modern Hispanic World*. Philadelphia: University of Pennsylvania Press, 2016.

May, Glenn. *Battle for Batangas: A Philippine Province at War*. New Haven CT: Yale University Press, 1991.

McCallum, Jack. *Leonard Wood: Rough Rider, Surgeon, Architect of American Imperialism*. New York: New York University Press, 2006.

McCammack, Brian. *Landscapes of Hope: Nature and the Great Migration in Chicago*. Cambridge MA: Harvard University Press, 2018.

McChristian, Douglas C. *Regular Army O! Soldiering on the Western Frontier, 1865–1891*. Norman: University of Oklahoma Press, 2017.

McCoy, Alfred, and Francisco Scarano, eds. *Colonial Crucible: Empire in the Making of the Modern American State*. Madison: University of Wisconsin Press, 2009.

McCutcheon, John. *Chicago* Record's *Stories of Filipino Warfare*. Chicago, 1900.

McEnroe, Sean. "Painting the Philippines with an American Brush: Visions of Race and National Mission among the Oregon Volunteers in the Philippine Wars of 1898 and 1899." *Oregon Historical Quarterly* 104, no. 1 (Spring 2003): 24–61.

McGrath, Autumn Hope. "'An Army of Working Men': Military Labor and the Construction of American Empire, 1865 to 1915." PhD diss., University of Pennsylvania, 2016.

McKenna, Rebecca Tinio. *American Imperial Pastoral: The Architecture of US Colonialism in the Philippines*. Chicago: University of Chicago Press, 2017.

——— . "Igorot Squatters and Indian Wards: Toward an Intra-imperial History of Land Dispossession." *Journal of the Gilded Age and Progressive Era* 18, no. 2 (2019): 221–39.

Mearns, Edgar A. "Ancient Dwellings of the Rio Verde Valley." *Popular Science Monthly* (October 1890): 745–63.

——— . "Some Birds of Arizona." *Auk* 3, no. 1 (January 1886): 60–73.

Meier, Kathryn Shively. *Nature's Civil War: Common Soldiers and the Environment in 1862 Virginia*. Chapel Hill: University of North Carolina Press, 2013.

Merrill, J. C. "In Memoriam: Charles E. Bendire." *Auk* 15, no. 1 (January 1898): 1–6.

Meyerson, Harvey. *Nature's Army: When Soldiers Fought for Yosemite*. Lawrence: University of Kansas Press, 2001.

Miller, Angela. *The Empire of the Eye: Landscape Representation and American Cultural Politics, 1825–1875*. Ithaca NY: Cornell University Press, 1996.

Miller, Bonnie M. *From Liberation to Conquest: The Visual and Popular Cultures of the Spanish-American War of 1898*. Amherst: University of Massachusetts Press, 2011.

——— . "The Incoherencies of Empire: The 'Imperial' Image of the Indian at the Omaha World's Fairs of 1898–99." *American Studies* 49, no. 3–4 (Fall–Winter 2008): 39–62.

Miller, Char. *Gifford Pinchot and the Making of Modern Environmentalism*. Washington DC: Island Press, 2004.

Miller, Daegan. *This Radical Land: A Natural History of American Dissent*. Chicago: University of Chicago Press, 2018.

Miller, Ian Jared. *The Nature of the Beasts: Empire and Exhibition at the Tokyo Imperial Zoo*. Berkeley: University of California Press, 2013.

Miller, Stuart Creighton. *"Benevolent Assimilation": The American Conquest of the Philippines, 1899–1903*. New Haven CT: Yale University Press, 1982.

Mitchell, Lee Clark. *Witnesses to a Vanishing America: The Nineteenth-Century Response*. Princeton NJ: Princeton University Press, 1981.

Morey, Michael. *Fagen: An African American Renegade in the Philippine-American War*. Madison: University of Wisconsin Press, 2019.

Morrissey, Katherine G. *Mental Territories: Mapping the Inland Empire*. Ithaca NY: Cornell University Press, 1997.

Moulton, Cindy. *Valentine T. McGillycuddy: Army Surgeon, Agent to the Sioux*. Norman: University of Oklahoma Press, 2011.

Moyd, Michelle. *Violent Intermediaries: African Soldiers, Conquest, and Everyday Colonialism in German East Africa*. Athens: Ohio University Press, 2014.

Muir, John. *Our National Parks*. Boston: Houghton Mifflin, 1903.

Munroe, Kirk. *The Painted Desert: A Story of Northern Arizona*. New York: Harper and Brothers, 1897.

Murolo, Priscilla. "Wars of Civilization: The US Army Contemplates Wounded Knee, the Pullman Strike, and the Philippine Insurrection." *International Labor and Working-Class History* 80, no. 1 (Fall 2011): 77–102.

Myres, Sandra L. "Romance and Reality on the American Frontier: Views of Army Wives." *Western Historical Quarterly* 13, no. 4 (October 1982): 409–27.

——— . *Westering Women and the Frontier Experience, 1800–1915*. Albuquerque: University of New Mexico Press, 1982.

Nacy, Michele J. *Members of the Regiment: Army Officers' Wives on the Western Frontier, 1865–1890*. Westport CT: Greenwood Press, 2000.

Nash, Linda. "Furthering the Environmental Turn." *Journal of American History* 100, no. 1 (June 2013): 131–35.

Nash, Roderick. *Wilderness and the American Mind*. 5th ed. New Haven CT: Yale University Press, 2014.

Nelson, Megan Kate. *Ruin Nation: Destruction and the American Civil War*. Athens: University of Georgia Press, 2012.

——— . *The Three-Cornered War: The Union, the Confederacy, and Native Peoples in the Fight for the West*. New York: Scribner, 2020.

Nielsen, Thomas Solevad, ed. *Inside the Fighting First: Papers of a Nebraska Private in the Philippine War*. Blair NE: Lur, 2001.

Nye, David. *American Technological Sublime*. Cambridge MA: MIT Press, 1994.

O'Brien, Jean M. *Firsting and Lasting: Writing Indians Out of Existence in New England*. Minneapolis: University of Minnesota Press, 2010.

Official Handbook of the Philippines and Catalogue of the Philippine Exhibit. 2 vols. Manila: Bureau of Public Printing, 1903–4.

Ontal, Rene G. "Fagen and Other Ghosts: African-Americans and the Philippine-American War." In *Vestiges of War: The Philippine-American War and the Aftermath of an Imperial Dream 1899–1999*, edited by Angel Velasco Shaw and Luis Francia, 118–33. New York: New York University Press, 2002.

Ostler, Jeffrey. *The Lakotas and the Black Hills*. New York: Viking, 2010.

——— . *Surviving Genocide: Native Nations and the United States from the American Revolution to Bleeding Kansas*. New Haven CT: Yale University Press, 2019.

Otis, George A. *List of the Specimens in the Anatomical Section of the United States Army Medical Museum*. Washington DC: Army Medical Museum, 1880.

Owen, Norman G., David Chandler, and William R. Roff. *The Emergence of Modern Southeast Asia: A New History*. Honolulu: University of Hawaii Press, 2004.

Paredes, Oona. *A Mountain of Difference: The Lumad in Early Colonial Mindanao*. Ithaca NY: Cornell Southeast Asian Program, 2013.

Parezo, Nancy J., and Don D. Fowler. *Anthropology Goes to the Fair: The 1904 Louisiana Purchase Exposition*. Lincoln: University of Nebraska Press, 2007.

Parker, James. *The Old Army: Memories, 1872–1918*. Philadelphia: Dorrance, 1929.

Parkman, Francis. *The Oregon Trail of Francis Parkman*. Edited by William Ellery Leonard. Boston: Ginn and Company, 1910.

Paulet, Anne. "The Only Good Indian Is a Dead Indian: The Use of United States Indian Policy as a Guide for the Conquest and Occupation of the Philippines, 1898–1905." PhD diss., State University of New Jersey–New Brunswick, 1995.

Pauly, Philip J. *Biologists and the Promise of American Life: From Meriwether Lewis to Alfred Kinsey*. Princeton NJ: Princeton University Press, 2002.

Pawley, Emily. *The Nature of the Future: Agriculture, Science, and Capitalism in the Antebellum North*. Chicago: University of Chicago Press, 2020.

Peavy, Linda, and Ursula Smith. "World Champions: The 1904 Girls' Basketball Team from Fort Shaw Indian Boarding School." *Montana: The Magazine of Western History* 51, no. 4 (Winter 2001): 2–25.

Peralta, Christine. "Medical Modernity: Rethinking the Health Work of Filipina Women under Spanish and U.S. Colonial Rule, 1870–1948." PhD diss., University of Illinois at Urbana-Champaign, 2019.

Phillips, Katrina. *Staging Indigeneity: Salvage Tourism and the Performance of Native American History*. Chapel Hill: University of North Carolina Press, 2021.

Pilcher, James Evelyn, ed. *The Military Surgeon: Journal of the Association of Military Surgeons of the United States*. Vol. 23. Carlisle PA: Association of Military Surgeons, 1908.

Pinchot, Gifford. *Breaking New Ground*. New York: Harcourt, 1947.

——— . *The Fight for Conservation*. New York: Doubleday, 1910.

Poliquin, Rachel. *The Breathless Zoo: Taxidermy and the Cultures of Longing*. State College PA: Pennsylvania State University Press, 2012.

Porter, Joseph. *Paper Medicine Man: John Gregory Bourke and His American West*. Norman: University of Oklahoma Press, 1986.

Potter, Constance, and John Deeben. "Care for the Military Dead." In *A Companion to American Military History*, vol. 2, edited by James C. Bradford, 1034–44. Chichester: Wiley-Blackwell, 2010.

Powell, Miles. *Vanishing America: Species Extinction, Racial Peril, and the Origins of Conservation*. Cambridge MA: Harvard University Press, 2016.

Prucha, Francis Paul. *Broadax and Bayonet: The Role of the United States Army in the Development of the Northwest, 1815–1860*. Madison: State Historical Society of Wisconsin, 1953.

Quintero, Camilo. "Trading in Birds: Imperial Power, National Pride, and the Place of Nature in U.S.-Colombia Relations." *Isis* 102, no. 3 (September 2011): 421–45.

Quintero Toro, Camilo. *Birds of Empire, Birds of Nation: A History of Science, Economy, and Conservation in United States–Colombia Relations.* Bogotá: Universidad de los Andes, 2012.

Raby, Megan. *American Tropics: The Caribbean Roots of Biodiversity Science.* Chapel Hill: University of North Carolina Press, 2017.

Rafael, Vicente. *Contracting Colonialism: Translation and Christian Conversion in Tagalog Society under Early Spanish Rule.* Durham NC: Duke University Press, 1993.

Raibmon, Paige. "Living on Display: Colonial Visions of Aboriginal Domestic Spaces." *BC Studies*, no. 140 (Winter 2003–4): 69–89.

Rakestraw, Lawrence. "George Patrick Ahern and the Philippine Bureau of Forestry, 1900–1914." *Pacific Northwest Quarterly* 58, no. 3 (July 1967): 142–50.

Redman, Samuel. *Bone Rooms: From Scientific Racism to Human Prehistory in Museums.* Cambridge MA: Harvard University Press, 2016.

Renda, Mary. *Taking Haiti: Military Occupation and the Culture of U.S. Imperialism.* Chapel Hill: University of North Carolina Press, 2001.

Report of the Secretary of War: Being Part of the Message and Documents Communicated to the Two Houses of Congress at the Beginning of the Second Session of the Forty-Eighth Congress. Vol. 1. Washington DC: Government Printing Office, 1884.

Rice, Mark. *Dean Worcester's Fantasy Islands: Photography, Film, and the Colonial Philippines.* Ann Arbor: University of Michigan Press, 2014.

Richmond, Charles. "In Memoriam: Edgar Alexander Mearns." *Auk* 35 (1918): 1–18.

Rico, Monica. *Nature's Noblemen: Transatlantic Masculinities and the Nineteenth-Century American West.* New Haven CT: Yale University Press, 2013.

Roberts, Brian. *American Alchemy: The California Gold Rush and Middle-Class Culture.* Chapel Hill: University of North Carolina Press, 2000.

Roberts, Nathan. "U.S. Forestry in the Philippines: Environment, Nationhood, and Empire, 1900–1937." PhD diss., University of Washington, 2014.

Robinson, Charles M., III, ed. *The Diaries of John Gregory Bourke.* Vol. 1, *November 20, 1872–July 28, 1876.* Denton: University of North Texas Press, 2003.

————, ed. *The Diaries of John Gregory Bourke.* Vol. 4, *July 3, 1880–May 22, 1881.* Denton: University of North Texas Press, 2003.

————. *General Crook and the Western Frontier.* Norman: University of Oklahoma Press, 2001.

Robinson, Michael C., and Frank N. Schubert. "David Fagen: An Afro-American Rebel in the Philippines, 1899–1901." *Pacific-Historical Review* 44, no. 1 (February 1975): 68–83.

Rosaldo, Renato. "Imperialist Nostalgia." *Representations* 26 (Spring 1989): 107–22.

Roth, Russell. *Muddy Glory: America's "Indian Wars" in the Philippines 1899–1935*. West Hanover MA: Christopher, 1981.

Runte, Alfred. *National Parks: The American Experience*. Lincoln: University of Nebraska Press, 1979.

Rust, Thomas C. *Watching over Yellowstone: The US Army's Experience in America's First National Park, 1886–1918*. Lawrence: University Press of Kansas, 2020.

Rydell, Robert. *All the World's a Fair: Visions of Empire at American International Expositions, 1876–1916*. Chicago: University of Chicago Press, 1987.

Sachs, Aaron, *The Humboldt Current: Nineteenth-Century Exploration and the Roots of American Environmentalism*. New York: Viking, 2006.

Sackman, Douglas Cazaux. *Wild Men: Ishi and Kroeber in the Wilderness of Modern America*. Cambridge MA: Oxford University Press, 2010.

Salman, Michael. *The Embarrassment of Slavery: Controversies over Bondage and Nationalism in the American Colonial Philippines*. Berkeley: University of California Press, 2001.

Sandweiss, Martha. *Print the Legend: Photography and the American West*. New Haven CT: Yale University Press, 2004.

Savage, Victor. *Western Impressions of Nature and Landscape in Southeast Asia*. Singapore: Singapore University Press, 1984.

Savoy, Lauret. *Trace: Memory, History, Race, and the American Landscape*. Berkeley: Counterpoint Press, 2016.

Schama, Simon. *Landscape and Memory*. New York: Knopf, 1995.

Schiebinger, Londa. *Plants and Empire: Colonial Bioprospecting in the Atlantic World*. Cambridge MA: Harvard University Press, 2004.

Scott, James C. *Seeing like a State: How Certain Schemes to Improve the Human Condition Have Failed*. New Haven CT: Yale University Press, 1998.

Sheridan, P. H., and W. T. Sherman. *Reports of Inspection Made in the Summer of 1877 by Generals P. H. Sheridan and W. T. Sherman of Country North of the Union Pacific Railroad*. Washington DC: Government Printing Office, 1878.

Silbey, David. *A War of Frontier and Empire: The Philippine-American War, 1899–1902*. New York: Hill and Wang, 2007.

Silva, Noenoe. *Aloha Betrayed: Native Hawaiian Resistance to American Colonialism*. Durham NC: Duke University Press, 2004.

Simpson, Audra. *Mohawk Interruptus: Political Life across the Borders of Settler States*. Durham NC: Duke University Press, 2014.

Simpson, Leanne Betasamosake. *As We Have Always Done: Indigenous Freedom through Radical Resistance*. Minneapolis: University of Minnesota, 2017.

Sledge, Michael. *Soldier Dead: How We Recover, Identify, Bury, and Honor Our Military Fallen*. New York: Columbia University Press, 2005.

Slotkin, Richard. *The Fatal Environment: The Myth of the Frontier in the Age of Industrialization, 1800–1890*. New York: Atheneum, 1985.

————. *Gunfighter Nation: The Myth of the Frontier in Twentieth-Century America*. New York: Atheneum, 1992.

Smalley, Andrea. *Wild by Nature: North American Animals Confront Colonization*. Baltimore: Johns Hopkins University Press, 2017.

Smith, Cornelius Cole, Jr. *Don't Settle for Second: Life and Times of Cornelius C. Smith*. San Rafael CA: Presidio Press, 1977.

Smith, Diane. *Yellowstone and the Smithsonian: Centers of Wildlife Conservation*. Lawrence: University Press of Kansas, 2017.

Smith, Henry Nash. *Virgin Land: The American West as Symbol and Myth*. Cambridge MA: Harvard University Press, 1950.

Smith, Sherry L. *Sagebrush Soldier: Private William Earl Smith's View of the Sioux War of 1876*. Norman: University of Oklahoma Press, 2001.

————. *The View from Officers' Row: Army Perceptions of Indians*. Tucson: University of Arizona Press, 1991.

Solnit, Rebecca. *A Field Guide to Getting Lost*. New York: Viking, 2005.

————. *Savage Dreams: A Journey into the Landscape Wars of the American West*. Berkeley: University of California Press, 1994.

————. *Wanderlust: A History of Walking*. New York: Penguin Books, 2000.

Spence, Mark David. *Dispossessing the Wilderness: Indian Removal and the Making of the National Parks*. Oxford: Oxford University Press, 2000.

Stanley, Peter W., ed. *Reappraising an Empire: New Perspectives on Philippine-American History*. Cambridge MA: Harvard University Press, 1984.

Stoler, Ann, ed. *Haunted by Empire: Geographies of Intimacy in North American History*. Durham NC: Duke University Press, 2006.

Stoler, Ann, and Carole McGranahan. "Refiguring Imperial Terrain." In *Imperial Formations*, edited by Ann Stoler, Carole McGranahan, and Peter Perdue, 3–42. Santa Fe NM: SAR Press, 2007.

Stoll, Steven. *Larding the Lean Earth: Soil and Society in Nineteenth-Century America*. New York: Hill and Wang, 2002.

Storey, Moorfield. *The Moro Massacre*. Boston: Anti-Imperialist League, 1906.

Summerhayes, Martha. *Vanished Arizona: Recollections of My Army Life*. Chicago: Lakeside Press, 1939.

Sutter, Paul. "Nature's Agents or Agents of Empire? Entomological Workers and Environmental Change during the Construction of the Panama Canal." *Isis* 98, no. 4 (December 2007): 724–54.

————. "The Tropics: A Brief History of an Environmental Imaginary." In *The Oxford Handbook of Environmental History*, edited by Andrew Isenberg, 178–204. New York: Oxford University Press, 2014.

Sweeney, Edwin R. *From Cochise to Geronimo: The Chiricahua Apaches, 1874–1886*. Norman: University of Oklahoma Press, 2010.

Taft, William, and Philippine Exposition Board. *Circular Letter of Governor Taft and Information and Instructions for the Preparation of the Philippine Exhibit for the Louisiana Purchase Exposition to Be Held at St. Louis, Mo., U.S.A., 1904*. Manila: Bureau of Public Printing, 1902.

Tan, Samuel K. *The Filipino-American War, 1899–1913*. Quezon City: University of the Philippines Press, 2002.

Tate, Michael. *The Frontier Army in the Settlement of the West*. Norman: University of Oklahoma Press, 1999.

Telfer, George. *Manila Envelopes: Oregon Volunteer Lt. George F. Telfer's Spanish-American War Letters*. Edited by Sara Bunnett. Portland: Oregon Historical Society Press, 1987.

Trafton, William Oliver. *We Thought We Could Whip Them in Two Weeks*. Edited by William Henry Scott. Quezon City: New Day, 1990.

Trouern-Trend, Jonathan. *Birding Babylon: A Soldier's Journal from Iraq*. San Francisco: Sierra Club Books, 2006.

Tuason, Julie A. "The Ideology of Empire in *National Geographic Magazine*'s coverage of the Philippines, 1898–1908." *Geographical Review* 89, no. 1 (January 1999): 34–53.

Tuggle, Lindsay. "The Afterlives of Specimens: Walt Whitman and the Army Medical Museum." *Walt Whitman Quarterly Review* 32 (2014): 1–35.

Twain, Mark. *Roughing It*. Hartford CT: American, 1872.

Tyrell, Ian. *Crisis of the Wasteful Nation: Empire and Conservation in Theodore Roosevelt's America*. Chicago: University of Chicago Press, 2015.

Utley, Robert M. *Frontier Regulars: The United States Army and the Indian, 1866–1891*. New York: Macmillan, 1973.

———. *Geronimo*. New Haven CT: Yale University Press, 2013.

———. *The Indian Frontier of the American West, 1846–1890*. Albuquerque: University of New Mexico Press, 1984.

Valenčius, Conevery Bolton. *"The Health of the Country": How American Settlers Understood Themselves and Their Land*. New York: Basic Books, 2002.

———. *The Lost History of the New Madrid Earthquakes*. Chicago: University of Chicago Press, 2013.

Velayo, Carlo Jones. "The Good, the Bad and the Friendly: America's Engagement with the Muslim Peoples of Mindanao in the Early 1900s." *Our Own Voice* 43 (June 2014). http://www.oovrag.com/oovnew/americas -engagement-with-the-muslim-peoples-of-mindanao-in-the-early-1900s/.

Ventura, Theresa. "'I Am Already Annexed': Ramon Reyes Lala and the Crafting of 'Philippine' Advocacy for American Empire." *Journal of the Gilded Age and Progressive Era* 19 (2020): 426–46.

Veracini, Lorenzo. *Settler Colonialism: A Theoretical Overview*. New York: Palgrave Macmillan, 2010.

Vetter, Jeremy. "Cowboys, Scientists, and Fossils: The Field Site and Local Collaboration in the American West." *Isis* 99, no. 2 (2008): 273–303.

———. *Field Life: Science in the American West during the Railroad Era*. Pittsburgh PA: University of Pittsburgh Press, 2016.

Waggoner, Josephine. *Witness: A Hunkpapha Historian's Strong-Heart Song of the Lakotas*. Edited by Emily Levine. Lincoln: University of Nebraska Press, 2013.

Watt, Eva Tulene. *Don't Let the Sun Step over You: A White Mountain Apache Family Life, 1860–1975*. With the assistance of Keith Basso. Tucson: University of Arizona Press, 2004.

Welch, John R., Chip Colwell-Chanthaphonh, and Mark Altaha. "Retracing the Battle of Cibecue: Western Apache, Documentary, and Archaeological Interpretations." *Kiva* 71, no. 2 (Winter 2005): 133–63.

Welch, Richard. *Response to Imperialism: The United States and the Philippine-American War, 1899–1902*. Chapel Hill: University of North Carolina Press, 1979.

West, Elliott. *The Contested Plains: Indians, Goldseekers, and the Rush to Colorado*. Lawrence: University Press of Kansas, 1998.

Wexler, Laura. *Tender Violence: Domestic Visions in an Age of U.S. Imperialism*. Chapel Hill: University of North Carolina Press, 2000.

Wheeler, Homer W. *Buffalo Days: Forty Years in the Old West; The Personal Narrative of a Cattleman, Indian Fighter and Army Officer*. New York: A. L. Burt, 1925.

———. *The Frontier Trail, or From Cowboy to Colonel: An Authentic Narrative of Forty-Three Years in the Old West as Cattleman, Indian Fighter and Army Officer*. Los Angeles: Time-Mirror Press, 1923.

White, Richard. *The Republic for Which It Stands: The United States during Reconstruction and the Gilded Age, 1865–1896*. New York: Oxford University Press, 2017.

Wilcox, Marion, ed. *Harper's History of the War in the Philippines*. New York: Harper and Brothers, 1900.

Williams, Michael. *Americans and Their Forests: A Historical Geography*. Cambridge: Cambridge University Press, 1989.

Williams, Walter L. "United States Indian Policy and the Debate over Philippine Annexation: Implications for the Origins of American Imperialism." *Journal of American History* 66, no. 4 (March 1980): 810–31.

Winker, Kevin. "Obtaining, Preserving, and Preparing Bird Specimens." *Journal of Field Ornithology* 71, no. 2 (2000): 250–97.

Wolfe, Patrick. "Settler Colonialism and the Elimination of the Native." *Journal of Genocide Research* 8, no. 4 (2006): 387–409.

Wood, Leonard. *Chasing Geronimo: The Journal of Leonard Wood, May–September 1886*. Edited by Jack C. Lane. Lincoln: University of Nebraska Press, 2009.

Wooden Leg. *Wooden Leg: A Warrior Who Fought Custer*. Interpreted by Thomas Marquis. Minneapolis: Midwest Company, 1931.

Worster, Donald. *A Passion for Nature: The Life of John Muir*. Oxford: Oxford University Press, 2008.

———. *A River Running West: The Life of John Wesley Powell*. New York: Oxford University Press, 2002.

Wyckoff, William. *How to Read the American West: A Field Guide*. Seattle: University of Washington Press, 2014.

Yochelson, Ellis, and Mary Jarrett. *The National Museum of Natural History: 75 Years in the Natural History Building*. Washington DC: Smithsonian Institution Press, 1985.

Yusoff, Kathryn. *A Billion Black Anthropocenes or None*. Minneapolis: University of Minnesota Press, 2018.

Zwick, Jim, ed. *Mark Twain's Weapons of Satire: Anti-Imperialist Writings on the Philippine-American War*. Syracuse NY: Syracuse University Press, 1992.

INDEX